Pannekoek and the Workers' Councils

by Serge Bricianer

Introduction by John Gerber

Translated by Malachy Carroll

TELOS PRESS • SAINT LOUIS

Library of Congress Catalog No. 78-50978

IBSN: 0-914386-17-4 (cloth)
        0-914386-18-2 (paper)

Printed in the United States of America.

TABLE OF CONTENTS

THE FORMATION OF PANNEKOEK'S MARXISM

by JOHN GERBER

The Dutch Marxist theoretician and astronomer, Anton Pannekoek (1873-1960), has remained a largely neglected and unknown figure in the history of European socialist thought.[1] Yet Pannekoek's long life and political career spanned several distinct stages of socialist history, resulting in some of the most significant and fundamental contributions to twentieth-century Marxist thought. His political maturity coincided with the rise of Social Democracy,

---

1. Obscurity was not always the case for Pannekoek. Prior to the First World War, and for a few years afterward, Pannekoek was a widely known figure in the international socialist movement. Commenting on the impact of Pannekoek's thought on the formation of American Communism, Theodore Draper has noted: "...Pannekoek and Gorter were familiar names to many American Socialists when Lenin and Trotsky were virtually unknown." Theodore Draper, *The Roots of American Communism* (New York: Viking Press, 1957), pp. 65-66. More recent interest in him has developed only after the May 1968 events in France. Because of this emphasis has been placed on the later "Council Communist" aspects of his career. Most work on Pannekoek thus far has consisted almost exclusively of anthologies of his writings. These include: Serge Bricianer, *Pannekoek et les conseils ouvriers* (Paris: Etudes et documentation internationales, 1969); Cajo Brendel, *Anton Pannekoek Theoretikus van het Socialisme* (Nijmegen: Socialistische Uitgeverij Nijmegen, 1970); Joop Kloosterman, *Anton Pannekoek: Neubestimmung des Marxismus* (Berlin: Karin Kramer Verlag, 1974); Fritz Kool, *Die Linke gegen die Parteiherrschaft* (Olten, Germany: Walter Verlag, 1970); Hans Manfred Bock, *Anton Pannekoek und Herman Gorter: Organisation und Taktik der Proletarischen Revolution* (Frankfurt: Verlag Neue Kritik, 1969). Also useful is Paul Mattick's short obituary, "Anton Pannekoek," *New Politics*, Winter, 1962. For an analysis—though somewhat misleading—of the impact of Pannekoek's thought on Lenin's political development see H. Schurer, "Anton Pannekoek and the Origins of Leninism," *The Slavonic and East European Review*, June, 1963. A valuable assessment of Pannekoek's pre-1914 activity is contained in Hans Manfred Bock, "Anton Pannekoek in der Vorkriegs-Sozialdemokratie: Bericht und Dokumentation," in *Arbeiterbewegung. Theorie und Geschichte*, Jahrbuch 3 (Frankfurt: Fischer Verlag, 1974). A major source of background material is Herman de Liagre Böhl's outstanding biography of Pannekoek's closest friend and political colaborator, *Herman Gorter* (Nijmegen: Socialistische Uitgeverij Nijmegen, 1973). Several factors account for Pannekoek's relative obscurity. The most important of these is that following his break with the Comintern Pannekoek lost touch with any movement of consequence. Another, perhaps, is that Pannekoek, unlike other theorists such as Lenin, Trotsky and Rosa Luxemburg, was more a "pure theorist" than a party leader (Pannekoek's highest party position was chairman of the Leiden branch of the Dutch SDAP). And finally, there is the problem of the inaccessibility of many of his writings. In the most immediate sense this arises from the fact that a large proportion of his writings are in Dutch. But this is further compounded by the variety of pseudonyms he used throughout his career (known pseudonyms include: Karl Horner, John Harper, P. Aartsz, Krable, J. Fraak and van Loo), and by the obscure nature of many of the publications his later writings appeared in.

his death with the rise of the New Left; his writings left their imprint on both movements. Despite his professional commitment to science, the contours of Pannekoek's political activity are almost without parallel. Prior to 1914 he participated as a militant in both the Dutch and German Social Democratic parties, taught in the German Social Democratic Party (SPD) schools, and collaborated with Kautsky on the *Neue Zeit*. Along with Rosa Luxemburg, he emerged as one of the leaders of the left wing of the German SPD, gaining fame with his 1912 *Neue Zeit* polemic against Kautsky. Pannekoek was one of the first in Europe to understand the fundamental contradictions and weaknesses of the Social Democratic movement and to anticipate its eventual collapse. Following the outbreak of the First World War, Pannekoek was the first to call for the formation of a new International, and later became a leading figure in the Zimmerwald anti-war movement. Although he had played a major role in the initial formation of European Communism and was a leader of the Comintern's Western European bureau, Pannekoek emerged in 1920 as a formidable left-wing critic of Leninism, becoming a leading theoretician of the left-Communist *Kommunistischen Arbeiter-Partei Deutschlands* (KAPD). Under the pseudonym Karl Horner he gained fame as Lenin's adversary in *Left-Wing Communism; An Infantile Disorder*. From 1929 until his death in 1960 he was the intellectual mentor of the quasi-syndicalist "Council Communist" movement.

Given its enormous circumfrence, it seems difficult to find a single entry into Pannekoek's theoretical work. Yet in seeking out those categories which unify his thought, one finds one particular area in which his thinking remains remarkably constant: the set of philosophical assumptions undergirding his political theories. Pannekoek's Marxism can, therefore, be made more intelligible by focusing on the key philosophical concepts he built his Marxism on early in his career and which he retained with only slight revision and reformulation throughout his life. The aim of this essay will be to explore these philosophical foundations and their implications through an examination of: (1) The basic Marx-Dietzgen synthesis on which his thought rests; (2) His extension and broadening of these categories into a conception of science and Marxism; (3) Some of the main implications these philosophical and scientific conceptions had for his political thought; (4) The final crystallization of these ideas in his unified philosophical, scientific and political assault on Leninism. In posing the question of Pannekoek as philosopher, it must be noted that his concern was not philosophy in the formal sense, but one of developing and understanding certain philosophical and scientific categories of analysis for practical application to a variety of more immediate political questions.

Pannekoek and Dietzgen
Unlike most Second International Socialists, Anton Pannekoek came to Marxism directly out of natural science, a fact that was to have considerable significance in the formulation of his thought. For Pannekoek, the personal transition to Marxism came in 1898, while a doctoral student at Leiden University, following a reading of Edward Bellamy's novel, *Equality*. The effect of this American utopian novel, he later noted, "was as if a blindfold had been removed." "For the first time it dawned on me that all theories have a social basis and significance and develop in response to real material interests rather than abstract reasoning."[2] The acceptance of Marxist ideology led him to undertake a painstaking study of Marx's economics in collaboration with Frank van der Goes, the major figure in the introduction of Marxian Socialism into the Netherlands. Dissatisfied with what he felt was the determinism inherent in Marxian economics and concerned above all with the problem of developing a scientific framework for analyzing the relationship of human consciousness and action to the material world, Pannekoek went on in 1900 to a systematic examination of the philosophical basis of Marxism.[3] It was at this point that he discovered the writings of the German autodidact ("the worker-philosopher") Joseph Dietzgen, which marked the decisive turning point in his theoretical development. To understand the precise nature of the impact of Dietzgen in Pannekoek's thought requires a brief summary of Dietzgen's philosophy.[4]

Like Pannekoek, Dietzgen has remained a largely neglected theorist. This

2. Anton Pannekoek, "Herrineringen uit de arbeidersbeweging," p. 2. This unpublished document was written by Pannekoek as a personal memoir for his family in 1944 during the Nazi occupation of Holland at a time when his personal fate remained uncertain. A copy is contained in the International Institute for Social History (Amsterdam).
3. *Ibid.*, pp. 4-5.
4. Joseph Dietzgen was born in 1828 near Cologne. His father was a tanner and it was in this profession that he was trained and worked. In his leisure time he studied literature, economics and philosophy and learned to speak French and English fluently. He became a class conscious Socialist upon reading the Communist Manifesto. A participant in the events of 1848, he was forced to flee to America where he worked at a variety of jobs. Throughout the next 30 years Dietzgen alternated between the U.S. and Europe, participating in the socialist movements on both sides of the Atlantic. In 1886, as an editor of several socialist papers in Chicago, he played a major role as a defender of the Haymarket martyrs. He died in 1886 and is buried at the side of the Haymarket anarchists in Chicago. For further information on Dietzgen see: Loyd Easton, "Empiricism and Ethics in Dietzgen," *Journal of the History of Ideas*, January, 1958; Adam Buick, "Joseph Dietzgen," *Radical Encyclopedia of the Social Sciences* (London: 1931); G. Bammel, "Joseph Dietzgen," *La Revue Marxiste*, April, 1929; Adolf Hepner, *Josef Dietzgens Philosophische Lehren* (Stuttgart: 1916); Henriette Roland-Holst, *Joseph Dietzgens Philosophie, gemeinverständlich erläutert in ihrer Bedutung für das Proletariat* (Munich: Eugen Dietzgben Verlag, 1910); Fred Casey, *Thinking: An Introduction to its History and Science* (Chicago: Charles H. Kree, 1926).

status, however, was not always the case. At the Hague Congress of the First International, Marx introduced Dietzgen as "our philosopher."[5] Although critical of certain aspects of Dietzgen's thought, Marx pronounced it "excellent and—as the independent product of a working man—admirable."[6] Engels, in *Ludwig Feuerbach*, subsequently credited Dietzgen—somewhat loosely in view of their different conceptions—with the independent discovery of "materialist dialectics."[7] Indeed, it was Dietzgen who first coined the term "dialectical materialism." Due in part to a major popularization campaign—in which Pannekoek played a prominent role—Dietzgen's writings also gained fairly widespread currency among rank-and-file working class militants.[8]

Considered in overall terms, Dietzgen was essentially a philosopher of science, attempting to develop the methodology for a comprehensive view of the world for the purposes of prediction and control, a fact which doubtless made a marked impression on the young Pannekoek. In particular, Dietzgen was concerned with establishing: (1) The objective reality and unity of both the natural and social processes; (2) The relative and tentative validity of all knowledge obtained about these processes; (3) The unity of human activity (particularly thought activity) with the natural and social environment and its importance as a factor conditioning it.

Although his dialectics rejected any rigid laws of a universal system, Dietzgen accepted (at least in a relative sense) Marx's social theories that explain social change and class ideologies in terms of the fundamental relations of economic production. But Dietzgen sought to clarify these theories by making explicit their psychological assumptions through an inductive theory of cognition. The human thought process, he felt, was as accessible to scientific analysis and elaboration as any other natural or social process: "If we could place this general work of thinking on a scientific basis, if we were able to discover the means by which reason arrives at its understanding, if we could develop a method by which truth is produced scientifically, then we should acquire for science in general and for our individual faculty of judgement the same certainty of success which we

5. Quoted in Eugen Dietzgen, "Joseph Dietzgen: A Sketch of His Life," in Joseph Dietzgen, *Philosophical Essays* (Chicago: Charles H. Kerr, 1917), p. 15.

6. Marx to Kugelmann, December 5, 1868. In Karl Marx, *Letters to Dr. Kugelmann* (London: Martin Lawrence, 1934), p. 55.

7. Friedrich Engels, *Ludwig Feuerbach and the Outcome of Classical German Philosophy* (London: Martin Lawrence, 1934), p. 54.

8. An examination of certain aspects of Dietzgen's influence on rank-and-file militants can be found in Stuart Macintyre, "Joseph Dietzgen and British Working Class Education," *Bulletin of the Study of Labor History*, Fall, 1974.

already possess in special fields of science."[9]

Dietzgen's first and best known study, *The Nature of Human Brainwork* (1869), represents his most systematic attempt to formulate such a scientific and materialistic theory of understanding. Summarily rejecting Kantian dualism, Dietzgen argued that since all knowledge derives from and cannot go beyond sensations, it cannot make definitive statements about objective reality; it can merely fill in the gaps in experience by the ideas, concepts and abstractions which experience suggests.[10] Conceptual thought is, therefore, formed out of the continuous clarification, systematization and classification of sensual data through a process of abstracting the particular qualities from the general qualities in such data. This abstraction process is dialectical in the sense that it mediates differences and distinctions in a particular object of thought. For Dietzgen, however, dialectical did not always mean absolute opposites or contradictions. These distinctions existed only through the mental separation of the component parts of a particular object of thought. Without the mental act there could be no contradictions. The mind merely constructs them and makes them relative and equal as part of the classification and systematization process. From this perspective, the objective world of matter, space, time and causality common to both "mechanical materialism" and Marxist materialism represented simply a set of artificial and relative conceptions.

For Pannekoek, the discovery of Dietzgen provided a critical link between Marxism and his professional role as a natural scientist: "Here I found for the first time everything that I had been looking for; a clear, systematic elaboration of a theory of knowledge and an analysis of the nature of concepts and abstractions. . . . Through this reading I was able to completely clarify my conception of the underlying relationship between Marxism and epistemology and develop it into a unified whole."[11] In his first major work as a Marxist,

---

9. Joseph Dietzgen, "The Nature of Human Brainwork," in *The Positive Outcome of Philosophy* (Chicago: Charles H. Kerr, 1906), p. 48.

10. *Ibid.*, p. 71. "The fact that the analysis of a concept and the analysis of its object appear as two different things is due to our faculty of being able to separate things into two parts, viz., into a practical tangible, perceptible, concrete thing and into a theoretical, mental, thinkable, general thing. The practical analysis is the premise of the theoretical analysis."

11. Anton Pannekoek, "Herrineringen uit de arbeidersbeweging," *op. cit.*, p. 19. Dietzgen's philosophy, more than any other factor, also served as the unifying thread for the so-called "Dutch Marxist school" as a whole. In addition to the works of Pannekoek other works from this group dealing directly with Dietzgen include: Herman Gorter, "Marx en het determinisme," *De Nieuwe Tijd*, 1904, pp. 57-58; Herman Gorter, *Het historisch materialisme voor arbeiders Verklaard* (Amsterdam: De Tribune, 1908). Gorter in 1902 had also made a Dutch translation of Dietzgen's *The Nature of Human Brainwork*. Cf. Henriette Roland-Holst, *Joseph Dietzgen's Philosophie, gemeinverständlich erläutert in ihrer Bedeutung für das Proletariat, op. cit.*, p. 206. Dietzgen's philosophy also exercised considerable influence on the literary work of Gorter

"De Filosofie van Kant en het Marxisme" (1901), Pannekoek sought to establish Dietzgen's real significance in the history of philosophy and socialist thought. This analysis was broadened the following year when, with Kautsky's assistance, he made contact with Dietzgen's son Eugen and was invited to write an introduction to a collection of Dietzgen's writings. Together these two works constitute the basic core of Pannekoek's early approach to Marxism.

In Pannekoek's view, Marx had elaborated only on the nature of the social process of production and its fundamental significance for social development without really concerning himself with the question of the human "spirit" (*Geist*), other than to show that it derived its content from the material world. The question thus remained open: what was the exact content of human consciousness and what was its real relation to the material world? This gap in Marxian theory, Pannekoek felt, coupled with the traditional influence exercised by bourgeois thought, was one of the main reasons for the erroneous understanding of Marxism by anti-Marxists and revisionists alike. Dietzgen, by making the human mind the special subject of investigation, and by attempting to show the exact content of the process of human consciousness, had made a major contribution toward filling this gap. Because it validated empirical methodology itself, Dietzgen's scientific and experienced-based theory of human thinking constituted the "essence and foundation" of Marx's theory of society and man. [12] By constructing out of philosophy a "science of the human spirit," Dietzgen "raised philosophy to the position of a natural science, the same as Marx did with history." [13] For this achievement, Dietzgen could be ranked "third among the founders of 'socialist science,' next to Marx and Engels." [14] As a result, Pannekoek contended that a "thorough study of

---

and Henriette Roland-Holst, in particular on Gorter's epic poems *Pan* and *De Arbeidersraad*. A useful discussion of this literary impact can be found in Robert Antonissen, *Herman Gorter en Henriette Roland-Holst* (Antwerp: De Sikkel, 1945); and Yves van Kempen *et al.*, *Materialistie Literatuurteorie* (Nijmegen: Socialistische Uitgeverij Nijmegen, 1973).

12. Anton Pannekoek, "The Position and Significance of Dietzgen's Philosophical Works," in Joseph Dietzgen, *The Positive Outcome of Philosophy, op. cit.*, pp. 30-31. This introduction first appeared in the 1902 German edition.

13. *Ibid.*, p. 28.

14. Anton Pannekoek, "Dietzgen's Work," *Die Neue Zeit*, 1913, vol. 2, pp. 37-47. In Pannekoek's view, Dietzgen's methodology was not limited to social science alone, but had equal relevance for physical science: "It is a proof of the deep validity of a clear Marxist insight that Dietzgen, a layman and an amatuer in the scientific area, fully clarified the basis of modern natural science long before the modern natural scientists themselves were able to do so. . . . The most well known of them, Ernst Mach, has admitted his astonishment upon learning that many of his newly developed theories had been discovered a quarter century earlier by Dietzgen." Anton Pannekoek, "Twee natuuronderzoekers in de maatschappelijk-geestelijk strijd," *De Niuewe Tijd*, 1917, pp. 300-314, 375-392. Throughout his career Pannekoek consistently attempted to apply a Dietzgenian methodology to his scientific research. For an example of this

Dietzgen's writings is an immediate necessity for anyone desiring to learn the philosophical fundamentals of Marxism and of the proletarian outlook on life."[15]

To lend additional credence to his assessment of Dietzgen, Pannekoek also attempted to render a critical and dynamic account of the development of "proletarian philosophy" itself, using both Dietzgenian and Marxist categories of analysis. Starting from Dietzgen's argument that the reduction of reality to ideas is essentially an historical and social mode of abstraction, Pannekoek outlined several distinct stages in the development of "proletarian philosophy."

The first stage in this process, Pannekoek maintained, began with Kant. The significance of Kantian philosophy was twofold: it was at once "the purest expression of bourgeois thought," and a precursor of modern socialist philosophy.[16] Since "freedom" of production, competition and exploitation were at the heart of the ideology of the developing capitalism of the late eighteenth and early nineteenth century, Kant's emphasis on "freedom" and "free will" corresponded to the needs and aspirations of a rising bourgeoisie. By challenging the mechanistic materialism of the French rationalists, Kant also provided a firmer foundation for religious belief, clearing the way for a revised form of faith and freedom of the will. Yet in focusing on sensory experience and on the organization of the human mind, Kant made the first valuable contribution to a scientific theory of understanding and human causation that was a necessary component of socialist thought.

A second stage in the development of a scientific theory of understanding came with Hegel. In strictly social terms, Hegel's thought was the product of the reaction against both bourgeois society and bourgeois philosophy that developed after the French Revolution. Historically, Hegel's aim of a practical critique of bourgeois philosophy was but one part of a large intellectual effort to develop a theoretical justification of the Restoration. Stripped of its social origins and transcendental character, the real significance of Hegelian philosophy lay in the fact that it provided an excellent theory of the human mind and its working methods: "The vicissitudes of the absolute spirit in the course of its self-development are but a fantastical description of the process which the real human mind experiences in its acquaintances with the world and its active participation in life."[17] A

---

see Anton Pannekoek, *De Evolutie van het Heelal* (Lieden: Venn Boekdrukkerij, 1918).

15. Anton Pannekoek, "De Filosofie van Kant en het Marxisme," *De Nieuwe Tijd*, 1901, pp. 549-564, 605-620, 669-688.

16. Anton Pannekoek, "The Position and Significance of Dietzgen's Philosophical Works," *op. cit.*, p. 17.

17. *Ibid.*, p. 27.

major corollary of this, as Pannekoek viewed it, was that the real dialectic was one of the encounters of the human mind with the external world, particularly in its attempt to gain an understanding of social development.

This quality of Hegel's work, however, could not be fully appreciated until Dietzgen had created the basis for a dialectical and materialistic theory of understanding. Viewed in the context of the history of philosophy, "the idealist philosophical systems from Kant to Hegel, which consist chiefly in the development of the dialectical method, must be regarded as the indispensible pioneers and precursors of Dietzgen's proletarian philosophy."[18] As an intellectual process this philosophy represents the "scientific culmination of former philosophies, just as astronomy is the continuation of astrology and of the Pythagorean fantasies, and chemistry the continuation of alchemy."[19] Dietzgen, therefore, "completed the work of Kant, just as Marx completed the work of Adam Smith."[20] Dietzgen's philosophy, moreover, was neither "his" philosophy nor a new system of philosophy, but merely one of the more systematic intellectual elements of the historical mode of abstraction of a rising working class (this concept bears a certain affinity with Engels' concept of *Weltanschauung*, or worldview, although the emphases and implications differ). Although this new "proletarian philosophy" was a direct and logical successor to previous bourgeois philosophical systems, it differed fundamentally from them in the sense that it sought to be less. Whereas earlier philosophical systems pretended to give absolute truth, Dietzgen offered only a "finite and temporary realization" of truth which could be further perfected only through the course of social development.[21]

Science and Marxism

As a professional astronomer, it was perhaps only natural that Pannekoek would devote a considerable portion of his theoretical efforts to an attempt to clarify the relationship between science and Marxism, starting with his 1904 *Neue Zeit* article, "Klassenwissenschaft und Philosophie." His conception is one which calls into question the meaning of orthodox Marxism itself.

---

18. *Ibid.*, p. 21.
19. *Ibid.*, p. 29.
20. *Ibid.*, p. 27.
21. Anton Pannekoek, "De Filosofie van Kant en het Marxisme," *op. cit.* There is a profound coincidence here between the way in which Pannekoek understood the relationship between Marxism and philosophy and the ideas of the Italian Marxist Antonio Labriola, though their emphasis and conceptual starting points differ. Close similarities also exist between their conceptions of socialism and science, particularly in their views of the relationship between Marxism and Darwinism. See: Antonio Labriola, *Socialism and Philosophy* (Chicago: C.H. Kerr, 1917); Antonio Labriola, *Essays on the Materialist Conception of History* (New York: Monthly Review Press, 1966).

The materialist conception of history, as formulated by Marx, was meant to be an anti-metaphysical theory based on the evidence of human sense data, to be examined "in the manner of the natural sciences." While the later writings of Marx reflected an increasingly positivistic trend, it was primarily Engels, and later his spiritual heir, Karl Kautsky, who generalized the historical materialism advanced by Marx into a form of natural science. This conception, which later became a theoretical cornerstone of the Marxism of both the Second and Third Internationals, was one which viewed the dialectic as the supreme science governing the general laws of movement and development of nature, human society, and thought. In Engels' words: "...that in nature, amid the welter of innumerable changes, the same dialectical laws of motion force their way through as those which in history govern the apparent fortuitousness of events; the same laws as those which similarly form the thread running through the history of the development of human thought and gradually rise to consciousness in the mind of man." [22] Marxism, through this methodology, had been turned into a cosmogony, a total scientific synthesis of universal validity for all questions of social, historical and natural development.

In developing his conception of the relationship between socialism and science, Pannekoek directed his inquiry on two levels: an examination of the methods, meanings and objects of inquiry behind scientific knowledge; and an analysis of the position of science in human social and mental activity.

Starting from Dietzgen's premise that human thought represents a mediation between the social factors that shape men and their expression in human action, Pannekoek advanced the proposition: "Thinkers can only work with the pre-existing conceptual materials of their era. The form in which new problems are posed often creates a consciousness about the insufficiency or falseness of the traditional views, and new 'truths' are then put forward as an improvement of the traditional views." [23] Among the various forms of "thought activity" of an historical epoch none has more importance than science, "which stands as a mental tool next to the material tools and, itself a productive power, constitutes the basis of technology and so is an essential part of the productive apparatus." [24] As part of a larger

22. Friedrich Engels, *Anti-Dühring* (Moscow: Foreign Language Press, 1962), p. 17.

23. Anton Pannekoek, "Klassenwissenschaft und Philosophie," *Die Neue Zeit*, 1905, pp. 604-610.

24. Anton Pannekoek, *Lenin as Philosopher: A Critical Examination of the Philosophical Basis of Leninism* (New York: New Essays, 1948), p. 19. On the concept of technology, Pannekoek has elaborated elsewhere: "The basis of society — productive power — is formed chiefly through technology, though in primitive societies natural conditions play a major role. Technology does not merely involve material factors such as machines, factories, coal mines and

historical mode of abstraction, science has always reflected a particular epoch in its subject matter, its laws, its metaphysical propositions and in its embedded values. The new scientific "truths" (or forms of consciousness) that evolve out of each epoch represent an important and indispensable source of "spiritual power," both for the development of new technologies and for the new social relationships that arise out of them. Consequently, the emergence of a particular form of scientific consciousness or structure of ideas cannot be separated from the social conflicts of its era: "A new rising ruling class is able to understand through its particular class situation the new 'truths' that serve its interests. These new 'truths' then become a powerful weapon in the struggle against the rulers of the declining social order, who have neither interest in, nor understanding of, the new doctrines and perceive them only as a threat. . . . So it was with the natural science that accompanied the rise of the bourgeoisie; so too is it with political economy, which is a science of the proletariat."[25] Viewed in such a manner, the scientific disciplines of the nineteenth century were all expressions of the growing historical self-understanding of an emerging bourgeoisie and a necessary pre-condition for industrial expansion. As such, they represented the "spiritual basis of capitalism."[26]

But such a conception of science as "class science" did not entail the view that every class maintains its own special set of scientific views, but "that a certain form of science can be both an object and a weapon of class struggle, and that a class has an interest only in the investigation and diffusion of

---

railroads but also the ability to make them and the science which creates this ability. Natural science, our knowledge of the forces of nature, our ability to reason and cooperate are all important as factors of production. Technology rests not only on material elements alone, but also on a strong spiritual elements." Anton Pannekoek, "Het historisch materialisme," *De Nieuwe Tijd*, 1919, pp. 15-22, 51-58. By analogy "socialist politics" could be viewed as the "technology of the proletariat" since it had a similar scientific and spiritual relationship to their productive relationships. Anton Pannekoek, "Sozialistische Politik," "Zeitungskorrespondenz" article, May 1, 1909. From 1908 to 1914, while a full-time militant in the German SPD, Pannekoek wrote a regular series of weekly articles which were sent to subscribing local SPD papers (the number varied between 15 and 30). Pannekoek's intention with these articles was to develop a body of popularized theory easily understandable to the average worker. Dates cited are those of the proof copies contained in the Pannekoek archives, International Institute for Social History (Amsterdam). These articles can be found most regularly in the *Leipziger Volkszietung* and *Bremer Bürgerzeitung*, usually several days to several weeks after the proof date copy.

25.   Anton Pannekoek, "Klassenwissenschaft und Philosophie," *op. cit.* Pannekoek's most detailed treatment of the question of scientific consciousness and social development is contained in his *A History of Astronomy* (New York: Barnes and Noble, 1969).

26.   Anton Pannekoek (pseudonym John Harper), "Materialism and Historical Materialism," *New Essays*, Fall, 1942. This article is a revised English version of his 1919 essay, "Het historisch materialisme," *op. cit.*

those truths which directly advance its own living conditions." [27] Thus, while the natural sciences of the nineteenth century could be termed "bourgeois" on the basis of their objects and interests, there could be, in strictly methodological terms, no such thing as a "bourgeois science" to be replaced by a "proletarian science." The question was one of a larger form of historical consciousness. What a Marxist critique of science must be directed against is the class-determined ideological interpretation and class-determined practical utilization of science whenever it conflicts with the needs of humanity. Historically, science, like the utilization of all other productive and human resources, was subordinated to the requirements of class relations within a given social system. As inheritors of a new social order, the proletariat will have a much greater interest in building upon the scientific traditions of the past since they would eventually reap the full benefits from it. The science and technology of the hypothetical socialist future—no matter how altered—could, therefore, only be based on all previous scientific and social developments.

In a more immediate sense, Pannekoek saw a major alteration in the social character of twentieth-century natural science which had potentially great significance. Whereas the natural scientists of the mid-nineteenth century "had stood in the avant-garde of the spiritual struggle as leaders themselves, or as spokesmen of the new class, professing the doctrines and ideals of a new form of progress," those of the twentieth century were "either isolated in their narrow specialities or bearers of reactionary ideas or old illusions." This did not mean that the natural scientists of the past were "a better breed of scientists," but illustrated simply "a difference of social significance caused by changed social conditions." [28]

This social decline and fragmentation of the natural sciences, Pannekoek felt, was paralleled by the development and expansion of a new and qualitatively different form of scientific consciousness: historical material-ism — "the class science of the proletariat." The principal gap in the scientific outlook of the bourgeoisie, he argued, was that a "science of society lay outside of its grasp," since it represented a class that could not see its own limitations and eventual downfall. [29] It could not, therefore, view the world in its interconnected unity, with complete clarity and without illusions. As in the case of the natural sciences of the nineteenth century the new "proletarian science" of Marxism was both a "theoretical expression" of a new stage of

---

27. Anton Pannekoek, "Klassenwissenschaft und Philosophie," *op. cit.*

28. Anton Pannekoek, "Twee natuuronderzoeker in de maatschappelijk-geesterlijke strijd," *De Nieuwe Tijd*, 1917, pp. 300-314, 375-392.

29. *Ibid.*

social development and one component of the worldview of a new ascendant class.[30] As representatives of a rising new class, and bearers of a new science of society, Marx and Engels were the first to transcend the limitations of bourgeois thought, and could, therefore, be viewed as "the first class scientists of the proletariat."[31]

The new science of historical materialism, moreover, could arise only with the development of the modern proletariat, since the bourgeoisie has no interest in allowing the truth about society to be discovered; a truth which would show the transient nature of its rule: "The proletariat, therefore, has every interest in discovering the inner laws of society and the sources of their endless torment. Because the working class is the only class which has nothing to conceal, and, therefore, can look at social phenomena in an unbiased manner, it alone is in a position to discover and advocate the truth about society."[32] Epistemologically, this new social or "spiritual science" (Pannekoek uses the terms interchangeably along with historical materialism and Marxism) also differed fundamentally in the sense that for the bourgeoisie science represented a system of abstract ideas and concepts for the intellectuals, while for the proletariat "his science" constituted an integral part of "his own life's experience." Viewing science in the broad Dietzgenian sense as the systemization and conceptualization of experience, this meant that for the worker "spiritual science" was merely a form of "ordered knowledge, a short summary of reality" based on his productive experiences, which both explains and clarifies these experiences and serves as a guide for his daily praxis: "It is very unlikely that many of the socialist workers have ever read Kant or Hegel, and perhaps not even Marx, Engels or Dietzgen. But they have something entirely different, life itself...it is their own life experiences which represent the study form that gives them their determined convictions."[33]

Although the new "spiritual science" of Marxism was linked with the bourgeois scientific methodologies of the past through the process of social and historical development, Pannekoek's fundamental distinction between social and natural science ruled out any connection between Marxism and physical theory: "The spiritual sciences differ from the natural sciences on the basis of both their object and method. The goal of natural science is to

30.   Anton Pannekoek, "Klassenwissenschaft un Philosophie," *op. cit.*
31.   Anton Pannekoek, "Twee natuuronderzoeker in de maatschappelijk-geestelijke strijd," *op. cit.*
32.   Anton Pannekoek, "Klassenwissenschaft und Philosophie," *op. cit.*
33.   Anton Pannekoek, "Die Arbeiter und die sozialistische Wissenschaft," "Zeitungs-korrespondenz," October 23, 1909.

develop an abstraction out of reality; while the goal of spiritual science is to discover and describe a fixed progression and unity in general and particular phenomena."[34] The central methodological question for both forms of science concerns the nature of their laws and predictions. Responding to those who claimed that physical science is characterized by the exactness of its natural laws and predictions, Pannekoek contended: "What certainty do I have that the event thus asserted and computed really takes place? The answer can only be: None. . . . No scientist assumes that for predictions on the basis of known laws there is absolute certainty. Hundreds of times it happened, contrary to expectations, that it did not come true, and on such cases depended the progress of science."[35] On this basis, it stood to reason that an even more tentative causal relationship between laws and predictions existed for the social sciences: "Through the immense complication of social relations 'laws' of society are much more difficult to discern, and they cannot now be put into the form of exact formulas. Still more than in nature they may be said to express not the future but our expectations about the future. It is already a great thing that, whereas former thinkers were groping in the dark, now some main lines of development have been discovered."[36] Thus, just as the history of astronomy, for example, was "full of predictions that did not come true, of disagreements that alarmed the scientists and had to be explained by new unforseen circumstances," so too would the new "class science of Marxism." [37] To speak, therefore, of Marxism as a set of absolute laws and predictions would be "a half-defeat, a laying down of one's arms." [38]

Pannekoek's most sustained effort to apply his conception of science and Marxism can be found in his treatment of the question of Marxism and Darwinism. Few questions had more centrality to the ideology of the Second International than the question of Darwinism. The link between Marx and

---

34. Anton Pannekoek, "Marx Studien," *De Nieuwe Tijd,* 1905, pp. 4-13, 129-142.

35. Anton Pannekoek, "Das Wesen des Naturgesetzes," *Erkenntnis*, 1933, pp. 389-400.

36. Anton Pannekoek, *Lenin as Philosopher, op. cit.*, p. 30.

37. Anton Pannekoek, "What About Marxism?" *Industrial Worker*, February 7, 1948. On the question of objectivity Pannekoek has noted: "Striving for objectivity as a principle of science is part of the struggle for self-preservation. Thus, for the bourgeoisie striving for objectivity in natural science is a class interest, a norm of action. In terms of maintaining themselves as a ruling class Marx's doctrine about capitalism and its development represents a pernicious threat since its validity would destroy their self-confidence and will to struggle. For the proletariat the scientific validity of Marxism is equally necessary as a means of self-preservation since it gives them the will to struggle. For the bourgeoisie it is a question of the validity of another doctrine. Both, therefore, strive for objectivity as defined within their class." Anton Pannekoek to Maxmillian Rubel, August 1, 1951, Pannekoek Archives, map 108, International Institute for Social History (Amsterdam).

38. Anton Pannekoek to Maxmillian Rubel, April 23, 1953, *op. cit.*

Darwin was officially formalized from a Socialist perspective when Engels, speaking at the graveside of Marx, stated: "Just as Darwin discovered the law of development of organic nature, so Marx discovered the law of development of human history." [39] This verdict of Engels on the fundamental parallel between Marxism and Darwinism was eventually to become a cornerstone of Marxist theory — orthodox and revisionist alike — receiving particular emphasis in the works of Karl Kautsky. As a young man, Kautsky, in fact, had initially come to socialism through his interpretation of Darwinist evolutionary doctrine, and some of his earliest theoretical efforts were devoted to developing a Marx-Darwin synthesis. [40] Early in his career Kautsky had written: "The theory of history wishes to be nothing else than the application of Darwinism to social development." [41] It was this conclusion which Kautsky derived from Darwin that was to serve as a major theoretical foundation of the deterministic Marxism of the Second International.

Unlike most Marxists of the Second International Pannekoek, however, rejected the determinism inherent in such a conception of Marxism and Darwinism. Pannekoek first addressed himself systematically to this question in his 1909 brochure, *Marxism and Darwinism*, a work he considered as among his best. His immediate practical aim was one of combatting, on the one hand, the "bourgeois Darwinists" who sought to use Darwinism as an intellectual justification for capitalism, and the orthodox Marxists, on the other, who saw it as "natural proof" of the inevitability of socialism. The basis of Pannekoek's analysis was outlined in his earlier distinction between the methodologies of natural and social science and their historical interconnection as scientific forms of class thought. "The scientific importance of Marxism as well as Darwinism," he wrote "consists in their following out the theory of evolution, the one upon the domain of the organic world. . . the other upon the domain of society." [42] What this meant was that: "Marxism and Darwinism should remain in their own domains; they are independent of each other and there is no direct connection between them." [43] To carry this theory from one domain into another where different

---

39.   Karl Marx and Friedrich Engels, *Selected Works* (London: Lawrence and Wishart, 1968), p. 435.

40.   Erich Matthias, "Kautsky und Kautskyanismus," *Marxismus Studien*, 1957, pp. 151-197.

41.   Quoted in *ibid.* For a discussion of the role of Darwinism in the ideology of German Social Democracy see Hans-Josef Steinberg, *Sozialismus und deutsche Sozialdemokratie: Zur Ideologie der Partei vor dem I. Weltkrieg, op. cit.,* pp. 45-56; Mattaus Klein, *et al., Zur Geschichte der Marxistisch-Leninistischen Philosophie in Deutschland, op. cit.,* pp. 438-45.

42.   Anton Pannekoek, *Marxism and Darwinism* (Chicago: Charles H. Kerr, 1912), p. 7.

43.   *Ibid.,* p. 35.

laws were applicable would necessarily entail wrong conclusions. This did not mean that they were opposed to each other, but that "they supplement each other in the sense that according to the Darwinian theory of evolution the animal world develops up to the stage of man, and from then on...the Marxian theory of evolution applies."[44] What was important in Darwin's work was the recognition that "under certain circumstances some animal kinds will develop into other animal kinds," through a mechanism of natural law.[45] The fact that this "natural law" became identified with a struggle for existence analogous to capitalist development did not affect the validity of his theory, nor, conversely, did it make capitalist competition a "natural law." The differences between Marx and Darwin were just as significant as their similarities. And the failure of Marxists to recognize them was a major weakness of their scientific position.

Darwinism, like all scientific formulations, was not mere abstract thought but an integral part of the class struggles of its epoch. In this case Darwinism functioned as a "tool of the bourgeoisie" in its struggle against both remnants of feudalism and the proletariat.[46] By undermining the entire foundation of orthodox Christian dogma, Darwin's theory destroyed the main ideological prop of the reactionary bourgeoisie. But Darwinism worked equally well for the new bourgeoisie as a weapon against the proletariat. By seeming to offer "scientific proof of inequality" and teaching that "struggle is unavoidable," Darwinism could serve as a powerful counterweight to the socialist doctrines of equality and cooperation.[47] What Marx and Darwin really had in common was to shatter an old, rigid, immobile worldview. For socialists, therefore, the real significance of Darwinism lay in the fact that it represented a precondition for the understanding of historical materialism, rather than a doctrine directly related to it in any way.

It will readily be seen that the conception of Marxism that emerges from Pannekoek's treatment of the problem of science and socialism represents a radical departure from the orthodox Marxism of his contemporaries. As early as 1901 Pannekoek had contended that it mattered very little whether or not

44. *Ibid.*, p. 33.
45. *Ibid.*, p. 11.
46. *Ibid.*, p. 22.
47. *Ibid.*, pp. 28-29. Pannekoek sought to expand upon the ideas expressed in *Marxism and Darwinism* some four decades later in a work entitled *Anthropogenesis*, in which he attempted to provide a more unified social and biological explanation for the rise of man in the animal world, examining in particular the question of the development of abstract thought. This effort can be seen as an attempt to provide a biological foundation for Dietzgen's theory of understanding. Anton Pannekoek, *Anthropogenesis: A Study of the Origin of Man* (Amesterdam: North Holland Publishing Co., 1953).

Marx's theories, or even his basic methodology, were completely valid, but rather that they produced results through practice just as the natural sciences had continually produced significant findings with wrong methods.[48] When Pannekoek addresses himself to the scientific character of Marxism, he conceives of it as a new science founded on the constitution of a new theoretical object: the social formation. For this reason, it has no connection with physical theory, neither by analogy with physical process, nor by inferring "laws of development" from nature. It is simply a set of practical hypotheses and not an abstract philosophy of the universe. Marxism is concerned with physical theory only insofar as such theory is used for specific class purposes. It is a science to the extent that the social development and revolutionary activity which it reflects and seeks to explain requires the comprehension of its own subject matter, methodological concepts and procedures. The conditional validity of its propositions depends both on the state of its external subject matter and on the internal articulation and development of its own discourse. The dialectic, rather than a special scientific theory, represents simply a "doctrine of historical development" which seeks to clarify and distinguish the "special properties" in a particular object by considering it as an interconnected totality.[49] From such a perspective, no statement about Marxism can ever be considered final. Marx's teaching does not stand outside the course of social evolution but undergoes a constant process of transformation, development and regression. In a broader historical sense, it is not the ideas of Marx *per se* that have the greater significance, but the fact that these ideas represent the first systematic formulation of the ideology of a rising revolutionary working class movement. The theoretical and philosophical fight of ideas is, from a proletarian point of view, not the basis, but just the transitory ideological form of the revolutionary class struggle. A Marxism ossified in the doctrines of Marx and Engels not only is not, but can never be, a theory of proletarian revolution.[50]

48. Anton Pannekoek, "Inlichting," *De Kroniek*, August 31, 1901. There is a certain similarity here with George Lukács' celebrated statement: "Let us assume for the sake of argument that recent research had disproved once and for all every one of Marx's individual theses. Even if this were to be proved, every serious 'orthodox' Marxist would still be able to accept all such modern findings without reservations and hence dismiss all of Marx's theses *in toto* — without having to renounce his orthodoxy for a single moment." George Lukács, *History and Class Consciousness* (London: Merlin Press, 1971), p. 1.

49. Anton Pannekoek, "Professor Treub over het historisch materialisme," *De Nieuwe Tijd*, 1904, pp. 87-97, 159-172, 295-308. Pannekoek also states elsewhere that it was Dietzgen and not Engels who developed the framework for a real Marxian dialectic. Anton Pannekoek, "Historischer Materialismus und Religion," *Die Neue Zeit*, 1904, pp. 133-142, 180-186.

50. In addition to the above, the most comprehensive source for Pannekoek's views on the nature of Marxism in his unpublished, 284-page manuscript "Historischer Materialismus," Pannekoek Archives, map 169, International Institute for Social History (Amsterdam). Also

Geist and Revolution: The Practical Implications of Pannekoek's Philosophy
Pannekoek's synthesis of Dietzgen and Marx also had more than abstract
political significance. The theoretical rejection of determinism and special
emphasis on the non-economic and "spiritual" factors in the revolutionary
process contained in this synthesis was only a starting point for Pannekoek,
who proceeded to apply it to a variety of more immediate political questions.

For Pannekoek, the ultimate political question was the problem of
working class consciousness. Its importance in his thought stems in part from
his early experiences in the Dutch Socialist movement where the lack of firm
working class roots was especially acute. Pannekoek's conception of the
relation of philosophy to economic reality led him to a view in 1901 which held
that the material world and the world of consciousness constitute an
inseparable entity in which each reciprocally conditions the other. Without
changing the structure of society one could not change the structure of
consciousness. But the converse also remains true: a revolutionary upheaval
in the economic and social structure of society is impossible without a
revolution of the societies' forms of consciousness. Proletarian revolution must
develop simultaneously in both the economic and the "spiritual" spheres: "As
never since the first advent of production of commodities there has been such
a fundamental revolution, it must be accompanied by an equally
fundamental spiritual revolution...the new understanding gains ground
step by step, waging a relentless battle against the traditional ideas to which
the ruling classes are clinging, this struggle is the mental companion of the
social class struggle." [51] Men must, therefore, think change before they can
accomplish change. Socialist revolution can only come into being as the
expression of the spontaneous consciousness of the workers. Although the
outcome of such a revolution will be decided by the physical power of the
working class, it is not this power alone that is decisive, but the "spiritual
power" which precedes it and determines its use. Revolution is thus a victory
of the mind, of historical understanding and revolutionary will. The

useful are the Pannekoek-Rubel and Pannekoek-Mattick correspondence, *ibid.*, map 108.
Toward the end of his life Pannekoek argued the need for a completely new socialist
terminology, starting first with the word Marxism itself: "So I think we must make a close with
the old slogans and traditions of socialism and make a new start.... The science of Marx, the true
lasting part of his work, remains the basis of all our opinions and thoughts. But to put it crudely:
the word Marxism should disappear from our propaganda. Everything we tell is based upon what
we see and what every worker can see. Every explication based on 'Marxism' floats over the heads
of the masses and disappears.... Future propaganda has to go to the masses because its contents
are, and are only, understandable by the workers themselves." Anton Pannekoek to Paul
Mattick, June 11, 1946, *op. cit.*

51. Anton Pannekoek, "The Position and Significance of Joseph Dietzgen's Philosophical
Works," *op. cit.*, pp. 12-13.

consciousness of the proletariat is as much a factor affecting historical evolution as the social and economic factors it arises from. The class struggle, while it corresponds to the material environment of society, is actually a struggle of consciousness.

It followed from these assumptions that the subjugation of the working class was not entirely due to economics and force alone, but in no small measure to "the *spiritual* superiority of the ruling minority" which "presides over all spiritual development, all science." Through its control over institutions such as the schools, the church, and the press, "it conataminates ever-larger proletarian masses with bourgeois conceptions." It is this "spiritual dependence of the proletariat on the bourgeoisie" that Pannekoek regards as the "main cause of the weakness of the proletariat." [52] As an obstacle to social revolution this "spiritual domination of the bourgeoisie" is just as dangerous, if not more so, as its power of material domination and exploitation. The proletariat is totally dependent intellectually and culturally on the bourgeoisie and acquiesces in its own enslavement. Viewed according to the traditional Marxist categories of base and superstructure, this formulation—which assigns an equal, if not predominant, role to the superstructure—represents a major departure from the traditional Marxist position expressed by Marx in "Preface to the Critique of Political Economy." The similarity of these ideas with Antonio Gramsci's theory of hegemony is also readily apparent. [53]

Given the "spiritual superiority" of the ruling class and the need for a "spiritual revolution" of the working-class, the corollary question arises: what is the precise nature of this proletarian consciousness and how is it developed? Proletarian class consciousness, according to Pannekoek's conception, was not identified with a particular set of doctrinal beliefs, but with a certain historical mode of abstraction. For Pannekoek, proletarian thought exists on two mutually interacting levels: the level of science (or theory) and the level of ideology or unconscious ideas. While both levels represent "abstract, generalized expressions of concrete reality," they differ in the sense that ideology (ideas) rests on unconscious feelings, perceptions and drives, while science (theory) is an attempt to give conscious insight and understanding to these spontaneous perceptions by abstracting the particular from the general

---

52. Anton Pannekoek, "Massenaktion und Revolution," *Die Neue Zeit*, 1929, pp. 541-50, 585-93, 609-16. See also Anton Pannekoek, "Der Sozialismus als Kulturmacht," "Zeitungs-korrespondenz," December 24, 1911.

53. For an elaboration of Gramsci's theory of hegemony see Gwyn Williams, "Gramsci's Concept of Egemonia," *Journal of the History of Ideas*, October-December, 1960.

and giving it concrete historical content. [54] What emerges from the interaction between the two levels is a series of "categories of understanding" unique to proletarian thought that Pannekoek considers the real content of proletarian class consciousness. Pannekoek, however, is vague in specifying precisely what these categories really imply other than to state that they are dialectical in the sense that they are based on conceptual opposites (which are later resolved in proletarian strategy and action) such as: revolution vs. evolution, theory vs. practice, end goals vs. daily activity. Although opposites, the categories are united in the sense that they are all different sides of the same process of development—the historical transition to socialism. They differ from bourgeois categories of understanding that are static and can only look at the present. [55]

Pannekoek's conception of "false consciousness" was tied to his view of the relation of ideas to economic reality. Rather than a direct reflection of economic conditions, ideas arise out of "present reality and the system of ideas transmitted from the past." [56] For the formation of proletarian class consciousness the "thought systems" of the past were of particular importance since, although detached from their material roots, they still constituted a major "spiritual force" of great social significance. That certain thought patterns persist long after the conditions of life which produced them have disappeared was not simply a consequence of the human mind, but of what might be termed the "social memory," or "the perpetuation of collective ideas, systematized in the form of prevailing beliefs and ideologies, and transferred to future generations in books, in literature, in art and in education." [57] It was this continued predominance of traditional thought that has caused the development of ideas to lag behind the development of society.

Although this "time lag" of ideas was viewed by Pannekoek as the main component of false consciousness, he foresaw it being eventually resolved through a process of "spiritual evolution" culminating in a sudden "ripening of new ideas." Through its encounter with new productive forces and relationships, "new and different impressions enter the mind which do not fit in with the old image. Then there begins a process of rebuilding, out of parts of old ideas and new experiences. Old concepts are replaced by new ones,

54. Anton Pannekoek, *Die taktischen Differenzen in der Arbeiterbewegung* (Hamburg: Erdmann Dubber, 1909), p. 130. This work represents one of the most developed and systematic products of Pannekoek's pre-war thought.

55. *Ibid.*, p. 27.

56. Anton Pannekoek, "Het historisch materialisme," *op. cit.*

57. Anton Pannekoek, "Society and Mind in Marxian Philosophy," *Science and Society*, Summer, 1937. Expressed more simply, it might be said that these ideas constitute "the mental store of the community."

former rules and judgments are upset, new ideas emerge."[58] This process is uneven in the sense that not every member of a class or group is affected in the same way or at the same time. Intensive ideological strife then arises which further accelerates the revolutionization of ideas. Since outdated ideas often prevent gradual adjustment of ideas and institutions, their continued predominance can also, under the impetus of certain unforseen events, lead to "explosions," to sudden "revolutionary transformations."[59]

For Pannekoek, the question of false consciousness also had a more immediate second dimension. Taking the view that tactical and ideological differences (i.e., anarchism and revisionism) within the international socialist movement had a distinct social base, Pannekoek sought to explain these differences as a struggle of social interests between different layers of the proletariat based on different modes of thought. Given the uneven course of social development, it stood to reason that the socialist movement would be heterogeneous, composed of several different social groups. From this perspective, anarchism could be viewed as the expression of the ideology of declassed petit bourgeois elements within the socialist movement. Their ideology was merely a continuation of bourgeois individualism and the tradition of bourgeois revolution. Their vision of a new society, unlike that of socialism, failed to recognize the necessity of establishing a completely new mode of production.[60] Revisionism, on the other hand, was based both in the petit bourgeoisie and in certain groups within the industrial proletariat who had achieved high wages and a shorter work week through strong organization and a relatively privileged position, and who consequently no longer felt the same need to overthrow capitalism as the other levels of the proletariat.[61] For them, "Socialism is not based on a completely new proletarian worldview but represents merely a framework for achieving

58. *Ibid.*
59. *Ibid.*
60. Anton Pannekoek, *Die taktischen Differenzen in der Arbeiterbewegung, op. cit.,* pp. 61-67. These ideas first appeared in less developed form in his earlier, "Theorie en beginselin de arbeidersbewegung" *De Nieuwe Tijd,* 1900, pp. 602-62.
61. *Ibid.,* pp. 125-126. Pannekoek was also among the first in Europe to employ the concept of the "labor aristocracy" which held that a certain segment of the trade union movement had been imbued with bourgeois values. This concept was first used in his 1905 article, "Lessen uit de mijnwerkerstaking," *De Nieuwe Tijd,* 1905, pp. 250-263. By 1910 Pannekoek had become embroiled in a series of controversies with the German trade union leadership which culminated in a public debate with the trade union leader Karl Legien before an audience of 2,000 persons. Further information on Pannekoek's "Zeitungskorrespondenz" articles: "Marx und die Gewerkschafte," November 13, 1901; "Unteroffiziere," November 27, 1909; "Amerikanische Arbeiterbewegung," January 10, 1910; "Gewerkschaftliche Demokratie," December 17, 1910; "Das Vertretungssystem in der Arbeiterbewegung," April 27, 1911.

practical goals, while the earlier bourgeois goals quietly continue to coexist."[62] Their peaceful evolutionary doctrines and narrow conceptions of day-to-day struggles remained unconnected to the larger goal of proletarian liberation. As a thought form, revisionist ideology was based on bourgeois moral categories such as freedom, justice and equality. Like anarchism, revisionism failed to perceive the need for new forms of productive relationships. For these reasons, "both anarchism and revisionism, by combining a bourgeois mode of thought with a proletarian temperament, represent bourgeois tendencies within the workers' movement."[63]

If there is a fundamental gap in Pannekoek's theory of class consciousness, it lies perhaps in his failure to work out the precise details of how false consciousness is transcended. His view, on one hand, is that it occurs spontaneously through "spiritual evolution," which is an outgrowth of the process of both historical development (in this case "large industrial concentration") and working class self-activity. Yet, from another perspective, he feels that it can be consciously accelerated by an organized socialist movement, through its education and propaganda capabilities, its ability to channel working class self-activity toward specific socialist goals, and by its capability to wage intense ideological struggles. Propaganda, here, was viewed as an "amplification and explanation" of what the workers already see and perceive rather than something directed at them. [64] The ultimate objective of this process of "clarification" was the development of a "social ideal" or "mental picture" of a subsequent, more highly developed social system: "Since everything which man does must first exist in his mind as purpose and will, therefore, every new order, before it becomes a reality, must first exist as a more or less adequate conscious ideal."[65] But shorn of their philosophical underpinnings, both of these views were little more than variations of standard Social Democratic assumptions of the era.

In view of his emphasis on consciousness and the ideological subjugation of

---

62. *Ibid.*, pp. 34-35.

63. *Ibid.*, p. 60.

64. Anton Pannekoek to Frank van der Goes, August 7, 1900, van der Goes archives, map 1803, International Institute for Social History (Amsterdam). It is perhaps of some significance that the bulk of Pannekoek's practical activity as a militant was devoted to developing and participating in socialist educational structures in Leiden, Berlin and Bremen. An account of his educational work in Bremen and its impact can be found in: Karl Ernst Moring, *Die Sozialdemokratische Partei in Bremen, 1890-1914* (Hanover: Verlag für Literature, 1968); and Gottfried Mergner, *Arbeiterbewegung und Intelligenz* (Starnberg: Raith, 1973). Pannekoek's efforts to develop a body of popularized theory with his "correspondence articles" can also be viewed as an attempt to address himself to this question.

65. Anton Pannekoek, "Socialism and Anarchism," *International Socialist Review*, February 1, 1913.

the working class, it is not surprising that Pannekoek would move to displace the problem of revolution from the party and trade unions to the masses. Prior to 1910 Pannekoek's theoretical work viewed party and trade union organizations as central factors constituting the "power of the proletariat," along with its size, role in the productive process, consciousness and theoretical knowledge. Organization, in this case, was conceived of as a "process" — one facet of the phenomena of social evolution — rather than as something independent and mechanically separated from the other factors. Integral to this conception was a theory of revolutionary parliamentarianism which stressed the subjective effects of parliamentary activity, in this case its possibilities as a mechanism for educating the working class on the nature of society and the state.[66] As early as 1908, however, in a document intended for the factional struggle in the Dutch SDAP, Pannekoek had expressed serious reservations about the utility of both traditional working class organizations and the strategy of parliamentarianism. Noting that "Dietzgen teaches us not to doubt the truth but to have doubts about the absolute validity of a truth," Pannekoek cautioned: "This truth is not absolute; it has its limitations. The labor movement has adapted itself to the strategy of parliamentarianism more than is really necessary and it is impossible to attain our goals through these methods alone. A revolutionary struggle with other more powerful mediums is necessary."[67]

Starting in 1910, Pannekoek, under the impetus of the sharpening factional struggle within German Social Democracy, and grounding his views in what he felt were "new experiences in the class struggle" (i.e., the growing wave of mass actions starting with the Russian Revolution of 1905), began to see the problem of revolutionary organization in a completely different way. By now it seemed clear to him that the fundamental problem of conscious revolution was no longer one of leadership, but one of direct organization for revolution at the level of class, with the party and trade union organizations acting as agents of the working class, especially on its assault on the state. Speaking of the capacity of the workers to undertake revolutionary mass actions on their own initiative, Pannekoek noted: "And it is not merely a question of the laboring masses simply acquiring consciousness of this task, but one of them grasping it firmly and decisively. The movement will never be able to take its proper course as long as they sit around waiting for their leaders to give the word. An acceleration of our struggle is possible only when

---

66. See in particular: Anton Pannekoek, "Algemeen Kiesrecht," *De Neiuwe Tijd*, 1906, pp. 1-10; Anton Pannekoek, "Theorie en beginsel in de arbeidersbewegung," *op. cit.*
67. Anton Pannekoek, "Joseph Dietzgen," *De Tribune*, April 18, 1908.

the masses themselves seize the initiative, leading and pushing their organizations forward." [68]

This conception was deepened and articulated during the following years into a full-fleged theory of revolutionary "mass action," which received its most detailed expression in his 1912 *Neue Zeit* polemic with Kautsky. What Pannekoek envisioned was a continuous and expanding series of mass actions, ranging from ordinary street demonstrations to the general strike. These actions would serve to educate, collectivize and strengthen the proletariat for the coming struggle for power while simultaneously weakening the foundations of the capitalist state. For Pannekoek, the main rationale of these actions lay not in their objective aims but in their subjective impact on the consciousness of the working class. Central to this process was his notion of "organizational spirit" (*Organisationsgeist*) or the spirit of solidarity, collectivity, commitment, self-sacrifice, sense of purpose and class identity inherent in working class organization: "The organizational spirit is the living soul of the labor movement which derives its power and capability for action from its body. But this immortal soul, unlike the soul of Christian theology, does not float around lifeless in the sky, but remains, in fact, always grounded in an organizational body, living in the common organized actions of those it joins together. This spirit is not something abstract, put forward in place of the 'real, concrete organization' of the existing organizational forms, but it is in fact something *just as real and concrete* as these forms. It binds individual persons just as firmly together as any principles and statutes could ever do so that even if the external bond of principles and statutes were removed these individuals would no longer be loose atoms competing against each other." [69] It is this spirit that creates the capacity to struggle and receives its fullest expression in mass actions. And it is this above all that would give a "completely new character" to the coming mass actions of the future. To ignore this principle, as Kautsky did, was to ignore what distinguished proletarian organization from any other form of organization.

68. Anton Pannekoek, "Die Organisation im Kampfe," "Zeitungskorrespondenz," April 9, 1910.

69. Anton Pannekoek, "Massenaktion und Revolution," *op. cit.* For further elaboration of various aspects of this theory see Anton Pannekoek, *Die Machtmittel des Proletariats* (Stuttgart: Sozialdemokratischen Vereins Stuttgart, 1910), and the following "Zeitungskorrespondenz" articles: "Proletarische Kriegstaktik," April 16, 1910; "Die Opfer des Kampfes," April 23, 1910; "Geist und Masse," February 10, 1912; "Zum neuen Kampf," May 25, 1912; "Der Instinkt der Massen," August 24, 1912; "Volksinteresse und Massenaktion," October 26, 1912. Pannekoek's theory of mass action also paralleled in many respects the revolutionary theories of Rosa Luxemburg and was an outgrowth of the same historical situation. The main differences lie in the lack of a philosophical base and the greater emphasis placed on the mass strike in Rosa Luxemburg's thought.

Several variations of this theme of socialism as a process of spiritual struggle were restated by Pannekoek as events pushed his theoretical development forward. Thus, in a 1916 article analyzing the collapse of German Social Democracy in 1914, Pannekoek rejected the notion that it collapsed simply because it was too weak. The weakness was not that of a material force but was much worse: "a general inability to struggle, a lack of spiritual force, a lack of will for class struggle." [70] The resurrection of a new International and the development of a qualitatively different "new socialism of the working masses" would only be possible through a long drawn-out process of spiritual renewal: "Now is the time to gather together everything in the way of new ideas, new solutions, new propositions, to inspect them, to clarify them by means of discussion and thus to make them of service to the new struggle....But this struggle is only made possible by a simultaneous relentless struggle against all the elements of the former Social Democracy, which would bind the proletariat to the chariot of imperialism...." [71] It was on these grounds that Pannekoek opposed Lenin's wartime tactics of splitting the existing socialist movement in favor of a strategy of appealing directly to the masses. [72] Here the germ of what was later to be at the root of the differences between Pannekoek and Lenin is already apparent. A similar view was again advanced in his analysis of the defeat of the German revolution in 1918. How was it possible, he asked, that victory eluded the workers at a time when the state was powerless and they were seemingly in control? This defeat, he felt, proved that "still another source of power of the bourgeoisie existed," which permitted them to newly construct their domination: "This secret power is the spiritual power of the bourgeoisie over the proletariat. Because the proletarian masses were still completely ruled by a bourgeois mode of thought they rebuilt bourgeois domination again with their own hands after its collapse." [73] It was a corollary of this that to return to an outdated strategy of parliamentarianism and trade unionism—as Pannekoek felt Lenin and the Third International were attempting to do—was to revert to a bourgeois mode of domination.

In shifting the problem of revolution to the subjective consciousness of the

70. Anton Pannekoek, "Der Imperialismus und die Aufgaben des Proletariats," *Vorbote*, number one, 1916.

71. Anton Pannekoek, "The Third International," *International Socialist Review*, February 1917.

72. These differing conceptions are detailed most concisely in Anton Pannekoek to William van Ravesteyn, October 24, 1915, van Ravesteyn archives, map 15, International Institute for Social History (Amsterdam).

73. Anton Pannekoek, *Weltrevolution und kommunistische Taktik* (Vienna: Verlag der Arbeiterbuchhandlung, 1920).

masses, it followed that Pannekoek would criticize with particular force the different nuances of "death crisis" theories of capitalist collapse which held that the collapse of capitalism was an inevitable consequence of the "laws" of capitalist reproduction. In Pannekoek's view, "nothing is more foreign to Marxism than the notion that capitalism will collapse through an unavoidable economic crisis." [74] As early as 1900, Pannekoek, in a letter to his mentor, the economist Frank van der Goes, had outlined what was to be the basis of his conception. For him, the critical link between economics and revolution was not crisis but the understanding and active intervention of the revolutionary class which translates changes in the economic structure into "social reality" through political action. Viewing all human actions as "equal products" of material conditions, Pannekoek ruled out a sharp distinction between evolution and revolution. Both form a "similar part" of the same process of development and it is only their external appearance that gives them the designations evolution and revolution. [75] This formulation was subsequently expanded to encompass an analysis of both the nature of economic "laws" and the particular mode of thought underlying "death crisis" theories. The fulcrum of his analysis is a rejection of what he terms "mechanical necessity" in the laws of capitalist reproduction in favor of the concept of "social necessity." Rather than either a predetermined and necessary course of development or pure voluntarism, "social necessity" represents a major connecting link between economic conditions and the desires and actions of men: "What has occurred economically must first be understood in the thoughts and desires of men and then translated into action." [76] Thus imperialism, for example, was not an absolute economic necessity for the reproduction of capitalism but was something capitalism understood as useful and desirable and had the capability to achieve. [77] Similarly, socialism would come only when the working class understands it as necessary, wills it and has the power and capability to attain it: "Only the self-liberation of the proletariat will signify the collapse of capitalism." [78] To

---

74. Anton Pannekoek, "Prinzip und Taktik," *Proletarier*, July and August 1927.
75. Anton Pannekoek to Frank van der Goes, August 7, 1900, *op. cit.*
76. Anton Pannekoek, "Prinzip und Taktik," *op. cit.*
77. Anton Pannekoek, "De ekonomische noodzakelijkheid van het imperialisme," *De Nieuwe Tijd*, 1916, pp. 268-285. The intended aim of this article was a critique of Rosa Luxemburg's *The Accumulation of Capital*. An earlier, less comprehensive, version first appeared as a book review in the *Bremer Bürgerzeitung*, January 29 and 30, 1913.
78. Anton Pannekoek, "Die Zusammenbruchstheorie des Kapitalismus," *Rätekorrespondenz*, June, 1934. This work, which was directed against the theories of the German economist Henryk Grossmann, was part of a series of polemics within the International Council Communist movement.

speak of a "final crisis" of capitalism apart from the intervention of a revolutionary class is to revert to a mechanistic bourgeois mentality, a dangerous illusion not based on revolutionary practice. In bourgeois thought capitalism is a mechanistic system which views men entirely in economic roles as capitalists, wage earners, buyers, sellers, etc. Their role is a completely passive one dictated by the structure of the capitalist market. Marxist thought, by contrast, views the social forces of development as not entirely economic, but as part of a larger totality of the human environment in which the thoughts, desires and actions of men, although externally conditioned, still play a prominent role. [79]

Pannekoek Against Lenin

The decisive turning point in Pannekoek's political career came with his break with the Comintern in 1920. [80] By the late 1920s Pannekoek's political development had carried him to a theory of the revolutionary self-organization of the working class based on the workers' council structure, which he counterposed to all other existing forms of working class organization. The "Council Communist" movement, according to this theory, represented both the beginning of a qualitatively new revolutionary labor movement and the embryonic structure for a socialist reorganization of society. Although this conception represented a major departure from his previous thought, many of his main Council Communist themes are directly related to the problems Pannekoek had worked out earlier. The Dietzgenian dialectical theory of knowledge is here broadened into a political-philosophical theory uniting subject and object, in this case a completely autonomous thinking and acting working class fully conscious of itself in the context of a particular stage of development—a stage in which historical consciousness is reunited with practical organization, one in which the workers are transformed from "obedient subjects" into "free and self-reliant masters of their fate, capable to build and manage their new world." [81]

For Pannekoek, this new consciousness could only arise through the daily experience of the proletariat, in particular through their experience in the shops: "In the factory the workers grow conscious of the content of their life, their productive work, their work community as a collectivity that makes it a

---

79. *Ibid.*

80. For details on the break with the Third International see: Hans Manfred Bock, *Syndikalismus und Linkskommunismus von 1918-1923* (Meisenheim: A. Hain, 1969); Herman de Liagre Böhl, *Herman Gorter, op. cit.*

81. Anton Pannekoek, *Workers' Councils* (Melbourne: Southern Advocate for Workers' Councils, 1951), p. 34.

living organism, an element of the totality of society. Here in shop occupations a vague feeling arises that they ought to be entirely masters of production, that they ought to expel the unworthy outsiders, the commanding capitalists, who abuse it in wasting the riches of mankind and in devastating the earth."[82] Within this process the role of the workers' councils was conceptualized as one of an "organ of collective thought"—in practical terms a mechanism for organization, clarification and discussion, and in a larger sense the "spiritual form of the proletariat."[83]

Complementing this theory was his view of the Soviet Union as a state capitalist society sustained by a pseudo-Marxist ideology. [84] Although others had advanced similar theories justified on social and economic grounds, Pannekoek sought to go a step further by giving his theory a philosophical base as well. To show what he felt the Marxism of the Russian Revolution really implied, Pannekoek undertook a detailed critical examination of the philosophical basis of Leninism, published as *Lenin as Philosopher* in 1938.

Lenin's philosophical ideas were first expressed systematically in his 1908 work, *Materialism and Empiriocriticism*, which was later to become a canon of Soviet Marxism. Shortly after the turn of the century certain intellectuals in the Russian socialist movement had taken an interest in Western natural philosophy, particularly in the ideas of the physicist Ernst Mach and Richard Avenarius. A kind of "Machism" with Bogdanov and Lunatcharsky as the leading spokesmen had developed as an influential trend within the Bolshevik party, which Lenin sought to undermine in *Materialism and Empiriocriticism*. Characterizing their position as a form of subjective idealism, Lenin defended dialectical materialism on what he regarded as the chief points at issue: the status and character of matter and the nature of knowledge. Opposing the view that matter is a construct of sensations, Lenin argued that matter is ontologically primary, existing independently of consciousness. Likewise, space and time are not subjective modes of ordering experience but objective forms of the existence of matter. On the question of knowledge Lenin affirmed a "copy theory," of perception which contended that sensations depict or mirror the real world. On this basis, Lenin defended the possibility of objective truth, emphasizing practice as its criterion.

Pannekoek's aim was to confront the scientific and philosophical content of Leninism by a consideration of the philosophical and social background out

---

82. *Ibid.*, p. 78.

83. *Ibid.* See also: Anton Pannekoek, "Five Theses on the Class Struggle," *Southern Advocate for Workers' Councils*, May, 1947.

84. Pannekoek's most succinct analysis of the social nature of the Russian Revolution and Soviet state is contained in his unsigned article, "Theses on Bolshevism," *International Council Correspondence*, December, 1934.

of which Lenin's *Materialism and Empiriocriticism* arose. Fundamental for Pannekoek's analysis is his attempt to establish a definition of matter based on a synthesis of the concepts of modern physics with the philosophical ideas of Dietzgen. For Lenin, matter was defined exclusively as a physical concept based on atoms and molecules, the movement of which was governed by unchangeable natural laws. Pannekoek, however, challenged this conception and sought to show that the physical matter which was so central to Lenin's work was in reality nothing but an abstraction. The whole course of modern physics, says Pannekoek, denies the material notion of matter and replaces it instead with an abstract mental concept (abstract in the sense that it is a concept based on an attempted expression of what is general and common in a particular set of phenomena): "Atoms, of course, are not observed phenomena themselves; they are inferences of our thinking. As such they share the nature of all products of our thinking; their sharp limitation and distinction, their precise equality belong to their abstract character. As abstractions they express what is general and common in the phenomena, what is necessary for predictions."[85] In a larger philosophical sense, this definition was broadened—following Dietzgen—to define matter as everything which actually exists, whether in nature or in the human mind: "If...matter is taken as the name for the philosophical concept denoting objective reality, it embraces far more than physical matter. Then we come to the view... where the material world was spoken of as the name for the entire observed reality. This is the meaning of the word *materia*, matter in Historical Materialism, the designation of all that is really existing in the world, 'including mind and fancies,' as Dietzgen said."[86] Lenin, therefore, in criticizing Mach and Avenarius (and for that matter Dietzgen to whom he devoted a chapter entitled: "How Could Joseph Dietzgen Have Found Favor with the Reactionary Philosophers?") for their alleged subjectivism (i.e., their view that reality is composed of purely mental elements) had failed even to reach the conceptual sophistication of their systems. This was not to say that Marxist criticism of Mach and Avenarius was not needed; it clearly was, but on different grounds than Lenin chose to do so.

Pannekoek, however, did not content himself with demonstrating the distance between Lenin's *Materialism and Empiriocriticism* and the developments in modern physics, but attempted to pinpoint the basis of these errors and assess their implications for the revolutionary movement. Pannekoek's main pole of reference was a distinction between bourgeois materialism and historical materialism. Bourgeois materialism, says Panne-

---

85. Anton Pannekoek, *Lenin as Philosopher, op. cit.*, p. 20.
86. *Ibid.*, p. 61.

koek, initially developed as an ideological weapon of the bourgeoisie in their fight against the aristocracy. For this reason, it was a type of materialism whose reference point was individualistic, a materialism whose principal tool was natural science and whose principal enemy was the religious ideology in which the absolutist status quo rationalized itself. According to this doctrine all phenomena of human life, including human ideas, have their origins in the chemical and physical processes of cellular substance and ultimately can be explained by the dynamics and movements of atoms. Historical materialism, on the other hand, was a weapon of the proletariat in their struggle against the bourgeoisie. Its reference point is society, and its science is a social rather than a natural science, which reveals to the proletariat their true relationships within the capitalist system. For these reasons it considers ideas a social rather than a physical phenomenon. Thus, for example, in the case of religion it seeks to explain its social base and does not fight it directly, but attacks the economic structure of society.

For Pannekoek, it was neither an accident nor an aberration that Lenin used an outdated form of mechanistic bourgeois materialism for his point of departure, but a natural outgrowth of the prevailing socio-economic conditions in pre-revolutionary Russia. In tsarist Russia the revolutionary intellectuals, Lenin among them, were confronted with the same task and problems as had been the bourgeois revolutionaries of a previous historical epoch: the overthrow of an absolutist land-based ruling class which was impeding the development of modern industry. But in Russia the bourgeoisie was too weak and too dependent upon tsarism to carry out this revolutionary task itself. This role, therefore, fell to the intelligentsia, a class composed of technical and professional people of non-noble origin often employed by the state, who were aided in their task by Russia's rather limited and backward proletariat. Lenin provided not only the organizational form (the vanguard party of professional revolutionaries) for carrying out an essentially bourgeois revolution, but also a philosophy suitable for its practical activity. Since a major ideological prop of the tsarist aristocracy was religion it was necessary that the militant wing of the rising bourgeoisie devote first priority to waging a campaign against it. Lenin's reversion to the militant bourgeois materialism of the past historical epoch provided the necessary ideological and philosophical basis for this struggle. Indeed, the last paragraph in *Materialism and Empiriocriticism* seems to suggest that the most important ideological struggle in the world is between materialism and religion. Consequently: "To the Russian Marxists the nucleus of Marxism is not contained in Marx's thesis that social reality determines consciousness but in the sentence of the young Marx inscribed in big letters on the Moscow

Peoples' House that religion is the opium of the people." [87] Both in his obsolete materialist philosophy and in his theory of revolution Lenin hid himself from the historical truth that the Russian Revolution was bound to remain a belated successor to the great bourgeois revolutions of the past. On these grounds, Pannekoek concluded that "the alleged Marxism of Lenin and the Bolshevik party is nothing but a legend. Lenin never knew real Marxism." [88] The question was not so much that Lenin was wrong or that his logic was fallacious, but that his thought was bourgeois. Leninism was, therefore, the theory of a new state capitalist middle class revolution installing a new ruling class which signified for the workers just another form of slavery and exploitation. This was the true significance of Lenin as philosopher.

How, then, shall one assess Pannekoek's legacy? The theoretical and political conceptions that evolved out of his basic Marx-Dietzgen synthesis, as we have seen, are far removed from the scholastic interpetation of Marx embodied in the Marxism of both the Second and Third Internationals. Rather than a finished theory in itself, Pannekoek's work represents a critical methodology open to all new social developments, in which all hypotheses are admissible, all conclusions tentative. Yet, viewed in its entirety, the architecture of Pannekoek's thought contains a collection of elements of critique, analysis and constructive conceptions with sufficient coherence to fit together into a single conceptual framework. And while it remains true that his theories never became identified with a political movement of any significance, or even any cogent political practice, it is Pannekoek's chief merit to have probed into the problems of both the nature of Marxism and working class self-activity far more persistently and coherently than perhaps any other revolutionary theorist before or since. It seems clear on these grounds alone that Anton Pannekoek, if nothing else, has appreciably widened the classical perspective of Marxist analysis.

---

87. *Ibid.*, p. 71.
88. *Ibid.* Pannekoek's analysis of the philosophical content of Leninism possesses certain close affinities with the theories developed contemporaneously by the German Marxist Karl Korsch, also a Council Communist. Although Korsch, like Pannekoek, concluded that Lenin was the philosopher of an essentially bourgeois revolution, he arrived at his conclusions from an entirely different starting point and through entirely different theoretical formulations. See in particular: Karl Korsch, *Marxism and Philosophy* (London: New Left Books, 1970).

AUTHOR'S INTRODUCTION

by Serge Bricianer

In a period marked by the eclipse of the revolutionary movement in the industrialized countries, Anton Pannekoek could scarcely have been the focus of much attention. This man never exercised the least power, nor did his life ever take a tragic turn. His name was, of course, mentioned with some frequency by the most prominent Marxist theoreticians of the early twentieth century, and today this earns him a footnote when early pamphlets are reissued. However, his own writings are muted by a thick veil of silence, since they contain nothing to captivate the refurbishers of old ideas—no ready-made aphorisms, no system to excite the exegetes, no manifest links with a state or with any organized political tendency. His was a body of thought attached solely to the cause of communist revolution, presenting an intellectual development linked with types of action whose very echoes had almost ceased to feed the panic and the hatred of the dominant classes.

Anton Pannekoek died, alone, in the little Dutch village of Wageningen on April 28, 1960. A few articles were then published about him,[1] and again a veil of silence descended. During the past few years, however, his name has been cropping up, not in learned works but in conversations among young people in quest of a new direction. Who, then, was this Pannekoek of whom Lenin speaks well in The State and the Revolution *and with suspicion in* Left-Wing Communism: An Infantile Disorder, *which, as it happens, are the only easily accessible sources?*

The aim of the present collection of his writings is to answer this question, not just to sing the praises of a dead man but to disengage broad outlines of a highly significant development. The life of Anton Pannekoek is inseparable from the various controversies which have raged since the beginning of the century among the ranks of the world workers' movement, especially in the midst of its most extremist tendencies—particularly within council

---

1. Cf. particularly H. Zanstra (a fellow of the Academy of Sciences) "Lebensbericht...," *Jaarboek der Koniglijke Nederlandse Akademie van Wetensrhappen* (1959-1960); G.B. Albada (disciple and longstanding political friend) "In Memoriam...," *Folio Civitas* (University of Amsterdam), 14:5, 1960, pp. 3-4; Paul Mattick, "Anton Pannekoek (1873-1960)," *New Politics*, Vol. 1, No. 2 (Winter 1962), pp. 107-114.

communism (as distinct from parliamentary communism) — also derogatively called "the ultra-left." Pannekoek, of course, was not intensively involved (quantitatively speaking) so much in these controversies as in the organizational patterns of which they were the special expression, except during the great period extending roughly from 1900 to 1920. This by no means precludes the fact that the most developed of his political writings — the part which today, especially since the May Days of 1968, assumes indisputable relevance — was written during subsequent periods.

Pannekoek's work includes two key interconnected ideas: 1) the idea of a development which is both anthropological and cosmological, based on historical materialism; 2) the theory of mass action, which, with the first great revolutionary crisis of the twentieth century, became the idea of the workers' councils. Hence the introduction to this collection will be devoted mainly to the first, and the anthropological part will be pivoted on the second.

This collection is presented, therefore, as a contribution to the history of ideas or, more precisely to the history of the formation of communist theory in the twentieth century. For this reason its method and organization will infringe somewhat the usual rules of the genre. In particular, the reader will not find a compactly organized biography, the biographical material being dispersed through the various chapters and interwoven more or less with the historical development or with that of theoretical problems. Of course, this formula will entail repetition; at the same time, limitations of space will constrain us to pass over questions of relatively minor importance within this framework. The introductory parts to each section of the book and the notes will attempt to meet any such deficiency. Where necessary, a summary of passages which had to be omitted will be given, remaining as close as possible to the original text.

In our view, the attempt to place the changing direction of the class struggle in historical perspective, especially in the developed countries, is infinitely more important than to inform the reader that Pannekoek was of rather small stature, that he had startling blue eyes, that the Pannekoeks were on calling terms with their neighbors, the Kautskys, during their stay in Berlin, or that they lived in an elegant bungalow in one of the best districts of Amsterdam.

Antonie (German form : Anton) Pannekoek was born on January 2, 1873, at Vassen, a little village of Gelderland, an agricultural region, then one of the most backward provinces of the Netherlands. From his rural childhood he seems to have kept a taste for a simple language little graced with literary artifice, and at times somewhat rough. He studied mathematics at the University of Leyden which, in 1902, was to confer on him a Doctorate in

Astronomy. Among the professors under whom he studied was the illustrious Kapteyn of Gronigen, one of the first to apply photographic techniques systematically to the observation of celestial bodies and to the study of their distribution in space. It was, then, to studies concerning the precise motion of the stars that the young Pannekoek first devoted his intellectual energies.

After several series of observations over a period of four years (1891-94), he published a paper on the brilliance variations of B Lyrae,[2] a binary star—one composed of two stars revolving around a common center of gravity. This movement entails partial eclipses which cause periodic brilliancy variations. The intrinsic luminosity of theses stars varies, therefore, with their period, in accordance with a law which can be experimentally expressed by a curve. Pannekoek's work consisted in correcting this curve, such as it had been established upon the basis of former series of observations and statistics. (His doctoral thesis—1902—is about another variable binary star, Algol—or B Persei—and belongs to the same field of research.)

He then carried out various geodetic undertakings as attaché to the Royal Dutch commission for the measurement of the meridian (1896-99). After that, he worked at the Leyden Observatory until 1906, when, married and with a family, he began a long stay in Germany—we shall come back to this—returning to live in Holland only upon the declaration of war. There he taught mathematics in various high schools, and in 1916 he was awarded his *agrégation* in the history of astronomy at the University of Leyden. In the same year he published a work of popularized scholarship, *The Wonders of the World* (*De wonderbouw der wereld*) which was to have a considerable and lasting success.

In 1918, his peers, in recognition of his competence, proposed him for the then vacant post of Director of the Leyden Observatory; but, "as though his propaganda activities might be a risk to the stars,"[3] the minister flatly turned down the proposal. Pannekoek remained, therefore, in that part of the educational field where nominations were in the hands of the municipal authorities rather than the ministerial bureaucracy. The University of Amsterdam, where he also gave courses in mathematics as part of the pre-degree course in chemistry, duly offered him a lectureship post. Assigned to the astronomy course in 1925, he became titular professor in 1932. Eleven years later, in 1943, he retired.

---

2. Anton Pannekoek, "Untersuchungen über den Lichtwechset von B Lyrae," *Verhandeligen der Kon. Neder. Akad. van Wetenschappen*, 1, V, 7, 1897.

3. Anders and Wauters, "Qu'est-ce que l'école hollandaise?," *la Correspondance Internationale*, 21:12, 1921.

"While still young," writes one of his biographers,[4] "Pannekoek was enthralled by the beauties of the Milky Way." Later, in his early twenties, he was to compose two authoritative atlases of these stellar groups. This body of work brought him fame in scientific circles; and, in 1925, he was elected to the Netherlands Academy of Science.[5] In 1927 he was appointed to lead a small research group on an expedition to Lapland to study the chromosphere—a classic undertaking on the occasion of a solar eclipse. As a result, he made some important observations concerning spectrum rays and the intensity variation of certain of these rays, works necessitating the adaptation of an appropriate method.

However, it was in the domain of research into stellar atmosphere that Pannekoek made his special mark. In 1921 (later we shall see in what political context), he established the Institute of Astronomy of the University of Amsterdam. Situated in the suburbs of the town, this institute was also quite close to Kapteyn's laboratory at Gronigen, whose equipment our researcher was therefore able to use; for, while the construction of models of stellar atmosphere involves an essentially theoretical problem, it would be inconceivable without empiric spectrographic verifications. As one specialist stresses, however, it primarily involves appealing to "the physical intuition of the theoreticians."[6] From the study of certain questions linked with such work (radiation), some of the fundamental laws of modern physics had already been derived.

By and large, it can be said that Pannekoek was particularly interested in the interatomic Stark effect, and that he proposed more sophisticated models designed better to account for the structure of hydrogen rays.[7] (The formulation of a statistical and physical theory of the expansion of rays demanded calculations of formidable complexity at that period.) In a passing reference to this research, Bruun Van Albada has some illuminating things to say: "It is not only what Pannekoek did that is characteristic, but also what he did not do. While showing a keen interest in theories about the internal arrangement of the stars, he made no personal contribution to the elaboration of such theories. In fact, as long as the origin of stellar radiation remained unknown, these theories could do little to advance the theory of

---

4. Van Albada, *loc. cit.*

5. Pannekoek, we note in passing, never saw fit to refuse academic distinctions: Doctor *honoris causa* of Harvard, Laureate of the American Astronomical Society, in 1951 he received the gold medal of the Royal Astronomical Society of England.

6. Daniel Barbier, *les Atmosphères stellaires* (Paris, 1952), p. 16.

7. Subsequently, the basic hypothesis adopted by Pannekoek proved inadequate along with its results, as is usual in science. Besides, the problem has long been "a nightmare for the theoreticians," and only recently has it begun to be clarified (Barbier, *op. cit.*, pp. 158ff).

evolution; and statistics never ranked among Pannekoek's primary concerns." That is why he centers his works on the physical nature of the stars, thus highlighting "the immense importance of the study of the spectrum in regard to the determination of mass."[8]

Besides astronomy proper, Pannekoek's scientific activities covered the whole history of this science,[9] a history to which he ascribed exemplary value: "In early times, when physical theory was only abstract speculation, astronomy was already an ordered system of knowledge giving practical orientation in time and space. In later centuries, astronomical research was directed more and more towards theoretical knowledge of the structure of the universe, far beyond any practical application, to satisfy the craving for truth, or, in other words, for intellectual beauty. Then the mutual relation of the sciences became the opposite of what it had been. Physics, chemistry, and biology took off with increasing rapidity. Through technical applications they revolutionized society and changed the face of the earth. But astronomy stood aside in this revolution. How could the stars contribute to our technical development, our material life, or our economic organization? So their study became more and more an idealistic pursuit tending toward a physical knowledge of the universe. While the other sciences won brilliant triumphs in a transformation of the human world, the study of astronomy became a work of culture, an adventure of the mind."[10] And, on this basis, Pannekoek presented "the development of the notion of astronomy as a manifestation of humanity's growth."[11]

This aspect of the biography of Anton Pannekoek can be sketched here only in broad outline. It would often supply his social-democratic or Bolshevist adversaries with an opportunity for facile sneers as "the Cosine scholar," implying that an astronomer cannot fail to have his impractical head in the clouds.[12] It did not matter that the man so contemptuously

---

8. Van Albada, *loc. cit.*

9. Cf. in particular Pannekoek's preface and erudite notes to an edition of the astronomical works of Simon Stevin (vol. III [Amsterdam, 1961]). Stevin was a famous Flemish mathematician and physicist of the second half of the sixteenth century.

10. Disciplines in astronomy have certainly taken a turn since World War Two. Celestial mechanics is used to calculate the orbits of artificial satellites; solar physics has brought to the fore the influence of solar eruptions on the propagation of radio waves on the surface of the globe; the most advanced study of the properties of the ionosphere will probably facilitate progress in the transmission of certain radio signals; etc. But Pannekoek's thesis in no way rules out this return to practical applications of astronomy (or rather of peripheral disciplines).

11. Anton Pannekoek, *A History of Astronomy* (London, 1961), pp. 14-15. (First Dutch edition, 1951).

12 As a sample of the type of denigration, cf. Radek, "An astronomer who spends his life contemplating the stars, and therefore never sees a flesh and blood worker," *Protokoll der III*

labelled was in his day the only Marxist theoretician of repute capable of tackling any question connected with the natural sciences. No claim is made, of course, that this competence automatically implies any superiority whatsoever; but it can be urged that this type of professional activity must have greatly developed certain intellectual qualities in Pannekoek: the gift of theoretical intuition, the power of intellectual abstraction, an impressive range and depth of knowledge, intellectual exactitude and mental serentiy, a sense of team-work. Such qualities, invigorated by revolutionary enthusiasm, would enable him to organize and to generalize ideas brought to the surface by the development of the proletarian struggles of the twentieth century. Consequently this Dutchman was one of the few Marxists to attempt a real assessment of contemporary scientific ideology.

In this connection, his article in *De Nieuwe Tijd*, published in 1917, is among the most interesting.[13] "There was a time," he writes, "roughly towards the middle of the nineteenth century—the period marked by the rapid development of the bourgeoisie—when the intellectuals, the scientific researchers, figured as leaders in ideological warfare, and, as the mouthpiece of the new class, provided new slogans and ideals of progress." This time has long passed. "Another type of researcher has now appeared," professing reactionary ideas and fostering old illusions. "Of course, this does not imply that these researchers have sold out to the existing order;" there is no question of abusing or deploring a degeneration "or a retreat, or of regarding yesterday's researchers as superior to those of today. This development is quite simply the result of the transformation of society."

In the eighteenth century, says Pannekoek, the bourgeoisie waged a merciless war against the crumbling old order, a war in which the natural sciences played a role of the first importance both as a factor of technical development and as forceful element in the combat of this new class against spiritual traditions, especially belief in God. However, as soon as the bourgeoisie, having strengthened its grip on society, saw the proletariat facing up to it, it abondoned what had up to then been its special war horse—the theory of evolution. While the natural sciences continued to progress, doubts were cast on the evolutionist optimism of the preceding era, on ideas such as the physico-chemical origin of all life processes, which were reducible—it had been maintained—"to a mechanics of atoms."

"There was no question, of course, of a complete and immediate about-face; these tendencies appeared at first sporadically and gradually

---

Kongress der K.I. (Hamburg, 1921), p. 259.

13. Anton Pannekoek, "Twee natuuronderzoekers in de maatschappelijk-geestelijke strejd," *De Nieuwe Tijd*, 22 (1917), pp. 300-314, pp. 375-392.

strengthened each other before emerging fully defined in a systematic, explicit form. In political and social practice the old progressivist or liberal tradition counted for less and less and was slowly reduced, in an almost imperceptible way, to a few basic representations; while the old formulas in their pristine purity were defended only by a few individuals, and the masses remained indifferent to them. The same was true at the spiritual level. The majority of scientific scholars stood aside from political and social life, seeing in the latter little more than sordid conflicts of interest and cheap demagogy. Some, for ethical or humanist reasons, joined the camp of the reformers, but from sentiment much more than from a critical knowledge of the social situation; others, on the contrary, reverted to the formulas of another age and were caught up in reactionary currents of Christian inspiration."[14]

Going on to analyze in detail the works of the two Dutch intellectuals, Lotsy and Kohnstamm, Pannekoek traced the conservative qualities in them. The first advocated a mystique of "life," generally very close to Bergsonian speculations—the *élan vital* and the rest. In other respects, Lotsy reduced human social behavior to impulses which were by nature essentially instinctive and incomprehensible. The masses, he said, act blindly, governed by a deep spirituality at once religious and patriotic. In Pannekoek's view, we have here another example of the necessity to unite the nation by diminishing class antagonisms in the age of imperialism. Kohnstamm, on his part, deduced from the Bolzmann theory—and from the substitution of statistical laws for the old causal determinism—that nearly all the accepted laws of physics had to be set aside, and that, in the last resort, the origin of the world was inconceivable without the existence of a Creator.[15] Against this view Pannekoek set the idea of the universe as a process of constant interactions. Not content, however, to argue within his adversary's field of modern physics, Pannekoek showed how "in the twentieth century, a positive Christianity arose in the ranks of the bourgeoisie and the intellectuals" which postulated an immutable order of things and fundamentally contested the idea of evolution. We have already seen the material reasons for this attitude. Twenty years later, in *Lenin as Philosopher*, Pannekoek was to criticize anew a reactionary attempt to base a theory of knowledge on data with scientific pretentions which, this time, was aimed at restoring the old bourgeois

---

14. *Ibid.*, p. 305.

15. Clearly, Kohnstamm did not make assertions of this kind without having previously attempted to buttress them with long considerations concerning various theoretical aspects of contemporary physics. Here we cannot enter into the details of this argument and its refutation. We merely note that Pannekoek, in support of his thesis, appealed to examples drawn from astronomy and from the kinetics of gases.

materialism. [16]

The special field for the application of the theory of evolution is, needless to say, the human sciences. Pannekoek devoted many studies to this subject. The following is a summary of one of the principal of these: *Marxism and Darwinism*. [17]

Both Darwin and Marx have placed the principle of evolution at the basis of modern science. The former has shown that the evolution of the species is subject to a law — the law of natural selection — by virtue of which the species best adapted to an environment survive in the struggle for life, while the others succumb. Marx, for his part, maintains that the basic cause of the evolution of societies was the development of the implement, and, in a broader sense, of technique. Technical progress issued in a modification of the social forms of labor through confrontations, at certain times, between the classes which make up society and to which men belong according to the place they hold in production. Thus, social development has a determined direction. For both thinkers, evolution is the outcome of a struggle: the struggle for life for Darwin; the class struggle for Marx.

Marx maintains, however, that while the tremendous forward surge of technique necessitates the replacement of capitalism by socialism, this substitution depends on the struggle waged by the masses — and that this, in turn, depends on the transformation, in and through this struggle, of the mentality of these masses. Like Marx's theory, Darwin's is something other than an abstract scientific truth. Did it not serve the bourgeoisie, especially, in Germany, as a weapon in their fight against the aristocracy and the priests, since it substituted the play of natural laws for Divine intervention?

In this sense, the Social Democrats could justifiably see here a confirmation of their materialist theses. However, "socialism has as its fundamental premise natural equality among men, and seeks to give practical expression to their social equality." On the other hand, Darwinism, having modeled itself on capitalist competition, constitutes "the scientific basis of inequality." [18] Hence it not only encounters socialist opposition, but also arouses the objections of reformers and other bourgeois philanthropists. They are concerned only with the ethical aspect of the social question and rely on certain legal improvements to abolish the most flagrant excesses which create the struggle for life in a capitalist régime, a struggle which they see as embodying a natural law. Is it not clear, however, that the laws governing the

---

16. Cf. below, Chapter Eight.
17. Anton Pannekoek, *Marxismus und Darwinismus* (Leipzig, 1909), p. 44.
18. *Ibid.*, p. 20.

animal kingdom are not applicable to human societies, since each society adapts to conditions peculiar to itself?

Certainly, man belongs to the animal kingdom, but he is a very special animal whose social existence, after a certain stage of development, is no longer entirely subject to the laws of nature. The cohesion of the human group is maintained by one power, the social instincts (which Pannekoek lists as "abnegation, courage, devotedness, discipline, loyalty, honesty"—all of which are ideas envisaging not the individual person but the group, the class). This power of social instincts is developed by the struggle for life, which tends to endow it with an absolutely primordial character. We have here, then, an altruistic consciousness which exists, though to a lesser extent, in the animal kingdom, and which is in basic opposition to the values of bourgeois egoism, especially to the nationalist sentiment.

What radically distinguishes man from all the other animal species is, on the one hand, the ability to make implements and to use them for pre-designed purposes; and, on the other, "language, and therefore abstract, conceptual thought, rational thought, the first having directly engendered the second and the implement serving as an extension of the human hand." In short, "practical life, labor, is at the origin of technique and of thought, of the implement and of science. It is thanks to labor that the ape-man has been raised to the condition of man." [19] Thus the division of labor, the distribution of functions linked with different applications of the implement, has opened up to man unlimited perspectives of development. And on this point Pannekoek concludes: "With the animal, the fight for life has led to a constant development of the bodily organs (for example, the muscles and teeth of the lion); this is the basis of the transformist theory, the nucleus of Darwinism. With man, it has led to a constant development of the implement, of technique, of productive forces; this is the basis of Marxism." In this respect, the two doctrines have a fundamental common principle: the law of evolution.

Life in society and the use of the implement, therefore, form the basis of man's evolution, a long evolution at whose end the vast majority are deprived of the implement, and become the machine for the benefit of a small minority. But the class struggle unites recently separated groups—no longer a struggle against nature by means of the implement, it is a struggle for the implement, a struggle to put technical equipment at the disposal of all humanity by means of organized action, the movement of the working class. And this struggle will end in the abolition of classes, in the emergence of a

---

19. *Ibid.*, p. 37. Engels, as we know, was the first socialist to stress "the role of work in the hominization of the ape."

single great community of united producers.[20]

On the whole, this booklet conforms with the views on the subject, at least at that time, held by the "orthodox" Marxists of Social Democracy. However, if it is compared today with one of the many works which Kautsky wrote at that time on the same question, one striking difference appears: the emphasis on "the social instincts" developed, according to Pannekoek, in the class struggle. Certainly, Kautsky stresses the "new moral ideal," the "ethical indignation," constituting a "power," a "weapon" for the socialist class struggle. But, in his view, this power is not a direct product of the class struggle and of a radical transformation of attitudes, but the product of a factor linked "with determined material conditions"—with the economic development which, he says, assures the imminent abolition of the classes.[21] We shall see later that this difference, scarcely noticeable at the time, is much more than a matter of words.

This, of course, does not imply that Pannekoek ever held that the ethic, the moral sentiments predominating in a given society, could be separated from the mode of production characterizing that society. On the contrary, indeed, he strongly emphasized this relationship in a booklet, *Ethics and Socialism*, published the same year as the one we have just been discussing. This was a contribution to a debate in connection with the great quarrel about revisionism then raging within German[22] and international Social Democracy. "Bernstein," wrote Pannekoek, "has frequently appealed to the ideas of Kant to combat the dogmatic materialism in our ranks; the neo-Kantians maintain that the historical-causal foundations which Marx and Engels have ascribed to Socialism operate with a certain coldness which should be countered with the warmth of Kant's moral ideal."[23] The

---

20. This latter theme is omitted in the much more searching study which Pannekoek later devoted to anthropogenesis, the "birth of man." The reason for this is simply that the work was published under the auspices of the Academy of Sciences. On the other hand, he there deals in detail with the connections between the use of the implement and the emergence of the upright position, the development of the brain, the gradual elaboration of articulate language, etc. ("Anthropogenese. Een studie over de onstaan van de mens," *Verhandelingen der Kon. Akd.,* II, 1, 1945; the current edition appeared in 1951 with the subtitle as title). By far the most outstanding work on anthropogenesis to appear recently is that of M. Leroi-Gourhan, *le Geste et la Parole* (Paris, 2 vols., 1965), a study somewhat marred, however, by an excessive "end of civilization" pessimism, whose social origins Pannekoek would no doubt have liked to trace.

21. Karl Kautsky, *Ethik und materialistische Geschichtsauffassung* (Stuttgart, 1906), pp. 141ff.

22. We refer the reader to Lucien Goldmann's summary of this discussion (*Recherches dialectiques* [Paris, 1959], pp. 280-298), from a viewpoint different in several respects from Pannekoek's.

23. Anton Pannekoek, *Ethik und Sozialismus* (followed by *Unwälzungen im Zukunftsstaat*) (Leipzig, 1906), p. 7.

Dutchman inserts in this connection a materialist critique of Kantian philosophy, the essential arguments of which we shall deal with soon.

But he also stresses that the moral sentiment had not been disposed of by having been presented "for what it really is: a mystified expression of class interests." He continues as follows:[24] "Just as immediately and vigorously as other men, we Social Democrats judge this or that act to be moral or immoral. Thus, therefore, the moral sentiment is a phenomenon linked with human nature, a sentiment which science can take into account without being subjected to its influence, and not an imposture or an illusion which it is the duty of science to eliminate. If moral ideas are engendered by class needs, they are not necessarily identical with such needs; that is why the analysis must be carried further. The immediate moral judgment cannot be replaced by a detailed and attentive consideration of what is useful or harmful to the community; there is a difference, therefore, between what is moral and what is useful to the community, and it is this difference which we shall now examine."

To make his point more clearly, Pannekoek uses a concrete example. "In 1903," he recalls, "the Dutch railway workers stopped work in sympathy with the striking dockers of Amsterdam. They had to choose between a struggle against the powerful private companies who owned the Dutch railways—a struggle involving considerable risk to their own interests—and a neutrality which would make them strike-breakers. They chose the first alternative, and the railway traffic in the western provinces was interrupted for a whole day. Had one asked a bourgeois person what he thought of this, no doubt he would have voiced his horror and indignation at seeing the personal interests of some individuals given precedence in this way, with chaos in society as a result. His view would have been that the government ought immediately to condemn such actions as criminal, a 'crime' being, in his view, anything which disturbs 'order'—the conditions necessary to peaceful profitmaking, allowing the rich to get richer while hunger torments the workers. By contrast, the workers would react very differently, applauding and admiring the courageous men who had sacrificed their own interests to solidarity with their class brothers.

"Thus the ethical judgments would differ completely in accordance with the class differences. The cleavage between these respective opinions was to be most clearly shown in the press controversy which followed. It was impossible to get the two sides to understand each other. The workers could not be made to understand what wrong they had committed by stopping work for a day in support of a group of workers at war with their employers. The bourgeois

---

24. *Ibid.*, pp. 20ff.

journalists argued along these lines: 'If it had been a matter of defending the legitimate and particular interests of the railwaymen, then nothing could have been more natural; but to go on strike for others, through solidarity! Sheer madness indeed! What would things come to if such ideas became widespread among workers in general! Do these people imagine that the splendors of exploitation could one day lose their luster? One thing at least was clear: while these journalists had their own particular way of understanding the interests of the workers, the working class virtues seemed to them to be expressions of insanity. This example shows clearly that, in practice, each regards as moral and good what suits the community, and therefore the class, to which he belongs. This is a fact of general application, and therefore the present experience throws light on the moral ideas of other eras and other nations."[25]

Returning a little later to this question—in order to illustrate, he said, the nature of ethics according to Dietzgen—Pannekoek writes: "After the railwaymen's victory, the bourgeoisie began to clamor for a special law which it would be the government's duty to implement. The working class, in a united front, declared their solidarity with the railwaymen, who had resolved to force the issue of their right to strike by again stopping work. This time, however, the strike failed. The workers sustained a terrible defeat which dealt a devastating blow to the whole workers' movement, from which it was able to make even a partial recovery only after several years of indefatigable propaganda. Thus, the first, glorious 'sympathy' strike set up repercussions which, for some years at least, proved more disastrous than advantageous to the workers movement. Does it follow that this strike was immoral? If it were true that whatever is useful to the community and therefore to the class involved is moral, and whatever is harmful is immoral, than one should regard this strike as immoral. And yet no worker would so regard it. He would say: 'Quite possibly this strike has been disastrous, but nonetheless it represents a beautiful, admirable action, a highly moral act.' So we see that an act can be regarded as good even if it has proved more harmful than useful to the class. This example will also enable us to highlight the difference between the useful and the moral.

"Let us then ask ourselves the question: Why did the workers see in this action a pattern of virtue? The answer is self-evident: because in this action solidarity—the individual's sacrifice of self-interest to what he regarded as the interests of his class—was plainly shown. But why regard as virtue the mere fact that he showed his solidarity? Because, as a general rule, a show of

---

25. *Ibid.*, p. 16.

solidarity is useful to the working class: not always (we have just considered a case in which solidarity had harmful effects), but nearly always it is useful and even indispensable to the extent that without it a definitive victory would be out of the question. In this sense there is virtue even in the exceptional cases where, because of special circumstances, the action is useful without involving risk. The difference between class interest and the moral element is therefore plain: what is moral is not what is useful to the class, but what is useful *in general* to the class, what *generally* serves its interests. A moral act is not always an act to be recommended, a rational act; in practice, one should not respond to the spontaneous promptings of the heart but act so that, as a result of mature reflection, the action is seen to be in accord with its purpose in the given circumstances. What is suited to its purpose, what is useful, is inscribed in our feelings and determines the moral judgment; but the rationality of an action is decided by the test of what, in the particular case, is suited to the purpose."[26]

Pannekoek sums up his account as follows: "Kant indicated the major outlines of ethics when he said that it serves as a general rule for immediately determining the moral judgment without a weighing of the *pros* and *cons*. He was unable, however, to discover its true origins; failing to take into account the division of mankind into classes, he saw only the antagonism between the individual and the human race as a whole. Kant had to believe, therefore, in the existence of an absolute ethic endowed with universal validity; and, since he was therefore unable to assign it an earthly origin, he was compelled to see it as something supernatural. Marxism had uncovered the origins of morality—namely, class interests—and has opened the way to the interpretation of ethics as a natural phenomenon. What essentially constitutes ethics becomes perfectly clear, thanks to Dietzgen's profound vision of the nature of the human mind.

"We set off from the everyday experience that the will, and therefore the conduct of man, are determined by two kinds of factors: on the one hand, his interests, his needs; on the other, ethics. When we undertook this investigation we did not as yet know what precisely the term *ethics* signified, but now we are able to give it exact definition. The opposition between *interest* and *ethic* can now be seen as an opposition between two types of interests: temporary, personal interest and permanent, general interest, which appears essentially as class interest. We are now in a position to assert that our will is determined by two kinds of factors: our own immediate interest, and the interest of our class. In our day, new and vigorous moral

26. *Ibid.*, p. 22.

motivations, new virtues, are developing within the working class. These motivations and virtues form a considerable source of power and are necessary for the transformation of the world, since without this power there can be no social upheaval of any magnitude, no passage to socialism. And if we now enquire into the source of this power, the answer is simple: it is not a power descending from the skies; it is the product of effective earthly conditions, and quite simply shows that each member of the working class has a potential which can enable him to rise above his own personal, limited interests and to lift his mind from the particular to the general, to the level of what is demanded by his class and by society as a whole." [27]

In these lines at least one fact is clear: we are not dealing with a university philosophy, a system of precepts primarily intended as logical speculation (in the final analysis obeying, like everything else, the class imperatives, a situation in the age). In another article on the same subject, [28] Pannekoek replies to those (then numerous among the intellectual revisionists) who, discovering in Marx the existence "of an indignation which erupts whenever he describes disgraceful exploitation," take this as evidence of an ethical attitude. Now, Pannekoek stresses, "the materialist theory of Marx does not rule out the ethical, and therefore does not deny the power of the moral sentiments. What it does deny is that these sentiments originate in an ethic which hovers above the human race. It sees the ethical itself as a product of material, social factors. The virtues which are now growing among the workers — solidarity and discipline, the spirit of sacrifice and of devotedness to the class community and to socialism — represent the basic condition for the abolition of exploitation; without this new proletarian morality, the active fight for socialism would be inconceivable. But this morality does not just appear without apparent cause in the worker; it is the fruit of capitalism, of exploitation, of the concentration of capital, of conflictual experience — in a word, of the whole of the material living conditions of the proletariat."

In fact, our author's target is precisely "the civil and unctuous morality of the preacher, the ideology of the self-contented bourgeois" who aspires only to conciliation between the classes without the need to censure the excesses of capitalism too severely. "The praxis of the workers' movement has nothing in common with this ethical way of looking at the world. When we denounce the frightful crimes of capitalism against the life and the health of the workers, and when we take a stand against governmental violence and injustice, our point of view is quite distinct from that of the redresser of wrongs who is

27. *Ibid.*, pp. 23-24.
28. Anton Pannekoek, "Marx der Ethiker," *Bremen Bürger-Zeitung*, Oct. 16, 1910. (One of the few Pannekoek texts whose title contains an explicit reference to Marx).

morally indignant at such flagrant wrongdoing. It is the cry of indignation of the victims and the oppressed themselves, the cry of hatred and of menace against the torturer; it is the shout of the fighter calling on his comrades, still drowsy and crushed with anguish, to join with him, reminding them of the torments they are enduring. And this cry of indignation, this rousing battle cry, has as little to do with ethics as has the anguished cry of a tortured animal or the exciting shouts of men fighting for their freedom. It is nature itself which decides the matter. A person who finds himself crushed and mastered *must* defend himself, and cannot do otherwise. There is no question of any moral indignation whatsoever toward the oppressor; such a person acts quite simply from the sheer natural instinct of self-preservation. The same is true of the workers' movement: it does not come forward like a valiant knight moved by ethical indignation, who seeks to free the human race from the immorality of capitalism; rather, it fights capitalism because it must, because for it there is no other way of salvation, because otherwise it will quite simply be pulverized by the enormous weight of capitalism.

"Thus the splendid discourses about Marx the ethicist are false for two reasons. Far from ethics being the basis of Marxism, it is the latter which provides a materialist interpretation of ethics. And the strong critical, fighting passion emanating from the works of Marx has just as little to do with ethics. It simply proves that, in his scientific works and in his critique of capitalism, he was merely the representative and one of the vanguard fighters of the proletariat who acted as the interpreter of their feelings and who gave them his works as a weapon in their fight for freedom."

Here we are poles apart from speculative research and exegesis. But this appeal to evidence of a primary kind, expressed in words as simple as they are vigorous (perhaps a little crude for the academic), should not be allowed to obscure the fact that Pannekoek, throughout his life, took a learned interest in philosophical questions. We can only make passing reference to the very first article he published at the time when he formally accepted Dutch Social Democracy: a detailed critical analysis of Kantian philosophy which was followed by a list of "the philosophical attainments" of Marxism according to Dietzgen and concluded with a discussion of neo-Kantian revisionism, particularly that of Bernstein. [29] Instead, we shall examine a more concise study of precisely the same subject, which serves as a preface to an American

29. Anton Pannekoek, "De Filosophie van Kant en het Marxisme," *De Nieuwe Tijd* (1901), pp. 549-564, 605-620, 669-688. (Pannekoek once said that the starting point of his political evolution had been the critique of Kantian philosophy [cited by Van Albada in "In Memoriam..."]; he also liked to remark, in conversation, that this evolution was in a sense a natural extension of his scientific activities.)

anthology of Dietzgen extracts. [30]

Essentially, Pannekoek says that the history of philosophy reconstitutes the various successive forms in which the ideas of the dominant classes have been clothed. Besides, in course of time, the philosophic and religious systems have integrated the discoveries made "by the human mind both about itself and about the universe." This is somewhat so in the case of Kant, who holds that "God and Liberty are concepts whose truth is non-demonstrable, unlike the natural truths drawn from experience." This attitude was in perfect accord with the contemporary condition of scientific and economic development. At the time, science was dependent on the inductive method with a strictly materialistic basis: experiment and observation. But religious faith persisted nonetheless, and ignorance concerning the origins of life and of man made it possible to uphold the ideal of a system of supernatural ethics.

"Kantian ethics mirrors the inner antagonisms of bourgeois society: the antagonism created by the fact that the character of production is individual on the one hand and social on the other, which engenders omnipotent but incomprehensible social forces which rule the destiny of mankind." This antagonism lies at the root of the contradictions and the pronounced dualism of Kantian philosophy.

Furthermore, these internal contradictions were to bring about the bankruptcy of the entire system at the very moment when the contradictions within the bourgeoisie were becoming obvious. However, to deal them a decisive blow it was necessary to grasp the material origins of morality, its relative and non-absolute character. "Marx's discovery of class struggle and capitalist production dislodged faith from its ultimate sanctuary."

Contemporary with the restoration of monarchic power in Germany, the philosophy of Hegel was triumphing over the "bourgeois dualism" of Kant. Pannekoek recounts the essential features of the Hegelian system, in which "the revolutionary dialectic, the theory of evolution, regarding all completed things as provisional, leads to a conservative conclusion by ending all new development as soon as absolute truth is attained. All forms of knowledge of the time were assigned a place at one of the stages of development. Many scientific concepts later discovered to be erroneous were presented within this framework as necessary truths resting on deduction rather than experience." Whence the impression, very widespread at the time, that Hegel regarded empirical research as useless and its influence on the natural sciences as insignificant. But it was quite otherwise as regards the "abstract sciences."

The Hegelian conception of history as a progressive evolution "in which the

---

30. J. Dietzgen, *The Positive Outcome of Philosophy* (Chicago, 1906), pp. 7-37.

previous state appears as a necessary and preparatory stage to the subsequent states, and therefore as natural and rational, represented a great advance for science." Furthermore, it uncovered the constant interactions and the contradictory relations existing between individuals and social units (the family, civil society, the state), moral precepts, expressions of the general will, "represented in the natural laws of civil society and in the authoritarian laws of the state." In its monarchic form, the latter appears as the ultimate consummation of social evolution.

The theory of the restoration, therefore, was bound to make a radical criticism of the revolutionary bourgeois philosophy without, however, rejecting it root and branch: like the latter, it preserved a faith in the supernatural tinged with scepticism. However, the Hegelian system could not survive the test to which it was subjected as soon as "capitalism, reaching maturity, began to revolt against the shackles which the reaction was trying to place upon it." Feuerbach set out to bring religion down "from the transcendental heights of abstraction to the physical man." Marx then showed that the ultimate reality of bourgeois society is class antagonism, and discovered that real historical development rests on that of material production. Nevertheless, "Hegel's philosophy is of very great importance even in our age, since it constitutes an excellent theory of the human mind as long as we strip off its transcendental character." This was the import of "the dialectical and materialist theory of knowledge" conceived by Dietzgen.

It is the merit of Dietzgen, writes Pannekoek, "to have raised philosophy to the position of a natural science, as Marx did with history. The human faculty of thought is thereby stripped of its fantastic garb. It is regarded as a part of nature, and by means of experience a progressive understanding of its concrete and ever-changing historical nature can be gained." There is no longer any question, therefore, of a philosophic system pretending "to give absolute truth," since, as Dietzgen emphasizes, one deals at best with "partial truths" which, however, deserve preservation insofar as they are valid. This new conception is fundamentally materialist, but not in the sense of the old bourgeois materialism: "matter to it means everything which exists and furnishes material for thought, including thoughts and imaginings." From this viewpoint, the human mind appears as a component of the universe, with "an equal place among the other parts of the universe," and "its content is only the effect of the other parts." Thus Dietzgen establishes a permanent, direct relation of the mind to the world, and highlights the way the mind reacts to the world in forming ideas. The cerebral activity of man comprises a constant systematization, one of whose expressions is science. Of course, as a result of the mode of production this systematization can take the form of transcendental beliefs, for instance, "the bourgeois idols: Freedom, Right, Spirit, Force, which Dietzgen shows to be only fantastic images of abstract conceptions with a limited validity."[31]

The present-day reader may not be familiar with the work of Dietzgen, which was published more than a century ago. But in a period such as ours—a period which, in many respects, is living on its capital of general ideas without being able to expand that capital—the reader may well accept these reflections on Dietzgen by Pannekoek, since, although their source is old, they are still valid as a categorical refutation of every species of dogmatism: "The mind is the faculty of generalization. Out of concrete realities, a continuous and unbounded stream in perpetual motion, it forms abstract conceptions that are essentially rigid, bounded, stable, and unchangeable. This gives rise to the contradiction that our conceptions must always adapt themselves to new realities without ever fully succeeding; that they represent the living by what is dead, the absolute by what is incomplete; and that they are themselves finite in partaking of the nature of the infinite. This contradiction is understood and reconciled by insight into the nature of the faculty of understanding, which is simultaneously a faculty of combination and of distinction, which forms a limited part of the universe and yet encompasses everything; it is solved, moreover, when the nature of the world becomes intelligible. The world is a congregation of infinitely numerous phenomena and comprehends within itself all contradictions, so that they become relative and balance each other. Within it there are no absolute opposites: it is the mind which constructs them, because it has not only the faculty of generalization but also that of distinction. The practical solution of all contradictions is the revolutionary practice of an infinitely progressing science which molds old conceptions into new ones, rejects some, substitutes others in their place, improves, connects and dissects, striving for an always greater unity and an always wider differentiation."

"If a worker wants to take part in the self-emancipation of his class," Dietzgen once remarked, "the basic requirement is that he should cease allowing others to teach him and should set about teaching himself." If Pannekoek did not specifically adopt this formula, he clearly acted on it, as on the rest of the tenets of proletarian materialism. Everything in his political writings, and therefore in his militant action, tends to provide instruments for

---

31. *Ibid.*, pp. 28-32. In *Lenin as Philosopher,* Pannekoek reports with approval this aphorism of Gorter: "Marx has clarified what the social matter makes of the mind; Dietzgen, what the mind itself does." H. Gorter, *Het historisch materialisme* (Amsterdam, 1920) first edition, 1907), p. 98, n. 1.

thought and for action. Was he not convinced, with Karl Marx, that "theory changes into material force as soon as it penetrates the masses?" He was, of course, aware that this penetration is linked with great historical conflicts, with an enormous upsurge of forces which itself is the fruit of a whole complex of circumstances; but he was equally aware that consciousness is an element of these forces. He said so—on one occasion among many, since every theoretician inevitably repeats himself—in one of his most remarkable studies: "Historical Materialism."[32]

Here especially one finds the idea, developed by Dietzgen, that spiritual factors such as "love of freedom, patriotism, conservatism, the feeling of frustration, the spirit of submission, the revolutionary will," act equally with material factors as determinants of human action. But this in no way implies the primacy of the one over the other since, in fact, they are inseparable. Thus, "the domain of technique includes not only machines, factories, mines, railways, and other material things, but also the capacity to create them and the science from which they issue. The natural sciences, what is known about natural forces, the capacity to implement them by work, must therefore be equally regarded as productive forces. Hence it is that technique includes not only a material element but also a powerful spiritual element. From the viewpoint of historical materialism this is self-evident since, in contrast to the fantastic abstractions of bourgeois philosophers, it places the living man and his corpus of physical needs at the center of evolution. The material element and the spiritual element in man constitute a unity so firmly established that they cannot be separated. Thus, when we talk about human needs, we are not referring merely to the stomach's needs but equally to the needs of head and heart, both types of need being by their nature at once material and spiritual. Human work, even at its simplest, inevitably exhibits these two aspects, and any attempt to separate them involves an artificial abstraction.

"No doubt this abstraction has an historical meaning. By the very fact that it has entailed division of labor and separation into classes, historical evolution has partly transformed the spiritual element linked with the labor process into a distinct function peculiar to certain people, to certain classes, and has thus induced a shrinkage of 'human quality' at both levels. Hence, these specialists, the intellectuals, are coming to regard their work, the spiritual, as a higher form; they are thereby becoming blind to the organic, social unity of these two elements. That is why their idea of historical materialism cannot fail to be wrong in every particular."

---

32. Anton Pannekoek, "Het historisch materialisme," *De Nieuwe Tijd* (1919). There is a French translation of this in *Cahiers du communisme de conseils*, 1 (1968).

It does not follow from this that ideas determine historical events; their influence, says Pannekoek, is beyond question, but cannot of itself account for such events. In an article published in 1937 [33] he offers the following solution: "The thoughts and aims of an active man are considered by him as the cause of his deeds; he does not ask where these thoughts come from. This is especially true because thoughts, ideas, and aims are not as a rule derived from impressions by conscious reasoning, but are the product of subconscious spontaneous processes in our minds. For the members of a social class, life's daily experiences condition, and the needs of the class mold, the mind into a definite line of feeling and thinking, to produce definite ideas about what is useful and what is good or bad. The conditions of a class are life necessities to its members, and they consider what is good or bad for them to be good or bad in general. When conditions are ripe, men go into action and shape society according to their ideas. The rising French bourgeoisie in the eighteenth century, feeling the necessity of laissez-faire laws, of personal freedom for the citizens, proclaimed freedom as a slogan, and in the French Revolution conquered power and transformed society."

Of course, this class saw in freedom only what suited its own interests. It was an abstract formula whose real meaning remained hidden. "The materialistic conception of history explains these ideas as caused by the social needs arising from the conditions of the existing system of production." However, to interpret the French Revolution "in terms of a rising capitalism which required a modern state with legislation adapted to its needs does not contradict the conception that the Revolution was brought about by the desire of the citizens for freedom from restraint. . . . Man is a link in the chain of cause and effect; necessity in social development is a necessity achieved by means of human action. The material world acts upon man, determines his consciousness, his ideas, his will, his actions; and so he reacts upon the world and changes it." [34] This is poles apart from the "mechanical materialism" which "assumes that our thoughts are determined by the motion of atoms in the cells of our brains. Marxism considers our thoughts to be determined by our social experience observed through the senses or felt as direct bodily needs." [35] Nor is there any absolute necessity acting on man "as a fatality to which man has to submit," but instead a constant interaction between man and the world through "historical activity." [36]

---

33. Anton Pannekoek, "Society and Mind in Marxian Philosophy," *Science and Society,* 1:4 (1937).

34. *Ibid.,* pp. 448-449.

35. *Ibid.,* p. 445.

36. *Ibid.,* pp. 449-50.

The bourgeois ideologists of the early part of the century attributed (indeed in a more primitive way than do their present successors) a unilateral determining role not to ideas alone but also to personalities. In this connection Pannekoek was to attack the ideas of philosophers such as Dilthey and Windelband as well as those of neo-Kantians à la Max Adler. [37] We are interested in this article only insofar as it contains the formulation of an essential concept — the popular masses, a concept which thoroughly scandalized the platitudinous orthodox Marxists. [38] Here, as elsewhere in his writings, Pannekoek does not strain after originality since, in his thinking, what is new is so intimately linked with classical elements — at least with their enduringly valid aspects — and is expressed in so straightforward a way, that it does not always emerge at the outset, and sometimes appears only in the conclusions.

". . . History is not the history of persons, but that of masses. Whereas with the individual personal qualities always play a considerable role, these qualities lose their prominence among masses, where exceptional traits merge into an average. We are dealing, therefore, with something general, something which can be the object of an interpretive science. Incidentally, here the reason comes to light why all bourgeois efforts to create a science of society are necessarily doomed.

"If one considers the mass in general, the mass as a unit, the people as a whole, one sees that the removal of mutually opposed ideas and wills does not by any means result in an indecisive, fickle, passive mass, constantly divided between apathy and frenetic activity, volatile, oscillating between irrepressible brutal impulse and the most dismal indifference — in accordance with the picture which liberal publicists see fit to present. In fact, this picture could not be otherwise as long as bourgeois writers continue to regard the people simply as a characterless mass, since such writers are convinced that, given the endless diversity of individuals, abstraction of the individual can lead only to the abstraction of everything which makes man an active being endowed with a will. They see no intermediate category between the smallest unit, the person, and the totality in which differences are obliterated, the inert mass. They are unaware of the existence of classes. In contrast, the strength of the socialist theory of history lies in the fact that it introduces order and system into the endless diversity of individuals, by means of the division of society into classes. Whatever its kind, a class brings together

---

37. Anton Pannekoek, "Teleologie und Marxismus," *Die Neue Zeit*, XXII, 2, 1905, pp. 428-35, 468-73.

38. Pannekoek took up the passage cited below during his famous controversy with Karl Kautsky in 1912.

individuals whose interests, aims, and feelings are to all intents and purposes identical and opposed to those of other classes. The chaotic representation to which we have just alluded disappears as soon as one distinguishes, within the mass movements, the classes which compose them. There immediately emerges a clear and distinct class struggle, whose aspects vary in the highest degree: offense, retreat, defense, victory, and defeat. In this regard it is enough to compare Marx's account of the 1848 revolution with those of bourgeois writers. Within society, the class constitutes a totality endowed with a particular content; suppress this particular content in order to secure an undifferentiated 'total man,' and even the slightest positive element no longer exists."

Pannekoek then stresses that "the spiritual behavior of classes stems from their material situation" in production, and that one can understand that behavior only "by visualizing oneself in the same situation." There is no attempt here to deny the role of personality but simply to place it, in each case, in its socio-historical framework. Besides, "every man lives only as a part of the mass;"[39] and, in this sense, he evolves with the world. But what exactly does this mean? Our author is repeatedly led to clarify "the process by which human consciousness adapts itself to society, to the real world." One of his fullest treatments of this question is found in the conclusion of his 1937 article: "When the world does not change very much, when the same phenomena and the same experiences are constantly reproduced, the habits of acting and thinking become fixed with great rigidity. New impressions on the mind fit into the image formed by previous experience and intensify it. These habits and concepts are not personal but collective: they survive the individual. Intensified by the mutual intercourse among members of a community who are all living in the same world, they are transferred to the next generation as a system of ideas and beliefs, an ideology—the mental apparatus of the community. Where for many centuries the system of production does not change perceptibly, as for example in old agricultural societies, the relations between men, their habits of life and their experience of the world remain practically the same. In such a static situation ideas, concepts, and habits of thinking will petrify more and more into a dogmatic self-enclosed ideological body of eternal truths.

"When, however, as a consequence of the development of the productive forces the world begins to change, new and different impressions enter the mind which cannot be adapted to the old representations. Thus begins a process of reconstruction, partly on the basis of old ideas and partly on new

---

39 Anton Pannekoek, "Teleologie und Marxismus," pp. 432-433.

experiences. Old concepts are replaced by new ones, former rules and judgments are stood on their heads, new ideas emerge. Not every member of a class or group is affected in the same way or at the same time. Ideological strife arises in close connection with class struggles[40] and is eagerly pursued, because all the different individual lives are linked in diverse ways with the problem of how to pattern society and its system of production. Under modern capitalism, economic and political changes take place so rapidly that the human mind can hardly keep pace with them. In fierce internal struggles ideas are revolutionized, sometimes rapidly by spectacular events, sometimes slowly by continuous warfare against the old ideology. In such a process of unceasing transformation, human consciousness adapts itself to society, to the real world.

"Hence, Marx's thesis that the world determines consciousness does not mean that ideas are determined solely by the society in which they arise. Our ideas and concepts are the crystallization, the essence, of the whole of our present and past experience. What was fixed in the past in abstract mental forms must henceforth be included with such adaptations to the present as are necessary. New ideas thus appear to arise from two sources: present reality, and the system of ideas inherited from the past. Out of this distinction arises one of the most common objections against Marxism: that not only the real material world but also to a lesser extent ideological elements—ideas, beliefs and ideals—determine man's mind, and thus his deeds and the future of the world. This would be a correct criticism if ideas originated by themselves without cause, or from the innate nature of man, or from some supernatural spiritual source. Marxism, however, says that these ideas must originate in the real world and are related to social conditions.

"As forces in modern social development, these traditional ideas hamper the spread of new ideas that express new necessities. In taking these traditions into account we need not abandon Marxism: quite the contrary. For every tradition is a fragment of reality, just as every idea is an integral part of the real world living in human thought. It is often a very powerful reality in determining human actions. It is an ideological reality that has lost its material roots with the disappearance of the conditions which produced them. That these traditions could persist after their material roots have

---

40. These lines no doubt refer especially to the religious form. In this connection, we note that Pannekoek traced the "irreligion" of the contemporary proletariat to "the state of mind engendered by intellectual participation in the present struggle for emancipation," and saw it as "a fruit of the knowledge acquired both by theoretical formation and by experience." Without abandoning a materialist propaganda clarifying the origins of religion, he stressed—as did the classic Social Democrats—that "in our party, religion remains a private matter" (*Religion und Sozialismus* [Bremen, 1906].

disappeared is not simply a consequence of the nature of the human mind, which is capable of preserving the impression of the past in memory or subconsciously. Much more important is what may be termed the social memory, the perpetuation of collective ideas systematized in the form of prevailing beliefs and ideas, and transmitted to future generations through oral communications, books, literature, art and instruction. The surrounding world which determines thought consists not only of the contemporary economic world, but also of all the ideological influences arising from continuous human intercourse. Hence comes the power of tradition, which in a rapidly developing society causes the development of ideas to lag behind the development of society. In the end, tradition must yield to the power of incessant battering by new realities. Its effect upon social development is that, instead of permitting a regular, gradual adjustment of ideas and institutions in line with changing necessities, these necessities, when they come too strongly in contradiction with the old institutions, lead to explosions, revolutionary transformations, by which lagging minds are drawn along and are themselves revolutionized."[41]

The activist critical intent of this set of ideas will become clear in the following pages. In one form or another, it constitutes an essential key to understanding not only our author, but also the Marxist revolutionary current in the twentieth century which Pannekoek appropriately called "West European communism." For, needless to say, the preceding relates to the very personality of Anton Pannekoek, whose ideas are inseparable from those of his comrades in arms, whether eminent theoreticians or rank-and-file militants.

That is why we shall not attempt to retrace ideational connections from individual to individual, but shall concern ourselves instead with agreements and divergences linked with the difficult ascent or decline, within a given phase, of new forms of organization and of theoretical awareness, as exercizing direct influence on the development of proletarian struggles. (However, space limitations necessitate a very sketchy, incomplete treatment. This is of little consequence in the case of Lenin and the Russian Bolsheviks, since there the reader has ready access to many and varied sources of information. Of greater consequence are matters concerning the German Leftists and others, especially Rosa Luxemburg and the Spartacus League; however, we have nonetheless decided to give a minimum of information about these tendencies which, at least for the moment, are entirely forgotten.)

This limitation will not prevent us from seeing Pannekoek as an exemplary

---

41. Anton Pannekoek, "Society and Mind...," pp. 452-53.

figure, and his life as a systematized epitome of the theoretical attainments of the emancipatory movement. He was one of the few Marxist thinkers of his day to follow his conclusions to their ultimate consequences, and to remain consistently faithful to them. According to political proclivities, one may view this attachment to principles which did not necessarily fit the demands of immediate situations either as an incurable utopian whim (we shall return to this) or as a display of personal integrity. However, in the second case, it must be remembered that Pannekoek, during the relatively short time he was a "professional revolutionary," had the advantage of a very special position; and that, generally speaking, his material situation enabled him to escape by the direct and indirect day-to-day restraints of party life. However, the guarantee of intellectual independence is one thing; the use made of it is something else—and at this level personality certainly intervenes. In this connection, to quote Van Albada: "Pannekoek was a man endowed with extraordinary capacities; but first and foremost, he was a pure and upright, courageous and devoted person." To these virtues, we shall add freshness of mind and revolutionary enthusiasm.

CHAPTER ONE

GERMAN SOCIAL DEMOCRACY

When the workers' movement made its appearance in the old countries of Europe in the nineteenth century before it spread with capitalism to most of the world, it took two basic forms: the trade union form and the party form. Both had the same purpose: to promote the specific interests of the workers. The first sought to secure the sale of labor power at its value within the framework of capitalist domination and the capitalist market. However, in the Western Europe of the second half of the nineteenth century—that is, in the course of a more or less completed bourgeois revolution—the workers and others among the most underprivileged sections of the population could not hope to make their interests prevail in a lasting way, or to secure for these interests the authority of law, except through political action whose instrument was the party form. This party form was born and developed, assuming very distinctive characteristics in consequence of the course of this bourgeois revolution during its phase of peaceful growth as a parliamentary system. (The same is true of the trade union form to a much more limited extent since it showed analogous traits, in general, in all the developed regions of Europe during the opening years of the present century.)

In Germany, therefore, the development of the party form was subject to the particular conditions of the bourgeois revolution and the spread of capitalism in that country. The bourgeois revolution—in the classic French meaning of the term [1]—had been effectively crushed in Germany in 1848; it continued, no doubt, but under the aegis of a semi-absolutist state power in the hands of the aristocracy (especially in Prussia). Politically vanquished, the bourgeois liberal element was integrally absorbed by an expansion of the economy, whose acceleration, at first irregular, became constant after the Franco-German War of 1871. The oppositional element, doomed to powerlessness at the political level by the relations of forces, took shape in the workers' party. But here let us yield to Pannekoek himself—the Pannekoek of

---

1. Free political growth of the middle class; administrative centralization secured at the expense of feudal privileges and those of the old state bureaucracy; development of military power; state intervention to facilitate the setting up of new industries; unfettered growth of banking, industry and commerce; etc.

1942, of World War II: "Left alone in their struggle against the oppressive police state, they were not attached to the middle class by the tradition of a common fight for political freedom. Whereas in other countries the hard industrial boss commanded respect by seizing power over the state and modernizing it, in Germany the gruff master in the shop proved the submissive coward in politics, giving examples in servility only. The German workers stood directly over against the allied classes of land owners and capitalists; they had to fight on the political at the same as on the economic field. Concentrated by the rapid development of industry in large numbers in the factories and the towns, they had to build their organizations and find their own way, independent of middle class influences and traditions.

"The rapid rise of social democracy demonstrated this political independence. Its name expresses the basic idea that socialist production must be won by means of democracy, by the masses conquering power over the state. Its propaganda of class struggle aroused the increasing numbers of workers to devoted fight, its papers and pamphlets educated them to knowledge of society and its development. It was the energy and rapidity of capitalist development that aroused the energy of the German working class and soon made them the foremost and directing power in the international workers' movement. It was the submissive politics of the German capitalist class, in placing them directly over against the entire ruling class, that rendered them class-conscious, that forced them by theory to deepen their insight in social forces, and that made them the teachers of the workers of all countries. Just as in France the sharp opposition between middle class and nobility had given origin to an extensive literature on political theory, so in Germany the sharp opposition between working class and bourgeoisie gave origin to an extensive literature on social theory, mostly based on the scientific work of Marx. This intellectual superiority, together with the gallant fight against oppression and despotism, alone against the mighty rulers, attracted all progressive and idealistic elements among the other classes, and collected around them all who longed for liberty and hated the degrading Prussian militarism. In Germany a deep gap, social as well as spiritual, separated two worlds, one of insolent power and wealth. where servility glorified oppression and violence, the other of idealism and rebelliousness, embodied in the workers' class struggle for liberation of humanity.

"The infiltration with idealistic middle class and intellectual elements tended to call up ideas of peaceful petty capitalist reform and democracy, though they were entirely at variance with the actual big capitalist conditions. Other influences went in the same direction. The increased power of the workers—politically, by finally, in 1912, mustering one-third of all the vote, economically by the rapid growth of the trade unions to giant organizations — awakened the desire for direct progress in social reform. Though traditional program and theory spoke of revolution as the goal of all activity, the real outcome was to ascertain to the workers their place in capitalism, acknowledged not officially, but actually, and only at the cost of continual fight. So reformist tendencies got an increasing hold on the workers. At the deepest root of reformist mood lay, of course, the economic prosperity that in the twenty years before the first world war enormously swelled German capitalism. All this meant a strong influence of capitalist and middle class ideas upon the workers.

"The spiritual power of the German bourgeoisie over the working mass was not due to its political, but to its economic achievements. Leaving politics and government to others, concentrating all its attention on industry and commerce, the capitalist class here unfolded such capacities and energy as to push German economy in an unrivalled tempo to the forefront of world development. This vigor commanded respect in the workers and carried them along in the feeling of participating in a mighty world process. They felt the enormous and enormously increasing power and brunt of capital, against which their organizations appeared insufficient and against which even their own ideals seemed to fade. So, in their subconsciousness, they were to a certain extent dragged on in the middle class stream of nationalism, in the desire for national greatness and world power that burst out in the first world war." [2]

This provides the best introduction to Pannekoek's *Die taktischen Differenzen in der Arbeiterbewegung* (translated in the next chapter), a work he published more than thirty years earlier (1909). It was born in the heat of controversy, in a blossoming of ideas whose richness the workers' movement in general was not to reach again.

The controversy, of course, was not centered in the realm of pure ideas. It immediately involved the orientation and even the very nature of socialist activity. Up to the end of the last century, a practical movement and a theoretical movement had coexisted within Social Democracy — not without clashes and even violent crises which, however, were nonetheless kept in bounds. While at local and sometimes even regional levels politicians and administrators waged savage war to win seats on municipal councils and other elective bodies, the theoreticians were slowly absorbing the substance of the writings of Marx and Engels.

The party was living on the Erfurt program (1891), which associated with the final purpose, "the abolition of the classes," a whole body of demands

2   *Workers' Councils* (Melbourne, 1948), pp. 125-26.

aimed at promoting immediate, day-to-day political action, the *Kleinarbeit*. The practical movement was interested almost exclusively in this second part of the program; it paid its due respects to the first part only during electoral campaigns in working class districts. The aristocrats and the bourgeoisie, for their part, were aware only of the first part and were extremely alarmed by it. The more informed elements among them, however, only made a pretense of being afraid. Bismarck had taught them that this very real fear enabled the state to keep a tight rein on the liberal bourgeoisie (and the princelings) and to administer certain branches of production in their place.

The Bismarckian brand of state reformism was to last only for a short time. As it concerns this discussion, it had two fundamental consequences: firstly, it established the bases of an economic expansion which ended by arousing at least the political ambitions of certain sectors of the bourgeoisie; secondly, over a period of some dozen years, it legislated to prevent Social Democracy from expressing itself as a "revolutionary party" while at the same time opening up the possibility that it could act as the sole legal opposition to the absolutist imperial regime, and thereby snatch electoral victory upon victory and implant itself deeply in the day-to-day life of the nation.

Ultimately, this development could not fail to have repercussions at the theoretical level. Bernstein—whom Engels had in a sense designated as his heir by making him and Kautsky his executors—took particular care to invite the party to bring its theory into line with its practice,[3] and to advocate henceforth the adaptation of English-type bourgeois liberalism to German conditions in the guise of an "organizing liberalism." That is why he urged the rejection of the "dictatorship of the proletariat" and other "decidedly outmoded" concepts associated with the idea of violent revolution:[4] in short, the ending of *a priori* opposition (in connection with the budget vote, for example), a permanent subject of discord.

Bernstein, as he himself admits,[5] did not expect his ideas to create a "sensation." In his view, "Marxist theory" had a twofold character: on the one hand it was "*Blanquist*," because of its insistence on the idea of an expropriation of the bourgeoisie resulting from "revolutionary brawls;" on the other, it had a "pacifically evolutionist" character and extolled "universal suffrage and parliamentary action as means of workers' emancipation." With

---

3. "In my view, the task of revision lies in the domain of theory, not in that of practical action" (at the Dresden Congress, 1903; *Protokoll über der Verhandlungen des Parteitages der Sozialdemokratischen Partei Deutschlands*, p. 391. Subsequent references here: *Protokoll...*).

4. E. Bernstein, *Socialisme théorique et social démocratie pratique* (Paris, 1912), pp. 202-237.

5. My articles, he wrote, "were beginning to attract attention in a completely unexpected manner" (*ibid.*, Preface to the French ed., p. vii).

the support of texts, he linked the first of these aspects with a past historical phase, on Engels' own admission.[6] Bernstein, however, was not just an expert Marxologist; he proposed a fresh analysis of contemporary social development. Rejecting the thesis of the rapid polarization of society into two antagonistic classes, he sought to show with statistics that the income of all social groups had increased, and that the rise in general living standards was bound to continue, given the mitigation of crises through cartellization and credit, or, in a word, through the progressive regulation of the market. Certainly economic expansion had not yet eliminated the distortion between supply and demand in workers' consumption; but with the devlopment of trade unionist, cooperative, parliamentary, municipal and other types of action, the exercise of democracy would remedy it. Thus, without meddling too much with private property (or "even with the principle of individual economic responsibility"),[7] there would be progress towards a higher civilization, morally more satisfying than the present one. "The movement is everything; the goal is nothing," he concluded in a famous formula.

In a sense, Bernstein touched Marxism at its vulnerable spot. It is a fundamentally critical theory, able to clarify the real significance of a critical phase of history and to incite the direct producers, on this basis, to take their affairs into their own hands. On the other hand, in growth periods, the periods of relative social harmony which Marxism foresaw, its basic concepts lost their critico-activist relevance and served only to describe the economic development after a fashion.[8] At that level, as a historically specific, dated theory, Marxism could cope with immediate situations only at the price of systematic adjustment. In this respect it is the form of political organization or the class to which the theoretician adheres which dominates the theoretical vision: Bernstein, a defender of the democratic party form, therefore stressed

6. *Ibid.*, pp. 50ff.
7. *Ibid.*, p. 220.
8. Karl Korsch said somewhat the same thing when he wrote as follows concerning the *Bernsteindebate*: "During the long period when Marxism was slowly expanding without having any practical revolutionary task to fulfil, the revolutionary problems had ceased, in the eyes of all Marxists, both orthodox and revisionist, to have any terrestrial existence, even at the theoretical level" (Korsch, *Marxisme et philosophie* [Paris, 1964], p. 100). Pannekoek reached an analogous diagnosis when, in 1919, he wrote: "In phases of accelerated development, the mind glows with enthusiasm; it grows in flexibility and in dynamism, and crushes old ideas more rapidly. In the course of the past few decades, the capitalist system and the proletariat have reached a high degree of development, and the effect of this has been to curb and even to halt the process of political revolution. That is also why, during this period, the process of spiritual development went on at a diminished rate, especially when one compares it with the headlong formation of ideas during the bourgeois revolutions of the past. This was bound to entail, after the preliminary and brilliant emergence of Marxism, a decided recoil: revisionist doubt, revival of the bourgeois critique, and dogmatic sclerosis among some of the radicals." ("le Matérialisme historique," *loc. cit.*).

factors calculated to justify the practical action of that party. However, when social evolution took a critical turn with the economic crises of 1901-02, 1907-09, and 1913, and then with the outbreak of World War I (followed by the first international wave of revolution in history), his thesis was completely enfeebled and his ethical utopian, optimistic prophecies were nullified.

Nonetheless, much to his own surprise Bernstein caused a tremendous hue and cry against himself throughout both the German and the international movement. Had he not invited that movement "to dare to appear as what it is: a movement of social and political reform?" A movement to seek an overt alliance with the liberal middle class whose first indications were only just coming into the open. "The Bebels and the Kautskys, the Victor Adlers, the Plekhanovs and their like heaped abuse on this insolent fellow who had divulged the carefully guarded secret. At the Hanover Party Congress of 1899, during a debate opening with Bebel's six-hour report and lasting four days, Bernstein was subjected to a formal trial. He just managed to escape expulsion. For many years, Bernstein was constantly abused by militants and constituents in the press and at party meetings." It was easy to attack the theory of a particular individual rather than the actual practice which he imprudently but faithfully expressed. With equal ease one thereby verbally safeguarded the revolutionary character of the party, as was to happen later in the "construction of socialism" in Stalinist Russia.[9]

Without going into the details of the discussion, we can note that the two most important critiques of Bernstein at the time were those of Karl Kautsky[10] and Rosa Luxemburg. Both sought to refute the dangerous errors of a *unique*[11] theoretician; both summoned a wealth of statistics[12] in their

9. On this point, we cite and follow Korsch ("The Passing of Marxian Orthodoxy," *International Council Correspondence*, 11-12, Dec. 1937). Korsch verifies and enriches a thesis previously advanced by Georges Sorel: "[Bernstein] saw, therefore, no other means to keep socialism within the frame of realities except to suppress anything misleading in a revolutionary program in which the leaders no longer believed. Kautsky, on the other hand, wanted to preserve the veil which hid from the workers the true activity of the party" (G. Sorel, *Réflexions sur la violence* [Paris, 1930, 3rd edition], pp. 328-29).

10. From the viewpoint that concerns us here, the best biography of Kautsky remains the short essay by Paul Mattick: "From Marx to Hitler," *Living Marxism*, IV, 7 June 1939, pp. 193-207.

11. "Bernstein's theory was the first, but also the last, attempt to provide a theoretical basis for opportunism" (R. Luxemburg, *Réforme ou révolution?* [Paris, 1947], p. 79); later, Rosa incidentally admits that "in the majority of the socialist parties of Western Europe, a link exists between opportunism and the intellectuals" (*Marxisme contre dictature*, [Paris, 1946], pp. 27, 30-32).

12. We note, with the writer of the preface to a Dutch version of *Éthique et socialisme* (*Daad en gedaachte*, Nov. 1966, pp. iv-v) that, unlike the other critics of Bernstein who essentially oppose an "orthodox" interpretation to a "heretical" one, Pannekoek gives priority to questions of method, to the materialist analysis of the revisionist current in the broad sense.

support. Kautsky cited Marx extensively, finally, and not without contortions, conceding an eminent role for parliamentary and trade union activity. Luxemburg declared, among other things, that the great days of trade union activity, that "labor of Sysiphus," belonged permanently to the past. But Rosa's expectations proved wrong: in Germany, the membership of the trade unions increased almost tenfold in the twenty years between 1891 and 1912.

At the time Pannekoek wrote *Tacitical Differences*, the framework of the discussion had changed profoundly. The avowed revisionist tendency as such remained an insignificant current whose members, generally intellectuals, could claim favor with university liberals; but the attitude toward them in the party was hostile. On the other hand, a radical tendency [13] firmly implanted in the most industrialized regions of the country—the "red belts" of the big towns—slowly gathered strength as a relatively autonomous force at the local level, where it often controlled the party machine, the body functionaries of permanent salaried officials, and partly controlled the editing of the publications of the party and its peripheral organizations (women, youth, etc.). Things were completely different at the central level. There power was in the hands of executives or administrative bodies which were essentially conservative, even if in times of social crisis they did temporarily rely on the radical tendency—the "leftists," as they were sometimes called. The latter, despite a mode of representation at the congresses which was highly unfavorable to them, [14] succeeded in certain circumstances in securing the adoption of a "line" which was in conformity with their ideas but was doomed to remain a dead letter. [15]

As a whole, the rather scattered radical organizations achieved only a poor degree of organic cohesion, which varied with the general situation (or indeed with local personalities). It was only from about 1910 that this current succeeded in taking on a clearer form, especially as a result of intense factional struggles. These confrontations occurred on the basis of a body of ideas inherited from the past: orthodox Marxist "tactics." These tactics sought to assign precise limits to parliamentary and trade union action and to subject that action, at least in its tendencies, to the realization of the "final goal"—socialism.

---

13.   We here translate the German *radikal* as "radical," "extremist," or sometimes, according to context, "Left." On the other hand, it seems inadvisable to render *Radikalismus* by "Leftism" or even "Ultra-leftism," both for this and the subsequent period, since these terms belong to the post-1920 Leninist vocabulary and have little to do with the ideas of Pannekoek and of his political comrades.

14.   Cf. Carl Schorske, *German Social Democracy 1905-1917* (Cambridge, Mass., 1955), Chapter V, *passim.*

15.   Thus the famous resolution of the Dresden Congress (1903) condemning revisionist attempts at "adaptation to the existing order," a resolution noted, however, by the revisionist delegates themselves.

Besides, looking upon parliamentarianism and trade unionism in themselves as the principal elements of reformist practice, the leftists vigorously stressed the general strike and mass actions as the supreme means of the class struggle and consciousness.

This was not a purely theoretical attitude. Between the onset of the century and the outbreak of World War I, industrial expansion constantly increased the size of the proletariat, and strikes and demonstrations were numerous and sometimes violent. With a few major exceptions, however, they remained limited in extent: especially in Germany, the leadership or the party and, even more so, of the trade unions was on the alert against any "excesses" and kept a firm hand on the organizational network. Faced with the power of this workers' bureaucracy, radical theoreticians worked out a new concept of organization as a process, whose elements derived largely from reflection on the 1905 Russian Revolution and the mass strikes in Western Europe but were also not unrelated — despite denials as vigorous as they were sincere — to the ideas of certain anarchist thinkers and French trade unionists.

Rosa Luxemburg formulated this concept as follows: "The rigid, mechanical-bureaucratic conception cannot conceive of the struggle save as the product of organization at the certain stage of its strength. On the contrary the living, dialectical explanation makes the organization arise as a product of the struggle. . . . Here the organization does not supply the troops for the struggle, but the struggle, in an ever growing degree, supplies recruits for the organization. . . . If the social democrats, as the organized nucleus of the working class, are the most important vanguard of the entire body of the workers and if the political clarity, the strength, and the unity of the labor movement flow from this organization, then it is not permissible to visualize the class movement of the proletariat as a movement of the organized minority"[16] of the party or the trade unions. She adds that this is the only way in which "that compact unity of the German labor movement can be attained which, in view of the coming political class struggles and of the peculiar interest of the further development of the trade unions, is indispensably necessary."[17] To take up a later notion born in completely different conditions, the "degeneration" of the workers organizations, inevitable in a period of calm, will be surmounted only through the most active class struggle. Although this consequence of the theory was rarely drawn in an explicit way at the time,[18] no one could doubt that the idea of the class

---

16. Rosa Luxemburg, "The Mass Strike, the Political Party and the Trade Unions" in *Rosa Luxemburg Speaks*, ed. Mary Alice Walters (New York, Pathfinder Press, 1970), pp. 196, 198.
17. *Ibid.*, p. 217.
18. Such, for example, was the perspective of Pannekoek himself, during the war.

consciousness process sought, as one of its aims, to "redress" the current course of the party and the trade unions, and to regenerate structures which had become rigid and reactionary. Hence the welcome it got within the party from both revolutionary workers and radical functionaries.

Neither of these groups was considering a breakaway. Fetishism of the organization was sustained by a number of circumstances: the breadth and constant growth of the movement; the extremely wide and varied field of activities it supplied for each and all; the day-to-day advantages it offered with its cooperatives, dispensaries, and cultural and other circles; the strength of habits; the keen hostility which the bosses and the authorities displayed towards it; the salaried or honorary positions secured within the different organizations; also the petty-bourgeois impregnation which Pannekoek noted; and even more, perhaps, the absence up to then of one of those "great historic battles" to which Marx traced the existence of classes.[19] All these circumstances contributed to maintain the unity of German Social Democracy. But it was very different in Holland.

The industrial development of Holland was slower than that of Germany, in whose wake it occurred. On the other hand, the process of bourgeois political and cultural revolution had reached a much more advanced stage in Holland. There the socialist movement had consequently presented, at least in its beginnings, a more "French" character, in the sense that it centered more on anarchism than on Marxism. Its leading light was the highly gifted ex-clergyman, Domela Niewenhuis. Elected deputy with the sole intention, originally, of using his parliamentary seat to propagandize the Social Democratic Movement (Sociaal-Democratisch Bond), this former correspondent of Marx soon realized that this was a forlorn hope. He turned to anti-parliamentarianism and became a zealous advocate of the idea of the general strike, regarded as the dawn of the "great day.[20]

Although it was far from securing electoral successes comparable to those of the German Party, the SDB's parliamentary power visibly increased towards the end of the century. After sustained controversies a split occurred in the party and, in 1894, the SDAP came into existence, formed on the German model but even more centralized and authoritarian. Soon the intellectuals lent it their support: Gorter and Henriette Roland-Holst in

---

19. In his famous letter to Weidemeyer (5 March 1852) published 1907 in *Neue Zeit*.

20. Much later on, Gorter, recalling with what enthusiasm the aged Nieuwenhuis had greeted the Russian Revolution, was to note: "The difference between him and us is that we are for revolutionary methods in a time of revolution, while he advocated them in a completely different period." (Anonymous, "Die Marxistische revolutionäre Arbeiterbewegung in Holland," *Proletarier*, II, 1, Feb. 1922, p. 16).

1897, Pannekoek in 1901 (the latter at first regarded as "one of the bigwigs of Marxist orthodoxy").[21] This group very soon clashed with the party leadership and with its chief, the lawyer Troelstra, one of whose favorite dicta was: "first life, then theory," meaning that support had to be given to the cause of the small peasants, or approval to government subsidies to the denominational schools.[22]

This antagonism increased after the big strikes of dockers and railwaymen in 1903. The party leadership gave lip-service support while attempting to curb the movement,[23] provoking the enraged criticism of Gorter, among others, who reproached the party with contemptuously despising "the proletarian instinct" and "the revolutionary energy" of the masses.[24] Things became worse when, in 1905, the party leadership (particularly Troelstra) brazenly violated a resolution adopted by the Party Congress prohibiting all parliamentary support for the liberal bourgeois government (whose political life depended on such supplementary votes.) The left wing, in which Pannekoek was very active, advocated intensive campaigns of agitation among the workers and an attitude of undeviating opposition toward parliament. Troelstra and his followers, the "majority group" who dominated the party machine, regarded the leftists as "dogmatists," "unilateral doctrinaires" unable to appreciate how useful it was to play "on the divisions among the bourgeois groupings," who if they were heeded would reduce the party to a "propaganda club."[25] Thus the differences were far more lively than in Germany, since they took on an immediate practical character. In 1907, the minority group financed an independent weekly paper, *De Tribune* (whence their name—"Tribunists"); two years later, the split was complete.

The new party (SDP) was tiny (400 members) and, in the 1913 elections, received ten times fewer votes than its rival. From the viewpoint of electoral effectiveness, which continued to be the viewpoint of the German leftists, this was a singular failure and an added reason for setting aside any idea of a schism.[26] While the majority party drew support from the "neutral" trade

---

21. W. van Ravesteyn: *De wording van het communisme in Nederland 1907-1925* (Amsterdam, 1948), p. 26.
22. Anonymous, *Die Gründung der "Sociaaldemocratische partij in Nederland"* (Berlin, 1909), pp. 4-5.
23. *Ibid.*, p. 7.
24. At the Ninth Party Congress; cited by A. C. Rüter, *De Spoorvegetakingen van 1903* (Leyden, 1935), p. 573. Ten years later, Rosa Luxemburg defined the strike in general in the same terms, as "the expression of a high tension of revolutionary energy" (*Gesammelte Werke*, IV [Berlin, 1928], p. 637; she also regarded it (1910) as "a means of moral and political education"—*ibid.*, p. 613).
25. *Die Gründung...*, p. 14.
26. As Paul Frölich notes in the introduction to Rosa Luxemburg: *Gesammelte Werke*, III

unions of the German kind, the major beneficiaries of the 1903 strikes, the minority party was working in conjunction with a relatively small and anarchistic trade union organization which was active in those years.[27]

The split of the Netherlands Party could not fail to have repercussions within the Socialist International. In fact, it provided the occasion on which Lenin, for the first time in his political career, took an active position in the organizational life of a Western European party — needless to say, on the side of the Tribunists.[28]

In the course of the long controversy which preceeded the split, Gorter and Pannekoek often criticized "opportunism" and urged their own conception of orthodox Marxism. At that time the special platform for their ideas was *De Nieuwe Tijd*, a leftist-controlled party theoretical organ. But, the two men differed greatly in temperament. Somewhat older than Pannekoek, Gorter (1864-1927) was already famous, perhaps the greatest poet then writing in Dutch. His verses combined rhythmic beauty and perfection of form with inspiration of a pansexualist kind, notably in *Mei* (1889), which was to develop (*Pan*, 1912) towards a lyricism celebrating "the unification of mankind and the cosmos"[29] in which the socialist universe appears as the final radiant goal of the human race. Gorter was to resume this theme in the often classically constructed poems of his posthumous collection *De Arbeidersraad* ("The Workers' Council"). Nevertheless, in politics the poet displayed more concrete thinking than the astronomer. An extremely active man, a great sportsman, tribunist, and agitator, Gorter deliberately directed his energies to practical matters and questions of organization, which may partly explain why, after 1920, he was more deeply involved in immediate political activity than was his friend.

The bonds between these two Marxists always remained the closest: in all, they complemented one another admirably. Pannekoek, absorbed in arduous theoretical problems, sometimes hesitated and ignored details of practical application; whereas Gorter flung himself on his adversary, and usually confined his attention to matters of immediate concern. Long after his

(Berlin, 1925), p. 28.

27. Van Ravesteyn, *op. cit.*, pp. 36, 127. "The NAS [trade union] was the body, and the SDP [minority party] the head," says even this author, himself of the majority party.

28. At the eleventh reunion of the Bureau of the International; in the article he devoted to this question (*Sotsial-demokrat*, 10 Dec. 1909; *Collected Works,* SVI, pp. 140-44), Lenin fully answered for his part the arguments of the Dutch Left. Rosa Luxemburg would hear nothing of a split. In August 1908 she wrote to her friend Henrietta Roland-Holst: "Nothing more fatal than a splitting of the Marxists. . . . One cannot remain outside the organization, lose contact with the masses! The worst among the workers' parties is better than no party at all!" (Cited by J.P. Nettl, *Rosa Luxemburg* [London, 1966], p. 656).

29. H. Roland-Holst, *Herman Gorter* (Amsterdam, 1938), p. 137.

friend's death, Pannekoek was still defending him against the accusation of having been "a poor politician." He reminds his readers that those who attempt "to help the exploited masses gain the strength to effect their own emancipation are labeled, in parliamentary jargon, poor politicians." [30] Undeniably, in this sense Gorter, Pannekoek, and many others were "poor politicians;" and this is to their credit.

Interrupting his university career in 1906, Pannekoek left for Germany accompanied by his wife Anna. They remained there until the delcaration of war. As an orthodox Marxist, Pannekoek had been invited to Germany by the party leadership to teach the history of materialism and of social theories at the school which they had decided to open in Berlin in conjunction with the leaders of the trade unions confederation. However, on the eve of the second school semester the Prussian police threatened to deport both Pannekoek and his colleague, Hilferding, also a foreigner; the two teachers had no option but to submit. [31] Pannekoek defined as follows the aims of the school (which were also those of all his own work): "We must clearly understand the nature of capitalism, not just to incite the workers to fight it but also to discover the best *methods* of combat. Where this understanding is lacking, tactics are governed by established traditions or by a superficial empiricism. When one merely takes account of the present, the immediate, appearances inevitably prove deceptive and coherence upon solid foundations is neglected." [32]

Having had to give up his Berlin teaching post, Pannekoek then became a salaried propagandist. As a journalist and traveling lecturer, he soon gained a considerable reputation as a theoretician in Germany and Eastern Europe. [33] In 1909 he settled in Bremen at the invitation of the party branch and the trade union coalition of that town, where the factional struggle was at its height. In Bremen, the local party machine had been organized "for action" by Friedrich Ebert. When Ebert left for Berlin in 1906 to take on the administrative leadership of the party—and to become, as he was justly called, "*mutatis mutandis*, the Stalin of Social Democracy"[34] — he left behind him an authoritarian structure of great strength. Nevertheless, the big Hanseatic town was experiencing lively social conflicts; in particular, there

30. "La politique de Gorter," *la Révolution prolétarienne*, 64, Aug. to Sept. 1952, p. 254.
31. The revisionist wing of the party strongly attacked this venture, alleging the "doctrinaire" quality of the teaching.
32. Anton Pannekoek, "The SD Party-School in Berlin," *International Socialist Review*, VIII, Dec. 6, 1907, p. 322.
33. A biography of translations of socialist "literature" into the Serbian language (up to 1914) gives 68 Kautsky titles as against 58 Pannekoek titles (W. Blumenberg, *Karl Kautsky's literarisches Werk* [The Hague, 1960], p. 16).
34. Schorske, *op. cit.*, p. 124.

were frequent strikes among the dock workers (we shall return to this). In the schools a nucleus of teachers was threatening to stir things up in order to suppress religious instruction.[35] The opposition, directed by young officials such as Heinrich Schulz, Wilhelm Pieck and Alfred Henke, had vigorous rank and file support. Despite a certain provincialism, the political life of Bremen presented a lively example of currect theoretical controversies.

Pannekoek, however, especially because of his scientific training, was inclined to generalize. His political views were those of the left, the orthodox Marxist tactic conceived in accordance with the basic principle which he himself formulated in *Tactical Differences* when he wrote: "The conditions for revolutionary transformation exist germinally in daily action," and with these conditions, the spread of reform into revolution. No doubt, in his own particular way he stressed the importance of spiritual factors, *geistlich*, in the class struggle and the direct link between the maturation of these factors and the form of organization. But in this as in others matters, the Dutchman was not a precursor; his originality consisted in deeply scrutinizing the theoretical achievement of a particular current of ideas in the spirit of Marx and Engels in close connection with the practical situation.

Some years ago Heinz Schurer, a London political scientist, drew attention to the role played by Pannekoek's ideas in "the origins of Leninism."[36] "In fact, commenting on *Tactical Differences*, Lenin said that it contains "deductions whose complete correctness cannot be denied.'[37] But Pannekoek himself once described this type of abstract research into the kinship of pure ideas as "sterile and misleading," as a distinctive mark of "official academic science," as "the fundamental vice of criticism as professed in modern universities" which ignored everything referring to real historical conditions.[38] Shurer has decided to apply this very "method" to the process by which ideas are formed and transmitted within the Marxist workers' movement. However, to regard this process as dependent on individuals is certainly a mistake. Schurer is mistaken when he writes in connection with Pannekoek's *Tactical Differences*, that here, "for the first time in the Marxist camp, an author established that the tactical differences between the right wing and the left wing of the workers' movement originated in the class structure of the latter — namely, that it was weighed down by "the new middle class," the intellectuals, and the "labor

35. Cf. H. Schulz, "Die Bremer Lehrschaft und der Religionsunterricht," *Die Neue Zeit*, XXIII, 2, 1905.

36. Heinz Schurer, "Anton Pannekoek and the Origins of Leninism," *The Slavonic and East European Review*, XLI, 97, June 1963, pp. 327-44.

37. Lenin, "Divergences in the European Workers' Movement," *Zvezda*, Dec. 1910; *Marx-Engels-Marxisme* (Paris-Moscow, undated), pp. 148-55.

38. "Teleologie und Marxismus," *loc. cit.*, pp. 471-73.

aristocracy." [39]

That theoreticians and militants closely linked with the movement should have remained blind to a phenomenon of such magnitude might seem strange—and indeed, such was not the case. As early as 1895 Kautsky pointed out the existence of "a whole party of 'intelligentsia' animated with reformist sentiments," and recommended that in dealing with them the positions of Democratic Socialism should be maintained unyieldingly in order to win over the best of them, especially among the students, on a clear, explicit basis. [40] Four years later, in a polemic with Bernstein, Kautsky noted that although the intellectuals who have reached the higher echelons become "the most reactionary of reactionaries," their constant numerical increase exposes them to the increasing risk of proletarianization, pushing them toward the party. However, these social groups, "regarding themselves as above class antagonisms," seek "to substitute social reforms for revolution"[41] and to transform the organization "into a party for everyone," a "popular party."[42] In this connection, as we shall see, Pannekoek's analysis brings him into direct line with a conception widely expressed in the party ranks. He was in no sense an innovator.

The same can be said about the "theory" of the labor aristocracy. Twenty-five years earlier Engels, discussing England and its monopolistic power, had described this social group as a factor in reformism operating through big trade union formations. "The metal lathe workers, the carpenters" and others, he wrote in 1885, "form an aristocracy within the working class; they have succeeded in creating a relatively comfortable situation for themselves, and they regard that situation as fixed and settled."[43] Clearly, therefore, judgments of this kind were current among Marxists of every tendency and in many nations—among German Marxists, needless to say,[44] but also, as Pannekoek himself pointed out, among

---

39. Cf. H. Schurer, *op. cit.*, p. 329. This very well documented article provides many indications of the connections between the theoretical work of Pannekoek and the evolution of the political thought of Lenin, Bukharin, and Zinoviev (Cf. also Robert Vincent Daniels, "The State and the Revolution," *American Slavic and East European Review*, XII, 1 Feb. 1953, pp. 22-43).

40. Karl Kautsky, "le Socialisme et les carrières libérales," *le Devenir social*, 1895, 2 and 3.

41. Karl Kautsky, *le Marxisme et so critique Bernstein*, (Paris, 1900), pp. 242-54; cf. also Chapter Two, note 18.

42. Letter to Victor Adler, May 5, 1901; Victor Adler, *Briefwechsel...* (Vienna, 1954), p. 355.

43. F. Engels, *Die Neue Zeit*, June 1885; *Marx-Engels Werke*, XXI, pp. 191ff. Considerations of this kind often recur with Engels in this period.

44. Thus about 1900 Bernstein (with qualified approval from Kautsky) stated that "trade unionism will always rest principally on those categories of the working class whom it is usual to call the workers' aristocracy" (in a preface to the German translation of the Webbs' "History of

Americans. [45] It could, of course, be argued that in every case the reference was to the Anglo-Saxon labor aristocracy; but if so, then Pannekoek — and later on Lenin — would merely have generalized an idea which had been kept within arbitrary bounds.

In any case, Pannekoek's attitude shows that, far from indulging in utopianism and mysticism, he always took his bearings from the realities of the movement and its development and bearings from the realities of the movement and its development and generalized them, not in an arbitrary way but in terms of its practical and theoretical attainments. Besides, he was ready to abandon an idea when it seemed to him ill founded; a case in point being this very notion of a labor aristocracy, to which he never again reverted to the best of our knowledge. [46] Perhaps, on reflection, he came to realize that in this way one gains only a very incomplete and historically limited truth, further increasing the division and confusion in the "proletarian" ranks (at the time, the worker aristocrat was a salaried artisan, and almost all the German workers' leaders, including the radicals, had come from this stratum. [47]

The conceptual core of *Tactical Differences* is elsewhere. In a positive way, it lies in a particular emphasis on spiritual factors, on *geistlich*, on social life generally, and on the fundamental role of class consciousness (and not of specialized organizations) in the revolutionary class struggle. Besides, it highlights the idea that the socialist movement does not have, or no longer has, a homogeneous class nature (whence, once again, the necessity for recourse to mass action as a basic cohesive factor). At the national level, in Western Europe and in America, the middle classes weigh on the development of this movement and crystallize in "opposed and unilateral tendencies," revisionism and anarchism, "although these labels leave much to

---

Trade Unionism" — a work translated into Russian by Lenin during his exile in Siberia). Cf. also K. Radek, *In den Reihen der deutschen Revolution* (Munich, 1921), p. 316.

45. Cf. Chapter Two, n. 24.

46. Pannekoek makes no allusion to the workers' aristocracy in an important text which can be regarded as the first sketch for *Die tatischen Differenzen*: "Theorie en beginsel in die arbeiders beweging," *De Nieuwe Tijd*, 1906. Nor does it appear in his article, "The New Middle Class," *International Socialist Review*, October 1909, pp. 317-36.

47. With Lenin and his disciples, on the other hand, this idea was to supply an essential key to understanding Social Democratic and trade unionist "opportunism" (for a recent treatment, cf. Eugène Varga, *Essais sur l'économie politique du capitalisme* [Moscow, 1967], pp. 138-56). However, with the spread of a minimum and uniform level of skill, the political and social weight of the workers' aristocracy, still very considerable at the beginning of the century, has clearly diminished, as Zygmunt Bauman has shown in connection with England (cf. *Studie Soziologiczno Polityczne*, 1958, 1, pp. 25-122). Something quite different, of course, would be a critique of the widespread division of the proletariat into categories with specific and anti-egalitarian demands at the material level and of the over-estimation of levels of competence, one of the ideological bases of the exploitation of man by man on the spiritual plane in the West as in the East.

be desired."[48] Similarly at the international level, in the East beyond the Vistula, [49] in an effort to emancipate themselves from the domination of foreign capital the emerging bourgeoisie is attempting to adapt socialism to its interests, given the proven imminent bankruptcy of liberal ideology.

This is a discerning extrapolation, even if it does not accord with immediate empirical data. There is no longer a special conern with refuting an individual theoretician (Bernstein), denouncing an ambitous politician (Millerand, Troelstra), or stigmatizing some controlling body of the party or of the trade unions. Instead, the effort is to move forward a critique of a specific social and historical process which is both detailed and linked with action.

---

48. Anton Pannekoek, "Theorie en beginsel in die arbeiders beweging," *op. cit.*, p. 13.

49. In Russia at the same period, Waclaw Machajski showed, following Bakunin, that socialism was the "class ideal" of intellectuals destined to succeed the capitalists (cf. the study by S. Utechin in *Soviet Studies*, XX, Oct. 1958, pp. 121-22); and Lenin, often regarded at the time as "anarcho-marxist," ceaselessly emphasize, with proofs, the deeply bourgeois character of other tendencies of Russian socialism.

CHAPTER TWO

TACTICAL DIFFERENCES WITHIN THE WORKERS' MOVEMENT [1]

I. *The Aim of Class Struggle*

"The tactics of the proletarian class struggle represent an application of science, of theory, which clarifies the causes and the tendencies of social development.

"The capitalist mode of production transforms the production of socially necessary use value into a means of enlarging capital. The owner of capital buys the labor power of the worker, who has no means of production; he uses this labor to set his means of production in motion; and thus appropriates the product of labor, the value created by labor. Since labor power creates a value greater than the value necessary to its reproduction, the exploitation of this labor power constitutes a means of amassing wealth. The surplus value — the value which the worker produces in excess of the value of his labor power — reverts to the capitalist and serves for the most part to augment capital.

"The most important quality of capitalism is not derived, however, from this structure, from this exploitive character in general, but from its constant rapid *evolution* towards new forms. *The driving force of this development is competition*.

"Through the operation of the laws of competition, the total surplus value created by the whole body of capitalist enterprise is not distributed proportionately among the enterprises. Those with the most productive machinery and methods, who therefore can produce at lowest cost, secure a surplus profit, whereas less productive ones make only a small profit, break even, or even register a loss.

"The first result of this situation is *a steady growth of the social productivity of labor*. The discoveries of the natural sciences and their rapid development lead to better methods of labor and improved machinery. The policy is to use the best techniques; less efficient techniques are abandoned; the production capacity of machinery and the labor yield continually increases. . . ."

The big firms are the beneficiaries of this evolution. This entails a decline

---

1. *Die taktischen Differenzen in der Arbeiterbewegung* (Hamburg, 1909), p. 132. Here as elsewhere, all italics are by Pannekoek himself.

of the middle class of small producers and independent merchants, and an increase in the proletariat, this increase comprising "both former members of the petty bourgeoisie and uprooted peasants absorbed into big industry. The natural growth of big capital is not sufficient of itself to secure *concentration of capital*; concentration is accelerated by the fact that the joint stock companies and the banks absorb small capitals and thus create large masses of capital. *Business organization* is transformed; the capitalist who hitherto personally directed production recedes further and further into the background;[2] control is placed in the hands of salaried employees, managers, commanding a whole staff of departmental chiefs, overseers, technicians, engineers, chemists, and so forth. These managers form *a new middle class* whose dependent situation distinguishes it from the old middle class. The capitalist thus loses all active part in the production process and is reduced more and more to *a mere parasite*.[3] Production goes on without him, but continues to serve his interests...."

Thus, while the mass of producers founder in misery and endure insecurity of employment, production is socialized and comes into conflict with the private form of appropriation. Ever-increasing concentration of capital entails a corresponding diminution of competition and the emergence of giant monopolies, which attack the unbounded anarchy of private production and establish a partial control of production. However, this development benefits only the big capitalists. There is no way to suppress them except by *"the socialization of the means of production — socialist production*. The evolution of the capitalist system itself reveals its ultimate end: the contradictions of the system are exacerbated to such an extent that they become intolerable and provoke an upheaval, a social revolution, which leads to the replacement of capitalism by a new mode of production — the socialist mode.

"But these contradictions do not bring about such a revolution in any mechanical way. The latter occurs only insofar as these contradictions are experienced as intolerable constraints. *All production relationships are human relationships;* everything that occurs in society is due to human intervention. The invention and utilization of new machines, the concen-

---

2. Marx, as we know, already speaks in *Capital* about the expropriation of the capitalist (I, Ch. 22 *in fine*) and emphasizes that the administrative function tends more and more to become separate from the property of capital (III, Ch. XV, 2 *in fine*). Hilferding, more particularly, has studied this problem in one of the most brilliant chapters of *Finanzkapital* (1910).

3. We recall that Pannekoek's analysis is perfectly classic; it was shared at the time by all the theoreticians of Marxist Social Democracy (Bernstein alone contesting the diminution of the competition and of the number of small enterprises). His originality lies in a particular, and highly characteristic, insistence on the human factor.

tration of capital, the creation of bigger and bigger factories, the formation of trusts—all of this is the work of humanity. Of course, these actions
are not deliberate parts of a great master plan. Each man sees only his
own situation and acts only in response to immediate necessity or need; he
pursues only his own interest, sets himself up against others, and tries to get
the better of them. Social development is the outcome of all these actions, of
all these individual wills. That is why the whole complex of these actions has a
result which, compared with that of each of the actions taken separately,
assumes the appearance of super human power. This global result emerges as
an inexorable, inflexible, natural force. *Society is like a headless body*, deprived of collective thought, in which, without conscious reflection everything
is governed by blind laws. Yet this organism is made up of people who, as
individuals, reflect in a conscious manner.

"All social events thus flow solely from the fact that men act. *The
contradictions of social development are contradictions felt by men, and
therefore the overthrow of a mode of production can only be the work of men.*
But this is by no means the work of men who regard themselves as above
society, as capable of transforming the social body through the power of
clearheaded conscious reflection; for in that case, each individual does only
what his immediate interests dictate. On the contrary, it is the actions taken
necessarily—in a sense, instinctively—in order to satisfy their interests, that
have as a global result the overthrow of the mode of production.

"The interests of members of the same class are compatible, whereas the
interests of different classes diverge or clash. This is the origin of *the class
struggle*. The interests of the exploited workers run counter to those of the
capitalist exploiters. The capitalist seeks to increase exploitation as much as
possible so that the surplus value supposed to increase his capital will be as
large as possible; in addition, he tries to lower wages, to increase working
hours, and to intensify the work. The worker, thus condemned to destroy his
health and his strength, resists; he wants higher wages and a shorter working
day so that he may lead a more human life. Working conditions thus become
the object of a struggle in the course of which workers and capitalists begin by
confronting one another; but gradually, as they come to understand the class
character of their interests, they join others of their own class to form
organizations.

"The *proletarian class struggle* develops gradually. It begins with a workers'
revolt in some factory against unendurable working conditions. Little by
little, these workers set up permanent associations, and perceive that their
interests do not just happen to run counter to those of the employers, but that
this conflict is permanent. They thus become aware that they form a

particular class, and their outlook widens to include the entire class. At once the battle moves to the political field, where general confrontation unfolds between the classes. [4]

"As long as they regard the State as a supreme power over society, the workers seek, by supplication or demand, to obtain laws designed to end their misery and, above all, to protect them from redoubled oppression. But in the struggle, experience teaches that the capitalists use their hegemony over the State to defend their class interests against the workers. The workers are therefore forced to take part in the political conflict. The more they realize that the State is under the thumb of the exploiting class, and that State power is of decisive importance from the viewpoint of economic interests, the more must they take *the conquest of political power* as their objective. As soon as the working class adopts this goal, it needs to know how it will use political power, and therefore it needs a program for the future. The experience of the class struggle, which gives insight into the nature of capitalism, shows that it is not enough to remedy some of the excesses of the system. . . . To make the revolution, the working class must destroy the existing order, adopting the inauguration of the socialist mode of production through the conquest of political power as their ultimate objective and political program.

"Socialism, therefore, will not come into existence because everyone acknowledges its superiority over capitalism and its aberrations. Since people respond only to their immediate class interests, it must be accepted that they form an unreflecting mass as concerns the conscious control of their social condition. The bourgeoisie knows that their immediate interests are necessarily linked to a system which gives them the means to live by exploitation, and so they want nothing to do with socialism. The latter, an inevitable consequence of a victory of the working class, can be born only of the class struggle . . .

"The *immediate goal* of every action connected with the day-to-day class struggle cannot be socialism, which is the final outcome of a long period of struggle and of that alone. *Socialism is the final goal of the class struggle*. It is therefore necessary to distinguish between final and immediate objectives. As a final goal, socialism helps the struggling class gain awareness of the course of social development; as a reality destined one day to become fact, it enables this class to judge capitalist relations by comparison and, while the grandeur

---

4. This scheme clearly follows the classic passage in *Poverty of Philosophy* (ch. 11, par. 5), in which Marx shows how the mass of the workers, with common interests, who form a class vis-à-vis capital, constitute themselves into a class for its own sake in the course of the political struggle. A perfectly orthodox schema, therefore, but the sequel shows that the concept "war of class with class" is here taken in the strictest sense.

of this ideal urges them to fight relentlessly, it gives a critical form to our scientific knowledge of the capitalist system. In contrast, the immediate objective associated with different aspects of day-to-day action can only be an immediate result.

"This immediate result is none other than *the increase of our strength*. . . . The most powerful class is always the one which wields power; therefore, a class seeking to gain power must aim to increase its strength to a degree that will enable it to vanquish the enemy class. Hence *the immediate objective of the class struggle is to increase the social power of the proletariat*."

In the era of their struggles against the feudal system, the bourgeoisie drew its strength from financial riches. In the modern states, its strength comes from the fact that it leads in all the principal branches of production, "whence their moral sway over all the social groups that acknowledge their role as leaders,[5] at least as long as groups have not become conscious of the antagonisms which set them in opposition to the class in power. . . ."

II. *The Power of the Proletariat*

"First and especially, this power consists in size. Increasingly, the proletariat forms the great bulk of the people; in developed countries, wage-earners account for a considerable majority of the population. But a majority dependent on a minority—a huge *lumpenproletariat*, for example— cannot develop into a group with independent power." The importance of the proletariat has an economic origin; it is indispensable to successful production, as the mass of petty bourgeois and small impoverished peasants are not. "In this respect, the power of the working class is all the greater for its not being dependent on numbers only.

"Numbers and economic importance cannot of themselves confer any power on a class, if that class remains unaware of them. When a class cannot discern its particular situation, its specific interests; when, in a dumb and paralyzed fashion, it endures the domination if its oppressors and even accepts such domination as part of the eternal order of things—then numbers and importance mean nothing. If these advantages are to mean anything, the class must become self-conscious. Only as a result of class consciousness does size take on significance for the class itself, and does it realize that it is indispensable to production; solely through this consciousness can the proletariat promote its interests and attain its goals. Class consciousness alone enables this vast, muscular, inert body to bestir itself into life and activity.

---

5. A note refers in this connection to the results of the last "American elections," a massive vote of the workers and of the petty bourgeoisie for the "trusts party" (and not for the socialist party).

"The knowledge which confers this power on the working class is not limited to a mere awareness of belonging to a particular class with specific interests. The struggle will be waged more efficiently and with greater success insofar as the proletariat has a basic knowledge of the social framework within which it is fighting. And in this respect, it has an advantage over its enemies: the working class possesses *a science of society* that enables it to elucidate both the causes of its misery and the goal of social development. Thus able to rely on forces that shape political events and to foresee what is about to happen, it gains a quiet energy, a serenity, which helps it through difficulties. The maturity it shows in political struggle has the same foundation. Does not this science enable it to foresee the consequences of its actions and to avoid being beguiled by immediate, passing appearances? The confidence of ultimate victory that this science gives it endows it with a moral solidity; whereas the other classes, which, lacking science, grope about in darkness and are terrified of falling, do not know what direction to take. Thus the knowledge of society—ranging from its simplest form, nascent class consciousness, to its highest form, the doctrine of Marx which we call scientific socialism, socialist theory, or Marxism—constitutes one of the most significant factors of proletarian power.

"Nevertheless, however knowledge is used, it is insufficient when the power to act is missing. What can the thinking head do without a strong arm to carry out what is thought? Large numbers alone are not enough to ensure strong action. The whole history of civilized mankind shows that the popular masses have allowed themselves to be ruled by small minorities and have tried in vain to free themselves, the minorities being strong due to their organization. As long as a class remains splintered in distinct units, each one having a different objective, they cannot pretend to exercise the least power. Organization unifies these disparate wills and roots them in a single will, that of the masses henceforth endowed with cohesion. The enormous power of an army, the power of the State itself, derives from a closed and compact organization which, like a single body, is animated by a single will.

"But what transforms a great number of people into an organization? *Discipline*—the subordination of the individual, of his personal will, to the will that governs the whole. In the army, submission to an external will is involved, military discipline being secured by the fear of severe sanctions for rebellion. In the ranks of the workers, the will to which the individual submits is the general will of the organization itself, expressed through majority vote decisions. Therefore, this is a freely accepted discipline, a ready and willing submission to the will of the organization. This does not mean that the individual renounces his opinions or abdicates his personality; rather does it show his conviction, the fruit of mature reflection, that the masses cannot become a force unless they are animated by a single will, and that the minority has no right to require the majority to bow to its views.[6] It is only by pooling his strength with others of his class that the individual can secure his objective. He can do nothing on his own, and that is why rational reflection, if not sheer instinct, impels him to join with others. But it is also necessary that the organization can count on all its members, even if some of them disagree with the majority attitude. Discipline, the cement of organization, thus means the spiritual bond which creates an energetic, compact mass out of hitherto scattered units.

"The power of the working class is thus made up of three essential factors: size and economic importance, class consciousness and knowledge, organization and discipline. Its growth is related to all these factors. The first factor is the fruit of development itself,. . .the effect of economic laws, and therefore increases independent of our will or our action.

"But the other two factors are dependent on our action. They are, of course, also induced by the economic development that helps us better understand society and obliges us to organize ourselves. But economic causes act through the agency of men, inasmuch as they compel us to work, through conscious reflection, for the growth of these two factors. *The purpose of our agitational campaigns, the objective for which we are fighting, is to heighten knowledge and class consciousness among the proletarians, to increase their organization and discipline. Insofar as it depends on our will, this is how proletarian power will increase; and this is the goal of the class struggle.*

"This, too, is the only rational meaning of that movement which Bernstein set up in opposition to the final goal. In our view, not only is the movement not everything, it is nothing, an empty word.[7] To swing in every direction

---

6. Within German Social Democracy, the extreme Left as a whole always advocated a rigorous discipline, absolute respect for resolutions adopted by the Party congress, these resolutions being generally inspired by the orthodox Marxist tactic. The extreme Left sought in this way to subordinate the behavior of the trade union chiefs, of the members of the parliamentary sector, etc., to the will of the Party, the primary purpose being the pursuit of the "final objective." (Cf. Carl Schorske, *op. cit.,* pp. 50-51 and 222-23). Vain hope! In fact, the German Left were to fall victim to their own ideas in this matter: it was they who, in the hour of truth, when the majority of the Party were wholeheartedly participating in the war effort, found themselves forced to violate this famous discipline. Despite the evidence, they resigned themselves slowly and only with difficulty to this.

7. In 1898, Rosa Luxemburg exclaimed: "The working class must not take up the decadent viewpoint of the philosopher: 'The final objective is nothing; the movement is everything!' On the contrary: the movement in itself and unrelated to the final purpose, the movement as an end in itself, is nothing; *the final objective is everything!*" (Le But final," in *Réforme ou revolution?* [Paris, 1947], p. 101). By "the final objective," she meant at that time the "destruction of the State," the "conquest of political power."

without taking a step forward or even backward is also movement. Nonetheless, every expression rests on a proper idea; this idea, in our context, is that here and now, day after day, a change occurs to which we devote all our energies: the increase of power. This in no way runs counter to the final objective, but, on the contrary, is absolutely identified with it. When we adopt as our aim the constant growth of our power, we are already working to achieve our final goal.

"One sometimes hears it said that *the immediate purpose of all our actions is to obtain reforms." In fact, certain reforms — the right of coalition, freedom of the press and, still more, universal suffrage — strengthen the working class, while other reforms are conceded by the bourgeoisie in order to weaken the workers' class consciousness.* "Social reforms, therefore, do not, as is often maintained, constitute stages on the road to the final objective, in the sense that this objective is something other than the sum total of a series of reforms. We are striving today to secure measures which in no way constitute a partial realization of what we intend to achieve in socialist society. For example, the legal sanction limiting the length of the working day, insurance against industrial accidents,[8] etc., are at present reforms of the highest importance; but when capitalism has disappeared these laws will become completely superfluous, as will all legislation protecting the workers against the arbitrary decisions of the capitalists. Social reforms *forcibly won by conflict* represent so many stages on the road to the final objective, in that they involve an increase of proletarian strength. It is only as such, as an increase in power, that they are of any interest for socialism. . . ."

A long development follows on "the science of society" — Marxism — "engendering for the first time among the proletariat something which may be called the self-consciousness of society."

III. *The Tactical Differences*

In its first phase, the socialist movement, both German and international, was split by two energetically opposed tendencies, in a confrontation that still continues. "It has often been said that this conflict was a kind of *childhood ailment*[9] which the movement had to put up with in its beginnings, when workers were still lacking in knowledge and experience. In a certain sense, this is true. The science of society, the knowledge of the objectives and the

---

8.   Under discussion at the time and finally promulgated in 1911, this law excluded the trade unions from acting as cashiers; it was very ill received by the Social Democrats of every tinge, who unanimously regarded it as an instrument designed to consolidate the imperial regime.

9.   I have before me a copy of the present pamphlet corrected by the author for a new edition (probably in Switzerland during the war). This phrase is underlined anew. It should also be pointed out that, in this copy, the term "revisionist" is everywhere replaced by "reformist."

method of the struggle, cannot be acquired in a quasi-academic way outside the conflict of which, in reality, they are the fruits. Subjected to oppression and exploitation, the workers find themselves stirred instinctively to resistance. However, they are still imbued with illusions and prejudices fostered in school and in church, which their present way of life continues to feed. When they set about defending themselves, they thereby show that they have lost one of their illusions, but only one: the illusion that the capitalists are fathers to them, and that they can rely on their humanitarian feelings. Later, experience of conflict gradually dissipates the other illusions and prejudices—their trust both in the bourgeois government and in the bourgeois opposition parties. In this way the tactical and political knowledge of the workers increases and, at the same time, their organization. The Marxist theories are increasingly well understood, because they correspond more and more closely to the experience of all. *Thus the battlefield represents both school and exercise yard....* The workers should, therefore, seek their way and deepen their knowledge through the class war; although the theoretical writings of scientific inspiration undoubtedly help toward a better and quicker understanding, they are no substitute for struggle. That is why differences and spirited conflicts, with resultant false orientations and deceptions, are inevitably involved in the development of the workers' movement...."

After the decline of anarchism around the 1890s, new differences emerged, this time between Marxists and revisionists. This occurred both in Germany and throughout the world; while in France and Italy revolutionary trade unionism—known in Germany as anarcho-socialism[10]—made its appearance. "The fact that the workers' movement has always been marked by internal conflicts shows that this is not a matter of anomalies, of mere childhood ailments, but of normal and inevitable reactions to natural situations. Hence one must take care not to treat them as childish squabbles and meaningless cavilling.... Among the most direct causes of the tactical differences are the following: the unequal rhythm of development in the different regions; the dialectical nature of social development; the existence of other classes besides capitalists and wage-earners." A passage, omitted here, maintains in effect that the mass of new party members, being raw

---

10. A current originally made up of trade unionists who rejected the ever increasing centralization of the trade union organizations (and their dogma of "political neutrality"), whence their name—"localists." They grouped themselves, in 1897, into a "Free Association of Trade Unions" (FVDG). Cf. Fritz Kater, *The Tendency of the Free Association of German Trade Unions,* (Berlin, August 1904), p. 7; Dr. Friedeberg, *le Mouvement socialiste,* nos. 139-140, Aug.-Sept. 1904; for a history of German anarcho-trade unionism, see the articles by Gerhard Aigte in *Die Internationale* (organ of the FAUD), nos. 7, 8-9, 10, (1931).

recruits, often repeated the errors committed by the movement in its early years and took up illusions that had long disappeared from the socialist movement.

"Socialism, both as an objective and as a class organization, is in every respect *a product of the conditions specific to large industry.* These conditions bring home to the workers the possibility and the necessity of a socialist order, also teaching them that, in the masses, they have the power to create this order. Confidence in their own strength and in their ability to take power are the fruits of these conditions.

"A movement that seeks to conquer the whole State, to transform the whole of society, cannot, however, be limited to the large towns and cities. It must also extend into small towns, villages, and rural areas. Besides, promoters will find such widespread discontent and oppression there that they will be heard eagerly. . . . But these people live in conditions that lead them to take quite another view of society and of our purposes. And since the immediate reality of their situation continues to shape their views, they may themselves come to doubt the validity of our theory—and of the tactics based on it—since this theory is linked with conditions in large industry. This is a primary source of differences that are as basic as tactical differences.

"Highly developed capitalism opens a bottomless gulf between the class owning the means of production and the working class, while the independent middle classes disappear or lose their autonomy. On the other hand, in the underdeveloped regions one still finds a large, well-off middle class acting as a buffer between the extreme classes. This middle class consists, on the one hand, of independent craftsmen, who rarely employ anyone; and, on the other, of petty bourgeois, who generally have very few employees. The line of demarcation between laborers and craftsmen is not very pronounced; they mix socially as a matter of course, and the relations between worker and employer are trustful and relaxed, or, in the larger business concerns, patriarchal. Often the capitalist himself has only just left the ranks of the skilled workers, so that there are workers who remember him working by their side and speaking familiarly with them. Hence, in these innocuous forms, where the wage-earning condition seems to be determined by personal circumstances and personal bonds, it would require great powers of abstraction to discern exploitation by greedy capitalism and the beginnings of the class struggle. The conditions of rural life are even less in accord with the picture of major industry presented by our theory. In the country the bonds between peasants, families, farm laborers, maid servants, remain primitive. Of course, the general norms of capitalism can be seen here in effective, widespread operation: exploitation, the thirst for profit, and the clash of interests; but, by comparison with their clear and indisputable form in big industry, here they must be traced under the cover of primitive appearances.

"In these regions, the workers form a scattered minority and the petty bourgeoisie frequently looks down on them. Socialism awakens in them the idea that they have rights and claims that should be pressed. But the idea of wishing to be everything, of wresting power from the other classes, seems to them *an unrealizable utopia*. The goal of the struggle—ceaselessly to increase class power—seems to them unattainable. Their objective is something quite different. In these regions, wages are generally very low, and consequently the living conditions of the worker are miserable. He sees the improvement of his immediate situation as an objective that has at least the merit of being feasible...since circumstances, personal relations, are matters that can be discussed, transacted, and understood.

"Again, a considerable part of the petty bourgeoisie feels threatened by capitalism and has every reason to hate it, the more so since the multiplication of factories makes competition more and more ruthless and life more and more harsh. The petty bourgeoisie is often forced to oppose the intrusion of big capital into the political field, and thus to ally itself with the workers—for example, in defense of democracy. In such circumstances, the theory of opposition between the classes can seem ill-founded and one-sided.

"Marxism, as a theory of the revolutionary proletariat, induces a complete change of mental attitude. Therefore it is welcomed warmly by those who have every reason to change their attitude in view of the considerable transformations of which they are at once the witnesses and the victims. The development of modern giant industry destroys ancient traditions, throws down old customs, and makes a *tabula rasa* of minds, which then become capable of accepting absolutely new ideas. But in the country, in remote corners where even the whisper of such mighty changes has scarcely been heard, the people continue to inhale deeply the poisonous air of tradition..., and there socialism does not appear as a completely new world-vision, but as a series of practical and limited objectives that can co-exist perfectly with the traditional ideas of the bourgeoisie.

"Furthermore, it is understandable that the penetration of our party into backward regions would provoke a reaction of doubt there about socialist theory and about certain aspects of our tactics as shaped in the large industrial centers." But ultimately, it is big international capital that is decisive and the middle class of the small towns who find themselves inevitably left behind. The workers of the large centers are destined to make their weight felt more and more, whence their preponderant influence as regards the transformation of society. "No doubt, the situation in the backward regions also exercises an influence, but its only role can be *to curb the movement....* That is why it would be absurd to attempt to gain new militants there by humoring prejudices. The work of theoretical explanation is, indeed, as necessary in such regions as it is difficult."[11]

IV. *Revisionism and Anarchism*

"*The dialectical character of social development* is a second reason why heterogeneous tendencies occur in the workers' movement. In this connection the importance of the philosopher Hegel should be stressed. He was the first to point out that the development of the world is effected through contradictions and that internal contradictions are the driving force of all evolution. Essentially, the world is simply the *unity of contraries.* In their content these contraries reciprocally exclude one another, and therefore appear to naive thought as irreconcilable contradictions. They do not coexist in peace, but, on the contrary, their disappearance as a result of development gives rise to new situations. Consequently, these contradictions form only transitory stages of the development; yet the whole of history consists only of stages of this kind, which follow one another and alternate. As a result of this dialectical mode of thinking, Marx was able to elucidate completely the nature of capitalism and to show that it involved a *development ceaselessly engendering new contradictions and actuated by them....*

"The dialectical nature of capitalism in turn determines the highly contradictory character of the modern workers' movement, so incomprehensible even to reflective bourgeois observers. Sometimes they see in the socialist movement a full-blown attempt to incite peaceful populations to replace an absurd social order by another order shaped by human sagacity. Sometimes they seek reassurance in the thought that Social Democracy is only a reform party representing the interests of the workers within the naturally stable pattern of capitalism, and to seek the suppression of certain disadvantages affecting the workers, but destined to disappear automatically once these errors have been corrected; in short, a 'temporary phenomenon.' The first of these ideas overlooks the fact that the new order develops organically from the old; the second, that the struggle to make the workers' interest prevail and to establish reforms will lead to a social revolution. Anyhow, both are wrong because they take into account only one aspect of the workers' movement. In reality, this movement comprises two inseparable aspects that are divided in appearance only (a completely superficial appearance).

---

11. Lenin had this passage in mind, perhaps, when he wrote: "If he [Pannekoek] seems to allude sometimes to Russia, it is only because the basic tendencies...are also appearing in our midst." Lenin, *op. cit.*, p. 152.

"Socialism is a *natural product* of capitalism and at the same time its *mortal enemy*. One cannot speak, therefore, of a power external to capitalism that will someday attack and overthrow it; on the contrary, socialism lives in the heart of the system and draws all its strength from the system. The struggle it wages is not artificial; it will last as long as capitalism itself; and its praxis consists in everyday action, which, however, is only one part of it. Because of the intolerable misery that it engenders, capitalism drives the working class to combat this misery; and, by so doing, it cannot prevent that class from improving its living conditions. But, at the same time, it constantly tends to reduce them to misery, and the workers must often fight hard to keep the advantages they have won. If at first sight it may seem that the answer is quite simply to put an end to these aberrations, and so at one stroke to make capitalism endurable and to perpetuate it — as bourgeois reformers believe — the whole course of the conflict soon shows that these 'aberrations' are at the very essence of capitalism, and that, to combat them, struggle must be waged against the system as a whole.

"These two aspects, which socialism harmoniously unites, may be called the *reformist* aspect and the *revolutionary* aspect.... One or other of these aspects prevails according to the economic situation and to both personal and social circumstances. When a situation favors the workers — even if only at a local level as in England during the 19th century, or exceptionally for a limited period — and when attempts to profit by this situation are crowned with success, awareness of the revolutionary character of the movement is lost; in other words, it comes to be accepted that a change of society by stages is possible, thanks to gradual improvement and to the cooperation of the class in power, or, at least, without bitter opposition from this class and without violent revolution. The opposite situation exists in times of crisis, when great political catastrophes awaken large-scale discontent and agitation. It then becomes easy to persuade people that capitalism can be leveled by a single revolutionary blow, without the need for partial, patient, preparatory day-to-day action.

"One of the two tendencies in which these sentiments and ideas are incorporated is *revisionism*. It is interested only in reformist social practice, and regards all talk about revolution and the revolutionary character of our movement as empty formulas serving only to distract praxis. In this view, not the final objective but the movement itself is what is important. Indifferernt to the sharp antagonism between socialism and capitalism, they focus attention only on their organic relationship. According to the revisionists, society transforms itself toward socialism gradually, insensibly and without sudden spurts; a slow evolution is guaranteed; the theory of political and social revolution is, in their opinion, simply a theory of catastrophes. They maintain that the reforms secured constitute an element of socialism within the capitalist system. That is why they refuse to make a clear distinction between our movement and the activities of bourgeois reformers whose aim is also to secure reforms (but for a purpose quite different from ours; that is, to strengthen capitalism against us), and why they see only a gradual differentiation between timorous reformers and consequential ones. For them, the passage to socialism is not tied up with a basic change in mental attitudes, nor does it involve a break with the past; all that is required is a new attitude toward simple, practical questions; hence they see with jaundiced eyes any exposition which recommends uprooting established middle-class traditions, since they fear that this would be a shock and a setback for the masses.

"The other one-sided idea of socialism is the very opposite of all this; its adherents reject day-to-day action and are concerned only with the final objective. The revolution, they say, will effect an immediate and complete change, will establish a new order; meantime, there is nothing else to do except keep insisting on this fact. In capitalism they see only unjust tyranny and exploitation, but they are completely blind to the organic relationship between the two systems that ensures that socialism develops naturally from capitalism. They consider social reforms not as progress but as danger, since the workers are thereby lulled into acquiescence and may well give a lukewarm reception to revolution. The slow work that secures progress does not interest them; their sole dream is to overthrow capitalism at one blow, and as soon as possible. This idea has lately spread among the anarchists. Today, the term 'anarchism' covers the most diverse tendencies, from the most pacific and unworldly Tolstoyism to the unfortunate rejects of society, feverishly hungry for homicide. Here we are concerned with anarchism only insofar as it plays a part within the workers' movement, and to the extent to which it is distinguishable from Social Democracy by the qualities we have listed. After the 1897 London congress, at which this current of ideas was outlawed from the workers' movement, the majority of these qualities reappeared in revolutionary trade unionism or anarcho-socialism, which has meantime undergone a certain development. . . ."

Since these anarchists regard parliamentary action as a source of corruption, they have turned to trade union action and have even come to regard the trade unions as organs of revolution. But they either entrench themselves in day-to-day action, in immediate demands and in these alone, or else their activity degenerates to the level of discussion circles in which they dream of 'the great day.' Since the revisionists, for their part, are solely concerned with reforms, they attempt at all costs to ally themselves with the bourgeois parties, at least with those which openly favor democracy and reforms; and lest they frighten off such parties, they studiously avoid any clear statement of their basic principles.

"In order to support the liberal and progressive middle class against the reactionary elements, the revisionists join them in a concerted policy to set up a coalition government. They scarcely realize that all this mere illusion. In effect, little or nothing of the hoped-for reforms will materialize, since it is necessary to mobilize all available forces to repel the attacks of the reactionaries. And even if they succeed in doing so and the day comes when a government is formed in which promises must be kept and substantial concessions made to the proletariat, the outcome will be reminiscent of the story of the man who sought to teach his horse to live without eating: at the very moment when the beast had become used to this, it was killed accidentally. Similarly, when the coalition government seeks to implement great reforms, it loses—quite accidentally, of course—middle class support, and the cabinet is overthrown.

"If, in one respect, the gain is so slight, in another the loss is great. When it tries to lead the workers to expect wonders from the alleged sympathy of the middle class toward them, revisionism *ruins the class consciousness so painfully won,* and plays the game of the ruling class; for, if the workers are induced to expect more from middle class good will and enlightenment from from their own efforts, they will be that much less inclined to form strong organizations. The external, organizational strength of the proletariat and its internal, spiritual strength will both be weakened. Besides, the movement will thereby lose its power to attract the proletariat. The large number of workers —who, while lacking any deep understanding of all that socialism stands for, have nevertheless a class consciousness as solid as it is instinctive—turn away from the party, which they now see parading under the colors of a middle-class party, and lay on it part of the blame for all the oppressive measures legislated by the government. In France and in Italy, the reformist tactics, the policy of coalition with the liberals and with ministerialism, strengthened anarcho-trade unionist sentiments—hostility toward all political action—in a section of the proletarian class, without consolidating organization or increasing class consciousness, those two pillars of working class power.

"Obviously, of course, these theoretical ideas are not the only basic cause of this development; on the contrary, indeed, the emergence of these limited conceptions of socialism can be explained by a mediocre degree of economic development and by specific political circumstances. On the other hand, in regions where big business is making giant progress, the workers are compelled to wage a fierce class war, to build up large organizations *and, in face of repression*, conduits to link up more and more closely the two aspects of the workers' movement, which are embodied in the Marxist theory. . . ."

Capital created the middle class society, whose juridical basis is the freedom and equality of all. It thus emancipated the masses of the people from the bonds of personal dependence that characterized the feudal system. The worker therefore became a free and equal partner with the capitalist, to whom he sells his labor. "His juridical freedom is the necessary condition of his economic bondage. Capitalism is a highly developed mode of production that has no need of slaves obedient only to the whip or of coolies deprived of all rights. Using a highly evolved technique and subject to commercial regulations, it needs workers with a high sense of responsibility and educated to a standard incomparably higher than that of a slave or a serf.

"This anomaly involved in the condition of the proletariat, the fact of being at once free and dependent, constitutes the most important contradiction of the capitalist system." On the one hand, capitalism finds itself compelled to acknowledge that workers' organizations have rights; on the other, it is constantly trying to limit those rights by force. But, in the second of these cases — to take a concrete instance, the prohibition in Bismarck's regime against the Socialist Democratic Party's propagating its ideas — the result does no more than arouse the workers' sympathy for the socialist cause. In the first, the result is much more positive: the workers' movement grows in numbers and in solidarity.

"Thus the ruling class constantly oscillates between two methods of government embodied in two opposed political tendencies. In the first place, the political antagonisms within the ruling class assuredly derive from clashes of interest between the different groups of that class. Historically, they stem from the antagonism between the two major middle class parties, found everywhere in the world: the antagonism between the magnates of industry and the wealthy landed proprietors, to which are then joined the clerical lower middle class. However, in reaction to the development of capitalism, the proletariat grows to be a threat to all its exploiters; furthermore, the extension of capitalism into the rural areas, with the participation of the rich nobility in industrial enterprises, gradually effects an eclipse of the old antagonisms. The result of all this is a continual lessening of the opposition between the middle class parties. But these antagonisms appear anew — imbricated, however, on what remained of the old — and associated with them are different ideas about the best way to repress the proletariat. The 'conservative' or 'clerical' party advocates strong measures; the liberal party, the maximum liberty of movement; nevertheless, the old party demarcations tend to become increasingly blurred, so that both parties are eventually composed of landed proprietors, manufacturers, farmers and the lower middle class. Hence the terms 'conservative' and 'liberal' take on a new meaning. The progressivist section of the middle class can no longer limit itself to the recognition of the workers' political liberty and certain rights; it must also seek a remedy for the 'aberrations' of capitalism, which are the causes of the workers' discontent. Hence, in contrast with the old dogmatic liberalism of the Manchester School type, the new liberalism finds itself compelled to opt for reforms, democracy, and the intervention of the State in the economic life of the country.

"Such transformation of political parties occurred in an integral way only in the countries of Western Europe which have a truly democratic constitution. Germany, for its part, ignores the constitutional regime; it is under a government which behaves as an autonomous power over which all the classes seek to exercise a determining influence, without ever succeeding in entirely doing so. Faced with the aristocrats and the workers, liberalism continues, therefore, to represent the exclusive interests of the industrial middle class; the new liberalism, the democratic current and the sympathy for the workers, are still at the stage of the fine phrase.

"It is in terms of given economic and political events that one or other of these tendencies is predominant, and that the mass of lower middle class electors opt for one or other of these methods of government. The development of the workers' movement is also governed by these factors, and that is why it is bound to stray to the right or to the left when theoretical knowledge is lacking, when it is without the sure means of recognizing the recurrence of the crisis by whose aid it can move towards its objective. When the ruling class resorts to reactionary policy, and represses the workers' organizations, the idea gains ground that nothing can be expected by legal measures, and that violence must be met by violence. The feeling of powerlessness which grips the workers pushes them towards nihilism; since ordinary political action is excluded and secret agitation alone remains possible, a contempt for day-to-day action sets in and the workers see the final solution as some far off 'day of wrath.' Very soon, the mere fact of sticking firmly to existing conditions of acting at the parliamentary level, seems a betrayal of the workers' cause.

"But everything changes with the circumstances, when the crisis has passed and the ruling class are now trying a policy of sweetness and light. When the vice-like grip is loosened, the working class can breathe again, can flex their muscles, and organize their forces—and the whole prospect becomes rosy.

The new attitude of the ruling class is regarded as an absolute law of development, signifying *a permanent softening of the class war, a lasting democratization of society, and an increasingly strong tendency towards reforms*, which will lead to socialism."[12]

The socialists, unanimous in desiring a real policy of reforms, approve of the following formula drawn up by Vollman (a declared revisionist): "The more the development takes place in a peaceful, orderly and organic way, the better is it both for us and for the collectivity." "But the development is in no way dependent on our wishes. At that time, no doomed class decided to go under with dignity and honor, nor any social order to founder, without first using up every ounce of strength in an attempt to remain afloat. And, today, the capitalist class is not showing any readiness to pave the way for socialism by means of real social reforms and of a democratic and progressive regime. There is no so-called 'logic of events' which, by shaping the course of history, will force this class to choose the way of democratic reform; on the contrary, concern for their economic interests will dissuade them from this, so long as they see such a step as strengthening and raising the enemy. For *the positive purpose of the liberal policy is to mislead the workers*. . . . Middle class social reforms are mere pretense and charlatanism. Only the vigilance of the workers' representatives, who ceaselessly urge the demands of the workers, can secure anything of value from such a situation. . . .

"At first sight, the two tendencies designated by the general names *anarchism* and *revisionism* seem to be absolutely opposed. However, since they have a common ground in both being distortions, but in contrary directions, of Social Democrat tactics, they are closely akin. Both, in effect, originate in a middle class outlook, radically different from the proletarian one. . . .

"The proletariat have their own dialectical idea of necessary social development, whose stages can be grasped only in terms of antagonist notions—for example, revolution and evolution, theory and practice, final objective and movement. Especially proletarian is the idea that all apparently opposed situations are simply movements in a major process of development. The proletariat does not reason along logical either/or lines—for example, either revolution or evolution—but sees in two such elements simply two aspects of one and the same development. . . . The middle class, non-dialectical way of thinking takes account only of the accidental, which

---

12. These clearly empirical considerations are primarily inspired by the experience of German Socialism both in the period of the "law against the dangerous intrigues of Social Democracy" (1878-1890), and afterwards. *Mutatis mutandis*, they still retain, however, some value as regards other countries, and even other times.

for the most part is merely a passing phenomenon, and so it swings from one extreme to the other. It notices contradictions only in the form of 'on the one hand...on the other hand,' but without seeing in them the driving forces of development; in its view, a development is to be seen as a slow evolution which, while it no doubt ends by effecting some change, leaves the essential quality intact.

"This first opposition is closely connected with the second. While the proletarian outlook is materialist, the middle class outlook is ideological; dialectic and materialism go hand in hand, as do ideology and non-dialectic. For the proletariat, it is material forces that govern the world, forces outside the scope of the individual; for the middle class, development depends on the creative forces of the human mind. The material reality is dialectical; that is, it can be truly grasped only as a unit made up of opposed ideas. By contrast, in the notions and ideas which, according to the middle class way of thinking, constitute the driving force of development, the terms of the contradiction mutually exclude one another *as notions*; for example, evolution and revolution, liberty and organization. *We are concerned in the middle class context with abstract ideas, with incompatible essences, no account being taken of the underlying material reality:* either revolution or evolution, without the possibility of a third term. So, when revolution is regarded as the only true principle, minor reforms are automatically declared anathema; or, *vice versa*, the minor reforms are alone considered as valid.

"*In this sense, anarchism and revisionism both represent middle class tendencies within the workers' movement; they unite a middle class view of the world with proletarian sentiments.* Standing shoulder to shoulder with the proletariat, they mean to espouse their cause, but without assisting to effect radical changes in mental attitudes and to substitute the knowledge which characterizes scientific socialism. They borrow their concepts and patterns of thought from the middle class world, and are distinguishable one from the other only by the fact that they derive from different periods of history. By and large, it can be said that the middle class, in the period of its ascension to power, professed revolutionary ideas; whereas, in the period of its decline, it no longer wants to have anything to do with upheavals, even in the natural sciences, and believes only in slow and gradual evolution. Anarchism, continuing the traditions of the middle class revolutions, thinks only about staging revolution; while revisionism adopts as its own the theory of slow evolution, proper to middle class decadence.

"More accurately, we are dealing with lower middle class rather than middle class tendencies For, unlike the complacent upper middle class, the lower middle class has at all times constituted a class of discontents, always inclined to oppose the existing order. Social development does not, in effect, favor this class. Left in the cold, it inevitably plunges from one excess to another. Sometimes it is intoxicated with revolutionary slogans and tries to seize power by means of putsches; sometimes it crawls shamefully at the feet of the upper classes and tries, by cunning and deceit, to wheedle reforms from them. *Anarchism is lower middle class ideology gone mad; revisionism, the same ideology with its teeth drawn.* This close kinship explains why each can be so easily changed into the other. The history of the workers' movement contains only too many instances of ardent 'revolutionaries' metamorphosed into peaceable reformists. In 1906, many revisionists suddenly become convinced of the possibility of engineering a minor reovlution; but, when they discovered the uselessness of the attempt, they then relapsed into a reformism of the most blatant kind.[13] Only the external form had changed; fundamentally, the conception had remained exactly as it was, opposed to Marxism and refusing to see development as the unity of contraries.

"Furthermore, these two tendencies have in common the cult of the individual and of personal liberty. Marxism regards the powerful economic forces which move the mass of mankind as factors of the social dynamic; while the middle class theory places in the heart of its philosophy *the free and unshackled personality.* "This was the doctrine of old style liberalism, and this is the doctrine of anarchism, always ready to defend the individual freedom of the producer against interference by the state, while ignoring the fact that the principal function of state power is to oppress the working classes, and that this power must be suppressed, as must all forms of authority in general, to give way finally to real freedom. While revolutionary trade unionism does not coincide on this point with pure, individualistic anarchism, because it developed in a milieu of already organized workers, it proclaims no less distinctly that its objective is the perfect autonomy of the individual. For its part, revisionism extols moral liberty, so dear to Kant. Besides, both anarchism and revisionism repudiate the Marxist conception of economy,

---

13. Toward the end of 1905, certain segments of the Social Democratic Party, under the impetus of the Russian Revolution (and, its repercussion on the level of ideas in the famous mass strike debate) launched an intensive press campaign with a view to securing the abolition of the suffrage restrictions. This movement took on vast proportions, and was accompanied by political strikes, demonstrations and clashes with the police. However, the party and, to a greater extent, the trade union leaders used every means to break it and succeeded some months later. The active campaigns against militarism, colonialism or the armaments race having been essentially the work of youth organizations, the campaign, resumed in 1908 and 1910 in support of voting rights constitutes one of the rare moments when the German Party took up toward the authorities an attitude other than one of peaceful criticism. However, the choice of this example shows that Pannekoek is here attacking general tendencies much more than political currents with clear contours.

according to which "capitalist production presents a twofold character, itself deriving in turn from the twofold character of the merchandise: its usage value and its exchange value. Consequently, all labor is simultaneously concrete, a creator of usage values, and abstract, a creator of exchange values. In the capitalist system, production is also production of usage values for society and production of surplus value. This second function, the formation of surplus value, constitutes for the capitalists the essential purpose of production, but the first is indissolubly linked with it. Hence it is that capitalist production is at once *production of necessary objects,* without which society could not exist, and *exploitation of the workers.* "

The anarchist persists in ignoring this twofold character. He sees modern industry, that "great organizing power," as an oppressive power and as that alone. Generally a highly qualified tradesman or technician, he feels that industry is threatening to declass him socially. Furthermore, he dreams of leveling the middle class by means of the general strike, in the anarchist sense, not realizing that, in conjunction with big business, certain elements of the future society are taking shape within the present society, and that these elements must be developed, not thrown in disarray. This is recognized by the revisionist; but, since for him the difference between the capitalist and the socialist modes of production is simply a matter of degree, he believes that the passage from one to the other can occur gradually, without preliminary conquest of political power. "Both involve *a relapse into the old utopianism....* Since they refuse to regard the coming of socialism as an inevitable result of economic development, they are obliged to resort to lucubrations and claptrap. We know that the anarchists delight in elaborate arguments in which they eagerly try to reconcile this or that communist system with freedom; they regard the Social Democrats as people who want to establish a definite social order, collectivism, with a purpose completely different from their own communist final objective. Similarly Bernstein is most anxious to know what must be understood, in our program by saying that we want to 'statize.' In both cases, this is to ignore the fact that a new mode of production must evolve of itself, and that it cannot be introduced ready made, in conformity with a plan fixed in advance.

"Revisionism and anarchism represent, therefore, opposite and one-sided distortions of socialism. Since neither understands what is meant by Marxism, which unifies in itself the two aspects of the workers' movement, each of these tendencies regards the other as Marxist and attacks it as such. The revisionists describe the Marxist tactics as revolutionary romanticism, and, though the facts give them the lie, regard the Marxists as enemies of immediate claims, of day-to-day action, and of reforms. This is only to be expected, seeing that for them reform and revolution are mutually incompatible, and that they cannot understand how one can advocate the revolutionary tasks of the proletariat without at the same time abandoning the idea of minor reforms. Anarchists and revolutionary trade unionists see things from a strictly opposite viewpoint: they regard revisionist tactics as the necessary consequence of Social Democracy, and they combat the latter by accusing it of reformist theories and actions."

V. *Parliamentarinism*

"Political institutions serve to establish both the laws which men must obey as members of society, and the laws required by the dominant mode of production for its proper exercise; they must also see to the implementing of such laws. These rules restrain the freedom of the individual in the interests of all, or of what it has been found convenient so to describe. The power of the State must necessarily originate in the division of society into the ruling class and the ruled, exploited class; it constitutes the instrument which the rulers use to repress the ruled. The more complicated the social machinery becomes, the more are the functions of State power extended, and the more does this power take on the appearance of an autonomous organization, ruling over the whole of social life. State power has become the objective of the class war, because whichever class possesses it has also at its disposal the immense strength of the State, and can, by means of laws, impose its will on the whole of society.... Legislation, the police, the judiciary, the administrative authorities, the army, are all institutions which are used more and more as weapons in the war against the working class. The proletariat is therefore compelled to adopt as its objective the conquest of the state.

"*Parliamentarianism is the normal form of political domination with the middle class....* But, if this is so, why do the workers wage the parliamentary war? Why do they go to such lengths to secure universal suffrage? The importance of parliamentarianism is to be sought in quite another direction. In effect, it constitutes *the best way to increase the strength of the working class.* If today, in every country dominated by capitalism, one sees great socialist parties forming to enlighten the proletariat and, above all, to lead the war against the dominant order, this power, grown to such considerable proportions, is due essentially to the parliamentary struggle.

"It is easy to understand why parliamentarianism has made these results possible. The first effect of the parliamentary conflict is to *enlighten the workers about their class situation.* Of course, this can also be done by means of pamphlets and public meetings, but it is difficult to use these means at a time when the movement is still weak and when it comes up against a veritable wall of prejudice and indifference: . . . whereas the voices of the workers' representatives in parliament echo in even the most remote areas. . . .

"That seats in parliament are of such importance is undoubtedly because they serve as a means of agitation, but still more because the outcome of parliamentary conflict is the enlightenment of the alerted workers. If our representatives go into parliament, it is not primarily in order to make stirring speeches, but to combat the middle class parties there. In so far as such a distinction is possible, seeing that we are discussing an activity which can only be verbal, it is by their actions, not their words, that the workers are educated to socialism. . . . It is by following the parliamentary debates attentively that the workers acquire the political awareness which they need. When, day after day, senators of every party, seeking to impose their views, attack the general theory and outlook of the workers' representatives, the workers gain a radical knowledge of their own attitudes as opposed to those of the others. The parliamentary conflict is not, of course, the class war itself: however, it does in a sense constitute *the essence of the class war*. In the speeches of a small group of labor members of parliament, the interests and ideas of the masses are expressed in a condensed form. . . .

"What is more, parliamentary conflict appeals not only to the understanding, but also to spontaneous feelings. Besides giving the worker political knowledge, it increases his moral sense, in the spirit of proletarian morality, of solidarity, of the feeling of belonging to a class. And organization is thereby strengthened. . . . The laborers feel themselves to be Catholics, progressivists, or Protestants, and not workers; they do not feel that they are members of one and the same class. The entry of a Social Democrat into Parliament, where he deals with their situation as the most important part of his policy, and where he therefore speaks *in the name of the working class*, can suddenly fan into flame the class consciousness that has been smoldering within them. This and this alone gives them an awareness of their common brotherhood in one specific body, even if as yet they cannot rise above the middle class ideas which are sundering them.

"The trade union movement also arouses a lively feeling of belonging; it unites the workers, but only at the immediate basis of trade and craft. Within the trade union movement, the working class fights in skirmishes and with small detachments against various capitalists or groups of capitalists. The political conflict musters all these battalions, and then the uncommitted workers begin to join in their thousands. It activates *the working class as a whole*, without regard to trade or condition, and throws them into the war against the whole middle class. For Social Democracy attacks not only industrial capital, but also banking, landed, colonial capitalism. *The political conflict is the class war generalized.* That is why participation in this war engenders in the workers, on a massive scale, the feeling of belonging to a class. *It sets the seal on class unity;* in its absence, as in 19th-century England, for example, the trade union organizations readily give way in a limited cooperative spirit. The political conflict unites together with secure bonds all the separate sections of the whole working class; it transforms it into a homogeneous body and thus increases its organizational strength.

Parliamentarianism has, in a sense, completely changed the proletariat created by the enormous development of capitalism, into a self-aware and organized class, ready for combat. It is there that its value lies, and not in the illusion that the electoral system can guide our ship through calm waters to the harbor of the future State.

"As against the idea of parliamentarianism just outlined, there is an opposite view, widespread among the revisionists, which regards it, not as *a means of increasing proletarian power,* but as *the battle itself for this power.* . . . If one holds that the political conflict should occur exclusively within parliament, then the parliamentarians are the only people called upon to wage it. It is not the working masses who are involved, but thier representatives who fight on their behalf. The masses figure only at the ballot boxes; the only contribution they can make to their own emancipation is to choose the proper candidates and campaign vigorously for them during the elections. . . .

"The party deputies thus take up a vanguard position; they become a special class, the 'guides.' It is only natural that the most capable comrades, having the profoundest knowledge of socialism, should by what they say exercise a powerful influence over the party." However, the comrades elected are not generally those whose attitude most clearly expresses class consciousness, but others who are chosen with the further aim of wooing the middle class vote. "The strength of our parliamentarians does not therefore reside primarily in the socialism which they profess and in the strength of the masses who support them, but in their personal qualities and in their political skill. Through their technical knowledge in juridical and administrative matters, through their familiarity with the petty combines, intrigues and calculations of day-to-day politics, they regard themselves as superior to the non-parliamentarians. In their view, they themselves are best able to judge as experts what are really matters for approval by all, since they alone can delve deeply into such matters. When their ideas clash with those of the rank and file, they simply override all criticism: the comrades must remember that, since as non-parliamentarians they do not know enough about these problems, they must trust their 'delegates' to reach decisions in their 'soul and conscience.' In this way, the parliamentary section places itself above the people and the party, by virtue of 'the superiority of their political knowledge.' When the masses accept such tutelage, democratic sentiments are doomed to disappear from within the party. . . .

"There are those who regard the Social Democratic Party as indistinguishable from the middle class parties, and are blind to its absolutely different character. Naturally, their methods move closer and closer to those of middle class politics. Under the name of 'politics of the workers,' they shape a policy designed to secure for the workers as many specific advantages as the other parties seek to obtain for the middle class — for heavy industry, finance, small holders. In this way, a mediocre 'policy of interests' replaces the Social Democratic policy which embodies the permanent revolutionary interest of the proletariat. Instead of a class war clearly rooted in principles, the aim is to exercise an indirect 'political influence' through parliamentary coalitions and blocs. This is to forget that Social Democracy, by the fact that its attitude is dictated by principles, covers directly the whole field of middle class politics. Hence it is that participation in a governmental majority or the entry of socialists into the government, becomes the natural consequence of this viewpoint. . . . The quest for immediate positive results, nearly always a vain quest, is pursued to the detriment of our great objective, which is to enlighten and unify the working class.

"This is so, in the first place, because the chief aim of these advocates of indirect political influence is to win over as many electors as possible. The floating voters are by no means socialists but, on the contrary, are imbued with middle class ideas. Some of them undoubtedly approve our immediate demands; however, deeply imbued as they are with their class prejudices, they do not adopt our ultimate aims, our ideas as a whole. Really to turn them into solid, convinced militants, requires a campaign against their narrowness of mind, a liquidation of their old, lower middle class prejudices, by a long and arduous process of education. But the immediate outcome of this may well be to frighten them off. It is much easier to win their votes, and much less embarassing to respect their prejudices. . . . It is even worse when, to win the votes of the peasants and of the lower middle class, they bind themselves to promises of an immediate improvement of their condition, promises which are poles removed both from our theory and from real development. Lower middle class ideas are strengthened and socialist enlightenment thwarted by a campaign of this kind, which sacrifices the essential objective to immediate electoral gains.

The tactic of "exclusive parliamentarianism" is also harmful to organization. When the workers are persuaded that their deputies will make all decisions for them, they have no further reason for forming a major organization to conduct their own affairs themselves. In effect, all they have to do is to vote in electoral years, and all the thinking they need to do is about the choice of the best candidate.... The result is that many workers of revolutionary leanings, disgusted at the sight of socialist deputies behaving exactly like those of the middle class, leave the organization.... The unilateral revolutionary wing of the workers' movement thus takes on an anti-political character, while the reformist wing expresses itself correspondingly in middle class parliamentarianism. In France and in Italy, coalition politics and ministerialism have increased the following of revolutionary trade unionism, and are causing trade unions to become inimical to the party."

Anarchism sees in oppressive institutions, such as the state, the source of all the trouble. "That is why it rejects our objective, the conquest of the state, since such conquest would involve only a simple transfer of powers, while the principle itself of authority would continue as before. It advocates the overthrow of State power, the abolition of all constraint, so that men become absolutely free. Finally, they refuse to participate in the politico-parliamentary conflicts, which in their view serve merely to corrupt the workers, since they only contribute *to replace one set of rules by another....* The parties are no more than politicians' groups for strengthening the deputies' positions and for securing their promotion to cabinet posts.

"From the anarchist viewpoint, the State constitutes an autonomous power, which rules at its summit thanks to violence and cunning, and at its base thanks to superstition and slavishness. The State, the parties and the politicians are no longer in any real sense in contact with their origins, and the classes subjacent to them sink into insignificance. One finds the same errors and the same basic idea among the revisionists. Both they and the anarchists are victims of the same politico-superstition: for the former, the 'democracy' or the 'republic' represents a saving divinity; for the latter, the State is the malignant devil....

"Marxism always tried to establish the causal nexus of all social phenomena; under the political forms, it never fails to trace the economic connections, the class connections. But this nexus cannot be expressed as a simple formula, straightforward and easy to remember. This is especially true of the State. The State, the government, is an organization created by the ruling class to defend their interests. But those who exercise State power do not use it solely in the interests of the ruling class, whose representatives they are, but also in their own immediate interests. State power in the service of the middle class takes on a certain autonomy, and suddenly seems independent. Bureaucracy is *a specific class with very special interests* which they seek to assert even against the middle class.

"This independence is, of course, merely a deceptive appearance. Bureaucracy can attempt to secure its own interests *in minor matters*, because *in major matters* it serves those of the middle class. The latter support it as a lesser evil, because they could not impose their interests to the same extent without this bureaucracy. In Germany, the government of *junkers* (aristocrats) is adapting itself to a bureaucracy which is enriching itself at their expense, because it needs strong State power against the working class. Bureaucracy is recruited among the middle class, who see in the many and ever increasing government and administrative posts, so many soft jobs for sons and relatives. It too is therefore an exploiting class who deducts its share of the overall surplus value from the proceeds of state duties and monopolies and, from time to time, opposes the other classes' right to its part of the surplus value. In countries with parliamentary government, such as France, the bureaucratic summit comprises a *clique of politicians*; in countries with a two-party system, such as England and the U.S.A., two cliques take turns in governing, and secure for their friends the plum State jobs. The middle class as a whole sometimes resents having to put up with such a band of parasites, but is nevertheless content with the system, since bureaucracy sees to its general interests and to its profit. It is in appearance only that the state power is independent of the middle class. . . ."

VI. *The Trade Union Movement*

"The trade unions are the natural form of proletarian organization, and the direct manifestation of its social function—i.e., to act as vendor of the merchandise represented by work. The worker's immediate interest strictly consists in selling his work at the best price. To him, his employer, his direct exploiter, is the embodiment of the capitalist class, and the war against the employer for an improvement of working conditions represents the first, instinctive form of the class war.

"However, the trade unions are not the direct organ of the revolutionary class war, since their objective is not the overthrow of capitalism. On the contrary, they form a necessary element for the stability of a normal capitalist society. In regions where workers are not yet organized and are therefore incapable of serious resistance, the employers simply dictate the working conditions. Consequently, they pay barely enough to keep the workers at the subsistence level and to enable them to work; the workers are prematurely exhausted by the excessive length of the working day. *The work is bought at a price below its value*; the purchaser takes advantage of the seller's weak position, and cheating takes the place of fair exchange. But it is precisely this inhuman exploitation which forces the workers to resist and to organize themselves. When the trade union succeeds in waging war on these barbarous practices and in imposing somewhat fairer working conditions, it is essentially doing no more than applying a fundamental principle of all normal capitalism — that exchange of values takes place on a basis of equivalence. Thus the trade union destroys the hegemony of the employer; henceforward, employer and worker confront each other from positions of equal strength, and reach agreements by which work is paid for at its value."

This is the principal task of the trade unions "and the reason why they should remain 'neutral' in the sense of not imposing any particular political or philosophic opinions on their members. They should muster all the workers who want to fight the employer for a betterment of their working conditions, and also demand higher union subscriptions because, *without well stocked coffers*, it is impossible to keep up a strike or to withstand a lock out. They also need *salaried officers*, because the administrative duties, the conduct of the war, and the negotiations with employers, cannot be discharged on a part-time basis, and demand very specific aptitudes and knowledge which can be acquired only by practice." Formerly, the strike was a spontaneous explosion of despair; but, with the development of trade unions, it increasingly becomes a carefully prepared undertaking, and the conflicts between the trade unions and the employers' federations come to resemble wars between two great powers.

"In the course of these wars, the trade unions do not act *by any means as adversaries of capitalism*, but take their stand *on the same territory* as capitalism. They do not deny the fact that labor is a type of merchandise, but, on the contrary, seek to obtain the best possible price for it. The trade unions cannot, in effect, end the reign of the capitalist at the factory, since the capitalist is of course the owner of the merchandise he has bought and uses it for his own ends; they can only curb any arbitrary conduct on his part, which is simply an excrescence, an abuse. *Their tasks do not carry them outside the framework of capitalism.* That is why one frequently finds middle class politicians or sociologists taking a sympathetic attitude towards them; the trade unions fight the greed of the *individual* capitalist, not the class as a whole or the system as such. On the contrary, when they secure better conditions for the workers, the misery and revolt of the exploited masses are to that extent reduced; and, in this sense, they even act as a conservative force consolidating capitalism.

"But this characteristic is *only one aspect* of their nature. The employers, against whom the unions war, also form the middle class, the class that exercises State power. The workers who wage this war are also those who must carry on the political conflict, the war for socialism.

"If capitalism were a peaceful, stagnant and unaltering form of production, the trade unions would present the same picture. A condition of equilibrium would therefore result, to the great satisfaction of the capitalists who, with the workers receiving fair pay for an agreed working week, could then quietly pocket all the remaining surplus value."

Under the spur of competition, however, capitalism is forced to move forward, to accumulate more quickly ever increasing masses of capital. That is why it vigorously opposes pay demands, replaces men by machines and qualified workers by unskilled labor from the country areas or from abroad. Periods of prosperity alternate with periods of crisis, during which massive unemployment enables the employers to take back the concessions yielded grudgingly under pressure from the unions. The latter are then obliged to renounce these conservative traits, "which delight their middle class friends," and to support the action of the political party. "The trade unions form, however, a necessary element of capitalism in its phases of rapid expansion; they alone can thwart, by constant warfare, the tendency of capitalist development to reduce the working class to misery and thus prevent production from sufering as a result."

"However, the trade unions also constitute an *element of revolutionary transformation of society*. This does not mean that they need to take on tasks in addition to those they are already fulfilling, but simply that they carry out their specific mission as well as possible. Far from being ascribable to a deliberate intention or to a program, *it is the reality of the situation itself that makes them organs of revolution*. Once more we see how intimately the proletarian's revolutionary objective is linked to and develops from daily practice."

No doubt, the trade union conflicts contribute less than does the political one to develop proletarian strength. But they do awaken class consciousness in the workers, make them recognize the need for constant combat, and shatter their illusions. Soon the worker develops beyond this still limited stage; he sees that he must confront not just an isolated employer but capitalist society in its totality. It is the political conflict which alone makes him capable of this wider view. But the trade union, "the natural organizational form of the working class," musters the workers within a strong organization and, more important still, inculcates in them the discipline necessary to the everyday struggle, the feeling of solidarity, and the conviction that collective interest must take precedence over personal interest. "Isolated until then, and still preserving through their lower middle class origins the habit of acting in an individualistic way, the workers see themselves changed into new men with new habits, into men who feel closely united with their comrades as integral parts of a body animated by one and the same will. It is in this new character that the fighting strength of the proletariat resides.... Of the two major factors of this strength, knowledge and organization, the second is essentially the result of trade union action. The work of the trade unions, in which their importance to the revolution consists, is the enormous task of moral education required to transform the weak worker into a conqueror of capitalism.

"This conception of the role and significance of the trade union movement is peculiar to Marxism, which is alone in proclaiming that the revolutionary transformation of society is germinally contained in the ordinary conflicts of today. The middle class view, however, is that the objective of these daily conflicts is a direct improvement of living conditions, without there being any question of their linkage with the great proletarian war of freedom; but it can also happen that, through a realization of the revolutionary meaning of trade unions, an effort is made to give a specific direction to their present practice. The English trade unions provide a classic example of the first of these conceptions; the second, the revolutionary trade union conception, is much more evident in the French counterpart.

"In France, the reformist policy of the socialist party despises the class viewpoint; the unions have therefore experienced in their ranks, under the guise of reaction, an explosion of very pronounced revolutionary sentiments, a lively opposition to parliamentarianism. Their objective is not the conquest of political power, but the seizure of workers' control over industry. The true workers' movement consists in a struggle whose course is decided by the workers themselves, not by their representatives. These trade unionists have as their slogan *direct action*.[14] Only the masses can win their own freedom; their leaders and representatives cannot do it for them. The working masses must think and feel for themselves; it is not enough that they unite, simply with a view to obtaining higher wages and a shorter working day.

"Trade union practice here and now should be in strict conformity with these ideas. The unions are the only genuinely working class organizations. It is also up to them to wage political war on the government — at least when the latter attacks them, for any question of the State leaves them otherwise cold.

---

14. For a good definition, see Victor Griffuehles, *l'Action syndicaliste* (Paris, 1908), p. 23: "Direct action means action by the workers themselves, that is, action directly taken by those directly affected.... Through direct action, the worker himself creates his struggle: it is he who conducts it, determined not to hand over to others his own task of self-liberation."

The conquest of social power is to take place through a general strike, during which the organized workers will stop all work and will quite simply let the capitalists founder. The mission of the trade unions is to develop the revolutionary sentiments necessary to the implementing of an action on such a scale, and to do so, not only by exhortation, but also and especially by the practice itself of the strike. Thus the latter becomes an end in itself, or rather a *revolutionary gymnastic exercise*, and that is why it matters little whether its immediate oucome is victory or defeat in relation to the improvement of living conditions.

"Experience has shown that these principles are not the basis for a strong trade union movement,[15] and that the objective it sets itself cannot be attained in this way. This allegedly revolutionary practice is not at all successful in mustering the proletarian masses who are still without class consciousness—for this is something which can be achieved only by a persevering conflict solely aimed at small and gradual improvements. It presupposed in the worker a revolutionary attitude of mind which can only be the *final* result of long practice. The trade unions continue to be small groups of workers with revolutionary sentiments, whose fervor does not make up for weakness of organization. Through lack of centralization, the progress noted from time to time remains a passing phenomenon. Seeking to take on a function other than its own—namely, to act as a political party—the trade union finds itself unable to fulfill its proper function, the improvement of working conditions. It neglects what is incumbent on it, the organization of the masses; and the revolutionary education which it does attempt, it does wrongly.

"As regards trade union action, revisionism has an importance of quite another kind. In effect, it finds, in the natural existential conditions of these unions, an area much more favorable to its expansion than that of the political movement." Of course, the trade unions do not, any more than does the party, separate the fight for immediate demands from the fight for the overthrow of capitalism; but the party action is at an infinitely more general level, and that is why it also demands more general ideas and arguments and

15. In 1910, the French CGT numbered 358 thousand members (an estimate probably greatly exaggerated), while the German "free trade unions," linked with Social Democracy, could claim a membership of more than two million. On the development of the *Freien Gewerkschaften* between 1890 and the war, see especially: Heinz Varain, *Freie Gewerkschaft, Sozial-Demokratie und Staat* . . . *(1890-1920)* (Düsseldorf, 1956) especially the bibliography; Gerhardt Ritter, *Die Arbeiterbewegung im Wilhelmischen Reich,* (West Berlin, 1959); and, above all, Heinz Langerhaus, "Richtungsgewerkschaft und gewerkschaftliche Autonomie," *International Review of Social History,* 11, 1 and 2, 1957. See also Emile Pouget, *la Confédération Générale du Travail* (Paris, 1908), pp. 47-48.

adopts objectives which are equally so. In the domain of trade unionism, however, "the arguments are ready-made and decided by the most immediate interest. It is not necessary, therefore, nor is it always desirable, to press the distinction any further. The task of trade unionism is to regroup the masses in relation to a common and immediate objective; therefore it does not take kindly to ideas which are in danger of not being understood, because it thereby clashes with certain prejudices and even shocks many people, the consequence being possible injury to the unity of the movement. So it is that the trade unions are led to confine themselves to the immediate, and to regard as disastrous, as revolutionary 'romanticism,' whatever goes beyond this.

"There is yet another reason why revisionism is so welcomed within the trade unions. The latter fight on the terrain of the middle class political order, of the liberal State. In order to develop, they need the right of coalition and a solidly guaranteed quality of rights, but nothing more. The trade unions *as such* have as their ideal, not a socialist order, but freedom and equality within the middle class State. *When they possess these fully, as in England, they become upholders of the status quo; when these rights are not fully acknowledged, as is still the case in Germany, they declare for political democracy, and hence make common cause with the revisionists and the middle class progressives.*

"Let a trade union movement succeed in wresting some notable improvements, and the idea easily spreads that the proletarian condition can be permanently improved within the framework of the capitalist system. In such circumstances, a conservative spirit makes its appearance, complacent and little inclined to share in revolutionary aspirations. A workers' élite forms who, while seeking to raise itself by its own efforts, profoundly distrusts the mass of miserable and unorganized laborers. At the same time, Social Democracy finds itself thwarted in its efforts to raise the workers to an effective level of class consciousness.

"The trade unions do, of course, constitute the organization of the proletarian masses. But unaided and lacking as they do any ideals and long-term view, which the political movement cultivates *par excellence*, they are incapable of inducing unity among the proletariat. The trade union organization, in effect, resembles certain federations of trade or of industry, which remain separate from one another, each rarely benefiting from the active help of the others. . . .

"However, as major industry develops, the class war becomes more and more lively, and large employers' associations come into being who meet partial strikes with a general lock-out, thereby further extending the war and speeding up the centralization of trade unions. Decision-making, the power to declare industrial war or to end it, reverts more and more to the trade union leaders and to the central bodies; and more and more the local groups lose their right to make such decisions. The conflicts change into giant clashes in the course of which, exactly as in international wars, huge armies are directed by a supreme command. To safeguard the democratic character of the organization, recourse is had to a system of representatives of the parliamentary type, thus provoking a new rise of bureaucratism. One is faced with a phenomenon similar to that connected with the parliamentary conflicts: the influence of the leaders becomes decisive, while that of the masses declines. Success or failure appears to depend on the personal qualities of the leaders, on their strategic skill, on their ability to read a situation correctly; while the enthusiasm and experience of the masses themselves are not regarded as active factors. Within the workers' movement, just as within the State, a whole hierarchy forms whose particular ideas often prevail over those of the masses.

"The revisionist tendencies in the trade union movement have the further disastrous effects...of inducing feelings of complacency and an anti-revolutionary attitude of mind, of strengthening the corporative spirit and weakening both democratic awareness and the confidence of the masses in their own strength. Since these tendencies originate directly in the very nature of the trade union movement, the powerful development of the latter" is bound to strengthen them in an equally natural way; on the other hand, a campaign of propaganda centered on principles may confine their growth. "For such propaganda is something quite other than a fully armed means of salvation. The reality of the situation not only engenders revisionist tendencies but also causes the ground to slip away beneath them. *Capitalism is not only an existing reality; it is one that constantly overthrows everything that exists.* It is in the nature of the *existing* capitalist reality to transform trade union wars into a carefully calculated skirmish..., but it does not necessarily follow that these conditions are eternal and immutable." On the contrary, they undergo incessant change and, "to the extent to which the latter urge toward revolution, the long-term revolutionary role of the trade unions becomes an immediate reality."

While industry grows at an increased rate and, with it, the number of workers, the class war takes on a massive character, with a multiplication of major strikes in every country and hundreds of thousands of men involved in them. "Every major strike now takes on the appearance of an explosion, of a minor revolution. [16] The trade unions find themselves forced to abandon

---

16. We again remind the reader that between 1903 and 1913, huge and violent strikes

something of their immediate demands in order to adapt to a political context. The old corporative limitations are shattered—and, of course, their overthrow will be the more effectively and readily secured if assisted from the outset by a lively propaganda."

The State power reacts to this by repression, and the workers must face up to this. "Political action and trade union action merge more and more into a united front of the working class against the ruling class. This shows, therefore, that only temporary conditions peculiar to a particular phase of the class war were separating the first time of action from the second and were causing each to develop its own characteristics in a distinct way. In the 'parliamentary' phase, the proletariat has to adapt its war tactics to exterior conditions—in other words, to the middle class hegemony within the State, a hegemony that had continued undisputed throughout a whole generation without undergoing any basic modification. Hence, these war tactics—the political type and that of trade unionism—were able to develop each in its own way, so as to assume independent existence. The conditions peculiar to this phase left so deep an impression that many considered it foolish to suppose that they could ever disappear, the domain of 'practical' politics and tactics being doomed in that case to destruction. These conditions were not, such people believed, destined to change in the foreseeable future, and merely to envisage a shifting of the war to another terrain was regarded as romantic illusion. To gauge the effects of this period, it is enough to recall the reluctance very often shown in trade union circles to discuss the conditions and the possibilities of the general strike.[17]

"But *a third period of the proletarian class war* is being inaugurated.... The mass strike as an everyday tactic, during the parliamentary phase, was, in its 'revolutionary gymnastics' form, a piece of childishness without practical value; henceforth, it is becoming something real." Political conflict and trade

occurred in succession in various European countries, and this in spite of the determination of the big workers' organizations to limit such movements; thus this formula corresponded to the facts. Did it not take a world war—engendered of course by other causes as well—to put an end, provisionally, to this social agitation?

17.   Theodor Bömelburg, the head of the stonemasons' union, declared at the Trade Union Congress of 1905: "We ought to suspend all discussion of the general strike, and postpone [the discussion of] future solutions until the appropriate time," since the present situation "requires calm within the workers' movement." The Congress adopted a motion inviting the workers "not to allow themselves to be deflected from the day-to-day activity of building up the organization, by the accepting and propagating of such ideas." Cited by Karl Kautsky, *Der politische Massenstreik* (Berlin, 1914), pp. 115-18; see also the dossier assembled by Günter Griek on this theme, *Zeitschrift für Geschichtswissenschaft*, 5, 1963, pp. 919-940. In a general sense, the trade union leaders, whose influence over the party was great, did all in their power to prohibit any discussion of these ideas in congresses, in the press and in public meetings.

union action are merging, thereby entailing a union of political expertise and trade union discipline; the old methods have had their day. "Embodied in the leaders, the two modes of action remained distinct, and yet, at both levels, the masses were made up of the same workers. The organized masses themselves are now entering into the fray, endowed with class consciousness, discipline, and the strength gained in previous conflicts—their organizations, the trade unions, their political knowledge, socialism."

VII. *The Other Classes*

"If the proletariat and the capitalists engaged in major industry were the only classes in our society, the conflict would represent the very simple pattern of two camps drawn up against each other. But this is not the case. Between the middle class and the proletariat there are *numerous intermediate categories* that shade gradually from one class to the other. On the one hand, there are the vestiges of the old independent middle classes: the small capitalists, scarcely distinguishable from the big ones through whom they have been brought into tight circumstances; substantial farmers and lower middle class people, who partly serve the interests of big capital, which tends to exploit directly the small farmers and the laborers. On the other hand, however, there are classes of recent growth, the officers and noncommissioned officers of the industrial army who range from foremen to technicians, through engineers, doctors, chief clerks, to end in directors. Here the members of the inferior rank are the exploited, the others being the exploiters.

"All these intermediate categories, with their own particular interests, take part in the class war. Some identify their aspirations with those of the proletarians; the rest opt for the other camp. Suddenly, therefore, the class war picture becomes more complicated, and divergences show within the party because of attitudes linked with different interests."

A long description follows about the condition of the lease-hold farmer and of the lower middle class person, forced to pay high rent to the capitalist, dreaming of a return to a society of small enterprises, but wishing in the interests of his business that the workers had more money to spend. While hating the capitalist, he feels that he is threatened by the workers' demands, to the extent to which he himself employs a staff. He would like to see competition regulated and military expenses reduced, and, to secure this, he relies on the parliamentary system. In this sense, he is a democrat. "The proletariat can sometimes benefit by these clashes of interests. It did so in England in 1847 to secure the 10-hour day; and in Germany in 1867 to win the franchise—even if these demands triumphed only at the cost of grim battles. But these clashes of interests remained always of a secondary kind in comparison with the one which separates the proletariat and the middle class..., and never amounted to anything more than differences about *the division of the spoils....*

"The *so-called new middle class*—intellectuals,[18] civil servants, salaried employees—form, for their part, a transition category between the proletariat and the middle class. This new variety is distinguished from the old by the following essential trait: since they have absolutely no ownership of means of production, and live by the *sale of their labor*, they have therefore *no interest in the maintenance of private production*, of the private ownership of the means of production. At this level, they stand with the proletariat, with just as little reactionary interest or desire for reaction; they look ahead, not backwards. We have here a *modern class* that is emerging and becoming more and more numerous with the growth of society itself.

"The situation of this class differs greatly, however, from that of the proletariat. As a rule, its members offer a highly qualified type of work, the result of years of costly study. They therefore command much higher salaries than those of the workers. Holding management or scientific posts, they can, if they prove to be highly competent, reach the *highest positions*, and thus the old saying of the independent middle class, 'Everyone is the architect of his own fortune,' is given a new setting. Unlike the situation of the proletariat, misery and necessity do not force them into an implacable war against capitalism; on the contrary, they find this system satisfactory in many respects.

"They do not deliberately decide to fight for an improvement of their condition. Those with top positions feel that they belong with capitalism, and have other means of achieving their objectives. The mass of these employees breaks up into so many groups and categories, with such a variety of salaries and aspirations that they do not form a solidly united body in the manner of the working class. They comprise, so to speak, all the ranks from general to adjutant, whereas the workers represent the mass of private soldiers. The employees do not work in great collectives, but as individuals; they therefore lack the vigorous awareness that the proletariat has owing to its work in common and in large groups. Unaccustomed to hardship, they fear

---

18. *Der Intelligenz*: the Social Democratic theoreticians have never tried to define exactly the limits of this category. Thus, in his controversy with Bernstein (Kautsky, *op. cit.*, pp. 242-54), Kautsky used "intellectuals" imprecisely to refer to office or commercial workers, the cadres of industry, and others; he later applied the term only to the cadres in general, and finally he limited it to the members of the intelligentsia as creators and manipulators of leftist ideas. It would be rash to claim that the term is any more precise today.

unemployment more than the workers do. All this makes them unfit for organized trade union action against their capitalist masters. Only the subaltern categories, who are both the worst paid and the most numerous, and whose lot is therefore very similar to that of the better paid workers, are gradually coming round to the idea of organization and of trade union action.

"The intellectuals are also separated from the proletariat at the ideological level. The production of middle class environment, they are naturally imbued with a middle class idea of the world, an idea which their theoretical studies have served only to strengthen. With the intellectuals, the middle class prejudices against socialism take on a scientific coloring. Their particular position within the process of production makes them increasingly convinced of the truth of the ideological idea that the *mind governs the world*. Looking on themselves, therefore, as the vessels of a culture from which everything proceeds, they are filled with a sense of their superiority to the working masses; in business, in their jobs as inspectors or overseers,[19] they regard themselves as at enmity with the workers. That is why they equally hate socialism, the ideal of the proletariat, fearing that the power of the uneducated masses may reach a level equal to that of the industrial hierarchy, and thus destroy the latter's privileges.

"There are numerous factors, therefore, which contribute powerfully to separating the new middle class from the proletariat, and this despite an identity of economic function. Social development will draw the lower categories of this class more and more into the conflict, but they will never be able to wage war with the vigor, the ruthlessness and the intransigence which the working class situation imposes. Their socialism will therefore be of a moderate kind; they will find the bitterness of the proletarian war distasteful, and will emphasize the reformist and civilizing character of socialism.

"It should be noted here that certain categories of workers, whose degree of qualification makes them indispensable, and who, being better paid than the others, constitute a working class elite, are close to and show the distinctive characteristics of these lower categories of the intellectual class."

If one is to believe the revolutionary trade unionists, only trade unionists are fit to conduct the war: "this is to limit the movement to the working class or even to the part of the proletariat who can adhere to union organization." But the proletarian war has wider horizons; furthermore, "Marxism does not repudiate the idea of making common cause with other classes. . . . When the

---

19. With the increased division of labor, this term has disappeared from the workers' vocabulary.

government and its sustaining social groups bring in measures of a particularly provocative kind, kindling the masses to rage, the members of these intermediate categories—and also the still unawakened proletarians—join our ranks in great numbers, and together we make the government think again. But this action cannot last long; as soon as their immediate interests remove them from us, their middle class character reappears, and we have to press on alone, with our compact proletarian battalions. This change of direction on their part is only to be expected. All things considered, therefore, the proletariat will succeed in securing power only if political events completely discredit the government and draw on it the hatred and distrust of both the middle class and the proletarian masses, and only if the ruling classes lose their confidence and therefore find themselves unable to resist the proletarian assaults. But for all that, it is still possible that a temporary phase of reaction will follow, if the clash of interests between the proletariat and its allies emerges after the common victory.

"However, the revisionists do not find it sufficient that other classes, urged by their own interests, come forward from time to time to stand with the proletariat." The working class, they say, is too weak to impose its wishes, and therefore needs the support of the other classes. This common action should assume a permanent character and consequently it is necessary to modify the Social Democratic program and tactics, to center them on reforms obtained through the parliamentary system, through electoral alliances. In their view, the only means of "transforming the mode of production is to win a majority in parliament. To do this, the party must adopt a policy that favors the greatest possible number of social categories, and therefore must emphasize only the interests common to the proletariat and to the other classes, and play down what sets them against each other. The lower middle class and the farmers find that they are not regarded as employers,[20] but ranked among those exploited by capitalism and therefore wholly with us in the fight.

"The basic question, at this level, concerns the farmers. We must win them to our cause; indeed, it cannot be too often repeated that we shall never reach our objective as long as the farmers are against us." To secure their support, the revisionists urge the party to support the protectionist demands of the farmers who, for example, want to see their produce defended, by means of high import tariffs, against foreign competition. "The more efficacious this protection proves, the stronger the situation will become—and the weaker

---

20. In 1901, at the Lubeck Congress, the question was discussed whether the small entrepreneurs, party members, should be expelled for having refused to meet the demands of their salaried workers; the motion was defeated. Cited by J. Delevsky, *les Antinomies socialistes...*, (Paris, 1930), p. 357.

will become their common interests with the proletariat.... If Social Democracy succeeds within a capitalist regime in freeing the farmers from exploitation, their interest in maintaining the existing order will be increased. Only when the system has been destroyed can the farmers escape from the grip of exploiting capitalism...

"The Marxist line of tactics in no way departs from the principle that all intermediate social categories are always within the camp of big capital, but it brings out clearly that the interests of such categories very often run counter to those of the big capitalists, without thereby enabling the proletariat really to count on their support. Revisionism would reconcile opposed interests and *serve two classes at the same time....* But this is merely the way to compromise the interests of the proletariat and to enable the other classes to take advantage of them."

VIII. *Ideology and Class Interests*

"Socialism is the ideology of the modern proletariat. Ideology signifies a system of ideas, conceptions and plans, a spiritual expression of the conditions of material life and of class interests. But these spiritual expressions do not exactly correspond to the reality of their context. The ideas and conceptions are expressed in an abstract manner in which the concrete reality whence the ideology has been derived does not always appear, or appears with a variety of different aspects. So the idea of freedom, as a political watchword, derives from middle class interest in free enterprise and free competition; but each class that uses it gives the idea a meaning of its own. Today the word 'liberalism' has a completely different meaning than it had 50 years ago. As an abstract generality, an ideology is apt to obscure real differences so that their existence is not suspected. If later on, in new conditions, these differences emerge clearly and with practical significance, an ideological battle rages to decide the meaning of this or that idea: for example, what precisely does 'liberal' mean and what is real freedom?

"Socialism, too, as a system of ideas, can cover a wide range of highly different contents and meanings according to what class is putting it forward. We have seen in the previous section how a class, by nature both proletarian and lower middle class, gives to the socialist ideas that it adopts a meaning absolutely different from that given them by the proletariat of big industry. Every class can shape its ideas only on the elements of reality it knows directly; it does not understand, and therefore ignores, whatever is foreign to its own experience. So it is that it projects upon the ideas and ideals it has adopted experiences and desires associated with its particular situation.

"It is easy to see why socialism is successful in winning support outside the class of workers in the big industrial concerns of Western Europe. Socialism signifies *anti-capitalism*; the socialist party wars against capitalism on principle, as its mortal enemy. But capitalism spreads its oppressive reign over the whole world, and everywhere nations are suffering from its hegemony, are revolting against it and seeking to overthrow it. They see socialism as their solution, and the workers of Western Europe as their natural allies against the common enemy. This is so, we have seen, with small farmers pressurized by capitalism, but it is equally so with overseas regions where capitalism, in its colonial form, has penetrated deeply and whose agricultural resources it is exploiting. The 'socialism' of New Zealand is simply the policy of local farmers and employers who want to neutralize European large-scale capitalism, and to enable a truly native capitalism to flourish. Similarly, the socialism of the Russian intellectuals at the time of the narodniks—which still survives within the revolutionary socialist party—assumed the character of a peasant socialism at grips with the exploitation to which Western European capitalism was subjecting the country. [21]

"Socialism stands for the right of nations to decide their own destiny in the face of all oppression and exploitation, and in the face of absolutism. That is why such a lively sympathy for the socialist cause is found in the oppressed countries. During the Russian Revolution, the oppressed nations—for example, the Caucasians—sent a strong contingent of socialist representatives to the Duma. Numerous Eastern revolutionaries, hunted by police and driven from their countries, escaped to Western Europe, where only Social Democracy vigorously aided and supported them.[22] Even when they do not show the least trace of proletarian character, they remain in constant touch with Social Democrats and adopt their slogans and their solutions. The Eastern revolutionary classes feel close to the Western revolutionary class, because they have an identical enemy or at least one of the same kind, Eastern despots being in effect the instruments of European capitalism. In the East, to

---

21. It could not be said that the *narodnik* theoreticians paid great attention to the penetration of foreign capital into Russia; nor did the subject figure prominently in the electoral propaganda of the many tendencies claiming to be socialist. It took the massacre of the Lena strikers (1912) and, above all, World War I and its disastrous course to raise the problem generally. Thus, years later Pannekoek was to stress that "only vague rumors of the intestine quarrels in Russian Socialism were reaching Western Europe"—and this indicates a more general lack of information. More *au fait* with Russian realities, however, Karl Kautsky had formulated early in the century the basic question: "How is a bourgeois revolution to be effected without the bourgeoisie?" In 1920, Pannekoek persisted in regarding resistance to foreign capital as the determinant factor (at least the only one on which he spoke at length) of the Russian Revolution.

22. See the dossier drawn up under the direction of Georges Haupt and Madeleine Rebérieux, *la Deuxième Internationale et l'Orient* (Paris, 1947).

wage a war both enthusiastic and implacable, the rising middle class has only just adopted the liberal ideology proper to a class which, in the West, has long exercised power and is prey to corruption; socialism, the ideology of freedom, can alone help them. Only when their ideology is hitched to practical tasks, when the revolutionary classes begin to show individual differences and to become conscious of their real interests, do their spokesmen change from red socialists into moderate liberals.[23]

"In a revolutionary era, especially where the existence of an absolutist regime demands vigorously conducted warfare, *the most energetic class, the proletariat, is at the head of the movement* to which their ideology serves as a program. In Finland, there is no large industrial proletariat, since this is a country of small farmers. But the latter send a big socialist group to parliament; 40 percent of the electors vote Social Democratic, simply because socialism is synonymous with implacable war against tsarist oppression. In other conditions, these farmers would not elect socialists. The same can be said of the Armenians voted into the Turkish parliament.

"It emerges from all this that it would be absurd to regard all the movements laying claim to socialism as being of one and the same nature. The adherents of Social Democracy, the militants of the Social Democratic party, do not form a homogeneous group with identical ideas about everything. Very diverse classes and groups, whose interests differ in certain respects, are indiscriminately covered by the words 'socialism' and 'socialist

---

23.   Three years later, writing in *Neue Zeit* (Jan. 12, 1912) about an article by Otto Bauer on the "Eastern revolutions" (*Der Kampf*, Dec. 1911), Pannekoek refined this general schema by distinguishing two revolutionary currents in the East: that of the intelligentsia won over to ideas from liberal Europe; that of the violently anti-European masses. The two tendencies, he says, have the same objective; but one seeks to base itself on the masses, the other on the leaders. That is why the first is attempting to fuse with the second by organically linking its political objectives with national traditions and religion. And Pannekoek concludes as follows: "The revolutions of Asia and Africa will give the signal to the European proletariat for their struggle for freedom." This idea, connected with the general theme of imperialism—one of the main axes of the theoretical discussion within the German Party at that time—appears in an article published a few days earlier: "The political revolution in Asia, the insurrection in India, the rebellion within the Arab world, are imposing a decisive obstacle against the expansion of capitalism in Europe..., bloody clashes are becoming more and more inevitable. There is a link between the Asian wars of independence and of cononialism and the general struggles among European nations." A. Pannekoek, "la Revolution mondiale," *le Socialisme*, Jan. 21, 1912 (cited by Haupt and Revérieux, *op. cit.*, pp. 36-37; German version in the *Bremen Bürger-Zeitung*, 204, Dec. 30, 1911). Lenin expressed an analogous idea when he wrote, for example, in 1907: "The Russian working class will win freedom and will give the impulse to Europe by its revolutionary actions." (Preface to *Lettres de J. Becker...*, in *Marx-Engels-Marxisme*, p. 111). On the other hand, Rosa Luxemburg proclaimed a little later: "It is only from Europe, it is only from the oldest capitalist countries, that the signal for the social revolution which will free all men, can come, when the time is ripe." *La crise de la démocratie socialiste*, (Paris, 1934), p. 157.

party.' They merge in a temporary or lasting way where their interests coincide, but, where their interests differ or even clash, they fight among themselves. *These clashes take the form of tactical differences within the party.*

"All the proletarians, all the exploited, have, of course, a basic interest in the overthrow of capitalism. . . . But it can be said that men in general, middle class or otherwise, have an interest in the socialism which will create *for all* the conditions of a better life. . . . However, by 'interests' must be understood immediate interests, such as are engendered here and now in society by a specific situation, and are accepted as such by people whose ideas and conditions are equally shaped by a particular class situation.

"In this sense, the proletariat, the class of the exploited and the oppressed, which Social Democracy regards as its greatest source of militants and which it represents at the political level, is *neither a clearly defined nor an absolutely homogeneous group.* There has been lively controversy about whether the lower middle class proletarian categories and the lower categories of salaried employees belong to it; in fact, the party is infiltrating these social groups, but with much greater difficulty than it meets with the industrial proletariat. The revisionists like to preach that we should unite around us *all* the oppressed and the discontents. Within the American party, there has also been discussion about the proper nature of the proletariat, in the course of which it was suggested that skilled workers attached to the great trade union federation led by Gompers did not properly belong to the proletarian group called upon by the Communist Manifesto to unite, because, it was said, when these workers are ultimately supplanted by machinery, they will lose their privileged position and will adopt reactionary sentiments. [24] This idea is on a par with the hostility which the trade union leaders are showing toward socialism. But in a strange way, there is a certain basic truth in the assertion that the proletarian nature of these workers is arguable. Apart from the obvious fact that there are differences of theoretical knowledge, the basic truth is that, within the class itself of industrial workers, there are still considerable divergences of immediate interests.

---

24. The controversy alluded to here took place in 1908-1909, after the publication in one of the party publications of an article which noted that the qualified worker has always been excessively conservative because he is not proletarian. Thomas Sladden, "The Revolution," *International Socialist Review*, Dec. 1908, pp. 426f. Nothing was so common among the American "industrial" trade unionists as the idea put forward by Bill Haywood, among others, that the qualified worker exploits the non-qualified exactly as the capitalist does. See, Brissenden, *The IWW* (New York, 1919), pp. 84-88. We note, in passing, that Pannekoek was to say a little later of the IWW that "their principles are perfectly sound." *Neue Zeit*, XXX, 2, 1912, p. 203.

"These groups of the industrial proletariat, having secured a privileged situation, a higher salary and a shorter working day through their powerful organizations, do not match the lower categories of the working class in their urgency to overthrow capitalism. There is no doubt that they adapt well to the existing order and form an acknowledged force for negotiating with employers and politicians. Their only ideal is a gradual but constant raising of their living standards; their ideas are close to those of the lower middle class, just as their situation resembles that of the lower categories of the new middle class. . . . It is notorious that the English and American trade unionists form a workers' elite of this kind. To the extent to which they have won political autonomy they advocate a moderate socialist workers' policy, and they will have no truck with class warfare and revolution. Their socialism is 'evolutionary'—the theory of the gradual advancement of the workers and of gradual growth toward the nationalization of the principal branches of production, by a State actuated by ethical and philanthropic principles: in short, revisionist socialism."

Within Social Democracy, revisionism represents the interests of these lower class categories as well as those of the highly qualified workers' elite, as distinct from the interests proper to the masses of the industrial proletariat. "The conflicts between tendencies not only aim at deciding the fitness of certain theories or ideas. . . ; they also represent battles between the changing groups who together make up the proletariat. This is the only explanation for the vehemence and passion with which these battles are carried on. . . , sometimes degenerating into personal attacks. Now, experience shows that from now on we are not dealing with situations of simple, personal destitution."

The interests of the proletariat must be considered before those of the other classes, "the latter's interests running counter to real development; a party which would allow its aims to be shaped by such interests would inevitably find itself drawn into the blind alley of a reactionary policy or, to change the metaphor, into adopting a capitalist policy in socialist clothing. . . ."

"The ideas and conceptions of the proletariat have as their basis a science of society that enables them to foresee the consequences of their actions and the reactions of the other classes. Up to the present, ideologies, lacking awareness of concrete reality, were simply an extravagant reflexion of the economic situation, whereas socialism constitutes a clear scientific theory. Ideology and science are both abstract, general expressions of concrete reality; but *the basic difference between them* is that an ideology constitutes an unconscious generalization, one in which awareness of the corresponding concrete reality is lost,[25] whereas science is a *conscious* generalization whose conclusions make it possible to discern precisely the concrete reality from which they have been drawn. Hence, therefore, ideology is above all a matter of sentiment, while science is a matter of intellection. . . .

"In the preceding sections, we have shown that, while the science of society effectively enables us to find the right way, the differences of opinion concerning tactics are attributable to something quite other than a lack of clarity. These differences, like socialism itself, flow in effect from material conditions. Consequently, they are linked with various stages of capitalistic development in different regions and branches of production, with the dialectic nature of this development, and with the clashes of interests within the working class proper. They are therefore so inevitable that such dissension cannot be credited to the good will or ill will of certain comrades; what comes to the surface in them are the internal clashes between the social interests that play a part in the life of the political organization.

"But this must not lead to stoic acceptance, to the idea that we must just resign ourselves to the fact that these clashes of interests are inevitable, without being able to do anything about them. This is true only to the extent to which one accepts that the classes act solely in terms of their immediate, spontaneously felt interests; in other words, to the extent to which a conscious science of society is lacking. But this is much less true in the case of the socialist proletariat. The working class is guided in all its actions not only by direct, immediately felt interests, but by the general interest of which the science of society enables them to acquire a deep and lasting knowledge. Unlike the other classes, the proletariat has not merely submitted to blind sentiments, but also to conscious reason; and this will be increasingly the case as their theoretical development is perfected and they come to understand socialist theory better.

"The role of theory in the workers' movement is to deflect the will from direct, instinctive, powerful impulses, and to render it responsive to conscious and rational knowledge. Theoretical knowledge enables the worker to escape from the influence of immediate and limited interests, to the great benefit of the general class interest of the proletariat; it enables him to bring his activity into line with the long-term interest of socialism. All tendencies that deflect

---

25. "Ideology," says Engels, "is a process which the self-styled thinker effects very conscientiously but with a false conscience. He remains unaware of the motive forces which actuate him; otherwise, there would not be an ideological process. Thus, he invents false or specious motive forces," Letter to Mehring, July 14, 1893; *Etudes philosophiques* (Paris, 1947), p. 134. The possibility that Pannekoek was familiar with this text is slight; but is it not one of the keys to the materialist theory of history? And had not Marx used this key in those of his writings already known in 1909?

the proletariat from its objective, thereby making the conflict more prolonged and more difficult, are increasingly rendered less harmful as the workers understand Marxism, the socialist theory, more deeply. If the influence of the labor aristocracy of the trade unions is demonstrably weaker in Germany than in England, it is due in great measure to the socialist theoretical development of the German workers.

"Here also is the means to secure a maximum reduction of the danger which, as a result of the internal conflicts within the exploited class, is threatening the workers' movement. Theoretical enlightenment, a propaganda campaign aimed at deflecting the workers' attention from their particular interests and fixing it on the general context of society, will diminish conflicts, calm passions, and blunt the edge of disagreements. *It is the implementation of theory, the scientific basis of socialism, that will contribute most effectually to both securing for the movement a tranquil and sure course, and to the transformation of unconscious instinct into conscious human action.*"

CHAPTER THREE

THE KAUTSKY-PANNEKOEK CONTROVERSY

By refusing to limit socialist parliamentary activity to the representation of the workers' immediate interests, Pannekoek was taking up again a subject dear to the Left. The difference, perhaps, is that he viewed success as relying not so much on the press or on appeals from party leaders [1] as on the rank-and-file. His revisionist critics were not too far wrong when they accused him of calling for parliamentary action to give way completely to the general strike. This was not wholly true, of course; Pannekoek, however, did not bother to refute the accusation, but instead invoked the resolutions of the congresses that approved the principle of the general strike. [2]

It might be noted that this conception of "revolutionary parliamentarianism" — designated by the term "orthodox Marxist tactics" — characterized German Social Democracy in its first phase. [3] But, as one of its principal leaders later pointed out: "In the early stages, when we had few adherents, we used to go to the Reichstag and used it exclusively or almost exclusively for the propagation of our ideas. But very soon we found ourselves involved in practical matters"[4] — meaning essentially, the urging of immediate demands." [5] The parties of the Third International were to follow a similar

---

1. For example, in the period of the mass strike debate, Rosa Luxemburg called upon the party press "to stress more and more the proper power and proper actions of the working class, and not parliamentary battles." And she continued: "We are not concerned with simply criticizing the policy of the dominant class from the viewpoint of the immediate interests of the people — that is to say, from the viewpoint of the present society; we are concerned with going beyond the most progressivist bourgeois policy, and constantly setting up against it the ideal of the socialist society. Hence, the people could be more frequently convinced than they are today of the partial character of the progressivist measures, and realize how necessary it is to overthrow this order in its entirety in order to establish socialism." Rosa Luxemburg, "Sozialdemokratie und Parlementarismus" (1904); *Gesammelte Werke*, Vol. III, (Berlin, 1925), pp. 395-396.

2. Cf. *supra*, Chapter Two, note 6. The text of this conference was published under the title: *Die Machtmittel des Proletariats* (Stuttgart, 1910). Pannekoek also stressed on this occasion that he intended to give his conference "the character of a scientific exposé," seeking to establish "what is and what will be" on the basis of "new experiences of the class struggle," and not "what the party ought to do," as defined by the Congresses and their resolutions.

3. Cf. the remarkable work by Kurt Brandis, *Die deutsche SD bis zum Fall der Sozialisten- gesetz* (Leipzig, 1931).

4. Wilhelm Liebknecht (1897), cited by Edgard Milhaud, *la Démocratie socialiste allemande* (Paris, 1903), pp. 200-201.

5. "Le P.C. et le parlementarisme," *Thèses, manifestes et résolutions de l'I.C.*, (Paris, 1934),

policy. At first, they regarded parliament as "a secondary prop" of the "war of the masses destined to become civil war." That was in 1920, and we know what followed.

Be that as it may, "the long established tactics" that the Left passionately defended (although even these varied from town to town) did not triumph just on paper in the resolutions passed by the various congresses. In 1910, they erupted in the street, in pitched battles and violent brawling designed to achieve universal suffrage and other social reforms.[6] These struggles strengthened the Left in the large industrial centers; in Bremen, for example, the radical Henke exercised greater and greater influence over the local section. Furthermore, he had editorial control over the town's Social Democratic daily, the *Bremer Bürger-Zeitung*, for which, beginning in March 1910, Pannekoek wrote a weekly column and frequently articles.[7]

In time, however, the Bremen radicals were to split; the line of demarcation became increasingly clear between the mechanistic radicals of Henke's type and the group of intellectuals that included Radek and Pannekoek as well as Johann Knief, the engaging teacher.[8] This group of intellectuals was at once informal and distinct. Its activities, when necessary, were applied to the problem of workers' conflicts. Pannekoek once again analyzed it as follows: "The fact that in Hamburg and Bremen a movement of leftist instructors came into existence, whose dynamic nucleus was composed of a group of Social Democratic teachers, proves that the atmosphere in those towns is very different from that of Prussia.... The greater freedom and tolerance, which characterized the old commerical cities — and still does so today though to a lesser degree — accompany the economic and political preponderance of mercantile capital."[9]

But let us return to 1910. The party leaders used every means they could to prevent the agitation from assuming proportions that in their view would be excessive. Suddenly, Leftist theoreticians returned to the battle, encouraged

---

pp. 66-68.

6. Anton Pannekoek, "Prussia in Revolt. Being Chapter One in the History of a Political Revolution," *International Socialist Review*, May, 1910, pp. 966-975.

7. We have only had access to a collection of proofs of articles intended for a Sunday edition of the paper, proofs corrected by the author (the initials A.P. are at the beginning of each text).

8. Knief (1880-1919) is a good example of one of these theoreticians, without whom socialist thought would never have been what it was: clear and bold ideas, deep honesty, infectious enthusiasm, these were some of his qualities. His "works" consist almost exclusively of newspaper articles, often anonymous, but one can also list a large study devoted to Ferdinand Lassalle (Johann Knief, "Lassalle, ein Apostel der Klassenharmonie," *Archiv für de Geschichte des Soz. u.d. Arb. bwg.*, X.

9. Anton Pannekoek, "Der Bremische Liberalismus," *Bremer Bürger-Zeitung.* (abridged: B.B.Z.), 264A, March 1, 1913.

both by the struggles and by increased support for their own attitude. More than ever, they stressed the need to urge the masses into action to develop their class consciousness. [10] Toward the end of May 1910, in *Neue Zeit*, the theoretical organ of German and international Social Democracy, Rosa Luxemburg was allowed at last to express the left-wing's criticisms of Karl Kautsky. Though this controversy was important and prolonged, [11] its historical interest is eclipsed by the one that arose between Kautsky, the incarnation of Marxist orthodoxy, and Pannekoek. This controversy gains its importance, perhaps, from the fact that Pannekoek forced into the open a truth that earlier controversies, concerned as they were with this or that particular type of action, had not led Kautsky to express clearly and directly.

This time — indeed for the first time with such explicitness — Kautsky unconditionally justified the tactics used up until then by Social Democracy: the struggle by delegates who, in the name of the masses, made decisions and negotiated with the various authorities without any desire to move the masses into action. On the other hand, Pannekoek, in line with the ideas of the Left, emphasized direct, mass action; however, he put very particular stress, as always, on the spiritual factor (the *Geistlich*) and on the emergence of organizational forms of a new, unitary kind, in and through the class struggle.

Needless to say, these propositions seemed senseless to anyone for whom the present order was the measure of all things and on which the action of the oppressed could have no effect. For the academic researchers of today, Pannekoek's ideas represent "an apocalypic spirit," [12] a "quasi-Platonic idealization of proletarian solidarity," the "imminent expectation of the parousia," [13] all of which serve conveniently to distort and dispense with his ideas that are otherwise patently unacceptable. The reactions of reformists naturally, were similar. Kautsky, using a phrase formerly applied to the utopians, spoke of "social alchemy;" and another old radical later expressed his shock at what he called "a metaphysical construction of history expressed in mystical, theological conceptions." [14]

Lenin followed the controversy with deep interest, and, in *The State and Revolution*, he used even certain extracts from it that he had made at the

---

10. Cf. Schorske, *op. cit.*, pp. 184-185.
11. This controversy in its entirety covers 93 pages of the *Neue Zeit*, as against 116 of the Kautsky-Pannekoek controversy. Additionally, however, there are two Pannekoek articles against Kautsky published in the *B.B.Z.* (115, April, 16, 1910; 126, July 2, 1919). The Luxemburg-Kautsky controversy appeared in the *Neue Zeit* in 1913.
12. Schurer, *op. cit.*, p. 332.
13. Schorske, *op. cit.*, pp. 248-249.
14. Curt Geyer, *Der Radicalismus in der deutschen Arb. bwg.* (Jena, 1923), pp. 9-29.

time. He was then concerned mainly with Kautsky (and the Mensheviks); but he did have a few things to say about Pannekoek's ideas. They "erred greatly" in their "lack of clarity and concrete character," even though their central thought remained "for all that, nonetheless clear," even though their author did not bother to give these ideas separate *concrete* identity. Thinking only in terms of a huge, backward country, Lenin saw no need to apply general principles (and therefore to advocate special tactics) that would conform with the more advanced stage of the class struggle in the major industrial countries.

The historians of the Soviet state are no more explicit about this than is their necessary source of reference, *The State and Revolution*. One of them[15] accuses Pannekoek of having written only about "elements of force" and not about the "dictatorship" of the proletariat. The basis of this accusation is clear—namely, that Pannekoek in no way envisaged replacing the old state power by a new one. (Sheer quibbling! Pannekoek had not waited until 1917, as had Lenin, to envisage the state's destruction.) In fact, in Pannekoek's view (and, in this respect, in that of the Marx of "The Civil War in France"), it is the class struggle itself that finally determines the form of social organization. Another criticism from the same source maintains that Pannekeok "ignores the experience of the Paris Commune as Marx summarized it[16]—but Pannekoek had already anticipated this criticism by saying elsewhere that what is justified in one phase is not necessarily justified in another. That is precisely why Rosa Luxemburg, Karl Liebknecht and the German Left, as well as many others, have never regarded as decisive the quotations that the Kautskys and the Bernsteins so skillfully dig up to support their cause.

In October 1911, Kautsky—no doubt in order to discourage activist tendencies—published a series of articles on "mass action."[17] Kautsky's starting point was a critique of Gustave Le Bon and of his mob psychology, according to which the masses can only be destructive; and a critique of Kropotkin, who, in his history of the French Revolution (1909), also regarded the masses as incapable of clear-thinking and organization, although he did

---

15. G.W. Brjunin, "Die Diskussion uber den politischen Massenstreik," *Sowjetwissenschaft, Geschichtswissenschaft*, 1955, 5, pp. 669-670.

16. *Ibid.* Pannekoek regarded the Paris Commune as an attempt at municipal self-administration whose extension to the whole country would have called in question the state power: "but it was not a revolution of the workers in the big industries.... The effective relationship of forces between the classes worked against it. The mass of the population was peasant, without the least mental receptivity." Anton Pannekoek, "Nach vierzig Jahren," *Bremer Bürger-Zeitung*, 163, March 18, 1911.

17. K. Kautsky, "Die Aktion der Masse," *Neue Zeit*, XXX, 1, pp. 43-49, 77-84, 106-117. In November 1911, Pannekoek began a critique of these articles in the Bremen newspaper (Nov. 11, 1911).

not think this all bad. In reality, Kautsky said, mass actions cannot be foreseen and controlled by any party whatsoever, at least during certain historical phases. But as the workers' party gradually organizes the masses, the masses simultaneously mature and learn to foil the provocations of the ruling power aimed at nipping the movement in the bud, Kautsky maintained. But do mass actions today have any chance of success? Engels answered this negatively, in the Preface to *Class Struggles in France*, when he wrote that "the time for blows, for revolutions carried out by small enlightened minorities at the head of unenlightened masses, is past." The proletariat is educated through electoral campaigns and through trade union action. The class struggle does, of course, continue to develop, and so too does action by the masses; but 40 years of exercising political rights and of organization have left an impact. The number of organized and enlightened elements among the masses is now sufficient to warrant a reliance in the future on something other than spontaneous explosions, no matter how powerful and effectively they are channeled. "Some of our friends," Kautsky adds, "think that the conditions of battle have changed, and want to revise their tactics. But is it not the very nature of a spontaneous action that it should escape all control? Hence, all we can do is to be prepared for any eventuality, and so strengthen the party by securing positions of power that will be useful if the need arises. Furthermore, "it is useless to speculate about the unpredictable, and even more so to try to decide on tactics in advance. For 40 years, our party has gone from victory to victory. To consolidate and extend these conquests, it is only necessary to continue along the same path."

Pannekoek opened the controversy in July 1912 in *Neue Zeit*. [18] The question of mass action, he maintained, had been on the agenda ever since the Russian Revolution of 1905 and the Prussian political strikes of 1908 and 1910 calling for the reform of suffrage laws. He saw such actions as indications of the increasing strength of the proletariat and as manifestations of imperialism, the new form of capitalism, with its inevitable consequences—impoverishment due to financial pressures linked to the arms race, and the triumph of political reaction.

"Imperialism and mass action are new phenomena whose nature and significance it is important to understand. Our only means of doing so is through controversy..., which provokes a lively exchange of ideas and feelings, thereby inducing a new orientation of minds. Up to now, those aware of insurmountable conflicts within the party have regarded them as

---

18. Anton Pannekoek, "Massenaktion und Revolution," *Neue Zeit*, XXX, 2, pp. 541-550, 585-593, 609-619.

deplorable and painful misunderstandings. That is why it is now necessary to focus these divergences clearly."

The conquest of political power is the precondition for the advent of socialism. But, when dealing with the working class, the exploiting minority has certain sources of strength. The first of these is none other than "its spiritual superiority. As a class living off the surplus value and directing production, it has an all-embracing system of education and indoctrination. Having, therefore, a position from which it can view the whole of society in one comprehensive glance, it can always find new means of duping the masses, even at times when the masses are most seriously threatening it." By its monopoly of education, the press, and religion, the ruling class can impregnate the masses with bourgeois ideas. "This state of spiritual dependence on the bourgeoisie constitutes the principal cause of proletarian weaknesses.

"The ruling class has yet another essential source of strength: its compact organization. A small, well-organized number always prevails over a large, unorganized mass of people. *This organization of the ruling class is state power. . . .* Its internal cohesion derives from the homogeneous will that animates it, starting from the summit"—the government, with an army of officials at its disposal. It gives the impression of being a single organism, in the face of which all men are reduced to powerless atoms, automatically seized and pulverized if they show the least sign of rebellion. "And the masses, conscious of this power, respect it."

However, when the spirit of revolt arises in the masses, dissipating their fear of the state, the "atoms" unite. They could, no doubt, get the better of what may seem a mere handful of officials, but they would then have to face up to the state's material forces—the police and the army, highly organized and heavily armed minorities against whom the masses are defenseless even if they try to arm themselves. But the power of the bourgeoisie is waning. Since its economic functions are becoming more and more superfluous, it is becoming socially parasitic and thus witnesses the gradual disappearance of its sources of powers. It is "losing its prestige and moral superiority, and, ultimately, all that it has left is its hold over state power and its means of repression. If the proletariat is to rule, it must seize state power, the fortress in which the ruling class has entrenched itself. The proletarian battle is not just a battle against the bourgeoisie for state power; it is also a battle *against state power*. The problem of the social revolution can be briefly formulated as the need to raise proletarian power to a level where it exceeds state power; the essence of this revolution is the proletariat's destruction and liquidation of the state's sources of power.

The proletariat's strength lies in its numbers and economic importance and also, says Pannekoek, in the two great sources of power—knowledge and organization—referring his reader to his work *Die taktischen Differenzen* for a more detailed description of how parliamentary and trade union action stimlates the growth of the second of these sources. The bond that unites the individuals, and which is the first requirement for organization, is the discipline that comes from working together in the large modern factories. "Organization is the most effective weapon of the proletariat. The enormous power that organization confers on a ruling minority can be overthrown only if the majority achieves an organization of an even stronger kind.

"Hitherto, the progress of the class struggle has been largely due to parliamentary and trade union action, not through direct political conflict with the state. Basically, the battles have been no more than vanguard skirmishes, while the main strength remains uncommitted on both sides. In tomorrow's battles for power, the two classes will have to use their most powerful weapons and draw upon their most effective sources of strength: *without such a confrontation, there can be no decisive change in the balance of forces.* Faced with a ruling class ready to use bloody repression, the proletariat will resort to mass action in its simplest form, public meetings and street marches, and pass on from these to the most powerful action of all, the mass strike."[19]

The state, then, will not hesitate to use the most extreme means; but what can it do against the general strike? In Russia, the transport strike of October 1905 was sufficient to sever all connection between the central power and the local authorities. Of course, it was only a phase of a struggle in which everything depended on the degree of cohesion among the proletariat. "However, battle must begin again, sooner or later. On the one hand, the government is trying to take back from the masses the rights it was forced to give to them and which are the sources of proletarian power; on the other hand, the masses can declare this war at an end only when they hold the keys to state power... The conflict will cease only when final victory has been won, when the state organization has been completely destroyed. The majority organization will then have proved its superiority by the fact that it has annihilated the organization of the ruling minority."

But to achieve this, mass action must first transform the proletariat. In periods of crisis and of intensive warfare, a greater measure of awareness is developed in a few days than was previously developed by a whole year of

---

19.   Lenin, reading with pen in hand, registered approval, most frequently in his *marginalia*. Here, however, he wrote: "wrong...but XII-1905." *Leninski sbornik*, XIV (Moscow, 1924), p. 371. Cf. Brujnin, *loc. cit.*, p. 670.

political and trade union action. "The supreme demands which these battles involve, automatically engender, through practical action and the experience of victories and defeats, the means to acquire this political clearsightedness."

And the same holds true for organization. "No doubt, one often hears the contrary asserted, born of the fear that the proletarian organization, the most important of its sources of strength, may well be annihilated in the course of such dangerous conflicts. This is urged most frequently by those who are against all recourse to the general strike, and who today exercise considerable influence in the leadership of the large proletarian organizations. They fear that, in the event of violent clashes between the proletariat's organizations and those of the state, the former may prove to be the weaker, even if the more numerous. For the state still has the power to dissolve the workers' organizations that have the audacity to stand up against it, the power to end their activities, to confiscate their funds, to imprison their leaders. Hence it would be more prudent to be guided only by legal or moral considerations. Such strong measures, however, would be useless to the state, which could use them to demolish only the exterior form, leaving the internal nature unaffected. The proletariat's organization—its most important source of strength—must not be confused with the present-day form of its organizations and associations, where it is shaped by conditions within the framework of a still vigorous bourgeois order. *The nature of this organization is something spiritual—no less than the whole transformation of the proletarian mentality.* It may well be that the ruling class, through legal measures and the police, succeeds in destroying the workers' organizations; but, for all that, the workers will remain as they were—just as effectively stripped of the old individualistic self which responded only to egotism and personal interest. The same spirit, compounded of discipline, cooperation, solidarity, the habit of organized action, will live in them more vividly than ever, and will create new forms of intervention."

Ideas of this kind easily disconcerted narrowly positivist people, such as Kautsky, who make a fetish of the existing organization. Lenin himself, who was not yet formally opposed to these ideas, would several times describe them as "not very adroit,"[20] another way of saying that he did not fully understand them. In fact, a fundamental theoretical intuition, linked with the development of a historical form, is sketched in these pages. However, this intuition contains no specific reference to the new form of organization, the Soviets, which had come into existence in a manner both spontaneous and ephemeral during the Russian Revolution of 1905. This omission arises, of

---

20.   For example, in a letter to Chliapnikov of Oct. 27, 1914; Lenin, *Works,* XXXV, p. 164.

course, from Pannekoek's lack of information about the Soviets, but such ignorance was then widespread, both in Russia and elsewhere. If an absolutely new "definite and specific" phenomenon is to be more or less clearly understood in its general significance, must there not first be "recurrence" — a repetition of significant events? [21] And did not Pannekoek love to stress that it is only very slowly that a new reality can take hold of men's minds? [22]

"From the beginning of his article," Pannekoek writes, "Kautsky makes it clear that, by mass action, he naturally does not mean that the action of organized workers will of itself become more and more massive with the growth of the organizations. For him, the term signifies the eruption of the great unorganized masses, assembled in a purely accidental way and therefore entirely liable to disperse again: in other words spontaneous action at street level. . . . Consequently, to say that political and economic action will be increasingly transformed into mass action is not at all the same as saying that any type of mass action — i.e., the type described as action at the street level — is also destined to play a bigger and bigger role. According to Kautsky, there are two extremely different forms of action. On the one hand, there is the present form of workers' conflicts, in which a small group of the labor aristocracy, the organized workers that form about a tenth of the proletariat, lead political and trade union actions. On the other hand, there is the action of the great unorganized masses at the street level who seize upon any chance to erupt into history. In Kautsky's view, it is a matter of deciding whether the first of these will in the future be the only form of the proletarian movement, or whether the second is also destined to play an important role.

"When, in discussions over recent years within the party, stress was laid on the necessity, the inevitability or the utility of mass action, the reference was not in any way" to either of the possibilities suggested by Kautsky, "but to a third possibility: *a new form of specific intervention by the organized workers.* The development of modern capitalism has imposed these new forms of action. Threatened by worse dangers from imperialism, fighting to obtain greater power and more rights within the state, they find it necessary to assert their will vigorously against capitalism, and to do so with an energy they have never shown in expressing their wishes to their parliamentary representatives. They must intervene personally; they must erupt into the political struggle and try to influence the government and the bourgeoisie by their sheer weight of numbers. When we speak of mass actions and their necessity, we mean by

---

21. J. Witt-Hansen, *Historical Materialism,* 1 (Copenhagen, 1960), pp. 68-70.
22. "le Matérialisme historique," *loc. cit.*

this an extra-parliamentary political intervention by organized workers, the latter acting directly at the political level instead of leaving this completely to their delegates. [23] This intervention is not synonymous with "street" actions; while street demonstrations do represent one of its aspects, the consequence of its most powerful form, the mass strike, is to empty the streets. Trade union battles, through which the masses have always directly intervened, are a transition to political mass actions, since they have considerable political repercussions. As for the practical question of mass action, therefore, it is simply a matter of extending the intervention area of proletarian organization."

The demonstrations of spring 1910 proved that the workers were not cowed by the violence used by the ruling class. The latter will no doubt hesitate to call in the army, "made up as it is of sons of the people and, to an ever increasing extent, of young proletarians who have already absorbed a certain class consciousness in the atmosphere of their own home." No doubt, military discipline, unthinking obedience, will continue to be respected for a certain time, "but nothing more surely destroys it than the obeying of a series of orders to fire on the people, on their own class brethren, merely assembled peacefully or on a peaceful march.... Like a shining sword, the army commands respect and can inflict terrible blows, [24] but when it is used unworthily, it soon becomes tarnished and its honor is discredited. And when the bourgeoisie loses its most effective instrument of power, it finds itself defenseless.

"The social revolution involves the gradual dissolution of all the power instruments of the ruling class, particularly the state, while simultaneously building up proletarian power to its fullness. At the beginning of this phase, the proletariat should already have reached a high level of class consciousness and enlightenment, of moral strength and of compact organization, in order to be able to face up to the severe conflicts ahead; but all this remains still imperfect. In the eyes of the masses, who see them as inimical to their own interests, the prestige of the state and the ruling class is beginning to diminish, but their material power nevertheless remains intact. At the end of the revolutionary process, nothing remains of this; the workers have attained

23. Lenin clearly understood the meaning of this formula, whether adroit or not, since he wrote in the margin: "*Neverno*" ("Not true!") *Leninski sbornik, loc. cit.,* p. 372.

24. The German Left was not backward in pointing to the connection between bloodshed and bourgeois repression. Thus, at the Jena Congress in 1905, Rosa Luxemburg said: "History shows that all the revolutions were at the cost of the workers' blood. The difference is that, up to the present, the people's blood has been shed for the benefit of the dominant classes, whereas now, when anyone suggests the possibility of the people shedding their blood for their own cause we get a cry of protest from the prudent ones, from the so-called Social Democrats: 'No, this blood is too dear to us!' " *Protokoll...,* p. 321.

a high level of organization, they have proved capable of shaping their own destiny, and henceforth they are capable of taking in hand the organization of production."

Pannekoek devotes the second part of a series of three articles to a critique of the "present praxis" of the workers' movement. "Elections, strikes, parliamentary action, indoctrination," he writes, "all continue in the same old way, gradually gaining political weight but making no essential change whatsoever—until the day when, thanks to an extraordinary combination of circumstances, a powerful rising of the masses will occur and will perhaps overthrow the regime. This will follow exactly the old pattern of the bourgeois revolutions, but with the difference that the party organization is fully ready to assume power and to hog the fruits of victory, by appropriating, as the new ruling class, the chestnuts which the masses have snatched out of the fire." Kautsky upheld a theses of passive expectation according to which, the general strike will overthrow the capitalist regime with one single blow and with the strength of an act of nature. Until this happens, it is sufficient to continue parliamentary and trades union practice as before, and it is wrong to criticize the leaders of the party as is often done. "Contrary to our thesis of the revolutionary activity of the proletariat, who build up their power through an ascendant period of mass action and increasingly demolish the bourgeois state power, this theory of *passive radicalism* looks for no decisive change through the active intervention of the proletariat."

Finally, as he would do often,[25] Pannekoek, in the third of these articles, links up mass action with the fight against war, "not against enemy invasion, but against war itself, and in order to forestall it." There is no question here, as is done at the international Congresses, of studying the means to prevent war by this or that particular kind of action—a strike in the arsenals, for example—but rather one of directing this protest against the established authorities and extending it, through every form of demonstration, to the whole of the exploited class. In short, the ruling powers must be opposed by a proletarian power built up by proletarian action.

Kautsky's reply was soon forthcoming,[26] and it was this which especially interested Lenin, who in *The State and Revolution*, saw Kautsky's attitude as "an abandoning of Marxism for opportunism" and discussed it as such at some length. We refer the reader to Lenin's book for this aspect of the matter.

25. For example, at the Chemnitz Congress (1912), he would stress the fact that mass action is the only practical measure against imperialism; and "the workers can look to themselves alone" to implement this measure (*Protokoll...*, pp. 421-23); cf. also, in the same connection, many articles in the *Bremer Bürger-Zeitung*.

26. K. Kautsky, "Die neue Taktik," *Neue Zeit*, XXX, 2, 1911-1912, pp. 654-664, 688-698, 723-733.

As for the rest—that is, the final form of the organization-process such as it had been presented by Pannekoek—Kautsky accused him of "simplifying Marxism" (and of manipulating quotations!) and of "spiritualizing organization." Taking up the passage which dealt with the nature (*das Wesen*) of the new organization, he wrote: "Pannekoek himself underlines this phrase, so extraordinary does he find the statement that the organization is not really an organization but something absolutely different, *the mentality of the proletariat.* After this master-stroke of social alchemy, he has no difficulty in showing that the class conflicts, while involving the annihilation of the organization, awaken the working masses and perfect their character, so that the destruction of the organization miraculously becomes the means" of strengthening it. Thus Kautsky reproached Pannekoek for not seeing that "the form of present day organizations and associations" is capable of a better adaptation, as an effect of the class struggle, to new conditions. It is true that the organization transforms the mentality of the proletariat, but Kautsky stressed, a theoretician ought to take into account that this transformation is the result, and not the nature itself, of the organization because otherwise the organization would not have the least consistency and would rest on nothing.

Kautsky categorically rejected the idea of the destruction of the state. If, he said, the general strike is a means of bringing effective pressure on the government, it in no way makes possible the annihilation of state power. Besides, the basic problem is not to discover what form is to be given to a future state, but to establish how the socialist opposition policy is to transform the present state. From this perspective, parliamentary power is daily diminishing, its mechanisms being fouled up by the conflicts of the bourgeois majority; but nonetheless "the majority may change and the machine be re-started." But in the meantime, since the executive is attempting to curtail the powers of the legislative, it is the latter we must try to consolidate. "The purpose of our parliamentary action remains therefore what it has always been: to win political power by securing a parliamentary majority and creating a government." That is why mass strikes and disturbances, if they occur sporadically, cannot be regarded as permanent and normal methods of class warfare. Marx once described a type of limited, unilateral action as "parliamentary cretinism;" today, Kautsky concludes that what we have is "mass action cretinism."

Pannekoek discussed this answer in the *Bremer Bürger-Zeitung* [27] and in the *Leipziger Volkzeitung*, [28] both large socialist dailies regularly

---

27. September 10, 11, and 12, 1912.
28. September 9, 10, and 12, 1912.

left-socialist in their views. He also published, in the *Neue Zeit*, [29] an answer from which we here extract only two points, one about method, the other about organization.

First, to the accusation of having "simplified Marxism," Pannekoek points out (recalling an elementary and much too frequently ignored truth): "when in science we wish to probe an aspect of reality, we must first highlight the essential, the basic, in its simplest form; only then do we introduce the particular aspects and secondary factors in order to correct the first sketch, to complete it, to improve and elaborate on it, and in this way draw closer to reality. . . . In a first approximation aimed at forming a general idea, there can be no question of only two classes — the bourgeoisie and the proletariat; that is why we have attempted to sketch, in its broad lines, the revolutionary process as a development of relationships of forces. Everyone knows, of course, that this reality is much more complicated and that a host of problems remain to be solved before the picture can be completed. The bourgeoisie are not more homogeneous than the proletariat, and in both classes traditions continue to carry weight; among the working masses, one must count the *Lumpenproletariat*, the salaried employees, the petty bourgeoisie and others, whose specific class situation requires the mode of action." Nevertheless, it is clear that the general tactics cannot be based on these particular aspects and therefore be focused solely on the clashes within the bourgeoisie — i.e., on parliamentarianism.

To Kautsky's complaint that he sees only the spirit of organization and regards its body as of no significance, Pannekoek replied: "In fact, the spirit of organization is one other than the soul giving vital energy to the body and making it capable of action. But this immortal soul cannot hover bodiless in the heavens, in the manner of Christian theology; it ceaselessly creates for itself a body, the organization, because the men into whom it enters unite with a view to common and organized action. Far from being an abstract, imaginary thing, in comparison with the 'real, concrete organization,' of the existing forms of association, it is just as real and concrete. . . . No statutory arrangements fixing the rights and duties of the militants, no magic power of well stocked coffers, no democratic constitution, can give unity to a proletarian organization; this can result only from the class spirit, from a complete change of the mentality and the human nature of the proletariat. This metamorphosis is primarily a consequence of the condition of the worker, already educated to common action by the collective exploitation he

---

29. Anton Pannekoek, "Marxistische Theorie und revolutionäre Taktik," *Neue Zeit*, XXXI, 1, 1912, pp. 272-281, 365-373.

undergoes as one of a group in the same factory, and then a consequence of his class struggle. For these reasons, the practical life of the organization — the election of officials, the payment of union dues — is reduced to a completely secondary role. . . .[30] The purpose of the organization is to engender, through action, men of a new type. The hitherto scattered forces are brought together; these men will now be able to create for themselves an order born of their own action. It will no longer be a question of associating together on the basis of the common and immediate interests of disparate sectors of the workers."

An explanatory parenthesis is needed here. The following year, a wildcat strike was to give Pannekoek a fresh opportunity to illustrate his theoretical views. From July 1913, in the big North Sea ports, the dockers of the naval dockyards were laying down their tools, while the trade union leadership was refusing to recognize their strike. The strikers therefore elected autonomous committees. We might note that the group of Bremen radicals, led by Henke, gave assistance to the trade union leaders in their conciliation efforts which, for more than six weeks, got nowhere; the leftists, needless to say, basically supported the striking dockers.[31]

Shortly after the complete resumption of work, Pannekoek wrote in the *Bremer Bürger-Zeitung:*[32] "The wildcat strike with its violation of that discipline which has hitherto been the ideal of a developed trade union shows how impossible it is to maintain perfect trade union discipline against the intense oppression exerted by capital. . . . Success of mass movements depends on their capacity for autonomous action, their unquenchable ardor for battle, and the boldness and initiative of the masses. But it is precisely these qualities, the primary condition of the struggle for freedom, that are repressed and annihilated by trade union discipline. In discussions about future political mass struggles, the accent has always been on the autonomous initiative of the masses, without which nothing can be undertaken. Is it not then, a good thing if this initiative leads the masses to take different paths?

---

30. For analogous ideas, see Rosa Luxemburg, *Leipziger Volkszeitung*, June 27, 1913. Cf. Also Kautsky, "Nachgedenke zu den nachgedenkliche Betrachtungen," *Neue Zeit*, XXI, 2, 1913.
31. Cf. Josef Miller, "Zur Geschichte der linken s.d. in Bremen, 1906-1918," *Zeitschrift für Geschichtswissenschaft*, 1958 (Sonderheft), pp. 202-217; August Winning, "Zum Streik auf dem Schiffswerften," *Neue Zeit*, XXXII, 1, 1913, pp. 55-59.
32. Anton Pannekoek, "Gewerkschaftsdisziplin," *B.B.Z.*, 297, Oct. 18, 1913: from the onset of the movement, he spoke against "the strict and slavish respect" for the least article "of the trade union rules," and urged "unshakable cohesion and solidarity." "Der Werftargeiterstreik," *B.B.Z.* 287, Aug. 9, 1913. In 1910, during a similar strike in the naval dockyards, Pannekoek noted that "the requirements of the mass conflict led the rank-and-file to impose their will on the leaders." "Gewerkschaftliche Demokratie," *B.B.Z.*, Dec. 17, 1910.

Was it necessary to condemn the initiative of the naval dockers simply because they did not conform to the prescribed forms? We need not fall out over this particular instance; but, generally speaking, when we see absolute respect for trade union discipline being exalted as a supreme end in itself, we must proclaim with the utmost urgency that this is a sure way to choke an essential source of the future proletarian victory."

Let us now return to the 1912 controversy. The two opponents shared at least one peice of common ground of accusation: each censured the other for clinging to a past phase of history. Pannekoek, for his part, maintained that, by avoiding trials of strength and by glorifying discipline and the role of the leaders, [33] one could not fail to discourage the masses and to precipitate the decline of the party. This attitude, he said, belonged to an epoch when, because of the weakness of the workers' organizations, they had "to be protected against the terrorism of the ruling power. In this sense, our divergences are the expression of different degrees of development within the organization."

Kautsky retorted [34] that this was to return to the idea of "revolutionary gymnastics," once dear to the French trade unionists but "rejected now that they have become strong." As for the idea of destroying the state, this is nothing less than anarchy. Moreover, "history shows that state power is not simply a means of maintaining the economic domination of any one class, but equally a means of breaking the economic power of and thereby dispossessing a certain class." This emerged clearly during the French Revolution, in the course of which "the state machinery was changed from an instrument of the old class into an instrument of the new." And the *Communist Manifesto* recommends nothing else. In the meantime, how could a political organization subsist which refused to interest itself in electoral activities? "I strongly suspect," concludes Kautsky, "that Pannekoek is actively gathering material for a book whose title could be: 'Mass action by the individual.' "

---

33. "Marxistische Theorie und revolutionäre Taktik," *op. cit.*, pp. 373f. On this point, Pannekoek had often expressed his ideas; for instance: "As long as a small group decided on matters of vital interest to the masses, there will always be the chance that the masses will suddenly refuse to respond to the group's orders, despite all considerations of prestige and trust. This would be so, especially, if, in such instances, the prudence of the leaders must expect always to prevail, thus giving their ideas precedence over that of the progress of the masses... The old type of party leadership and of trade union leadership, at both local and national level, has given and is still giving good service. However, for some years now, the development of political mass conflicts is imposing new tasks on the party.... The idea is increasingly gaining ground, of the need for a close connection between the representative body and the profound changes occurring in the forms of conflict." Anton Pannekoek, "Das Vertretungsystem in der Arbeiterbewegung," *B.B.Z.*, 168, April 4, 1911.

34. K. Kautsky, "Der Jüngste Radikalismus," *Neue Zeit*, XXXI, 1, 1912, pp. 636-46.

This is the classic approach of reducing political differences to a mere matter of personalities whose views are no one's but their own.

Be that as it may, Pannekoek, given the last work in this phase of the controversy,[35] quietly disposed of the *Communist Manifesto* quotations which Kautsky was invoking with such ardor. In 1847, he recalled one could envision "the proletarian revolution only in the form of a minority dictatorship using the coercive power of the state for the benefit of the working class. Today, a revolution is possible only in the form of revolt and self-government of the masses." The accusation of revolutionary syndicalism, "a term which Kautsky uses because it is repugnant to the comrades," brought this reply from Pannekoek: "Well, so much for revolutionary syndicalism!"

Shortly after the outbreak of World War I, Pannekoek returned to the subject of this controversy. He then noted that the "whole method" of criticism used by the socialist press (*"Vorwärts* and other newspapers") was "at bottom an attack on the politics of modern grand capitalism from the petty bourgeois standpoint of 'small business' and shows that all understanding of modern political development was lacking. Connected to this was the theory expressed in the scientific organ of the party, the *Neue Zeit*, that the doctrine of Marx, that fiery revolutionary champion, meant a *passive waiting* and that all revolutionary *activity* was nothing but unscientific anarchism." Rejecting out of hand "all autonomous initiative of the masses, every strike declared without the consent of the leadership," the Social Democrats revealed their position: "While the old radicals continually repeated the dictum, 'Governments do not dare to begin war for fear of the proletariat, for war means social revolution,' the revolutionary Left emphasized the fact that the proletariat cannot prevent war by standing passively by, but only by energetic, active intervention." In these circumstances, it was highly improbable "that the masses, accustomed to do only what the party ordered, would now come forward independent of the leaders of the party.... The question of how the war could be resisted was never even raised, because the question of whether the war ought to be resisted was not even answered with a decisive *Yes*." Worse still, "in *Vorwärts* and many other party papers the war was termed a 'war against the bloody-czar,' a war against Russian barbarism. They cited Karl Marx, who in 1848 had urged Germany to a war against Russia; they overlooked the fact that it applied only so long as Russia dominated and threatened Europe as its most powerful military state. Thus the war was made popular among the working masses."

In complete contrast to this was the anti-war strategy advocated by the two

---

35. Anton Pannekoek, "Zum Schloss," *Neue Zeit*, XXXI, 1, 1912, pp. 611-12.

radical newspapers of Leipzig and Bremen—the organs of those with "a clear insight into the fact that today, Russia, as well as Germany, is a capitalist country pursuing a policy of commercial imperialism." They urged that "as soon as danger of war appears and nationalistic demonstrations in favor of war begin, the workers should fill the streets in masses and chase away the nationalists. If the danger becomes more threatening, the demonstrations must become more energetic; under a general strike the masses must be sent into the streets instead of going to the factory, and for these few days they can live wholly for the great political struggle. If the government tries to forbid the demonstrations and to prevent them by force, then they must be kept up all the more. Even if thousands perish, what is that compared with the hundreds of thousands who fall in war? And in war they fall for capital, in the street they fall for the proletarian cause." Pannekoek points out that "the fact that this tactic came to an end after the brilliant conflicts of 1910 means an acknowledgement by the party of its own weakness. Since then, a lukewarm spirit, averse to sharp conflict, gained the upper hand in the movement. The bureaucracy at the top became even stronger and was disinclined to risk itself in revolutionary struggles." He admits that, during this period, "there was an external growth of the organization, which is the necessary prerequisite for a fight," but asserts equally that "they shunned that fight more and more in order not to endanger this precious organization. Every independent initiative of the masses which occasionally broke out in the struggles of the labor unions against the wishes of the leaders, was branded as a 'lack of discipline' and as 'anarchism.' " The main concern, then of the Social Democratic "bureaucracy at the top" was to shield "the precious organization" at all costs.[36]

It would never have crossed the minds of the Social Democratic notables that the party's attitude was one of the principal reasons why the working masses accepted the war. On the contrary, they maintained that the party itself was simply responding to popular pressures. In reply, Pannekoek deliberately rejected the old excuse about conditions always being unfavorable for action, an excuse which has always been the hallmark of the forces of conservatism. He sought instead to stimulate the development of new forms of conflict and of organization, hitherto embryonic and ephermeral, by means of propaganda, the only weapon of the leftist theoreticians. Analysis and practical conclusions will no doubt seem inadequate to some people, but Pannekoek was not the man to raise, in the name of alleged clarity, questions calling for no answer other than evasion, resignation and complicity.

---

36. Anton Pannekoek, "The Great European War and Socialism," *International Socialist Review*, XV, Oct. 4, 1914, pp. 201-202.

As for Kautsky, he too was to allude again to this controversy. "How I would love Pannekoek to have been right!" he exclaimed, in refering to the idea that "the socialist worker never said *yes* to the war." [37] And yet, who was it then who had sagely declared: " 'The inevitable attempts of the proletariat to prevent the war,' of which Pannekoek tells us, are notably conspicuous up to the present by their inevitable absence?" [38] Was not that the very reproach leveled against the party?—the refusal of all practical initiative, in the name of certainties never seriously put to the test; the crass passivity of a powerful, tentacular organization with enormous resources but acting only as a supplementary mechanism of integration?

37.   K. Kautsky, *Sozialisten und Krieg,* (Berlin, 1927), p. 346. Cf. *International Review of Social History*, XI, 2, 1960, pp. 197-227; and Pannekoek, "Deckungsfrage und Imperialismus," *Neue Zeit*, XXXII, 1, 1913, p. 114.

38.   K. Kautsky, "Die Neue Taktik," *op. cit.*, p. 663.

CHAPTER FOUR

THE WORLD WAR AND THE WORKERS' MOVEMENT

After the controversy with Kautsky, Pannekoek, like most other left-wing Social Democratic theorists, constantly returned to the central issues: the wave of imperialism and of nationalism, the fight against reformism, and the danger of war.

In 1933, in connection with the armaments race, a wave of unprecedented chauvinism swept Europe, with almost the entire workers' movement caught up in it. Displays of patriotic and militaristic delirium in Germany during celebrations marking the centenary of the great resistance against the French invader encouraged Franz Mehring, a prominent radical, to publish two brochures praising "the fight against pitiless exploitation and oppression."

According to Mehring, the working class had "every reason" to glorify "a war comparable to its own," and that, besides, "the ossification of Marxism into ready-made formulas could through its dogmatism, only strengthen revisionism." [1]

Pannekoek, for his part, had already pointed out the connection between growth of nationalist ideology and the rise of imperialism. "The fight against militarism," [2] if it is to be effectively conducted, demands a concomitant spiritual fight; for only thus can we properly discover the significance of these traditional (patriotic) ideas. . . . The idea of the *patria* has radically changed. Originally, it signified the bond between the peasant or the petty bourgeois and the place where he lived: anyone threatening his prosperity was the enemy. In contrast, the *patria* of the bourgeoisie covers the full extent of the national territory and becomes emotionally identified with the material interests of that class—interests that the bourgeoisie successfully present as those of the nation as a whole. . . . On the other hand, the workers' *patria* is their class, and this *patria* extends far beyond national frontiers; it includes the proletarians of every country in an international network and unites them

---

1. Cf. Josef Schleifstein, *Franz Mehring* (East Berlin, 1959), p. 191.
2. Anton Pannekoek, "Patriotismus und Sozialdemokratie," *B.B.Z.* April 5, 1918, which argues against the English socialist Hyndman, who maintained that Germany was as reactionary as Russia had been in Marx's time. Cf. also "Patriotismus vor 100 Jahren und jetzt," *B.B.Z.*, April 4, 1913 (directed against the patriotic celebrations); and the pamphlet, *Klassenkampf und Nation*, Reichenberg, 1912 (aimed in particular against the Austro-Marxists).

in a common battle against the capitalist system as a whole.... The present military projects call for more than a campaign against heavy taxes; in addition, they offer an opportunity to fight against disastrous traditional ideas."

The outbreak of the war caused Pannekoek to repeat these arguments. Like the entire international left-wing,[3] he saw that imperialism was rooted in the competition among the great powers for raw materials and new markets. Armaments production was linked to this economic competition and exacerbated the national antagonisms in Europe. "The fact that war has broken out proves the extent to which the now soldier-workers (both Social Democrats and revolutionary syndicalists) and their spokesmen in every country have come under the influence of bourgeois patriotism and have joined with the bourgeoisie in sentiments about love of the *patria* and the duty to defend it, while at the same time they are trampling under foot the international solidarity of the proletariat.... The outbreak of war is proof of the power of imperialism, proof of the organizational and, especially, the spiritual weakness of the workers' movement.... Only a tireless socialist propaganda, urging heartfelt and enlightened commitment to conflict and unity, can in the future create the conditions needed to prevent another war."[4]

The small party of Dutch Tribunists, in an attempt to reorganize, associated with various other radical and leftist activities. It participated in the Zimmerwald Conference of 1915, which laid the foundations of a sect later known as the "Left-Zimmerwaldians," dedicated to the creation of a third International, and it authorized several publications, among them *Vorbote*, edited by Henriette Roland-Holst and Pannekoek.

Pannekoek, in his "Introduction" to the first edition of *Verbote*, wrote:

---

3. But not without marked divergences of opinion at the level of basic analysis.

4. Anton Pannekoek, *De Oorlog zijn oorsprong en zijn bestrijding* (Amsterdam, n.d.), compiled from articles published in *De Tribune* at the beginning of the war. Shortly afterward, Pannekoek wrote a pamphlet specifically on the problem of imperialism — *Uit de voorgeschiedenis van de wereldoorlog* (Zuitphen, 1916). He was also again to deal with the subject of nationalism in later writings. For example, in his *Workers' Councils*, composed during World War II, he has this to say: "For the time being nationalism exists as a strong power obstructing the way. For the workers it is necessary not only to destroy all nationalist tradition in themselves, but also in order to avoid illusions, to understand its strength in the hostile class. Nationalism does not belong to the ideologies that as traditions of the past times are gradually extinguished under modern conditions. It is a living ideology, drawing its forces ever anew from a fertile economic soil, standing in the center of fight, the flag of the foe." Anton Pannekoek, *Workers' Councils. op. cit.*, p. 185.

5. "Zur Einführung," *Vorbote,* Jan 1, 1918, pp. 1-4. The English version of this text was published under the title "The Third International" in *International Socialist Review*, Feb. 1917, pp. 460-462.

"The collapse of the International caused by the world war is not simply a surrender of international sentiment before the power of intensified nationalism.... The present catastrophe indicates more than the proletariat's inability to prevent the outbreak of war: it means that the methods of the era of the Second International failed to increase the intellectual and material power of the proletariat to the point where it could break the power of the ruling classes. Therefore, the world war must be a turning point in the history of the working class movement...." As a result of oppression and suffering caused by the war, "the masses are inspired; they must raise themselves if they are not to be completely submerged." In other words, they must strive for a new spiritual orientation. The proletariat, acting under unprecendented conditions, cannot rely on old ideas and old norms; hence the absolute need for an organizational break[6] with "those who would make social-democracy a tool of imperialism." And to elaborate the new solutions, the revolutionaries have Marxism: not the "Marxism regarded by the socialist theoreticians as a method to explain the past and the present and degraded progressively into a dry doctrine of mechanical fatalism,"[7] but a Marxism "which has regained its birthright as a theory of revolution."

In another article,[8] Pannekoek again stressed that "the proletarian masses should themselves intervene, using methods of active warfare." And he recalled how "the bureaucracy of officers and of leaders, naturally identifying their specific group interests with those of the proletariat, strenuously opposed 'the anarcho-trade-unionist actions.' " Then, speaking of mass actions and of the primordial need to combat state power, he returned to the theme that "the new character of modern capitalism demands a *new socialism*, a new workers' movement."[9]

In short—and Pannekoek stresses this—"*the increasing cohesion which the conflict gives to proletarian solidarity and organization makes it possible to shatter, by means of mass actions, the elements of force and the state organization. At the same time, political power comes into the hands of the proletariat, since it is able to create the organs necessary for economic reconstruction. To make the proletariat ripe for socialism through harsh conflict, and thus make it capable of abolishing bourgeois domination—that is the historic meaning of imperialism.*"

---

6. A small minority of the "Zimmerwaldians" (among them the Bolsheviks) held this idea.

7. A similar judgment, supported by ample theoretical and historical justification, can be found in the already cited works of Korsch and Brandis. Cf. also Erich Matthias, "Kautsky und der Kautskyanismus," *Marxismusstudien*, 11 (1957), pp. 151-97.

8. Anton Pannekoek, "Der Imperialismus und die Aufgaben des Proletariats," *Vorbote*, pp. 7-19. The article was first published in Russian in *Kommunist* (1-2, 1915).

9. "Zur Einführung," *op. cit.*, pp. 13ff.

By comparing such views with those of Lenin (in the article in *Verbote* that follows Pannekoek's introduction) on the "overthrow" and "betrayal" of Social Democracy, [10] one can get some idea of where their views converge — in their diagnosis of the problem — and where they diverge — on the prognosis for the communist movement. Lenin aims for the restoration, pure and simple, of the old orthodox Marxist tactics which, according to him have been betrayed by "the opportunism" of the labor aristocracy. Pannekoek, for his part, appeals to an essentially different tactic, in which traditional forms of organization no longer figure prominently, and in which the idea of the administration of the future society is beginning to undergo a profound change.

That is why Pannekoek regards the question of new tactics and of the formation of a new international "of supreme importance." However, one thing is certain: the structure of the traditional workers' parties "of which Social Democracy is the model. It takes the form of a gigantic and powerful organization, almost a state within a state, with its own officials, finances, press, spiritual universe, and specific ideology (Marxism). By its general character, it is adapted to the pre-imperialist peaceful phase. The thousands of officials, secretaries, agitators, parliamentarians, theoreticians and publicists [11] — who already form a distinct caste, a group with very distinct interests — rule the organization on both the material and spiritual levels; and express its general character. As such, and with Kautsky leading them, it is no accident that they will not hear of a genuine, bitter struggle against imperialism. Their vital interests compel them to oppose new tactics that would endanger their existence as officials. Their tranquil work, in conferences and committees, in offices and editorial rooms, is threatened by the storms of the imperialist era.

"Kautsky's theory and tactics represent an attempt to shield the whole bureaucratic apparatus from the risks of social revolution. In fact, he simply seeks to survive by keeping clear of the hurly-burly, untouched by the revolutionary combat and therefore unaffected by the larger world outside. If the party and its leadership were to aopt the tactics of mass action, state power would undoubtedly strike back at the organizations — the bases of their whole existence, destroying them perhaps, confiscating their funds, imprisoning their leaders. Of course, the state would be quite wrong if it assumed that this would break the back of the proletariat: the workers'

---

10.   Lenin, "Der Opportunismus und der Zusammenbruch der II Internationale," *ibid.*, pp. 19ff. The French text of this is in *Oeuvres*, XXII, pp. 115-128.

11.   It is difficult to establish precisely the number of individuals in this famous "apparatus." The estimates vary considerably.

organizational power does not lie in the exterior form of political associations, but in the spirit of comradeship, in the discipline and unity that enable them to create new and better forms of organizations. [12] For the officials, however, this would be the end of everything; the organization is their whole world, and they cannot exist or act outside it. The instinct of self-preservation, the interests of a specific group, force them, therefore, to adopt a tactic yielding to imperialism and making concessions to it. Consequently, what happened both before and at the time of the declaration of the world war was by no means an extraordinary accident. How often had not the officials proclaimed that such dangerous mass struggles would ruin the organization and that care must be taken not to provoke them? That is why the organizations they lead did not resolve to fight imperialism to the utmost. The struggle remained one of words, of accusations, of exhortations—a *fictitious battle* avoiding anything remotely resembling a real one. The most cogent proof of this has been given by Kautsky himself who, while having long hesitated about coming out against social-imperialism, [13] did not hesitate to describe the workers' street demonstrations as 'reckless actions.' In other words, they fight imperialism with words, but don't dare pass on to action. [14]

---

12.   Zinoviev cites this passage in his analysis (1917) of the material bases of Social Democratic policy. Zinoviev, *Der Krieg und die Krise des Sozialismus* (Vienna, 1924), p. 525. He drew on the impressive mass of material assembled by Roberto Michels in his now classic work of 1911 on the "sociology of the political parties." A little later on, Zinoviev writes: "This certainly does not mean that the workers' movement can in the future do without a large organizational apparatus, a whole category of people placed at the service of the proletarian organization. It is a question. . .of a new stage, in the course of which the spontaneous movement of the masses will subordinate itself to this stratum of officials, destroy the fixed routine, and cause the bureaucratic fungus to disappear and new men to rise up." *Ibid.*, pp. 526-527. This, in a sense, coincides with Michels' theory of the inevitable growth of a "bureaucratic oligarchy," because of "the need felt by the masses to be led and because of their inability to act except through an impulse coming from outside or from above," of "the masses' inability to look after their own interests, an inability which necessitates the existence of officials who act on their behalf." R. Michels, *Les Partis politiques* (Paris, 1914), pp. 36 and 62. Pannekoek, for his part, takes up a position which is not as clear and which, on his own admission, even contains an element of contradiction: on the one hand, he cites the necessity of a new political organization, at both the national and the international levels, but not for an apparatus of a new type; on the other hand, he reaches a final position pretty close to the general idea of the German Left that the development of a new spirit, born through revolutionary class struggle, will make possible the regeneration, the "redressing" of the old party. Need we recall that this undoubted ambiguity is due to the real situation in Western Europe, that is, to the existence of political, trade unionist and other organizations whose spirit deeply impregnated the masses? In Russia, conditions were leading the Bolsheviks to ignore, at the theoretical level, the existence of this contradiction.

13.   An extreme tendency of avowed revisionism, which even went so far as to support the colonialist ambitions of the imperial government. Cf. A. Ascher, "Imperialists within German Social Democracy," *Journal of Central European Affairs*, XX, 1961.

14.   A well-known reformist simultaneously reached a similar diagnosis: "The leaders are obliged to remain radicals in words, in order to conciliate the masses; in fact, they content

"Clearly, therefore, it would be useless to expect the present party bureaucracy to proclaim a revolutionary struggle against imperialism. Instead, it will limit itself to futile discussion in Parliament and in the press, to long-winded speeches about secondary matters, to concern with the technicalities of trade union action. Although the reformists are sympathetic to imperialism and the center-leftists are its enemies,[15] they still share a concern with mere criticism and an absence of any desire to engage in combat. They will soon attempt to change the party into one of bourgeois reforms based on the English model, which is satisfied with a few revolutionary phrases and which energetically pursues the day-to-day demands of the workers, without, however, being involved even slightly in any major revolutionary struggle.

"It is incumbent on the revolutionary Social Democrats to show the workers the meaning of mass action and to take every opportunity to enlighten them, to help them, and to draw them into the struggle. However, if this new tactic is propagated only by minorities while the big parties have nothing to do with it, then mass action—by definition inconceivable without the participation of the masses—will surely come to be regarded as mere wishful thinking. This incongruity proves one thing: the kind of mass action that was directed by the Social Democratic Party and praised before the war by the radical German Left is now impossible. Such action is spontaneous, breaking out suddenly when misery and revolt finally compel the masses to react. It may be the involuntary consequence of an affront emanating from the party, an affront small in itself but sufficient in itself to burst the dikes; or it may take the form of opposition to the declared wishes of the leaders (violating discipline). Nonetheless, if it spreads sufficiently, it can involve the organization itself and can force it, for a time, to go along with the revolutionary forces. It is not impossible that, when the war has continued for a while, something of this kind will occur; the symptoms are already appearing.

"One can foresee, therefore, that, in the near future, the existing organizations (parties and trade unions) will play a restraining role in conformity with their nature but counter to the objectives and tasks of the proletarian masses. However, if the new tactics are increasingly used, and if the power of the proletariat gradually increases through mass conflicts, both

themselves with minor reforms which can be secured without much trouble." G. Eckstein, "Bureaucratie und Politik," *Neue Zeit*, XXXIV:1 (1916), pp. 483ff.

15. There is question here of two main currents which were then showing themselves within German Social Democracy, one leftist, the other pacifist; the split was to occur early in 1917 and was confirmed some months later with the founding of the independent Social Democrat Party (USPD).

party and trade unions will find themselves unable to play this role. From then on, their rigid leadership organs will increasingly form a subordinate sector within a larger class movement and within a larger class organization that welds the masses into a powerful fighting collectivity, not through the membership card, but through consciousness of a common purpose."

The second issue of *Vorbote* carried an article in which Pannekoek tried to forecast the effects that the end of the war would have on the workers (widespread unemployment) and on the economy in general (renewal of military equipment and, therefore, a new stage in armaments production).[16]

In this connection he writes: "The wartime experience gained during state control over industry and commerce has developed, in a large part of the bourgeoisie, *the idea of state 'socialism.'* The advantages of a centralized system of production over private ownership are well known today. The major industries could quite easily be nationalized and reconverted to war production. The bourgeoisie could find this an answer to the problems that would arise with the return of soldiers looking for jobs.... And this would have other advantages. In the first place, it would lower prices through the elimination of middlemen. Everyone knows what economic benefits would derive from a state organization of production. It would be the means of preserving all the technical and organizational improvements developed during the war, and of regulating unemployment. Equally, of course, the wages and salaries could be fixed, and the trade unions would find themselves powerless against a new employer with enormous powers. As for the workers, their dependence would be increased and their freedom of labor-mobility would be less than it was under the regime of private property. The nationalization of these major industries would also signify militarization..., a means of taking the masses in hand and of repressing their inclination toward political opposition.

"This state socialism can only aggravate the proletarian condition and strengthen oppression. In spite of this, one can foresee that a large sector of Social Democracy will not oppose it, and will even support it. Its old ideology will, in effect, link Social Democracy with the new system of state exploitation.... *Nationalization of enterprises is not socialism; socialism is the force of the proletariat.*[17] But since, in the ideal world of present Social

16.   Anton Pannekoek, "Wenn der Krieg zu Ende Geht," *Vorbote*, April 2, 1916, pp. 22-27.

17.   Pannekoek already had occasion to broach this problem, as when, for instance, he wrote: "Nationalization of the big industries would mean merely the replacing of private capitalists with a much more powerful entrepreneur, against whom the workers would be much more effectively stripped of their rights.... socialism is the force created by workers consciously united by the struggle against the capitalist class, within powerful and self-administering organizations." Anton Pannekoek, "Sozialismus und Verstaatlichung," *B.B.Z.*, May 27, 1917. We might note in

Democracy, *socialism* and *state-controlled economy* are more or less regarded as synonymous, this party will find itself without spiritual arms when brought face to face with state socialist measures intended to reduce the proletariat to a condition of slavery.

"The task of revolutionary socialism is to lead the proletariat to declare war on this new servitude. The slogan 'fight state *socialism!*' should serve to explain to the proletariat its condition under the new imperialism. If the imperialist state increasingly emerges as the oppressor and exploiter of the workers, a situation will automatically occur, which, by its very nature, will cause the proletariat to see the state as the supreme enemy against which they must fight, primarily with the weapon of mass action. Thus the Kautsky tradition, which seeks above all else to preserve the state and to bend it to socialist purposes, will be shattered by the sheer logic of events.…

"When, both during the after the war, the workers resume the political battle, they will need *a clear program of action*. The fight for socialism cannot be other than the class struggle for the immediate and essential interests of the proletariat, and its character is decided by the methods and means used. No doubt, some of the old demands will still have their place in the new program of action: for example, the struggle *for complete and full democracy* within the state, and the struggle against *militarism*. Both of these, however, will take on a new strength and a new meaning when, as a result of the accelerated progress of state socialism, economic exploitation and militarist servitude are seen as clearly bracketed with political oppression."

Vorbote went out of existence with this second number. On one point at least, clear divergences of opinion were emerging. Radek's theses on imperialism and oppression unequivocally condemned the call for the right of national self-determination, while Lenin took the very opposite viewpoint, letting it be known privately that *Vorbote's* failure of the enterprise was due to the "intrigues" of Radek, who, he said, "deprived us of our editors." [18] It seems clear, however, that in reality, neither Lenin nor the editors of the review had decided to subscribe unconditionaly to Radek's view.

---

passing that one of the principal theoreticians of the Hamburg Left, Heinrich Laufenberg (1872-1932) also said something similar. "Sozialdemokratie und Verstaatlichung," *Die Neue Zeit*, XXXII, 2, 1914.

18. Lenin, *Works, op. cit.*, pp. 407-408.

CHAPTER FIVE

RUSSIAN SOVIETS AND GERMAN RAETE

World War I marked a decisive state in the transition from liberal capitalism to modern Western capitalism. In disarray following the war, the new economic structure nevetheless resulted in permanent changes, especially in the institutions serving the workers' immediate political and economic interests.

Prior to the war, party and trade union leaders had found it necessary to challenge economic and political power, as a result of the pressure from the large industrial centers and the authorities' impassioned concern to retain undiminished power. The war changed that; not only did it clearly reveal the deep patriotism of party and trade union leaders—i.e., their attachment to the status quo and their lack of any practical will to revolution—but it also made it imperative for the state to maintain social peace.

When German Social Democratic deputies (with one ludicrous abstention) approved the war credits on August 4, 1914, they sealed a choice that the majority of them had made much earlier, at least unconsciously. "The party had long before chosen its way, the way of reformism," wrote fromer editor in chief of *Vorwärts*, the central organ of German Social Democracy, in the bitter hour of defeat and exile.[1] In the midst of the agony, a Bremen Leftist could say of the vote: "This was no accidental disaster; on the contrary, it was a logical step for a movement whose evolution, since the Erfurt Congress, had been in this direction."[2] An observer noted at the time: "The mortal enemies of the bourgeoisie are accommodating well to being members of the state order."[3]

Certainly, the absorption of party and trade union leadership into

---

1. Friedrich Stampfer, *Die vierzehn Jahren der ersten deutschen Republik* (Karlsbad, 1936), p. 19.

2. Johann Knief, *Arbeiterpolitik*, June 24, 1916. In the eyes of leftists such as Pannekoek and Knief, to merely denounce the "treason" (as the *Spartakusbund* was doing) avoided the issue of the future form of organization and its purposes; they therefore linked the treason with the old form of organization. Knief unhesitatingly described as "social traitors" those who postponed fulfilling their solemn commitments because of the circumstances (cf. *infra*, final section of this chapter).

3. Cited by Werner Richter, *Gewerkschaften, Monopolkapital und Staat . . .1914-1916* (East Berlin, 1959), p. 66. This represents the most important work on the subject.

officialdom, as organizers and representatives of labor, was the culmination of a process begun long before; but it was now undergoing astounding development. With the continuation of the war, this body gave increasing support to the war effort, together with the municipal and industrial authorities. When the draft was introduced in 1916, Legien, the leader of *Kraft-Zentrale*, a major trade union council, secured from the war minister concessions—the recognition of trade union rights and the setting up of industrial committees and parity organs of arbitration—in recognition of "the workers' active cooperation." [4] Thus, without recourse to "mass action," the traditional form of organization had achieved its major goals. Two years earlier in August 1914, its administrators were trembling with apprehension, convinced—not without reason—that the associations were in danger of being dissolved, their newspapers suppressed, their funds confiscated,[5] and their militants placed under the control of the state.[6] The new status of party and trade union leaders banished these fears.

It was quite otherwise for the workers. Many had patriotically cheered the declaration of war; now the price had to be paid. In 1913, there had been 300,000 days lost through strikes; in 1915 there were 15,000. The threat of prompt dispatch to the front was sufficient to calm rebellious spirits, but working conditions soon became intolerable. Undernourishment, fear, inflation, in contrast to the huge profits of the employers, the arrogance of both minor and major authorities, and the luxurious living of the black market profiteers—all this, was the price workers had to pay for renouncing the class struggle.

However, this trend was gradually reversed with the onset of wildcat strikes. In April 1917 and January 1918, major strikes were called by committees elected by the rank and file. Workers also took an active role in the old party, now organizationally split into the Majority Party (SPD-M) and the Independents (USPD), corresponding respectively to the old Center-Left (Kautsky) and to the radicals. The latter, claiming fidelity to traditional tactics and program, increased their protest against the war and became more and more frustrated at their lack of political power that resulted from the dictatorship of the General Headquarters, in league with the large industrialists.

To the left of the two major political organizations of the workers' were various splinter groups persistently swimming against the stream. Their

---

4.   Robert Armeson, *Total Warfare and Compulsory Labor* (The Hague, 1964), pp. 73ff.
5.   Cf. Fritz Opel, *Der deutsche Metallarbeiterverband*...(Hanover, 1957), pp. 38-40.
6.   Cf. Johannes Kampfer (J. Marchlewski), *Kriegssozialismus in Theorie und Praxis* (Berne, 1915).

"literature" appealed to confirmed militants, [7] and their contacts scarcely reached beyond personal relationships in a country that continued to submit to the constraints of war. One of these splinter groups, the *Spartakusbund*, while maintaining contact with the masses through the Independents, published internationalist pacifist pamphlets denouncing the Majority Party and its open alliance with the bourgeoisie. These attacks, under the direction of Leo Jogisches (Tyszko)—a friend of Rosa Luxemburg—were expressed in the language of the old left and broke little new theoretical ground.

A second splinter group, the *Internationalen Kommunisten Deutschlands* (IKD), made up of communists from Bremen and various other local groups, moved in a different direction. From December 1916, the Bremen group severed all ties to the two major factions of Social Democracy (which were both seeking to gain control of the local organization), vigorously denouncing them. Its official organ, *Arbeiterpolitik*, was devoted to "scientific discussion" of theoretical problems. It sometimes opened its columns to "outside" contributors, notably Radek, Zinoviev and Pannekoek. Renewed worker interest encouraged the Bremen section and it opened once again debate on the structure of workers' organizations.

The Bremen section advocated not only a decentralized party separate from Social Democracy but also a "unitary organization" (*Einheitsorganisation*) linking the workers on both a political and a trade union basis. Thus, they argued against a "new party of leaders" on the old model. [8] "One must choose the tactics of mass action unfettered by leaders, or one must keep the leadership structure, as the Spartacus League is doing, and thereby renounce a proletarian policy." [9] Even so, *Arbeiterpolitik* (or at least some of its editors) was not yet rejecting "revolutionary parliamentarianism." *Arbeiterpolitik* welcomed news of the October Revolution, emphasizing that the victory had occurred because "in Russia, there was an independent, left-wing party, which fought for social revolution." [10]

In Holland, too, the Dutch Social Democratic Party—the "tribunist"—was

---

7. Cf. Gilbert Badia, *le Spartakisme* (Paris, 1967), pp. 280ff.

8. This idea made its appearance in *Arbeiterpolitik* in March 1917 (11, 16, March 21, 1917); it was taken up again there, and simultaneously in the publications of the other IKD "local groups" and of the Hamburg group; in November 1918, it also appeared in *Rote Fahne*, the organ of the Berlin *Spartakusbund* 1, 15, November 21, 1918; reproduced in *Dokumente und Materialen zur Geschichte der deutschen Arb.bwg.*, 11, 2, p. 431).

9. *Arbeiterpolitik*, 11, 12, June 9, 1917.

10. J. Knief, December 15, 1917. It seems, however, that the Bremen group had no precise idea of the Bolshevik conceptions of the party, as can be seen through Radek's "memoirs" ("I pointed out to him [Knief] that his ideas had nothing in common with Bolshevism;" cited by Badia, *op. cit.*, pp. 404-405). We shall see later that this lack of awareness was also shared by Pannekoek (and by all the rest of Western European Leftists, with few exceptions).

sharply divided into a parliamentarian faction characterized by militant francophilia (and which won two seats in the 1917 legislature) and a faction centered around Gorter, which advocated a strict internationalism. Pannekoek, however, appears to have refrained from aligning himself with either group.[11] On the other hand, it was he who wrote a series in *Nieuwe Tijd* tracing the significance of the Russian Revolution.[12] The author's solidarity with the Bolsheviks is clear from the first lines; and the main characteristics of the February Revolution are emphasized.

"What has never occurred in earlier revolutions in Western Europe—where fragmentation and powerlessness always followed political action—has become an enduring reality in Russia: the revolutionary masses are forming a powerful organization. As in 1905, the delegates of factories and revolutionary regiments are building in the form of *workers' and soldiers' councils*, a people's representation which speaks out vigorously against brougeois government and exploiters."

Various political viewpoints are found in the councils; but the Bolshevik Party, "which under the Czar already had great influence over the proletariat, is becoming increasingly the representative of the Petrograd workers, albeit they are a small minority in proportion to all the country's workers. The soldiers' councils, mainly peasants, are dominated by Mensheviks and revolutionary socialists.[13]

"Russia, with its huge peasant population and its limited capitalist development, is not yet ripe for socialism; power must remain in the hands of the bourgeoisie. This is at least what some dogmatic quasi-Marxists maintain, unaware that socialism can only result from a long process in which the maturity of a society is measured by the proletariat's ability to struggle for power. But even in Russia they were intimidated by the enormity of the task, which was augmented by the confusion resulting from the war and Czarist legacy of administrative deficiency. They imagined the bourgeoisie alone to be capable of bringing the country out of chaos and relied on its leadership to do so. Such quasi-Marxists saw only one solution: a capitalist government that would keep all its power, with the proletariat continuing to allow itself to be exploited. They failed to understand the central issue—that the government's lack of power arose not from its 'socialism,' which consisted of empty rhetoric, but from the absence of a true socialist character.

"The Bolsheviks have shown what a truly socialist government would have

---

11.   Van Ravesteyn, *op. cit.*, pp. 136-137; this author, however, is not always reliable.
12.   Anton Pannekoek, "De russische revolutie," *De Nieuwe Tijd*, XXII, 1917, pp. 438-52, 548-60, XIII, 1918, pp. 31-46, 119-42.
13.   These lines are dated August 1917.

done. Faced with the submissiveness of the social patroits, who only paid lip service to socialism, the Bolsheviks drew up a program of direct reform designed to meet specific problems, to free the country and the proletariat, from intolerable coercion and to open the path to socialism. Thus, the Bolsheviks became the vanguard of revolutionary socialism, on the rise throughout the world.

"And, first of all, regarding the organization of production, if capitalists close their factories in a move against the workers or in response to decreased profits, these factories must be confiscated and production resumed, but under the direction of workers and technicians. If the landed proprietors refuse to cultivate their lands, their lands should be seized and returned to the peasants. Unconcerned with property rights, the peasants can be counted on to place their products at the disposal of the general population, and would be supplied with low-cost agricultural tools and machinery.[14] Rigorous surveillance of commercial transactions would reduce interest rates, while the nationalization of profitable war industries and major banks would create a sizable source of revenue. Moreover, a revolutionary government ought to start by cancelling war debts, which enable the shareholders of Europe and of the West to exploit the Russian people through exorbitant rates of interest.

"However, one measure overshadows all the others: a swift end must be put to the war, which is causing millions of deaths, exhausting the country, and sacrificing production to the needs of armaments manufacture. That is why the Bolsheviks have focused their program around the call for peace—peace, not just as an escape from bankruptcy and famine but also as a rallying cry against the bourgeoisie.... And for these reasons the revolutionary proletarian party challanges the Provisional Government."

Pannekoek, while emphasizing the need for and the difficulties of a reorganization of production and distribution, carefully examines the evolution of the political situation in Russia. In general, he justifies the measures recommended by the Bolsheviks and defends them, at least implicitly, against the criticisms of the pro-Entente "Tribune." However, in his view and in that of the German and Russian left wing, the future of the Russian Revolution is tied to the development of the revolution in Western Europe. This perspective emerges in the following postscript to an article

---

14. Three months later, Knief expressed a similar opinion when he stressed that the Bolshevik slogan, "The land to those who cultivate it!" while not having a socialist character, did aim at closing the gaps between town and country—gaps in herited from Czarism. But, "State support and the supplying of farm implements will establish solid bonds between the peasants and the industrial workers" (*Arbeiterpolitik*, November 17, 1917; and *Dokumente und Materialen* . . . , II:1, pp. 16-17).

dated October 1917: "What we were hoping for has just been realized. On October 24 and 25 the workers and the soldiers of Petrograd swept away the Kerenski government. It is likely, but not yet certain, that this revolution will spread to the whole of Russia. A new age is dawning, not only for the Russian Revolution, but also for the proletarian revolution in Europe. For the first time since the Paris Commune, the proletariat, allied with the petty bourgeoisie, has seized political power, not just in one city, but in a large country. For the first time, modern social leaders have invited the proletariat to take part in reconstructing a society. But it is an extremely difficult task, especially in light of the complete disintegration and bankruptcy of the social order, all within the framework of world war. But none of this precludes the establishment of peace. There are still more remote difficulties, connected with Russia's predominantly agricultural character. Whether the Bolsheviks succeed or fail, at the very least they will have served as a model to the international proletariat. We salute the victory of our Russian comrades as that of our brave advance troops on the road to socialism."[15]

Rosa Luxemburg's views differed in certain respects from Pannekoek's. Publicly she delcared her solidarity with the Bolsheviks; privately, as the Russian experiment progressed, she criticized its principles.[16] On two points — the questions of land reform and national self-determination — she condemned the Bolsheviks for having succumbed to the "spontaneous movement" of the peasants who were taking over the land and to nations seeking to establish their independence; she also believed that the legitimization of these "two petty-bourgeois slogans" violated the principles of socialism. Pannekoek was in favor of the first point; he never declared himself on the second.[17] On the other hand, he unreservedly approved the Bolsheviks' dissolution of the constituent assembly, the third and principal area of Luxemburg's criticism. In this connection, she said, "Trotsky and Lenin reject in principle national representations established by general elections and want to rely only on soviets."[18] Primarily concerned with the development of the new institutions that had just reappeared in Russia, i.e., the workers' councils, Pannekoek agreed with the Russian revolutionaries, as is evident in a 1919 pamphlet:[19]

"Democracy, it is said, is government by the people, but the people as such do not exist; in reality, society is divided into classes...When we talk of the

15. Pannekoek, "De russische revolutie," *De Nieuwe Tijd*, XXII, p. 560.
16. Rosa Luxemburg, *la Révolution russe* (Paris, 1946).
17. Cf. below, Chapter 9.
18. Luxemburg, *op. cit.*, p. 34.
19. Anton Pannekoek, *Bolschevismus und Demokratie* (Vienna, 1919), p. 8.

people, we mean the masses as distinct from the propertied minority. It is this people, the poor and laboring people, the proletarian class, who should govern themselves." The present parliamentary system can ensure only the triumph of the interests of capital.

"We have recently criticized universal suffrage. Men are not equal, and therefore their votes cannot all be of equal value. A man who lived solely off his capital without working, a social parasite, cannot be equated with a worker whose labor serves to keep society in existence: in a certain sense, this is an ethical concept. Going a step further, our policy is aimed at organizing society on socialist foundations. So completely opposed to the interests of the bourgeoisie is this policy that they will seek to put every obstacle in its way and make it fail." All collaboration with the bourgeoisie must therefore be ruled out.

In Russia, "a form of democracy superior to formal democracy, enabling the masses to express their vital interests" has begun to develop: "the workers' councils in the towns, the peasants' councils in the rural areas, the councils charged with various administrations that form the basis of the government. The municipal bodies are elected by the workers' councils of the towns, and the workers' councils of a given branch of production elect the administrators of this branch for the whole country. A general congress of soviets is held from time to time and decides on general policy, but congresses are also held about matters concerning each branch: industry, agriculture, transport, health services, education. The local soviets send their most competent members as delegates to these congresses, experiences are compared, and decisions are made in common.

"It is the real need to reorganize social life that has led the Russian people to establish this flexible administrative machinery, which also constitutes the organ of the the dictatorship of the proletariat in which the bourgeoisie cannot participate. The bourgeoisie will not be excluded in any artificial way from government, for instance, by losing its right to vote; quite simply, it will be barred from this organization, which is based not on the people but on labor. . . . The ex-manager or owner of an industry who cooperates as a technical officer under the guidance of the workers' council can claim equality with other factory personnel. The intellectual workers—doctors, teachers, artists—form their own councils, which collectively decide about matters concerning them. All these councils remain in close, permanent contact with the masses, their membership constantly renewed and replaced. The formation of a new bureaucracy is thus prevented, and a monopoly in administrative skills is broken.

"In comparison to this true self-government, one sees how even the most democratic of parliaments is unable to create a people's government, and ends up as a government of parliamentarians. Periodically, parliamentarians must win the trust of the people; they gather votes with eloquent speeches and promise-crammed programs; then they are the masters once again. Then, after they escape the direct influence of the masses and face pressure only from their peers, they do as they like throughout the parliamentary session. But only in appearance are they all-powerful; the ministry depends upon bureaucrats. In all the democratic republics of the world, the alleged separation between the legislative and the executive branches is the means of ruling the masses, while giving them the impression that the masses themselves are exercising power, and is therefore the means for ensuring the domination of capital. In France, America, Switzerland, and elsewhere, in spite of all the talk of democracy, the masses are dominated and exploited by capital. And, despite universal suffrage, the masses are reduced to impotence, from which they cannot escape...."

Meanwhile, World War I ended, and changes that leftists were hoping to see in Germany remained at an embryonic stage. A network of workers and soldiers councils suddenly covered the country, but the old order remained intact under the appearance of sharing power.

Shortly before the end of the war, the German Admiralty's decision to force a final battle with the English Navy met with a collective refusal: the crews of the third squadron mutinied, raised anchor and sailed for the Baltic; on November 3, 1918, they sailed into Kiel harbor, flying the red flag, disembarked and, after a bloody encounter with a detachment of midshipmen, took over the town. Soon the soldiers made common cause with the rebels, and the following day, both in the ships riding at anchor and in the barracks, committees of delegates were elected. In a general assembly, the latter adopted a 14-point program demanding the liberation of political prisoners, a halt to disciplinary prosecutions, the restoration of freedom of the press and assembly, and the right to take "any necessary measure for the protection of private possessions."[20] On November 5, the local sections of the socialist parties (Majority Socialists and Independents) and of the trade union cartel merged to form a workers council.[21]

In response, the commandant of Kiel sought the intervention of the imperial government, which requested that Majority Party leaders send a delegation led by Gustav Noske. During an assembly of the soldiers

---

20. Cf. Kurt Zeisler, in *Revolutionäre Ereignisse und Probleme...1917-1918* (East Berlin, 1957), pp. 185-212.
21. Walter Tormin, *Zwischen Rätediktatur und sozialer Demokratie* (Düsseldorf, 1954), p. 58. Note the charts showing the spread of the movement.

committees, Noske, with the support of the trade union officers, had himself elected prisident of the central council, whose membership was determined by Noske or by his cohorts (the more resolute sailors had already left town). Since the military governor of the big war port had been removed, Noske took his place. As a result of a deal made with the Independents, a representative of that group succeeded him on November 7, as president of the local council. "At Kiel," Johann Knief worte to a friend, "there is a workers and soldiers council, with the socialist traitor Noske at its head! The sailors are full of enthusiasm. But are they social revolutionaries?"[22]

Enthusiasm? Certainly. The sailors took to the trains by squads, occupied stations, and, after some clashes, swarmed out to encourage the formation of workers and soldiers councils. But this enthusiasm was due less to precise political convictions than to the sailors' fear of ruthless repression if they remained in Kiel. They were warmly greeted in Hamburg and in Bremen, where an assembly held at the trade union headquarters resulted in the establishment of a 180-member workers' council. Leftist delegates were rare; the majority of the leftists were still fighting or were in prison, far away.

In a constantly volatile atmosphere, huge demonstrations occurred in the large cities. The proclamation of the republic, a major aim of the demonstrators, was realized on November 9, when Social Democratic "people's commissars" of both wings of the party took power. As a rule, the Majority Party and the trade unions ratified hastily formed slates of candidates in local assemblies. Often slates were produced after hurried telephone calls to party leaders in Berlin or nearby towns. In some instances, where Independents were strong or had political leverage, a slate was laboriously drawn up and later "elected" at a public meeting. Sometimes the slate contained leftists, more frequently leaders of the liberal bourgeoisie. The new political administrative organs corresponded to those of Kiel in their genesis and program: "to guarantee order;" to end blatant injustices; to restore democratic life.

To a considerable extent, the civil authorities kept control of public affairs (notably, of finances). Military authorities themselves ordered the establishment of councils[23] whose pressing task, especially in the rationing zone, was to calm the conquered army. Later, in large, rear-guard towns, councils were generally manipulated by their noncommissioned officers into respecting the status quo.[24] The rank and file were simply concerned about

22. J. Knief, *Briefe aus dem Gefängnis* (Berlin, 1922), pp. 94-95.
23. Cf. the appeal of Hindenburg in *Dokumente und Materialen...*, II:1, p. 356.
24. Especially when the leftists were exerting a palpable influence within the local grand council, for example at Hamburg. Cf. Heinrich Laufenberg, *Die hamburger Revolution*

getting back to their homes.

The traditional organization saw its new power affirmed both on the political level, due to the active cooperation between the "people's commissars" and the German High command, and on the economic level after the agreement of November 15 between large industrialists and trade unions, which provided for collective conventions, procedures for parity arbitration, industrial committees, and other units, opening up an immense field of bureaucratic activiteis to trade unions linked with Social Democracy. Within this framework, the "power" of the councils represented a kind of counter-fire, prudently continued by the authorities, including major socialist and trade union figures. As Knief observed toward the end of 1918, the workers and soldiers councils, far from "devoting themselves to revolutionary activities, were entirely taken up with political controversies."[25]

Nevertheless, obvious powerlessness did not prevent the new form from continuing to exist. Leftists called for a change in its function, initially at the local level, to include effective social administration. In factories and workshops, employers' authority remained intact. Often at the street level things were different: mass demonstrations were frequent; strikes broke out, greatly scandalizing the new masters ("socialism means hard work," said Ebert, president of the Council of People's Commissars); officers were molested when they went out in uniform. Faced with this agitation, often organized by the young communists, who were gaining support, the counter-revolution gathered its forces: the socialists painted a black picture of the Russian Bolsheviks and their German comrades and created a national guard recruited among the mass of ex-officers and reactionary students. Casulties began to occur, and arms appeared among the crowd of demonstrators.

The revolutionary tendency arose from the idea of the self-education of the masses through action. Its *leitmotiv*—the Faustian cry of *"Anfang war die Tat"* ("in the beginning was the deed")—contained the whole of its political philosophy, the basic principle of the proletariat as a revolutionary class. The old divisions among splinter groups, while continuing, became much less distinct. The Spartakus League, transformed by a massive influx of young militants who wanted to act personally and directly, not to issue orders, gradually moved away from traditional viewpoints. The organ of the Bremen socialists declared its sympathy with the League, provided it would break with the Independents, and added: "Unity of revolutionary action is the

(Hamburg, 1919).
25. Peter Unruh (J. Knief), *Von Zusammenbruch der Imperialismus*... (Berlin, undated, probably Jan. 1919), pp. 24-25.

fundamental condition for the development of the reovlution. This unity cannot be achieved in the present situation by a central body. On the contrary, it must be sought in the moral unity of groups enjoying complete organizational autonomy. The methods of the Spartakus group (as they are beginning to sense),...the launching of actions submitted to the sole leadership of a Berlin *Kraft-Zentrale*,[26] have had their day." [27]

Street actions enabled the splinter groups to develop visibility, publicize their ideas, and gain the active sympathy of some of the young workers and declassé (unemployed, deserters and others). But this growing influence stopped at the factory gates, for inside the factories, employers and their agents were allied with trade union delegates in seeking to curb every "ringleader" as quickly as possible. Communist marches would file past factories, but no worker would emerge from the gates to join in. Only rarely did workers' councils go on the offensive, e.g., temporarily suspending bourgeois papers.

Hence, the policy suggested by this situation was self-evident: "The revolution," said *Rote Fahne*, the Spartakus newspaper, "should try to mobilize the masses, and by educating them through conscious activity, shape them into a decisive political force." [28] In January 1919, and not without some reluctance and soul-searching, the splinter groups united. At the formative congress of the German Communist Party (KPD), a majority of the delegates (62 of 85) rejected the idea of participating in the elections to the National Assembly, an idea supported by the Spartakus leaders, Rosa Luxemburg, Karl Liebknecht and their friends. [29] However, the latter were elected to lead the party; Liebknecht even persisted, against the majority's wishes, in carrying on secret and useless negotiations with leaders of the Independents and with left wing trade union officials.

Rote Fahne called for a rededication to the revolution: "The rapid transformation of the revolution of November 9, in which soldiers predominated, into a revolution of working class character, requires...from the revolutionary class a degree of political maturity, education and passionate dedication much higher than was sufficient during the first phase. Revolutionary feelings must stiffen into inflexible conviction; the systematic must replace the merely spontaneous; the workers and soldiers councils,

---

26. Tyszko was nicknamed "Doktor Kraft" by the Bremen group, for he was a great advocate of the "strong (*kraft*) approach."

27. *Kommunist* (Bremen), Dec. 6, 1918; cited by S.I. Spiwak, *Die Presse der Sowjet Union*, 144, 1956.

28. *Rote Fahne*, 1, 8A Dec. 19, 1918.

29. Cf. André and Dori Prudhommeaux, *la Commune de Berlin* (Paris, 1949). This work contains a report of the Congress and an excellent chronology of events.

improvisations of the moment, must become a breastplate of steel." [30]

Having decided to strike the enemy in a critical phase at the source of his power—the machinery of propaganda and agitation[31]—and deprived, through lack of funds, of the means to spread their ideas widely and systematically, the spartacist demonstrators (anarchists, left-Marxists, Independent socialist militants, and other rebels) attempted to occupy the offices of reactionary newspapers and of the Majority Party. The latter gave the generals the go-ahead for repression, and there followed the "bloody week" in Berlin, the assassinations of Rosa Luxemburg and Karl Liebknecht, the ebbing of the Spartakus movement, and the holding of elections. Fighting continued, mostly underground, but with large and prolonged strikes, notably among the miners of the Ruhr and of Upper Silesia, with temporary seizures of power (Bavaria, Bremen), with scattered street fighting, an effort to stand against a bestial repression. [32] And these fighters, armed with little but their revolutionary passion, standing alone and unaided[33] and unwilling to die like dogs, faced up to well-armed mercenaries, trained to kill, behind whom skulked the treacherous leaders of German Social Democracy and the trade unions, products of a period of peaceful conflict and, for the moment, the last ramparts of capital. These desperate fighters were crushed mercilessly.

In the course of this revolutionary phase, the ideas that were propagated, especially after November 1918, developed naturally. In particular, the *Räteidee*, the idea of councils, was clarified through practical experience and through a great number of public meetings and discussions whose proceedings then became subject matter for newspaper articles[34] and

---

30. *Rote Fahne*, 11, 3, Jan. 3, 1919.
31. See, for example, the following statements by a trade unionist leader of the Ruhr: "The Spartakists are exercising unlimited domination in the whole district [of Duisberg]. They are supported by the big bosses of industry...whose plan is to destroy the trade unions with the help of the communists, to divide the miners and so reestablish their own power..." *Niederrheinische Volkstimme*, 66, March 1919; cited by Hans Spethmann, *Zwölf Jahre Ruhrbergbau*, 1 (Berlin, 1928), p. 253. See also, *L'Humanité*, May-June 1968, to find a tone and an inspiration which is analogous. Over a period of fifty years, there has existed, it would seem, a "spontaneous" continuity in the words an the behavior of the workers' bureaucracy.
32. According to Eberhard Kolb (*Die Arbeiterräte in der deutschen Innerpolitik* [Düsseldorf, 1962], p. 302), the councils were incapable of taking on the functions of real and full administration, because of "putschist elements who were opposed to the stabilization of order;" this author then states unblushingly that, even if "order" had not been disturbed, the local leftist-activist strongholds—for example, Bremen—"would not, in any case, have been able to subsist." This amounts to saying that their only expedient was action.
33. "In practice, there were no definite links between the Russian Communists and the German Communists from November 1918 to spring 1919," writes Kolb (*ibid.*, p. 157); cf. especially A. Prudhommeaux, *op. cit.*, p. 12.
34. For example, the series of articles, "Gewerkschaften und Rätesystem" which appeared in

pamphlets.[35] Linked to the needs of mass conflict and the contemporary image of the Russian soviets, a similar process was going on in England [36] and in Italy where anarchists [37] and Marxists [38] elaborated on the idea of revolutionary factory councils. The quintessence of all this is contained in the pamphlet, *Sozialdemokratie und Kommunismus*, to which we now turn. [39]

Rote Fahne (from no. 27, Feb. 13, 1919), whose editorial control was in the hands of the leftists and not of the *Zentrale* set up at the Congress, and in which the critique of the trade unions was the basis for the idea of constructing new organs both for the revolutionary struggle and for the administration of the society of the future.

35. For instance, that of Karl Schröder (1885-1950), who was to become one of the first leaders and one of the principal theoreticians of the KAPD. *Betriebsorganisation oder Gewerkschaft?* (Hamburg, 1919).

36. Cf. J.T. Murphy, *The Workers' Committee* (Sheffield, 1918).

37. Cf. "l'Autogestion de l'Etat," *Noir et Rouge*, 242 (Supp.), May 1968, pp. 5-8. The German anarchists with one or two exceptions were to remain faithful to the traditional trade unionist ideas.

38. The *Ordine Nuovo* group, and particularly Antonio Gramsci. Pannekoek's work was published in Amadeo Bordiga's paper, *Il Soviet*.

39. Notably: K. Horner (Anton Pannekoek), "Kommunismus und Sozialdemodratie," *Arbeiterpolitik*, IV, 7, Feb. 15, 1919; "Die neue Welt," *Die kommunistische Internationale*, 1-2, May-June 1919; "Die Sozialisierung," *Die Internationale*, 1, 13-14, Sept. 1919, pp. 254-259. (See footnote 4 of next chapter). There was also a pamphlet dealing with the division of the surplus-value within the dominant class, a pamphlet in which the role of the state bureaucracy is especially highlighted. *Die Teilung der Beute* (Moscow, 1918).

CHAPTER SIX

SOCIAL DEMOCRACY AND COMMUNISM

"The war," writes Pannekoek,[1] "has transformed social relationships." Socialism, "which is not a doctrine laid down once and for all," should therefore also continually renew itself. Having made its appearance for the first time in the class struggles that accompanied the 1848 Revolution, "the proletarian movement, the communist movement" was pushed into the background during the long period of prosperity which followed. The expansion of the workers' movement was then as vigorous as it was large, but its activities were limited. In effect, the class struggle was no longer being fought to achieve "the final goal, socialism," but to raise the standard of living. After 1870, the headlong development of the German economy gave rise to energetic clashes. It was at that time that Social Democracy became impregnated with the old communist ideas and came to adopt Marxism. However, this new Marxism depended on a gradual evolution, and postponed indefinitely any pursuit of proper communist objectives. Pannekoek points out that Social Democracy and the trade unions that grew up with it were expressions of the will of the working masses to escape pauperization. Taking on the task of representing the workers in Parliament, Social Democracy became an enormous, highly organized body within the bourgeois order and was dominated by an army of bureaucrats, all concerned with promoting their own specific interests above all else. Their highest ideal, as Kautsky clearly implied,[2] was to secure for themselves at some future point the posts held by the bourgeois parliamentary ministers.

It was the war that brought Social Democracy to power. At a time when the whole world was lapsing into bankruptcy and misery, this party saw salvation only in the preservation of the old capitalist order. "But the war had also enormously increased the demands of capital for profits. The national debt came to be counted in as many thousand of millions as it had previously numbered in millions alone. This meant that the holders of war credits expected to reap a rich harvest on the produce of the people's work and, as

---

1. K. Horner (i.e., Pannekoek), *Sozialdemokratie und Kommunismus* (Hamburg, undated [probably autumn 1919]).
2. *Ibid.*, p. 8. This is a clear allusion to the 1912 controversy.

revenue pocketed without work, on the interest on their thousands of millions, which the state was collecting in the form of taxes."

Increased worker exploitation was inevitable. That was why "even during the war, the communists were pointing out that it would be impossible to pay the enormous war debts, so that their declared policy was the cancellation of war debts and war indemnities." [3] But it was not enough to oppose the capitalists' thirst for profit in the area of armaments production, while giving them complete freedom in all other matters. Now that the reconstruction of the economy had become a matter of great urgency, "the profits from capital, whatever the source, represent for production a charge that increases the difficulties of its reorganization.... That is why the basic principle of communism — that all attempts of capital to monopolize profits must be resisted — is the only effectively realizable principle. The economy can be reconstructed in real terms only through the elimination of capital.

"This used to be the basic viewpoint of Social Democracy. What, today, is the position of the Independents, the left-wing of Social Democracy, claiming to be authentically Marxist and faithful to principles? They are campaigning for the socialization of industrial enterprises and indemnifying the owners with state treasury bonds. In other words, these capitalists are to receive from the state part of the product of labor, without at the same time having to work. The exploitation of the workers by capital will thereby be perpetuated.

"This runs counter to the whole concept of socialism, which involves two basic elements: abolishing exploitation, and setting up production in a socialist order. The first indicates the essential objective of the proletariat; the second points to technical organization, the national method for increasing the revenues of society. If one accepts the present Social Democratic plans, exploitation continues and the expropriation of industrial enterprises leads quite simply to a kind of state capitalism. This socialization — in the form in which it is urged today by the Social Democrats — is tantamount to duping the proletariat, since it involves just the façade of socialism, behind which exploitation continues to operate. The reason for this attitude is, no doubt, fear of a severe clash with the bourgeoisie at a time when the proletariat, still awakening, has not yet gathered all its forces. But in practice these plans can serve only to reorganize capitalism on new foundations." [4]

---

3. This was one of the points in the program of the left Zimmerwaldians. Pannekoek developed it in the second article he published in *Vorbote*, in passages not included here.

4. *Ibid.*, p. 13. In the article on socialization cited in note 41 of Chapter Five, Pannekoek emphasized that the only possible "expropriation of the expropriators" lies in abolishing profits for the capitalist; and that the only possible means of doing so is the class struggle. And he added

In the final analysis, "both majority socialists and independents are aiming only at maintaining capitalist exploitation. The first is doing so openly; the other, by a furtive trick. The first allows the capitalists to do as they wish; the second looks to the state to implement and organize exploitation. This is why both have only one solution to offer the proletariat: 'Work! Work! Work! harder and longer till you are completely exhausted!' For the reconstruction of the capitalist economy is possible only if the proletariat resigns itself to exploitation at its worst.

"The absolute antagonism between communism and Social Democracy was already evident before the war, though under other names. The question at issue then concerned the tactics to be followed in the class conflict. Under the name of 'left-wing radicals,' an opposition grew up within the ranks of Social Democracy (it was from this opposition that today's veteran communists come); in opposition to the radicals and the revisionists this left-wing faction argued the need to resort to mass action. These confrontations ended by highlighting the counter-revolutionary character of the ideas and tactics advocated by the radical spokesmen, with Kautsky at their head.

"Parliamentary and trade union action had enabled the workers to gain some slight improvement in their condition at a time when capitalism was undergoing a vigorous expansion, while at the same time this action was protecting them against the permanent tendencies of capitalism toward impoverishment. But, over the course of ten years, and despite an organization showing both lively and steady growth, the effectiveness of this protection had been gradually reduced: imperialism had strengthened the industrialists and the army, weakened the Parliament, threw the trade unions back on the defensive, and paved the way to World War. It was clear, therefore, that the old methods of class struggle no longer amounted to very much. This was something that the masses realized instinctively; in many countries, they suddenly resorted to direct action, frequently against the wishes of their leaders, this action taking the form of huge trade union clashes, transport strikes paralyzing the economy, and political demonstrations. Sometimes, these explosions of proletarian rage shook the complacency of the bourgeoisie to the point of forcing them to make concessions; sometimes, too, they were crushed in blood. For the party, Social Democratic leaders sought to utilize these movements for their own ends; they

---

that this socialization, conceived as "juridical expropriation of the capitalists, with payment of indemnities but without economic expropriation," shows that the proletariat are masters only in appearance and are consenting to be exploited anew. Just as the "socialist" government is the continuation of the old bourgeois domination, so too does socialization amount to pursuing the old bourgeois exploitation under the flag of socialism.

acknowledged the usefulness of political strikes for securing specific objectives,[5] but only on condition that such strikes did not exceed the predetermined limits, that they began and ended on the leaders' orders, and, above all, that they conformed to the official tactics laid down by these leaders. Strikes of this orthodox kind did sometimes take place, but without much effect. Forced to pursue a policy of compromise, the impetuous violence natural to spontaneous explosions of the masses was mitigated. The element of class action that immediately creates panic in the ruling bourgeoisie—the fear that the workers' movement might take on a revolutionary character—disappeared from these 'disciplined' mass actions, since every precaution had been taken to ensure their harmlessness.

"The Marxist revolutionaries, who are communists now, had emphasized at that time the extreme narrowness of the dominant conception of Social Democracy. They pointed out that, throughout history, the classes themselves have constituted the motive force of the great social upheavals. Never, in fact, has a revolution occurred as a result of a wise decision reached by an acknowledged leader. When their situation becomes intolerable, the masses go into action for any reason whatsoever, and sweep away the ruling power; then the new class or social category, called to rule the state, adapts that state to its own needs. Only during 50 years of peaceful capitalist development did the illusion arise and flourish that industrial leaders, thanks to their superior clearsightedness, are able to shape hsitory. As members of the central bodies of the party and of trade unions, the deputies take it for granted that *their* acts, *their* speeches, *their* decisions fix the course of events; the masses are to intervene only on *their* invitation and only to lend more weight to *their* words, and then disappear as quickly as possible from the political scene. The masses are to play only the passive role of electing leaders who are to constitute the sole active and real agents of development."

And Pannekoek emphasizes that, if this conception was already too narrow to explain the bourgeois revolutions of the past, it was even less adequate in regard to the proletarian revolution, since the latter required the masses' fullest initiative. He continues with a critique of parliamentary and trade union action, whose main ideas, as repeated in his pamphlet on communist tactics, we shall deal with later. In what follows, we will consider the fifth and final section of the pamphlet now being discussed, a section entitled 'Proletarian Democracy, or the System of Councils.' "[6]

---

5. Thus Bernstein, during the great 1905 debate, personally advocated the general strike as a means of forcing the imperial power to abrogate restricted suffrage. Cf. Eduard Bernstein, *Der politische Massenstreik* (Breslau, 1905), p. 3.

6. *Op. cit.*, pp. 23-29.

"Social Democracy viewed the proletarian conquest of political power in terms of the workers' taking over the state machinery. The state machinery was, therefore, to remain intact and be put at the service of the working class. This was also the opinion of the Social Democratic Marxists—Kautsky, for example—despite the fact that Marx had always taken a completely different attitude. According to Marx and Engels, the state constituted a weapon of oppression created by the ruling class and which was then developed and perfected by them as the proletariat began to revolt in the 19th century. Marx's view was that the proletariat should destroy this state machinery and create completely new organs of administration. He was well aware that the state fulfills many functions that at first sight seem to serve the entire community—protecting the citizens, providing means of transportation, education, administration—but he also knew that all these activities had only one purpose: to look after the interests of capital, to guarantee its domination. That is why Marx could not nurse the illusion that, to emancipate the population, one need only assign other objectives to the state. The proletariat must themselves forge the instrument of their own liberation.

"It was impossible to foresee what form this instrument would take, since this would show itself only in practice. In fact, it did show itself in the Paris Commune, when the proletariat won state power for the first time. Bourgeois and working class Parisians then elected a parliament on the old model; but this parliament immediately became something very different from our types. It did in any way beguile and subdue the people by means of splendid speeches that would allow the clique of capitalists and leaders to continue in peace with their own personal affairs. Far from being a purely parliamentary institution, this assembly was transformed into an institution where everyone really worked. Newly formed commissions saw to it that the new laws were carried out properly. The bureaucracy disappeared as a special, independent class ruling the people, and the separation between the legislative and executive branches was abolished. Those senior civil servants who might have been tempted to frustrate the will of the people now got their mandate from these same people and could be dismissed at any time.

"The short life of the Paris Commune did not allow this new creation to mature. It was born, as it were, instinctively and only as a kind of by-product, within the context of feverish struggle for existence. It took the genius of Marx to see it as the embryonic form that proletarian state power should assume in the future.[7] A step just as novel as it was important was taken in Russia, in

_____

7. Clearly, while the Pannekoek-Kautsky controversy indirectly enabled Lenin to clarify his views in *The State and Revolution*, Pannekoek in turn was affected by the way in which Lenin constructed the Marxian interpretation of the Paris Commune. We might recall that, in a

1905, with the creation of the councils, the soviets, as organs of proletarian revolutionary intervention. These organs, however, did not give political power to the proletariat, even when the conflict was directed the central Workers' Council of Petersburg, which, for some time, exercised considerable power. But when the new revolution broke out in 1917, the soviets then made their appearance as organs of proletarian power. The second historical example of proletarian state power occurred in the German November Revolution, when the proletariat took over the political direction of the country. However, the Russian example revealed much more clearly the forms and the principles that the proletariat would have to adopt to achieve socialism. These are the principles that communism sets up against those of Social Democracy.

"The first principle is the dictatorship of the proletariat. According to Marx, who returns to the subject several times, the proletariat should establish its dictatorship as soon as it has assumed power. Dictatorship means the exercise of power by one class to the exclusion of the others. This, of course, seldom fails to arouse protests: we must demand democracy and equal rights for all, they say, and therefore a dictatorship of this kind, which deprives certain social groups of their rights, is contrary to justice. But such objections have little to do with the foundations of equality. Every class feels it has a right to whatever seems to be good or necessary for it; the exploiter inveighs against injustice whenever it affects his own class. Not long since, the proud aristocracy and the rich, arrogant bourgeoisie were denying equality and political rights to the low, poorly educated worker ground under foot and reduced to slavery; and, at that time, it was already a very clear symptom of the proletarian aspirations towards human dignity that their cry became: 'we have the same rights as you!'

"The democratic principle was the first display of class consciousness within the proletariat, which did not yet dare to say: 'I am nothing, but I want to be everything!' When the general body of workers seeks to control public life and to make supreme decisions, are the criminals, the thieves, the war profiteers, the traders, the landed gentry, the usurer, the stockholders—in short, all who do no useful work and live as parasites on the working population—are they justified in invoking some law or other claimed to be natural or sent down from the heavens? If the ordinary man has the same rights as anyone else to

---

different period and therefore from a different viewpoint, Pannekoek had broached the question of the Commune in 1911 (cf. above, Chapter Three, Note 16). However, the method followed above differs from that of Lenin, to the extent to which it is concerned, not with "restoring" a given body of doctrine valid for all times, but with synthesizing the most advanced forms of action developing out of the class struggle.

decide political questions, then he has surely an even more natural right to live without misery and hunger. And when, to secure the second of these rights, he must violate the first, the democratic spirit is soon reconciled to this.

"The validity of communism does not depend on any abstract right but simply on the needs of the social groups. The proletariat's task is to build up socialist production and to organize work according to a different pattern. But, in doing so, it meets with passionate resistance from the ruling class, which does its utmost to hinder and disturb the realization of these aims. That is why the ruling class should forfeit all rights to have any say in politics. When one class seeks to push ahead and the other to drag its feet, they can only paralyze each other and bring society to a standstill by any attempt at cooperation. In the first phase of capitalism, in the period of full development and consolidation, the bourgeoisie established its dictatorship by establishing property qualifications for the right to vote. Subsequently, it became necessary and prudent to change to a democratic regime, which conceded a pseudo-equality of rights to the workers in order to keep them quiet. This democratic form in no way affected the dictatorship of the bourgeoisie, but merely camouflaged it; it did, however, enable the rising proletariat to unite and to fight for their class interests. After the first victory of the proletariat, the bourgeoisie still retained a number of weapons, both of moral and material, which, if given complete freedom of political action, they could use to disrupt severely, even paralyze, the work of setting up the new proletarian order. It would be necessary to dominate the bourgeoisie and to repress with the utmost vigor any attempt to hinder or to undermine the reorganization of the economy, the worst wort of crime against the people.

"It will perhaps be objected that the exclusion of a particular class always takes on the character of a completely arbitrary and unjust act. This undoubtedly applies to a parliamentary system. But as far as the specific organization of the proletarian state—the system of councils—is concerned, it can be said that all the exploiters and parasites automatically eliminate themselves from participation in the administration of society.

"The system of councils, in effect, forms the second principle of the communist order. Within this framework, the political organization has for its foundation the process of the economy of labor. The parliamentary system rests on the individual in his capacity as citizen. The historical reason for this is that, originally bourgeois society was composed of individual producers isolated from one another. They each produced their merchandise on their own, an the ensemble of these small industrial concerns made up the whole process of production. But in modern society, with its giant industrial complexes and class antagonisms, these foundations are becoming increasingly obsolete. In this connection, the sharp criticisms of the parliamentary system from the theoreticians of French revolutionary syndicalism (Lagardelle, for example) are completely justified. According to the parliamentary idea, every man is primarily a citizen, an individual theoretically equal to everyone else. But in practice man is a worker; the practical content of his existence resides in his activities; and the activities of all these individuals complement one another to form the social process of labor.

"It is neither the state nor politics, but society and labor that form the great human community. The politico-parliamentary practice is to divide up the electorate into electoral districts; but, within the same district, workers, stockholders, shopkeepers, factory hands, in fact all classes and all trades, are haphazardly lumped together simply on the basis of living there. The natural human groups forming part of one an the same whole are production groups, workers in a particular factory or branch of industry, the peasants of a village, and, on a more general level, the various classes. Of course, certain political parties succeed in recruiting their supporters principally from a given class, and represent them; but their success is very limited, since joining a party is decided by one's political convictions, not by one's class. Do not great sectors of the working class unfailingly choose to vote for candidates that are not Social Democrats?

"The new society makes labor and its organization a conscious objective and the basis of all political life, where 'political' signifies outward arrangement of economic life. In the capitalist system, such arrangement is done covertly; in the society of the future, it will be done with complete openness. People themselves act directly within their work groups. The workers of a particular factory select one among themselves to express their will; this representative remains in permanent contact with the rank and file, and is replaceable at any time. Those delegates decide on all matters within their competence, and hold meetings whose composition varies according to whether the agenda is about matters relating to a particular profession, or a particular district, and so forth. The central directive bodies for each area stem from these; at need, they can supply one another with experts.

"These flexible organizations do not offer the least place for bourgeois representation. There is no need to take formal steps to exclude such representation, since the mere fact that someone does not directly participate in a production group precludes his participation in decision making. On the other hand, the former bourgeois who cooperates with the new society according to his capacities—as a factory manager, for instance—can have his say, like any other worker, at the personnel meetings and can decide in common with the others. The professionals at a high level of general culture, such as teachers and doctors, form their own councils, which, within the areas of their competence, education and health services, make decisions jointly with representatives from other areas of labor. In every domain of society, self-administration and total organization represent the means to direct all the forces of the people towards the grat objective; at the summit, all their various energies are synthesized into a central body that insures that each and all are adequately brought into play.[8]

"The system of councils is a state organization, but without the bureaucracy that turns the state into a power external to the people it governs. Engels once remarked that in the proletarian state the government of men will be replaced by the administration of things; this formula is applied here. The subordinate officials, always necessary to the efficient discharge of day-to-day matters, are secretaries holding little desired posts accessible to anyone who has been adequately trained. Administration proper is in the hands of delegates, who can be removed at any time and who receive the same salary as the workers. During some transition periods, it may be difficult to keep strictly to this principle, since every delegate does not necessarily have, from one day to the next, the required aptitudes. However, with a bourgeois press continually praising to the point of absurdity the ability of the present bureaucracy, it is worthwhile recalling that, in November 1918, the German workers' and soldiers' councils successfully carried out such formidable tasks

---

8. By comparing this passage with an earlier one (cf. Chapter Four) the reader will see how Pannekoek, following his usual practice, carries similar ideas and formulas from one text to another, in a particular period. It is, of course, impossible here to compare his views with those of other theoreticians of a similar tendency, each of whom, naturally, emphasizes slightly different aspects within the framework of an overall similar group of problems. However, we shall glance at a few lines here and there in the articles which the Italian, Antonio Gramsci, contributed in 1919 to the *Ordine Nuovo*: "The system of councils tends to assemble all the producers into a unitary organism which, on the basis of the place of work, brings together the laborer and the skilled worker, the office worker and the engineer or technical director.... These organisms form the cells of a new state, the workers' state, founded on a new system of representation, the system of councils. And this state is destined to disappear as a state through its organic incorporation into a world system, the Communist International.... By their struggles, the trade unions have secured labor legislation which has undoubtedly improved the material living conditions of the working class, but they have done so on the basis of a compromise which ensures that the relationships of forces are always unfavorable to the proletariat. The trade union appears, therefore, as an institution of the existing order, destined to hold back the class struggle. Unlike this bureaucratic form, the councils tend to inculcate an active spirit and to create a new world of production and of work, not to carve up the old one." Antonio Gramsci, *Opere*, IX, (Turin, 1954), p. 46, 126, 134. Too fragmentary to have really significant value, these extracts do suggest the idea of a "spontaneous" theoretical convergence, from one region to another, under certain historical conditions.

that the state and military bureaucracy recoiled from them. In the councils, there is no place at all for bureaucrats and career politicians, those complementary instruments of bourgeois domination, because the power to legislate and the power to execute are merged, so the delegates must themselves implement what they have decided. The communist party is therefore very far from having the usual objectives of a political party, or, in other words, of an organization of career politicians — namely, to take direct control of the state machine. Its purpose is not to seize power for its own sake, but to propagate communist principles in order to show the proletariat why and how the system of councils should be established. There is absolute opposition, therefore, between the immediate, practical objectives of Social Democracy and those of communism: the first relies on the organization of the old bourgeois state; the second is laying the foundations of a new political system."

CHAPTER SEVEN

THE SPLIT IN EUROPEAN COMMUNISM

World War I marked a decisive stage in capitalist development in Western Europe, where its immediate aftermath (especially in Germany) was an equally remarkable phenomenon: the emergence of proletarian organs of self-emancipation and the theoretical elaboration of almost completely new strategic perspectives.[1]

At this level, the Western European workers movement converged in some areas with the Russian Revolution; but in both cases, and for very different reasons, the new movement of ideas and of action underwent a rapid regression. It had arisen during a feverish crisis of the state and of society in general. In Germany, however, this crisis in no way affected capitalist relations and the fear that was constantly engendered in the masses through the very conditions of social life in general and of work in particular. This is behind Rosa Luxemburg's remark that: "No proletariat in the world — including the German proletariat — can overnight completely eradicate the traces of an age-old serfdom."[2]

Because all classes have a historical task, they forge for themselves, through impassioned conflicts, a more or less clear-sighted awareness of their objectives. Furthermore, in modern times, the propertied class, because of its social situation, holds a permanent position of strength it can fall back upon when the inevitable reverses come, and which supplies it with a basis for a new historical offensive. On the other hand, the proletariat has no strength, even if at first sight it would seem that the law accords them some. Properly considered, however, these legal guarantees serve merely to protect the conditions that ensure the reproduction of labor. The classical forms of organization such as found in parties and trade unions could only secure the satisfaction of immediate demands and the legal legitimation of social progress at the cost of limited battles led by specialists. In contrast, orthodox Marxist tactics called for — in addition to parliamentary and trade union

---

1. Dirk J. Struik, a Dutch Communist, wrote in 1919: "Three years ago, the most clearsighted minds of the International were still showing themselves to be almost incapable of appreciating the importance of the councils." The allusion to Pannekoek's *Vorbote* articles is clear. Cf. Struik's article in *De Nieuwe Tijd* (1919), p. 466.

2 Rosa Luxemburg, *Rote Fahne*, Dec. 3, 1918.

action—the use of more radical methods, such as mass actions (according to Rosa Luxemburg) or armed insurrection (according to Lenin). In other words, such tactics envisaged a completely different historico-social context, and therefore were based on a different conception of the role of the specialized leaders. In the first case, we are dealing with classical social democracy; in the second, with radical social democracy.

At this point, a new set of tactics made its appearance in Germany and other industrialized countries, which, feeble as it was, rejected both radical and classical tactics of social democracy. We have seen, very briefly, the essential reason for its eventual failure: the conflict had involved only a small fraction of the working class, most of which was imbued with a tradition of peaceful methods incapable of shaking off its daily, age-old habit of servitude. And, although radical social democrats agreed with the emphasis placed on councils by the new tactic, in practice, they gave absolute and unquestioned priority[3] to parliamentarianism—but without admitting it too openly, seeing that such an approach was utterly repudiated by the rank-and-file militants.

By a substantial majority, the young communists decided to resign *en masse* from the trade unions (they were being systematically expelled in any case) and to develop workers unions (*Arbeiterunionen*). These associations had sprung into life with particular force among sailors and miners, particularly those of the Ruhr, after the major wildcat strikes of 1919.[4] Animated by a fighting spirit and violently opposed to the trade union leaders and to the police (who returned the hate in good measure), the workers unions demanded socialization on the basis of the councils system, disarming the *Freikorps* and formation of a workers militia, and the resumption of relations between Germany and Soviet Russia. Based on the direct representation of the workers through a network of delegates, they were also demanding labor reforms, such as the seven-hour day.[5]

The social democrats of the two parties had at that time one sole concern:

---

3. At the Heidelberg conference, Paul Levi, the perfect "gentleman-dandy" who coopted to the Central Committee of the KPD, defended the radical theses on parliamentary and trade unionist action: "They contain nothing new; they even contain what should be self-evident to those who are united in a political party." *Bericht über den 2. Parteitag der KPD* (October 1919), p. 25.

4. Cf. P. von Oertzen, "Die Grosse Streiks der Ruhrarbeiterschaft in Früjahr 1919," *Vierteljahrshefte für Zeitgeschichte,* 1958.

5. Cf. especially H. Bötcher, *Zur revolutionären Gewerschaftsbewegung in Amerika, Deutschland und England* (Jena, 1922), which gives a complete account of the movement and its ideas. Cf. also Peter von Oertzen, *Betriebsräte in der Novemberrevolution* (Düsseldorf, 1963), which devotes a chapter—unfortunately very short (pp. 207-218)—to the "role of the unions in the council movement."

"return to normal," to the old type of administrative structure, suitably democratized to meet their new needs. Within this framework, the workers councils served a dual purpose; but, in a period marked by turbulence, they were still able to avoid strong leaders.[6] That is why the leaders asked Parliament to "anchor" the councils in the republican Constitution. Parliament was happy to oblige, adopting on February 4, 1920, a definitive legal statute relegating the status of industrial committees (*Betriebsräte*) to that of a mere extension of the trade unions, a sort of training ground for their future officials. This is why the left-communists, seeking to adapt to the situation, wholeheartedly supported the workers unions (*Arbeiterunionen*), those associations born naturally from the struggle against the traditional organizational forms.

The majority of the left-communists were in no way challenging the need for a political party.[7] But in their view, this party should be that of an elite, firmly linked to principles, adapting them to the situation and propagating them—something impossible for a mass party, inevitably subjected to a bureaucratic apparatus, dedicated to the representation of the immediate interests of the workers, and therefore committed to sacrificing the ultimate objective in favor of conciliatory methodds. The opposite was true of the workers' unions: animated by the Communist Party and possessing a rigorously independent class consciousness, they transformed themselves through the class struggle into revolutionary workers councils, into organs of the proletarian dictatorship. The old methods had had their day; the capitalist system was moving toward its fatal crisis; it was necessary to prepare the way for new forms, to build the "unitary organization."

The tension between the radicals and the leftists became more acute. Indeed, the radical current scarcely existed outside the circle of party leaders, the Berlin *Zentrale* and a few provincial committees—a clique, but one supported by the executive of the Third International, and having as its sole objective a merger with the socialist independents. The latter were at a crossroads: on the one hand, nothing fundamental separated them from the classical tactics of the Majority Socialists; on the other hand, most of them

---

6.   A jurist, Brigl-Matthias, in *Das Betriebsratprobleme* (Berlin, 1926), p. 2, stresses that the law was intended to curb the attempts at "wildcat" occupations on the basis "of political workers councils and of revolutionary industrial organizations."

7.   In this connection, Wolfheim declared at the Heidelberg Congress: "Let me say emphatically, we have never regarded the existence of the KPD as superfluous.... Today, the proletariat forms, not a unified party, but a unified class. That is why its dictatorship cannot be a dictatorship of the party.... To those who say: 'You are trying to transform the party into a propaganda center,' we answer, 'Certainly! In our view, the party's mission is to enlighten,...to propagate the idea of the unions as an organizational basis of a system of councils.' " *Op. cit.*, pp. 31-32.

were convinced that cooperation with the bourgeois parties would almost obliterate the prospects for effective reforms. Moreover, the independents did not favor direct action, any more than did the Central Committee of the German Communist Party or the leadership of the International. They called such action putschist tactics, which would frighten the voters and therefore injure their parliamentary tactics.

The *Zentrale* took steps to exclude its opponents wherever possible, but this was not enough. Determined to deliver a decisive blow, they held a Party Congress at Heidelberg in October 1919 despite laws forbidding it. Making use of such secrecy, Paul Levi assembled some of the most reliable members and got most of them to vote to exclude the opposition elements. But it was a paper majority, purely bureaucratic. Thus, at Berlin, where the party claimed 12,000 members, an eye witness noted, [8] "there were 36 people in the room" when William Piek returned to report on the Congress.

In the months that followed, the excluded members vainly called on the party to convene a truly representative congress. In the meantime, in March 1920, a reactionary attempt was made at a coup d'état, known as the Kapp Putsch. A general strike, ordered by the trade unions, quickly put an end to this. At that time the sentiment among the workers favored formation of a "workers government" involving a coalition of groups extending from the Christian trade unionists to the independents. After some hesitation, the *Zentrale* chose to support the official strike under prescribed conditions, urging the workers not to take to the streets, and solemnly promising its "loyal opposition" to the eventual "workers government." [9]

The "excluded" members resorted to a campaign of posters and handbills. But they were excluded not only from the party. Doomed for the most part to unemployment because of their political activities, they were also excluded from production—an additional reason for their being, once again, the spearhead of the movement "at the street level," especially in the insurgent Ruhr. Shortly afterward, a formative congress was held in Berlin, and, on April 3, the Communist Workers Party of Germany (KAPD) came into existence, with about 30,000 members. [10] The new party drew from a party of workers unions which—at the Hanover Congress, where it claimed to have 80,000 adherents—had just joined together to form the Central Workers Union of Germany (AAUD). [11]

8. Ruth Fischer, *Stalin and German Communism* (Cambridge, Mass., 1948), p. 119.

9. O. Flechtheim, *Die K.P.D. in der Weimarer Republik* (Offenbach, 1948), pp. 62-66.

10. Cf. Bernard Reichenbach, "Zur Geschichte der K.A.P.D.," *Archiv für die Geschichte des Sozialismus und der Arbeiterbewegung*, XIII (1928), pp. 117-40.

11. For a complete account, see the anonymous study, "Le Mouvement pour les Conseils in Allemagne," *Informations Correspondance Ouvrières*, 42 (Aug.-Sept. 1965)—a translation of an

Needless to say, Pannekoek followed these events very closely, since similar confrontations were occurring in different sections of the International. In Holland itself, a split was about to take place that created the KAP-N and the AAB-B (comprising especially the textile workers of Friesland) but with the new organizational form being a minority group in relation to the parliamentarian Communist Party. The whole range of problems raised by these internal conflicts was the center of the debate at the Second Congress of the International (July 1920). It was in this chaotic context that Pannekoek wrote the pamphlet presented in our next chapter.[12]

---

article first published in *Radencommunismus*, 3 (1938).

12. Cf. the two articles he wrote in 1919 for *Nieuwe Tijd*: "Strijd over de Kommunistische Taktiek in Duitsland," pp. 693-99; "Het Duitse Kommunisme," pp. 777-85.

CHAPTER EIGHT

WORLD REVOLUTION AND COMMUNIST TACTICS [1]

> *"Theory, too, changes into a material force only when it penetrates the masses. Theory is capable of penetrating the masses...only when it becomes radical."*
>
> Marx

I.

"The transformation of capitalism into communism depends on two forces, one proceeding from the other: a material force and a spiritual force. The material development of the economy clarifies the real course of things, and this, in its turn, engenders a revolutionary will. It was from general tendencies within the capitalist system that the Marxist system was born. Originally a theory of the Socialist Party and later of the Communist Party, Marxism confers upon the revolutionary movement a powerful spiritual homogeneity. While Marxism slowly penetrates a part of the proletariat, the masses are led, through direct experiences, to see that capitalism is in an untenable position. The World War and the accelerated economic collapse reveal the objective need for revolution, even while the masses have not yet understood the idea of communism. This basic contradiction underlies the various clashes, interruptions and waverings that make the revolution a slow and painful process. Undoubtedly, theory is taking on a new urgency and is penetrating the masses with increasing effect; but despite all this, when confronted with practical tasks that have suddenly become gigantic, these two phenomena themselves also slow down.

"In Western Europe, the development of the revolution is principally

---

1. Anton Pannekoek, *Weltrevolution und kommunistische Taktik* (Vienna, 1920), p. 50. This edition includes a "postscript" absent from the other versions. The text first appeared in *Nieuwe Tijd* beginning March 15, 1920 (no. 6, pp. 161-69; then 193-207 and 257-71). It bears the pen name K. Horner, as does the German version published in Petrograd, entitled *Die Entwicklung der Weltrevolution und die Taktik des Kommunismus*. This version was also published in *Kommunismus*, the theoretical organ of the Communist International for southeastern Europe (*Kommunismus*, Aug. 1, 1920, pp. 976-1018).

determined by the stagnation of the capitalist economy and by the example of Soviet Russia. We need not dwell on what enabled the Russian proletariat to succeed in a relatively quick and easy manner: the weaknesses of the bourgeoisie, the alliance with the peasants, a wartime crisis. The example of a state where the workers exercise power, where they have triumphed over capitalism and are thus in a position to build up communism, was to make a deep impression on the proletariat of the whole world. Of course, this example by itself would have been insufficient to incite the workers of other countries to revolution. The spirit of man is responsive, above all else, to the influence of material conditions of the existing milieu; consequently, if the forces of the different types of international capitalism had remained intact, the interest in what happens in Russia would have been much less intense. When Rutgers[2] returned from Russia, he described the masses as having a 'respectful but timorous admiration' for the Russian Revolution, but as lacking 'the will to act to save Russia and the world.' At the end of the war, a prompt expansion of the economy was generally expected in the West, while the lying press continually described Russia as in the grips of chaos and barbarism. But since then the opposite has occurred: chaos is increasing in the old, civilized countries, while the new order is consolidating itself in Russia. And now, in these countries, too, the masses are on the march. Economic stagnation is the principal motive force of revolution."

The crisis raged throughout Western Europe, culminating in widespread strikes that gradually assumed the appearance of conscious revolutionary battles; "without being communists, the masses nevertheless pursue communist objectives."[3] An advance guard formed, which adhered to the Third International and severed its organizational links to social democracy, both in Western Europe where protection of the bourgeois state required the formation of socialist governments, and in Italy where "the will of the masses to revolutionary combat, which shows itself in a permanent minor war against the government and the bourgeoisie, makes it possible to accept without question a mixture of left-wing socialist, revolutionary trade-unionist, and communist ideas." And the unexpectedly strong resistance of Soviet Russia to

2. S. J. Rutgers, a Tribunist, went to Russia with his wife toward the end of 1918, via the United States and Japan. A delegate for Holland and the United States, with consultative vote, at the First Congress of the Communist International, he left Petrograd for Amsterdam in October 1919, his mission being to organize there the auxiliary Bureau of the Third International, whose creation had been envisaged at the Congress. For a time, he made common cause with the ultra-leftists. An agronomist engineer, he was later to return to Russia during the Stalinist era.

3. A few days after these lines were written, the Ruhr insurrection occurred, accompanied by the formation of a "red army" in which the Communist Workers' Party militants were the most active. Cf. Gerhard Colm, *Beitrag zur Geschichte und Soziologie des Ruhraufstandes vom Marz-April 1920* (Essen, 1921), especially pp. 69-83.

the assaults of world reaction increased still more Russia's influence over the socialist left. "Many communists, however, tend to see only the steady increase of positive forces, without taking the weaknesses into account. The proletarian revolution clearly seems to have taken shape as a result of the appearance of communism and of the Russian example. But powerful factors have also appeared that will make this revolution an extremely difficult and complicated process."

II.

"Slogans, programs and tactics do not flow from abstract principles but are determined solely by experience, by real praxis. What the communists think about their objectives and about the road to be followed ought to conform to actual revolutionary praxis. The Russian Revolution and the unfolding of the German Revolution offer us a body of revealing facts about the motive forces, conditions and forms of proletarian revolution.

"In the Russian Revolution the proletariat seized political power with an impetuosity, which, at the time, took Western European observers completely by surprise. And today, considering the obstacles we face in Western Europe, it still seems extraordinary, even though the causes are clearly discernible. In the enthusiasm of the early days, it was natural that the difficulties of the revolution would be underestimated. The Russian Revolution had, in effect, set before the eyes of the world proletariat the principles of the new world in all their purity and splendor: the dictatorship of the proletariat,[4] the system of soviets as the form of the new democracy, the reorganization of industry, of agriculture and of education. In many respects it presented such a clear and almost idyllic picture of the nature and content of the proletarian revolution that it could seem almost simplicity itself to follow this example. But the German Revolution has shown that it was not as simple as all that, and that the forces at work on that occasion are at work throughout Europe.

"When German imperialism collapsed in November 1918, the working class was completely unprepared to assume power. Exhausted both spiritually and morally from four years of war, and mentally imprisoned within the traditions of social democracy, they were unable, in the few weeks following the disappearance of bourgeois governmental power, to understand their

---

4. In his major pamphlet, *Workers' Councils*, Pannekoek returns to this idea, pointing out, however, that if it has taken on "the ominous sound" with the dictatorship of a totalitarian party, "as in Russia," it remains nonetheless true that: "When production is regulated by the producers themselves, the formerly exploiting class automatically is excluded from taking part in the decisions, without any artificial stipulation. Marx's conception of the dictatorship of the proletariat now appears to be identical with the labor democracy of council organization" (p. 51).

tasks clearly. Although communist propaganda had been intensive, it had not been in operation long enough to remedy the lack of working class preparation. The German bourgeoisie learned the lessons of the Russian Revolution much better than did the proletariat; while draping themselves in red to lull the suspicions of the workers, they immediately set about reconstituting their means of domination. Of their own accord, the workers relinquished their powers to the leaders of social democracy and parliamentary democracy.[5] Far from disarming the bourgeoisie, the worker-soldiers allowed themselves to be disarmed; the most activist of the workers groups were overcome by the new units of volunteers and by the bourgeoisie in the ranks of the national guard."

While this experience remains unique in Western Europe, it "nevertheless has characteristics of a general kind and repercussions of considerable importance. It highlights *the nature of the forces* that will necessarily make the revolution in Western Europe a long, drawn-out process.

"...In the phases of accelerated revolutionary development, tactical differences are quickly reconciled in the course of action, or even fail to emerge distinctly; a work of systematic agitation enlightens the minds, while the masses spontaneously erupt and action completely overthrows the old ideas. However, when a phase of accelerated stagnation sets in, when the masses allow anything at all to be inflicted upon them, and when the revolutionary movement seems to have lost its attraction; when obstacles accumulate and when the enemy seems to emerge stronger than ever from each encounter; when the Communist Party is weak and suffers defeat after defeat—then divisions appear and there is a search for new ways and new strategies. Two tendencies have emerged and are essentially the same in every country, despite minor local differences. The first is a tendency that seeks to radicalize the minds of men, to enlighten by word and action, and therefore attempts with the utmost vigor to challenge old ideas with new principles. The second tendency, in order to woo the reluctant masses to practical activity, assiduously seeks to avoid shocking them, and therefore emphasizes what unites rather than what separates. The first seeks to provoke a clear and distinct cleavage, while the second is concerned only with gathering the masses together; radical would be an appropriate name for the first, and opportunist for the second. In Western Europe at the present time, the revolution is meeting with considerable resistance, while the power of Soviet

5.   Held in Berlin Dec. 16-21, 1918, the "General Congress of Soldiers' and Workers' Councils of Germany" was dominated and manipulated by Social Democratic delegates of the type most aligned with the state. It refused to set itself up as an executive body, declared in favor of a National Assembly, and elected a "central council" composed of former "Kaiser Socialists." Cf. Kolb, *op. cit.*, pp. 197-216.

Russia, still intact after numerous attempts of the Entente governments to bring it down, is making a deep impression on the masses. Therefore certain workers groups, hitherto hesitant, are turning more and more toward the Third International;[6] it is beyond doubt, therefore, that opportunism will take on a singular importance within the Communist International.

"Opportunism does not necessarily resort to easygoing, reassuring and engaging words giving radicals the monopoly on more aggressive language; on the contrary, it all too often indulges in frenetic declamations to hide its lack of clear, principled tactics; furthermore, its nature causes it to rely in revolutionary situations on a single action. It tends to look only to the immediate without bothering about the future, so that it remains at the surface of things instead of probing into their depths. When available forces prevent it from achieving its objective, it does not try to strengthen these forces, but seeks to reach the objective by roundabout ways. Seeking immediate success, it sacrifices to that success the conditions of a future, lasting achievement. There must, in its view, be a union with other 'progressive' groups, and concessions made to their outmoded ideas, if nothing else in order to divide the enemy—the coalition of capitalist classes—and thus create more favorable conditions of struggle. However, it emerges clearly that such power can only be the shadow of power, the personal power of a few leaders, not that of the proletarian class, and that this contradiction begets only confusion, corruption and dissention. Were the working class to come into governmental power without having really acquired the maturity needed for its exercise, they would inevitably either lose power very soon or be forced to make so many concessions to backward tendencies that this power would crumble from within. Dividing the enemy—the recipe of reformism *par excellence*—is not a tactical move that destroys the internal unity of the bourgeoisie, but one that deceives, misleads, and weakens the proletariat. Of course, it can happen that the proletarian communist *avant-garde* must necessarily assume political power before the normal conditions exist for it to do so; but in that case, the clarity, knowledge, unity and autonomy that the masses have acquired will serve as a basis for a later development toward communism.

"The history of the Second International abounds in examples of this policy of opportunism, and the latter is already beginning to show itself within the Third International. For the Second, it consisted of striving to achieve the

---

6.   The reference is to talks between the Communist International branches of the socialist left in different countries—negotiations which, in Germany, led to merger of two-thirds of the Independents with the meager troops of the Central Committee of the German Communist Party in December 1920.

socialist objective through a coalition of non-socialist workers groups and other classes, and employing every means to win them over. These practices were bound to lead to the decomposition of the movement and its ultimate collapse. At the present time, the Third International is in a very different situation, because the phase of the harmonious expansion of capitalism is over — the phase in which social democracy could do nothing but enlighten the masses through a policy based on principles, in preparation for the revolutionary phase to come. Capitalism has collapsed; the world cannot wait for the day when our propaganda will have led the majority of men to understand exactly what communism is; the masses must intervene as soon as possible to save the world and to save themselves. Of what use is a small party and its loyalty to principles when what is needed is the intervention of the masses? Has not opportunism, which seeks a rapid grouping of large masses, some reason to claim that it is bowing to necessity?

"However, a huge mass party or a coalition of different parties is no more capable of leading a successful rebellion than is a small radical party. Revolution is the work of the masses; it begins spontaneously. Certain actions decided upon by a party can sometimes (rarely, however) be the point of departure, but the determining forces lie elsewhere, in the psychic factors deeply embedded in the subconscious of the masses and in the great events of world politics. The task of a revolutionary party is the advance propagation of clear knowledge, so that, within the masses, some may come to know what should be done in a crisis and will be able to judge the situation for themselves. And, during the revolution, the party should establish the program, the slogans and the directives that the masses spontaneously recognize to be correct and appropriate — as the precise formulation of their own revolutionary objectives. It is in this sense that the party directs the combat. As long as the masses are inactive, the party's efforts may seem useless; however, the principles propagated reach many people who for the moment are outside the party, and, in the course of the revolution, these principles take on an active force which helps guide such people along the desired path. On the other hand, to soften these principles as a preliminary step to forming a more broadly based party through coalitions and concessions enables people with confused ideas to acquire, in time of revolution, an ascendency that the masses cannot challenge because of their own deficient education. To compromise with outmoded conceptions is to move toward power without first securing its fundamental condition — the complete transformation of ideas. And this ultimately hinders the course of the revolution. Moreover, the effectiveness of such a policy is extremely illusory, since the most radical ideas can penetrate the masses only during a period of revolution; at other times, the masses tend to be moderate. A revolution is always accompanied by a profound upheaval of ideas among the masses; it thus creates the precondition for the revolution. That is why it is incumbent on the Communist Party to direct the revolution on the basis of clear principles aimed at transforming the world.

"What divides the Communists from the Social Democrats is the intransigence with which the Communists give priority to the new principles (the system of soviets and the dictatorship of the proletariat). Opportunism in the Third International uses as much as possible the forms and methods of warfare bequeathed to it by the Second International. After the Russian Revolution had replaced parliamentarianism by a system of soviets and built up the trade union movement on a factory basis, certain attempts — the first of their kind — to copy this model were made in Europe.[7] The German Communist Party boycotted the Reichstag elections and propagated the idea of an organized withdrawal from the trade unions.[8] But in 1919, when the revolution began to ebb and stagnate, the party leaders decided on a new tactic, reverting to parliamentarianism and supporting the old trade union organizations against the new organizations of workers unions (*Arbeiter-unionen*). As a decisive argument, they urged the party not to cut itself off from the masses. The masses, they argued, continued to think in parliamentary terms, and therefore the best means of reaching them was through electoral campaigns and parliamentary speeches, as well as mass entry into the trade unions, with about seven million members...." According to Radek,[9] "in Western Europe, the proletarian revolution will be a long drawn-out process during which communism should use every means of propaganda. Parliamentarianism and the trade union movement are the principal weapons of the proletariat, to which should be added, as a new battle aim, the gradual securing of workers' control.

---

7. Pannekoek, when alluding to the workers' councils of Germany, Italy and Scotland, was clearly unaware that from January 1918 on the Russian trade unions had taken back from the factory committees — at least on the juridical level and with the latter's more or less qualified consent — the powers which they were exercising within the industrial enterprises. Cf. P. Avrich, "The Bolshevik Revolution and Workers' Control in Russian Industry," *Slavic Review*, XXII:1, 1963. At the time, however, such ignorance was general among the few Communists in Western Europe who were at all interested in the effective power structure of the U.S.S.R.

8. Cf. A. and D. Prudhommeaux, *op. cit.*, pp. 45-56.

9. Pannekoek refers here to a pamphlet "composed in prison by our friend Radek" and dealing with "the development of the world revolution and the tasks of the Communist Party." In fact, Radek wrote two such pamphlets at the time: one before the Heidelberg Congress (*Die Entwicklung der deutschen Revolution und die Aufgaben der K.P.*), the other after (*Die Entwicklung der Weltrevolution und die Taktik der K.P. in Kampfe um die Diktatur des Proletariats*). No doubt Pannekoek's reference is to the second and more complete of these; he also borrowed the title for his own pamphlet.

"An examination of the principles, conditions and the difficulties of the proletarian revolution in Western Europe will show whether or not this line of argument has any justification.

III.

"It is often maintained that, in Western Europe, the revolution will continue for a long time because the bourgeoisie is much more powerful there than it was in Russia. Let us analyze this strength. Is it numerical? The proletarian masses are far more numerous than the bourgeoisie. Does it lie in the fact that the bourgeoisie dominates all of economic life? This is indeed a primary element of strength, but such a domination has perceptibly lessened and, in Central Europe, the economy is completely bankrupt. Is it ultimately the result of the bourgeoisie's grip on the state and on the means of repression? Certainly this has enabled the bourgeoisie to prevail continually over the proletariat, which is why the conquest of state power is the first objective of the proletariat. However, in November 1918, state power in Germany and Austria did fall into the hands of the working class. The state's repressive machinery was absolutely in abeyance, and the masses were reigning as masters. Despite all this, the bourgeoisie succeeded in reconstructing this state power and in replacing the yoke on the workers. This shows the existence of another factor of the power of this class, a hidden factor, one which remained intact and which enabled them to re-establish their domination, however shattered it may have seemed. This hidden factor is the spiritual power of the bourgeoisie over the proletariat. It explains why the masses still remain totally subject to bourgeois ideas, to the extent that, when bourgeois domination collapses, the masses rebuild it with their own hands.

"The German experience clearly raises the great problem of revolution in Western Europe. In these countries, the bourgeois mode of production and the advanced culture linked to it for centuries have deeply impregnated the way the masses feel and think. That is why the spiritual characteristics of these masses are completely absent in the countries of the East, which have never known this domination by bourgeois culture. And herein lies the primary reason for the different directions taken by the revolution in the East and in the West. In England, France, Holland, Scandinavia, Italy, Germany, a strong bourgeoisie has flourished since the middle ages, on the basis of petty bourgeoisie and primitive capitalist production. After the overthrow of the feudal system, a strong class independent of the peasants and masters of their own goods, developed in the rural areas. This basis enabled the spiritual life of the bourgeoisie to blossom into a vigorous national culture, especially in the maritime countries, such as France and England, the first to undergo capitalist development. In the 19th century, capitalism, encompassing the whole of the economy, and bringing even the most remote farms within the framework of the world economy, perfected still further this national culture, and, with the help of its propaganda mechanisms — press, school, church — drummed it into the minds of the masses, both the newly proletarianized and urbanized elements and those remaining in the rural districts. This was the situation, not only in the countries where capitalism had originated, but also, in slightly different forms, in America and Australia, where the Europeans had founded new states, and in the countries of Central Europe — Germany, Austria, Italy — where the new capitalist development was grafted onto a small, stagnant landholder economy and petty-bourgeois culture. When it penetrated into Eastern Europe, capitalism encountered a completely different situation and completely different traditions. In Russia, Poland, Hungary, and in Eastern Germany, there was no powerful bourgeoisie with a long established spiritual domination; the pattern there was defined by relationships within a system of primitive agricultural production — the big landed proprietors, patriarchal feudalism, and the village community. Communism there found itself dealing with a people more primitive, more simple, more open, and therefore more receptive. The socialists of Western Europe would often express their amused surprise at seeing the 'ignorant' Russians in the front line of the workers' cause. In this connection, as an English delegate to the Amsterdam Conference[10] rightly pointed out, it may be that the Russians are ignorant, but the English workers are so stuffed with prejudices that communist propaganda among them is much more difficult. These 'prejudices,' however, constitute only a primary aspect of the mode of bourgeois thinking that saturates the English masses and the American masses of Western European origin.

"This mode of thinking, in its opposition to the proletarian-communist conception of the world, involves conceptions so varied and so confused that one can scarcely sum it up in a few words. Its primary quality is an individualism that goes back to the first petty bourgeois and peasant forms of labor, and which yields only reluctantly to the new concept of proletarian community. In the Anglo-Saxon countries, this individualism deeply impregnates both the bourgeoisie and the proletariat. The outlook does not reach beyond the workplace; it certainly does not embrace the whole social group. Steeped in the principle of the division of labor, these individualists do

---

10. Cf. note 24 below.

not regard 'politics,' the direction of the whole society, as a matter that concerns everyone, but as a monopoly of the ruling class, as a branch of activity reserved for highly specialized career politicians. A century of assiduous interaction of a material and also of a spiritual kind through art and literature has inculcated in the masses a sense of belonging on the national level, a sentiment that can sometimes take the form of class solidarity at that level, but which in no way facilitates international action. This feeling remains firmly implanted in the subconscious, as is seen in the indifference shown about what is happening elsewhere, or, at best, by a façade of internationalism.

"Bourgeois culture in the proletariat is first manifested in the guise of a spiritual tradition. The masses, prisoners of this tradition, think in terms of ideology and not of reality; bourgeois thinking always assumes an ideological character. But this ideology and this tradition in no way constitute a homogeneous whole. As the result of innumerable and age-old class confrontations, spiritual reflexes develop in political and religious systems. The proletarians that adhere to them are therefore subdivided into distinct groups according to their ideological conceptions, churches, sects, parties. In addition, the bourgeois past of the proletariat is manifested in an organizational tradition that runs counter to the class unity reqired for the coming of a new world; the workers are reduced, within these traditional organizations, to the role of followers of a bourgeois vanguard. During these ideological conflicts, it is the intellectulas who become the direct leaders. The intellectuals — churchmen, teachers, writers, journalists, artists, politicians — form a large class which serves to uphold, develop and propagate bourgeois culture. They transmit this culture to the masses and serve as intermediaries between the power of capital and the interests of the masses. Their spiritual authority over the masses strengthens the hegemony of capital. Conseqently, the oppressed masses cannot rise in revolt under the leadership of the intellectuals. And when these leaders openly pass into the capitalist camp, the cohesion and discipline they acqired through conflict then makes them the strongest mainstays of the system."

This was the case with Christian ideology, which showed itself to be reactionary after having supported the conflict of the petty bourgeoisie with the state — that of the Catholics at the time of the *Kulturkampf*, for example.[11] The same is true of Social Democracy, which has helped to

---

11. In fact the trade union associations — most notably in the Ruhr — first came into existence, in the late 1860s, through the initiative of Catholic priests. Ridiculed by the Protestant authorities and frowned on at that time by the bosses, they were incapable of assuring an autonomous representation of the workers and soon yielded to formations inspired by Social

extirpate the old ideologies but which, "on the other hand, is grounded in the spiritual dependence of the masses on political and other leaders, whom the masses regard as specialists and to whom therefore they hand over the conduct of major class matters of a general kind, instead of seeing to them themselves. The cohesion and discipline forged by 50 years of impassioned conflict could not destroy capitalism, because they were linked to the power that organizations and leaders exercised over the proletarian masses. This was the power that, in August 1914 and in November 1918, made the masses a passive instrument of the bourgeoisie, imperialism and reaction. The spiritual hegemony that the bourgeois past exercises over the workers has led to a splitting of the proletariat into ideologically antagonistic groups in different countries of Western Europe, thus precluding any class unity. Originally, Social Democracy tried to establish unity, but because of its opportunist tactics, these efforts were useless.

"The domination of bourgeois ideology over the masses does not rule out the fact that, in times of crisis, when the masses are driven to despair and to action, the power of tradition is temporarily eclipsed — as in Germany of November 1918. However, the ideology soon reasserts itself and becomes one of the factors contributing to the re-emergence of the bourgeoisie. The German example shows the concrete forces at work, forces that we will refer to as the hegemony of the bourgeois: the veneration of abstract forumulas, such as 'democracy'; the force of habit in thinking, such as in the idea that socialism can be established by parliamentary leaders and through a socialist government; the proletariat's lack of self-confidence, as shown by the influence exercised over it by the monstrous dissemination of false reports about Russia; the proletariat's lack of faith in its own resources; but above all else, the belief in the party, the organization, the leaders who, over several decades, personified the revolutionary conflict and its objectives. The enormous material and spiritual power of these organizations, these gigantic machines created by the masses themselves through long years of hard work — machines that embodied the tradition of forms of conflict appropriate for the entire period that the workers' movement had been a part of the vigorous development of capitalism — now crushed all the revolutionary tendencies that were awakening among the masses.

"This case was not to remain an isolated one. The contradictions between the proletariat's spiritual immaturity, as evidenced by the strength of bourgeois traditions within it, and the rapid collapse of the capitalist economy can be resolved only through the process of revolutionary

---

Democracy. Cf. Walter Neumann, *Die Gewerkschaften in Ruhrgebiet* (Cologne, 1951), pp. 10ff. They degenerated into paternalism and parochialism.

development, by revolts and seizures of power, and with many reverses; for this contradiction is not an accidental one, since the spiritual maturity required to win power and freedom is inconceivable within the framework of a flourishing capitalism. That is why the idea of a revolutionary course of action—during which the proletariat would long and vainly besiege the fortress of capital with both old and new methods of warfare, and then one day conquer it completely—is among the least likely of hypotheses. Suddenly, the tactic of the well-organized and prolonged siege led by clever strategists is without foundation. The tactical problem is not one of establishing the feasibility of a quick conquest of power, since in this case there would be an illusion of power. But, rather, this problem is one of developing the preconditions within the proletariat for a permanent class power. No minority agitators can solve this problem, since its solution can come only through the action of the revolutionary class as a whole. Even if the prospect of such a seizure of power seems to kindle little enthusiasm in the populace, this does not mean that they are categorically opposed; on the contrary, it indicates that, to the extent to which the population has not been won over to communism, they are ready at all times to close their ranks, with the utmost vigor, in support of the reaction against the revolution. A party dictatorship of such fragility can only mask itself behind an alliance that strongly suggests the proverbial 'hangman's noose.' "[12]

"When the proletariat has succeeded, through a powerful insurrection, in breaking the bankrupt domination of the bourgeoisie and when its more clear-sighted vanguard, the Communist Party, has assumed political leadership, then its imperative mission is to use whatever means necessary to combat the weaknesses of the working class and to strengthen its power, so that it can meet the challenge of the revolutionary conflicts to come. The main objective should be to raise the masses to the highest level of activity, to stimulate their spirit of initiative, to increase their self-confidence, enabling them to decide for themselves the task they must fulfill and the means to do this. To achieve this, the predominance of the traditional organizations and old leaders must come to an end—and this precludes any type of coalition government, since it can only weaken the proletariat. New forms of organization must be perfected; the material strength of the masses must be

---

12. These lines refer primarily to the Hungarian Commune. This partly explains why this text appeared in *Kommunismus*, which was predominantly the voice of those who saw in the collaboration of the Hungarian Communists and Socialists one of the main causes of the collapse of August 1919. Cf. Ladislaus Rudas, "Die Proletarierdiktatur in Ungarn," *Kommunismus*, 1, 1921; and the documents published by Helmut Gruber in the collection, *International Communism in the Era of Lenin* (New York, 1967), pp. 135-69.

increased. Only in this way will it be possible to reorganize production as the most effective defense against the attacks of foreign capital; for, if this is not done, the counter-revolution will reappear in strengthened form.

"The power held by the bourgeoisie in this phase is simply the spiritual dependence of the proletariat. The development of the revolution lies in the process of the proletariat's emancipating itself from this dependence, from this tradition of past ages, an emancipation possible only through the direct experience of class struggles. When capitalism has held sway for a long time, and when, in consequence, the workers' struggle extends over several generations, the proletariat is compelled, in each period, to forge for itself the methods, forms, and means of combat suitable for the stage of development reached by capitalism. But soon these forms cease to be viewed for what they really are: instruments with a time limit to their usefulness. In fact, they are overvalued, viewed as permanent forms, absolutely valid and ideologically sanctified — only to become later on chains from which the proletariat must struggle to free itself. While the working class is undergoing an accelerated transformation and development, its leaders remain fixed in the mental attitudes of an earlier completed stage, and become spokesmen for a bygone phase. Therefore these leaders' influence is liable to hinder the movement; the old forms of action, hardened in dogmas and organizations, are elevated to objectives in themselves, and this makes a new orientation and adaptation to new conditions of conflict more difficult. This is equally true of the present period. In each phase of its evolution, the class struggle should shake off the traditions of the earlier phases, in order to focus clearly on its own tasks and to carry them to completion. The revolution, therefore, developes through a process of internal conflict. In effect, then, it is within the proletariat's own ranks that the main obstacles are generated over which the proletariat must triumph. Once these obstacles have been overcome and the proletariat has risen above its own limitations, the path is open to communism."

IV.

"During the period of the Second International, the two main forms of the class conflict were parliamentarianism and trade unionism.

"It was the first International Workingmen's Association that originally formulated the principles of this tactical approach. It thus took up a position (in a manner consistent with Marxist theory) toward the ideas born in the precapitalist, petty-bourgeois phase, and which were therefore outmoded with the passing of that phase. According to those conceptions, the proletarian class struggle should take on the character of an uninterrupted struggle to improve the workers' conditions, culminating in the conquest of political power. Since the era of bourgeois revolutions and armed insurrections was completed, political action could be pursued only within the framework of national states, and trade union action only within an even narrower framework. The First International was doomed to break up for this reason and also because of the division between the new tactical approach, which it was not attempting to implement, and anarchism, in which the old ideas and methods of struggle survived. It bequeathed this new tactical approach to those charged with carrying it out—that is, to the Social Democratic Parties, which were springing up everywhere simultaneously with the trade unions. When the Second International developed from this legacy, in the form of a rather loosely knit federation, it had to confront once again the traditions of the preceding period, embodied in anarchism, and, it regarded the heritage of the First International as a foundation to be adopted without question.

"Today, every militant communist knows why these methods of struggle were necessary and useful. When the working class first effectively emerged and grew with capitalism, it was not yet in a position to create organs allowing it to direct and control social life, nor indeed would the idea of doing so have occurred to it. It first had to discover its own way and understand what is meant by capitalism and clas power. Through propaganda, the Social Democratic Party, vanguard of the proletariat, had to unmask the nature of the regime, and, by establishing class demands, point out to the masses what their objectives should be. That is why it was necessary for their representatives to go into Parliament, the center of bourgeois domination, to voice their views there and to participate in the conflicts of the political parties.

"Things are different now that the proletarian struggle has reached a revolutionary stage. We shall not discuss here whether parliamentarianism, as a system of government, has any value whatever for the self-government of the masses, or whether it weakens rather than strengthens the system of soviets. At the point we have reached, it is a matter of using it as an instrument for the proletarian conflict. Parliamentarianism constitutes the typical form of struggle waged through leaders, with the masses themselves playing only a subordinate role. In practice, it boils down to handing over effective leadership of the class struggle to special people, to deputies; and, this naturally fosters the illusion among the masses that others can wage the struggle on their behalf. Yesterday it was assumed that such deputies were able to secure by parliamentary activity important reforms benefitting the workers. The illusion was even fostered that they could achieve the socialist revolution through a few parliamentary decrees. Today, when the system appears to be in decay, it is noteworthy that the utilization of the parliamentary seat holds an extraordinary interest for communist propaganda. In both cases, power reverts to the leaders, and it goes without saying that the shaping of policy is left to the specialists—if need be, under the democratic guise of discussions and congressional motions. But the history of Social Democracy is one of a constant succession of vain efforts aimed at enabling the militants themselves to determine party policy. As long as the masses have not created the organs for their own action, and as long as revolution is not the order of the day, this is inevitable. On the other hand, as soon as the masses show that they are capable of actively intervening, and therefore of deciding for themselves, the damage caused by parliamentarianism is of unprecedented seriousness.

"As we have already emphasized, the tactical problem boils down to the essential question: How are we to uproot among the proletarian masses the traditional bourgeois mode of thinking that is paralyzing them? Anything that strengthens routine ideas is harmful. The most tenacious, the most solidly anchored, aspect of this mentality is a dependence on leaders which induces the masses to abandon to such people the power to shape and to direct matters pertaining to their class. . . .

"The revolution requires that the proletariat itself solve all the major problems of social reconstruction, make difficult decisions, and participate completely in the creative movement. It follows that the vanguard, and then the ever increasing masses, should take matters into their own hands, should regard themselves as responsible agents, should investigate, propagandize, fight, experiment, weigh and then dare and be involved to the utmost. But all this is difficult and painful; and that is why, as long as the working class believes that there is an easier way, that of having others act for them. . . , they will evade the issue and will remain inactive, imprisoned in old ways of thinking and old weaknesses."

Parliamentarianism not only insures the absolute predominance of leaders over the masses, but also corrupts the masses by leading them to make a fetish of legality and of party coalitions and to regard means as essential, and not ends. "From being a vanguard uniting the whole working class for revolutionary action, the Communist Party is changing into a parliamentary formation, with a legal existence equal to that of other parties—in fact, a new version of the old Social Democracy, but with leftist slogans. . . ."

V.

"On the spiritual level, the dominance of the leadership over the masses is embodied in parliamentarianism; on the material level, it is embodied in the trade union movement. In a capitalist system, the trade unions constitute the natural proletarian form of organization—and Marx, in a period now remote, stressed their importance as such. With the development of capitalism and, still more, in the era of imperialism, the trade unions were transformed increasingly into huge bureaucratic associations with a tendency to proliferate, analogous to that of the former bourgeois state organism. A class of officials, a bureaucracy, was created among them, which had at its disposal all the means of power: money, the press, the promotion of junior personnel. In many respects, they had extensive prerogatives, so many that their members, originally intended to be the servants of the masses, have now become their masters and identify the organization with themselves. The trade unions also resemble the state and its bureaucracy in this respect, so that, despite a democratic set-up, the rank and file trade unionists have no means of imposing their wishes on the leaders; in effect, an ingenious system of regulations and statutes smothers the least sign of revolt before it can become a threat to higher echelons."

Years of incessant efforts on the part of a trade union opposition are required to secure any gains, which are often only a change of leaders. "That is why, in recent years, both before and after the war, revolts occurred on several occasions in England, America, and Germany, in which the rank and file unionists went out on strike despite their leaders' intentions and the decisions of their organizations. This occurred in a wholly natural way and was regarded as such. It shows that trade unions, far from unifying their members, became estranged from them. We have here another point in common with the state: the workers are no longer masters in their own house, but find themselves as opposed to their own organizations as they are to external powers above them and against which they see themselves compelled to revolt, even though such organizations were produced by their own efforts and wishes. When the revolt dies down, the old leaders resume their place and continue to maintain their power, despite the hatred and powerless exasperation of the masses, because they can count on their indifference, their lack of foresight, united will and perseverence. The old leaders have in their favor the intrinsic need for the trade union, since these organizations represent for the workers the only means of combatting capital.

"By limiting capitalist tendencies toward absolutism, thus ensuring the existence of the working class, the trade union movement fulfills its role within the system and thereby becomes a major foundation of the system. But from the moment that revolution breaks down the proletariat assumes a different role and is transformed from a force stabilizing capitalist society into an agent of its destruction. Consequently, the proletariat must also come into conflict with the trade unions."

The trade union bureaucracy does not limit itself to dealing with the state bureaucracy. It also encourages workers to approve the agreements it has reached with the capitalists. In Germany it resorts to demagogy, to violence, and to the most shameless lying; in England, it uses more subtle methods so as "to give the workers the impression that it is using every means to achieve their demands, while in reality it is sabotaging them.

"Marx and Lenin have repeatedly said of the state that its mode of functioning, despite the existence of formal democracy, precludes its use as an instrument of proletarian revolution. The same, we believe, can be said of the trade unions. Their counterrevolutionary power will not be destroyed or even impaired simply by a change of leadership, by the substitution of leftists or 'revolutionaries' for reactionary leaders. Rather, the form of organization itself reduces the masses to impotence and prevents them from making it the instrument of their will. The revolution can conquer only if the trade union is overthrown, or rather, wholly shattered so as to become something completely different.

"Arising from within the proletariat, the system of soviets (workers councils) can uproot and supplant both the state and trade union bureaucracies. The mission of the soviets is to serve as new political organs for the proletariat in place of parliament and as the nucleus for new trade unions. During the recent lively controversies within the German Social Democratic Party, certain people derided the idea that an organizational form could have a revolutionary character, since the whole question centered on the attitude of the militants. However, if the revolution is one in which the masses assume control of their own affairs — the direction of society and of production — any form of organization that excludes the possibility of their ruling and directing themselves is counterrevolutionary and harmful. It must be replaced by a revolutionary organization, revolutionary in the sense that it enables the workers to make all decisions. This in no way implies that a new form of organization should be created and perfected — but without their help — so that they may then be able to use it to manifest their revolutionary will. On the contrary, this new form can be created only within the revolutionary process, by the workers radicalizing themselves. It is necessary, however, to know the real nature of the present forms of organization in order to determine the attitude of communist militants toward subsequent attempts to weak or to destroy the old forms.

"In the revolutionary syndicalist tendencies and even more in the 'industrial' trade union movement is to be found the greatest evidence of a desire to restrain the bureaucratic machinery and rely on the activity of the masses. For this reason, the majority of communists support these organizations instead of the centralized federations. As long as capitalism continues, these new formations will have only a limited following. The IWW is important because of a special circumstance: the great many unskilled workers, mainly recent immigrants, who made a mass exodus from the old federation.[13] The English *shop committees* and *shop stewards* represent an example much closer to the practical organ of struggle created by the masses confronting bureaucracy.[14] By design, the German unions conform even more to the idea of workers councils but remain weak because of the stagnation of the revolution. To the extent that it succeeds in weakening the cohesion of the centralized associations and the counter-revolutionary power of the trade union bureaucracy, every new formation of this kind clears the way for revolution. The idea of unifying all opposition forces within these associations to secure a majority there and to transform them completely is certainly attractive. But, in the first place, it is just as absurd as the idea of conquering the Social Democratic Party from within (since bureaucracy is so adept at strangling an opposition before it really becomes a threat). In the second place, a revolution does not unfold

13. Pannekoek would return to this subject in an article published in the United States. An extract from it will show his skill to get to the essence of a revolutionary current, assessing its strengths and its weaknesses. He first recalls that the IWW came about in response to the narrow conservatism of the American Federation of Labor and the multiplicity of trade union organizations within the same industry, to which they counterposed their slogan: "one big union." "Contrary to the haughty disdain of the well-paid old American skilled labor toward the unorganized immigrants, it was these worst paid proletarians that the IWW led into the fight.... By a glorious series of big battles it infused the spirit of organization and self-reliance into the hearts of these masses.... Instead of the heavy stone-masoned buildings of the old unions, they represented the flexible construction, with a fluctuating membership, contracting in time of peace, swelling and growing in the fight itself. Contrary to the conservative capitalist spirit of the trade unionism, the Industrial Workers were anti-capitalist and stood for revolution. Therefore they were persecuted with intense hatred by the whole capitalist world. They were thrown into jail and tortured on false accusations; a new crime was even invented on their behalf: that of 'criminal syndicalism.'

"Industrial unionism alone as a method of fighting the capitalist class is not sufficient to overthrow capitalist society and to conquer the world for the working class. It fights the capitalists as employers on the economic field of production, but doesn't have the means to overthrow their political stronghold, state power. Nevertheless, the IWW so far has been the most revolutionary organization in America. More than any other it has contributed to rouse class consciousness and insight, solidarity and unity in the working class, to turn its eyes toward communism, and to prepare its fighting power." Pannekoek wrote this under the pen name of J. Harper, "Trade-Unionism," *International Council Correspondence*, II:1, Jan. 1936, pp. 18-19. Cf. also, *Workers' Councils*, pp. 170-71. For an excellent account of this, cf. Daniel Guérin, *Mouvement ouvrier aux Etats-Unis, 1867-1967* (Paris, 1968), pp. 36-46, 51.

14. Cf. Branko Pribicevic, *The Shop-Stewards' Movement and Workers' Control, 1910-1922* (Oxford, 1959).

according to a well-ordered program. Rather it is the spontaneous explosion of committed, active groups that is the major motive force. If the communists opposed these attempts by opportunists to obtain immediate advantages by glossing over the different trade union tendencies, they would then find that the obstacles presented by the opportunists are larger than ever.

"When the workers have succeeded in creating the soviets, their own organs of power and action, it can be said that the state is already disintegrated, abolished. The trade unions, a modern form of self-generated organization, will survive the state for a time because they are rooted in more recent traditions, based on intense personal experience. They will continue to function as representative organs of the proletariat, even though the illusions of the democratic state have dissipated. The new formations will appear as attempts to adapt trade unions, which, after all, are the products of working class activity, to new conditions. As a result of the revolutionary process, the new forms of proletarian struggle and organization will develop on the soviet model through constant metamorphoses and new developments."

VI.[15]

It is a neo-reformist idea to suppose that capitalism will succumb to a well-ordered siege, using methods proven by the army of the Communist Party and mounting wave after wave of assault, while workers gradually take control in the factories. Such thinking is out of touch with reality in Western Europe. First the old conditions must be dissolved and the workers must free themselves from old ways of thinking; bourgeois power must be crippled by strikes; the peasants must sweep away the vestiges of feudalism. Put simply, "a period of social and political chaos is inevitable. . . .

"However, two questions can be dealt with briefly. The first, concerning industrial technicians, will cause only passing difficulties. Even though these specialists think in an absolutely bourgeois manner and are passionate enemies of proletarian power, they will necessarily come around in the end. The proper functioning of transportation and industry involves, above all else, the supply of raw materials. It coincides, therefore, with the problem of replenishing supplies, an essential problem of the revolution in Western Europe, where highly industrialized capitalist countries cannot subsist without imports. In the context of the revolution, the problem of renewing food supplies is closely linked to the agrarian question; from the beginning of the revolutionary period, a communist reorganization of agriculture should

---

15.   This section and the following have been substantially cut. They deal with problems of the "transitional phase" in immediate, concrete terms and therefore have at best a historical interest. However, we have included one passage to give a general idea of Pannekoek's concerns.

take precautions against famine. The big landed estates of the nobility are ripe for expropriation and collective administration. The small peasant class will find itself freed from all capitalist exploitation and encouraged toward intensive cultivation through state cooperation and assistance. The middle peasant class, which, for example in western and southern Germany,[16] holds half of the land, thinks in highly individualistic terms and is therefore anti-communist. But because it holds an unshakable economic position and cannot be expropriated, it must be integrated into the whole economic process by controlling the exchange of foodstuffs, and encouraging productivity. In agriculture, communism will pursue a policy of increasing productivity and of restricting individual cultivation, similar to the policy it pursues in industry. It follows from this that the workers should regard the landed proprietors as their enemies, the agricultural labors and lower peasant class as their allies, while taking care not to alienate the middle peasant class, although the latter might well be hostile to them at first. Thus, during the chaotic first phase when the economy is badly disrupted, the requisition of food supplies produced by these categories of peasants should be resorted to only as an exceptional measure and solely for the purpose of securing a scarcity balance between urban and rural areas. It is imports, above all else, which will win the battle against famine. Soviet Russia, with its abundance of agricultural products and raw materials, will be the savior and the sustainer of the revolution in Western Europe. Therefore, it is vital to its own interests that the working class of Western Europe should defend Russia.

"The reconstruction of the economy, however formidable, is not a problem to be solved by the Communist Party. It is the proletarian masses who will solve it, as soon as their spiritual and moral capabilities are brought into play. The Party's task is to arouse these forces and accelerate their development. It should seek to uproot all the accepted ideas that intimidate the proletariat and threaten its confidence; it should discredit everything that fosters the illusion that there is an easier and which therefore dissuades the proletariat from using radical methods, limiting them to half-measures and compromises.

VII.

"The transition from capitalism to communism will not be achieved by the simple conquest of political power, the establishment of soviets or the abolition of private property, although such measures do provide the broad

16. On the peasants' councils in Bavaria, cf. Paul Werner (Frölich), *Die bayrische Räterepublik,* undated (1919), pp. 36-37; and especially Wilhelm Mattes, *Die bayrischen Bauernräte* (Stuttgart, 1921).

outlines of development. This transition will be made possible only through the power to build anew. At the present, the forms of enterprise and organization created by capitalism are solidly grounded in the minds of the masses, and it will take political and economic revolution to change this. Within the working class under capitalism, forms of organization have come into existence whose power cannot be immediately and fully measured and which, therefore, will play a fundamental role in the course of the revolution.

"The primary such form is the political party. The notorious role of Social Democracy in the present crisis of capitalism is nearing its end.[17] Its left-wing factions (such as the USP in Germany) are harmful, not only because they divide the proletariat, but even more because they foster confusion and prevent the masses from resorting to action due to their concept of Social Democracy, according to which the dominant political leaders shape the destiny of the people by their acts and negotiations. And if a communist party opts for the parliamentary road and aspires, not to class dictatorship, but to party dictatorship—in other words, dictatorship by the party leaders—this, too, may shackle development. A case in point is the attitude of the KPD during the March revolutionary movement; by favoring a 'loyal opposition' in the event that a 'purely socialist government' should come into power— their pretext being that the proletariat was not ready to exercise its dictatorship—they deflected any vigorous mass opposition to this kind of regime. . . .

"Not only is such a government incapable of actively promoting the revolution, but its only purpose can be to arrest its development at some halfway stage. Seeking by every means to prevent enlarging the divisions in capitalism and the emergence of workers' power, it behaves in a deliberately counterrevolutionary fashion. The communists have no choice but to combat it vigorously and with no concern for the consequences."

In the Anglo-Saxon countries the leftist trade union leaders such as those of the IWW, who adhere to the Third International, "do not regard the system of soviets as the purest form of the dictatorship of the proletariat but, on the contrary, as a government of politicians and intellectuals whose permanent basis is supplied by the workers' organizations. In their view, then, it is the trade union movement. . .that should exercise power. If the old ideal of

---

17. This prognosis was by no means an exaggeration at the time, at least in regard to Germany, as election results show. While by the Constituent Assembly elections of January 19, 1919, the Majority Party had secured 11.5 million votes, or 38 percent of the votes cast, compared with 2.3 million votes—8 percent—received by the Independents, in the next year's National Assembly (June 6, 1920), the USPD polled nearly 6 million votes (18 percent), only 700,000 more than that (21 percent), and the KPD just 442,000 votes (2 percent); in Berlin 456,000 electors voted USPD; only 186,000 voted SPD.

'industrial democracy' is realized, if the trade unions become masters of the factories, economic administration as a whole will return to their common organ, the congress of trade unions. Thus the workers' parliament will replace the parliament of the bourgeois parties. But, in such situations, some will recoil at the idea of an exclusive and 'unjust' class dictatorship, regarding it as a violation of democracy: by all means led the workers accede to power, they say, but the others must not be deprived of their rights. Consequently, in addition to the workers parliament, which administers everything connected with labor, they suggest a second chamber, elected by universal suffrage, representing all classes and invested with certain powers over matters of public and cultural life as well as political questions in general."[18]

Pannekoek is not concerned here with the idea of a 'labor' government endorsed in England by the official trade union movement, since such a government could only serve the bourgeoisie. "However, it still remains to be seen whether the discerning English bourgeoisie, with their liberal views, will prove capable by themselves of deceiving and choking the masses more effectively than is done by the workers' bureaucrats."

The leftist trade unionists, for their part, express "a limited ideology, which was developed in the course of trade union conflicts and which hinders them from seeing in world capital a totality with multiple interlocking forms—financial, banking, agrarian, colonial—since they are aware only of its industrial form.... As a result of their failure to see that the whole abstract domain of political and spiritual life is conditioned by the mode of production, they are ready to hand over that domain to the intellectual bourgeoisie, provided that it agrees to allow labor to predominate. Such a workers' government would be, in reality, a government by the trade union bureaucracy, aided by the leftist sector of the old state government, the first handing over to the second, because of its specialized ability, control over the domains of culture, politics, etc. Its economic program would surely have nothing in common with communist expropriation, but would merely seek to expropriate big capital, the larger banks and landed capital, while leaving untouched the 'honest' profit of the small employer, fleeced by big capital and dependent upon it. It is even doubtful whether this government would support full and complete freedom for the Indies, whereas this demand is an essential part of the communist program.

"One cannot foresee the manner in which a political form such as this will be realized. In effect, it is possible to discern the motive forces and the general

---

18.   In this connection, cf. Max Adler, *Démocratie et conseils ouvriers* (Paris, 1967). Originally published in 1919.

tendencies—the abstract characteristics—but not the concrete aspects it will assume from one country to another, the particular combinations on which it will rest. Thus, the English bourgeoisie has always shown its skill in making timely concessions that take the steam out of the revolutionary thrust; and that is why the limits of this tactic will vary in terms of the intensity of the economic crisis at any given moment. If rank-and-file revolt threatens trade union discipline while the masses are opting for communism, the reformist or radical trade union leaders will adopt a middle course; if the opposition against the old political policy of the reformist leaders is accentuated, the leftist leaders and the communists will walk hand in hand.

"These tendencies are not peculiar to England. In every country, the trade unions constitute the most powerful workers' organization; and after a political conflagration, when the old power is overthrown, they are the ones that emerge as the best organized force and that have the greatest authority." The old trade union leaders then try to increase still more their grip on governmental power, but this has the effect of compromising them with the masses. In these circumstances, other, more leftist leaders seek to form a workers' government; in Germany, their chances of succeeding are by no means negligible. But this regime would be unstable, since a new split is inevitable: some would simply aim at consolidating their positions of strength within the bureaucracy and, eventually, at the parliamentary level; others would strive to extend the system of soviets. "It may be that the road taken by the communists often skirts that of certain leftist leaders, but, nonetheless, it would be a mistake not to stress the differences of principles and objectives. This is relevant to the communists' attitude toward the present trade union organizations, since everything that contributes to strengthening their cohesion and power also strengthens a force destined one day to be a stumbling block in the way of the revolutionary movement.

"When communism wages a bitter struggle against these transitional political forms, it represents the living revolutionary tendency within the proletariat. This same proletarian action, which, by shattering the old machinery of bourgeois power, opens the door to workers' bureaucracies, is the action that simultaneously leads the masses to create their own organs, the councils, and set about undermining the nucleus of this bureaucratic machinery in the trade unions. Thus, the creation of the system of soviets also represents the struggle of the proletariat to replace the incomplete form of class dictatorship with its complete form.

"Due to the problems involved in 'reorganizing' the economy, a bureaucracy of leaders could retain a great measure of power for a long time while the ability of the masses to rid themselves of this bureaucracy slowly develops. These diverse forms and phases of development, however, do not gradually evolve in the logical succession we have outlined here. On the contrary, they parallel, intermingle with and crisscross each other in a chaotic mix of complementary tendencies and separate conflicts so that it is impossible to grasp the course of development in its entirety. As Marx pointed out, the proletarian revolutions 'constantly criticize one another, interrupt at every moment their own course, turn back to what seemed disposed of in order to begin on it anew, pitilessly ridicule the hesitations and weaknesses and miseries of their early attempts, seem to knock down their enemy only to allow him to draw new strength from the ground and to rise up again in formidable opposition . . . .'

"Those forms of proletarian power that insufficiently express its strength must be overturned as part of the process of developing this strength — a process that occurs through the oppositions and catastrophes of class struggle. At the beginning there was action, but the action was only a beginning. A moment of unanimous determination is enough to sweep away one form of power; but only permanent unity — whose necessary condition is clear-sightedness — can ensure that the victory is not dissipated for those who have won it at such cost. In the absence of this unity, a complete reversal of the situation occurs, not the return of the old masters, but new forms of domination, with new people and new illusions.

"Every new phase of the revolution sees the emergence of a new category of leaders who hitherto did not have any leadership role. They now emerge as the representatives of specific forms of organization whose triumph corresponds to a new, more advanced stage in the self-emancipation of the proletariat.

VIII.

"While capitalism in Western Europe is collapsing, in Russia the productive apparatus is making progress under the new regime despite great difficulties. The existence of a communist regime does not imply that production has been completely collectivized, for this can only be the end product of a prolonged process of development. It does signify, however, that the working class is deliberately directing production toward communism. This process cannot exceed the present level of technical and social development. That is why it necessarily assumes transitional forms in which vestiges of the old bourgeoisie take on a special importance. On the basis of what we know in Western Europe, this is what has happened in Russia.

"Russia constitutes an immense peasant region, where industry has not developed to the point where exports and expansion are a vital necessity, as they are in Western Europe, the 'workshop' of the world. Despite that, Russia's social development has still provided it with a working class that has progressed to the point of being able to take over the administration of society. Since most of its population are agricultural workers, the big modern industrial enterprises employ only a minority of the workers. While small enterprises still predominate, they no longer constitute a factor of exploitation and misery as in Western Europe. On the contrary, they are industrial enterprises that are attempting to improve the peasants' living standards, and which the Soviet government is seeking to link more closely with the whole society by providing them with needed products and implements, as well as by accelerating scientific and cultural education. In spite of all this, it is understandable that this form of enterprise engenders a certain individualist spirit, which can foster communism among the 'rich' peasants. The Entente was certainly relying on this when it made certain commercial propositions to the agricultural cooperatives in order to draw these social categories into the profit cycle and thereby create a bourgeois opposition movement. But the fear of feudal reaction is the stronger motivation, and their loyalties are therefore with the present government. That is why these attempts are doomed to failure, and if Western European capitalism collapses, this danger will vanish completely.

"Industry, now largely centralized, is devoid of any kind of exploitation; it is the heart of the new order, and the state leaders rely on the industrial proletariat. But this production, too, is in a transitional situation; the technical and administrative cadres of state factories and services have considerable powers, an understandable phenomenon in this developing communist regime. The need both to secure a rapid production growth and to raise an army to meet the reactionary assaults demanded that something be done with all urgency to remedy the dearth of highly skilled personnel. The threats of famine and enemy attack precluded full dedication to the much more prolonged task of developing the necessary skill and raising the cultural level of all citizens in order to lay the foundations of the communist collectivity. That is why a new bureaucracy had to be constructed out of political leaders and high officials; and why it was necessary to include what remained of the old order—of that class whose existence had, up to then, been regarded as a threat to the new order.[19] The only effective way to counter this threat is to work zealously to develop the masses, but there will be no permanent foundations for this development until the time of abundance

---

19. The problem of the administration of industrial enterprises had at that time (March-April 1920) been discussed at the Ninth Congress of the Communist Party of the Soviet Union. Cf. Léonard Schapiro, *Les Bolchéviks et l'Opposition* (Paris, 1947), pp. 184-98.

comes, when man will cease to be a slave to his work. Abundance alone creates the conditions for freedom and equality. As long as the struggle against nature and capital remains undecided, excessive specialization cannot be avoided.

"It is notable that our analysis of the different situations in Western Europe (insofar as one can foresee the resumption of the revolutionary process there) and in Russia uncovers the same politico-economic structure: a basically communist industry, within which the workers' councils form the organs of self-administration, but which is subject to the technical direction and political domination of a workers' bureaucracy; while alongside this, agriculture, dominated by small and medium landed property owners, preserves an individualist and petty bourgeois character. There is nothing surprising about this coincidence, since such social structure is not decided by political prehistory but by basic economic and technological conditions—the degree both of industrial and of agricultural development and of the formation of the masses; and this level was identical in both places. But apart from this similarity there is a great difference of direction and of aim. In Western Europe, this politico-economic structure constitutes merely a passing stage in the bourgeoisie's last-ditch effort to avoid downfall, whereas in Russia it represents a deliberate attempt to move toward communism. In Western Europe, this structure represents a phase of the class struggle between the proletariat and the bourgeoisie; in Russia it is a phase of economic reconstruction. Although externally similar, Western Europe is a civilization moving toward decline, whereas Russia is on its way to a new civilization.

"When the Russian Revolution, still very recent and weak, was placing its hopes of success in a prompt outbreak of the European revolution, in the West a very different idea of Russia's significance was taking shape. Russia, it was then asserted, was just the advance post of the revolution. Circumstances as favorable as they were fortuitous enabled the Russian proletariat to seize power, but this occurred too soon. In effect, this proletariat, small and uneducated, counts for little compared with the enormous mass of peasants. In view of Russia's economic backwardness, it can only lead the way for a while. As soon as the revolution occurs among the proletarian masses of Western Europe, with their experience and education in matters of technology and organization, we shall see a blossoming of communism against which the beginnings of Russian communism, however worthy of interest, will seem poor by comparison. It is in England, Germany, America, the countries where capitalism has reached its highest stage of development, where the possibility of a new mode of production has been raised that the center and the strength of the new communist world will be found.

"This way of viewing the question does not take into account the difficulties faced by the revolution in Western Europe. In a situation where the proletariat progresses only slowly in strengthening its power, and where the bourgeoisie is capable of continually regaining power or sectors of power, there can be no question of economic reorganization. In a capitalist context, the reason for this is simple: every time the bourgeoisie sees that the possibility is becoming real, they create a new chaos and destroy the foundations for a communist system of production. Resorting always to bloody repression and to ruthless destruction, they prevent a new proletarian order from developing any kind of strength. This has been the pattern in Russia. The destruction of the industrial and mining installations of the Urals and of the Donetz Basin by the armies of Kolchak and of Denikin and the need to mobilize the cream of the workers and the bulk of productive capacity against these armies have seriously injured and delayed the construction of the communist economy. . . .

"In Russia, the Soviet Republic nonetheless remains impregnable . . . , while in Western Europe, where the destruction has been equally severe, the best proletarian forces not only have been annihilated, but they also lack that source of power supplied by the existence of a great soviet state. As long as chaos and misery prevail, there can be no question of construction. Such is the fate of countries where the proletariat has not immediately grasped its task with a clear understanding of its nature and with a unanimous will—i.e., the countries in which bourgeois traditions have weakened and divided the workers, making them timorous and destroying their ideas. In the old capitalist countries, it will take decades to overcome the stupefying influence exerted over the proletariat by bourgeois culture; and, in the meantime, production will be doomed to stagnation and the land to economic sterility.

"While Western Europe is painfully struggling to free itself from its bourgeois past," stagnation is eroding its material riches and diminishing the productive capacities of its population. "The indestructible forces, the knowledge, the technical skills, are not linked with these countries; those who possess them are finding a new fatherland in Russia, where the importation of European material goods and technology can also have liberating effects. The probable outcome of the commercial agreements that Russia has concluded with Western Europe and America—if they are seriously and extensively carried out—will be a deepening of these contrasts, since they will stimulate the economic construction in Russia while in Europe they will delay the day of destruction, allow capitalism to get a second wind, and paralyze the action of the masses. Neither the duration nor the extent of this process is presently foreseeable. At the political level, this will probably lead to stagnation, expressed either in a bourgeois government or in one of the forms of government we have described above, accompanied by a rapid spread of opportunism in the communist movement. Resuming the old methods of struggle — participating in parliamentary activities and acting as a loyal opposition within the old trade unions — the communist parties of Western Europe will adapt to the institutions exactly as did Social Democracy before them, and they will attempt to suppress the radical, revolutionary tendency, now reduced to a minority. The idea of a new and real development of capitalism seems, however, extremely unlikely. . . . While it is possible to hold back an aggravation of the crisis" — due in large part to trade with Russia, "a permanent amelioration is out of the question, and sooner or later the crisis will recur. While the process of revolution and civil war will initially be retarded, they will come and when they do, they will involve a long, protracted struggle. . . . Meantime, in the East, the economy is developing unhindered, and new perspectives are opening up. Mankind's newly acquired domination of social forces is drawing support from the most developed natural sciences — which the West does not know how to use — and is being united with the social sciences. And these forces, multiplied a hundredfold by the new energies engendered by liberty and equality, will make Russia the center of the new communist world order.

"Of course, this will not be the first time in human history that, during the transition to a new mode of production or to one of its phases, the center of the world has shifted. In antiquity, it shifted from the Near East to Southern Europe; then, in the Middle Ages, from the South to the West. With the appearance of mercantile capital and colonialism, first Spain, then Holland and England, took the lead — a lead that would remain with England alone after the birth of the industrial revolution. In seeking to understand the causes of these changes, one must also be guided by the general principle that, when the primitive economic form has reached its full maturity, the material and spiritual forces, the political and juridical institutions guaranteeing its existence and necessary to its development, become almost irresistible obstacles to any development toward new forms. For instance, toward the end of antiquity, the slave system held back the development of the feudal order; subsequently, guild regulations, in force throughout the great and rich cities of the Middle Ages, compelled capitalist enterprise to establish itself only in places hitherto devoid of economic importance. Similarly, the political order of French absolutism, though encouraging industry under Colbert, was later in the 18th century to shackle the expansion of new major industry, which in England was in the process of transforming the country into a manufacturing economy.

"Everything occurs, therefore, as though there exists a law of the 'survival of outmoded forms,' analogous to Darwin's law of 'the survival of the fittest' in organic nature. When an animal species—for example, the saurians of the second era—evolved into a great variety of forms, perfectly adapted to the living conditions appropriate to a particular epoch, they became unable to evolve into a new type, because they had lost all their ability to develop. At the time of the origin of a new type, one always finds primitive forms that, because they have remained in an undifferentiated condition, have kept their evolutionary potential, while the adaptive abilities of the old species have disappeared. In society we see the phenomenon that bourgeois science shrugs off by terming it an imaginary 'exhaustion of vital energies' among a people or race in which economic, political and cultural primacy constantly passes from one people or country to another.

"We have just seen the reasons why the predominance of Western Europe and of America—a predominance that the bourgeoisie so readily attributes to a racial superiority that is both spiritual and moral—has vanished; we have also seen where there is a major possibility of a new predominance emerging. The countries destined to constitute the center of the new communist universe are those new countries where the masses, far from being intoxicated by the ideological miasmas of the bourgeoisie, have emerged, with the onset of industrialization, from their old, resigned passivity, acquiring at the same time a sense of community, which the communist spirit was awakening among them; countries in which there exists the raw materials necessary for the modern technology they have inherited from capitalism, now used for the renovation of traditional forms of production; countries where oppression inevitably engenders conflicts and the will to struggle, but where there is no bourgeoisie with the power to block it. Russia, a veritable subcontinent, is destined henceforth to figure in the first rank. These conditions also exist in other countries of the East—the Indies and China. Even if these Asian countries are still quite underdeveloped, any consideration of the world communist revolution must take these regions into account.

"To consider the world revolution only from the Western European perspective is to miss its universal significance; Russia is not just the eastern part of Europe, but is, to a far greater extent, the western part of Asia, both economically and politically as well as geographically. The Russia of former times had almost nothing in common with Europe. Compared with the West, it seemed close to those political and economic formations that Marx called 'oriental despotism,' a genre to which all the giant Asian empires, old and new, belong. In that genre, an aristocracy and princes with absolute power reigned over a largely homogeneous peasantry that varied little from one region to another. Equally important, they also had full control of commerce, which, though relatively modest, was important at this primitive stage. Despite frequent changes of masters, which in no way altered the basic structure, the same mode of production continued unaltered for thousands of years. Western European capital has burst upon these countries as a disruptive factor, bringing about their overthrow and impoverishment, and the subjugation and exploitation of their masses. . . .

"Although Russia has been numbered among the large world powers since 1700, it too has become a colony of European capital. Its contacts with Europe, often warlike, made it choose the same road that would later on be followed by Persia and China. Before the last war, 70 percent of the iron industry, most of the railways, 90 percent of platinum production, and 75 percent of petroleum extraction were in the hands of European capitalists.[20] Furthermore, the enormous debts of the czarist state forced the European capitalists to squeeze the Russian peasants almost to the point of starvation. While the working class in Russia labored under working conditions similar to those in Western Europe—whence the emergence of a proletarian community with revolutionary Marxist ideas—their economic situation as a whole made the country still just the most western of Asian lands.

"The Russian Revolution marks the beginning of the great Asian revolt against Western European capitalism, concentrated in England.[21] As a general rule, Western Europe has been interested only in the reactions of the West to this revolution, in which Russian revolutionaries, because of their high level of theoretical development, have become the educators of a proletariat aspiring toward communism. But the revolution's effects in the East are more important still, and that is why the policy of the Soviet Republic is governed by Asiatic considerations as much, or nearly so, as by European. From Moscow, where Asiatic delegations arrive one after another, there issues a constant call for liberation, for the peoples' right to self-determination, and for constant struggle against European capitalism throughout the whole of Asia. . . .

"The Asiatic cause is the cause of humanity. In Russia, in China and in the

---

20. For statistical data showing that the essential sectors of pre-1914 Russian industry were largely in the hands of foreign capital and that foreign banking capital had penetrated into all domains there, see Peter Lyaschchenko, *History of the National Economy of Russia to the 1917 Revolution* (New York, 1949), pp. 712-17.

21. Such sentiments were also repeatedly expressed by Lenin. For instance, at Zurich in 1917, he said: "The 1905 Revolution not only signified the awakening of the biggerst and most backward of the Asian countries . . . ; it also set all of Asia ablaze." Cited by Stanley Page, "Lenin: Prophet of World Revolution from the East," *The Russian Review*, XI, April 1952; cf. also the collection edited by Stuart Schramm and Hélène Carrière d'Encausse, *Le Marxism et l'Asie* (Paris, 1965), pp. 170-94.

Indies, in the Russo-Siberian plain and in the fertile valleys of the Ganges and the Yangtse-Kiang, are 800 million people, more than half the earth's population, almost three times as many as in Europe. Outside Russia, the revolution is germinating everywhere: on the one hand, major strikes are breaking out in towns where the industrial proletariat are penned up, such as Bombay and Hangkow; on the other hand, national movements led by intellectuals are emerging but are still weak. As far as one can judge from the sparse information that the English press allows to filter through, the World War has greatly facilitated national movements, even though they are still violently repressed, while industry is undergoing such a level of development that American gold is copiously flowing into the Far East. The wave of economic crises, when it reaches these countries—it seems to have already reached Japan—will provoke a fresh outbreak of conflict there. It may be questioned, therefore, whether support should be given to the purely nationalist movements in Asia, which aim at restoring a capitalist regime and which are opposed to movements to free the proletariat. However, it is probable that this development will take a different course. Up to now, the emerging intellectual class has certainly drawn its inspiration from European nationalism, and, inasmuch as it is composed of ideologists of the nascent native bourgeoisie, it propagates the idea of a bourgeois-national government modeled after the Western type. But this ideal is losing its attraction as Europe declines; and doubtless the intellectuals are bound to feel strongly the influence of Russian bolshevism, thereby will be led to join the proletarian movement of strikes and insurrections.[22] Thus, sooner perhaps than one might suppose, the Asiatic movements of national liberation will adopt a communist outlook and a communist program, on the solid material basis offered by the class struggle of workers and peasants against the barbarous oppression that world capital is exercising over them.[23]

22. This is an allusion to two articles published in German in *Vorbote* on April 2, 1916: Radek's "Theses on Imperialism and Oppression"; and Lenin's "The Socialist Revolution and the Right of Peoples." We shall return to this question shortly.

23. Rudi Dutschke, *La Révolte des étudiants allemands* (Paris, 1968), pp. 95-96, cited in a flippant way certain lines from the end of this section, omitting among other things any reference to the links between intellectuals and the bourgeoisie in the national liberation wars in underdeveloped countries. According to him, Pannekoek's analysis remains "descriptive" while taking on a "prophetic" aspect. And Dutschke comments on this as follows: "This passage vaguely outlines the need for a prolonged cultural evolution, especially in the highly developed countries of Central Europe, as a prelude to a possible revolutionization of the whole of society." Then, after having cited long extracts from an article by Lenin on the emergence of the revolution in Asia, he adds in connection with the Bolshevik leader: "One searches his work in vain for an answer to the very essential questions posed by the need to transform the consciousness of the European proletariat." One could not find a clearer example of what has separated Russian Bolshevism from Western European Communism.

"The fact that these societies are mostly peasant does not pose an insurmountable obstacle, any more than it did in Russia. The communist collectivity does not form a dense network of manufacturing towns, for the capitalist division between industrial and agricultural areas does not exist in Russia; on the contrary, agriculture must occupy a major position there. No doubt, the predominance of the agricultural sector makes the revolution more difficult, since the necessary mental attitudes are not quite as strong among the peasants as the proletariat. Certainly, therefore, a longer period of political and spiritual upheavals will be required. In these countries the difficulties are completely different from those found in Europe. More passive than active, they are less concerned with the effort of resistance than they are with the delay in the formation of the homogeneous force required to rout the foreign exploiter. We shall not dwell here on their specific traits: religious and national divisions in the Indies, or the petty-bourgeois character of China. In whatever way the political and economic forms develop, the basic and preliminary problem is to end the domination of European and American capital.

"The great task of the workers of Western Europe and the United States, united with the Asian multitudes, is to accomplish the final destruction of the capitalist system. This task now is only in its beginning stages. When the German revolution has taken a decisive turn and has successfully joined Russia; when the wars of the revolutionary masses break out in England and in America; and when the Indies are in the grip of insurrection; when communism extends from the Rhine to the Indian Ocean— then the world revolution will enter into its most violent phase. The English bourgeoisie, masters of the world, supported by their vassals in the League of Nations and by their Japanese and American allies, will find themselves attacked both from within and from without. In the colonies, upheavals and wars of liberation will threaten its hegemony, while at the center, its power will be paralyzed by strikes and civil war. England will be compelled to mobilize all its forces and to raise armies of mercenaries in order to hold out against these two enemies. When the English working class, vigorously supported by the rest of the European proletariat, moves to the offensive, it will fight in two ways for communism—by opening up the way to communism in England, and by helping Asia emancipate itself. In return, it can count on the support of the communist forces when the bourgeois mercenaries attempt to drown the proletariat's struggle in blood—for Western Europe, including Great Britain, is simply a large, island-like extension of the immense Russo-Asian geographical unit. It is through the common struggle against capitalism that the proletarian masses of the world will be united. And on the day when, after many difficult struggles, the exhausted European workers at last see the radiant dawn of Liberty, they will be greeted from the East by the emancipated peoples of Asia. At the center of everything will be Moscow, capital of the new humanity."

Postscript

"Drawn up in April, the preceding reflections were sent to Russia so that they might influence some of the decisions to be made by the Executive Committee and the Congress of the Communist International. Since then, the Moscow executive and the Russian leadership have wholeheartedly rallied to opportunism, thus insuring the dominance of this tendency during the Second Congress of the Communist International.

"This policy was first applied in Germany, where Radek became its most zealous advocate. It consisted of imposing on the German communists — over whom he exercised control through the leadership of the German Communist Party (KPD) — his tactics of parliamentarianism and of support for the trade union federation. The effect of this was to divide and weaken the movement. Since Radek has become secretary of the executive, this policy has become that of this organ as a whole. Although fruitless thus far, the attempts to persuade the Independents to attach themselves to Moscow have been pursued with the utmost vigor. On the other hand, the anti-parliamentarian members of the German Communist Workers Party (KAPD) have been treated in a completely different way, although it cannot be doubted that they naturally belong with the Communist International. The KAPD, it was said, had taken positions against the Third International in all important matters, and it was admitted as a member only on certain conditions. The auxiliary bureau in Amsterdam, which was once looked upon as its equivalent and treated as such, has been reduced to silence.[24] Talks have begun with

---

24. This auxiliary (or provisional) bureau was set up in January 1920 at the initiative of the executive of the Communist International (and of Radek) to serve as a liason among the various groups or parties of Western Europe and America that claimed membership in the International. Its objectives were to serve as a regional propaganda center, to publish a theoretical organ, and to organize exchanges at the regional level. Due to a lack of funds, only the last of these objectives was achieved. In addition, an international conference was held in Amsterdam in February 1920, but the police intervened and the assembly had to disperse. Cf. James Hulse, *The Forming of the International* (Stamford, 1964), pp. 152-60. The leadership of the bureau (Wijnkoop, Roland-Holst and Rutgers) was up to its neck in the controversy within the Dutch Communist Party between the majority parliamentarian sector led by the deputies Wijnkoop and Ravesteyn (who had the upper hand in the editorship of *De Tribune*) and the partisans of the council form. Cf. van Ravesteyn, *op. cit.*; and H. Gorter, *Het opportunisme in die N.C.P.* (Amsterdam, 1921). The Bureau's first and only *Bulletin* published "Theses on Parliamentarianism," whose author could easily have been Rutgers. According to these theses, parliamentary action is useful for propaganda, but not in a revolutionary period, when Parliament "can serve only as a rallying

delegates of the center of the French Socialist Party with a view to their admission.[25] According to Lenin, the English communists should not only take part in the legislative elections, but also join the Labor Party—a political association affiliated with the Second International and with the majority of the reaction trade union leaders as its members. These various options show the determination of the Russian leaders to establish close relations with the workers' organizations of Western Europe, even though they are not yet communist. While the radical communists still try to enlighten the masses and to inculcate revolutionary ideas in them through a vigorous and principled struggle against all bourgeois, social-patriotic and wavering tendencies, the leaders of the International are trying to win them over *en masse*, without demanding that they fundamentally revise their basic ideas.[26]

"The Russian Bolsheviks, who only recently were actively advocating radical tactics, have therefore taken a position squarely opposed to that of the radical communists of Western Europe. This emerges notably and clearly in Lenin's recent pamphlet: *Left-Wing Communism: An Infantile Disorder.* The importance of this pamphlet lies in the stature of its author rather than in its content, since there is little new in the arguments put forward; for the most part, they are identical to the ones others have long been using. The novelty lies in the fact that Lenin is now espousing them. There is no need, therefore, to refute them. Their basic error lies in establishing a similarity between the conditions prevailing in Western Europe—parties, organizations, parliamentary activities, etc.—and that which in Russia goes by the same names. What all of this points to, of course, is the crystalization of a particular policy.

"As can readily be seen, the needs of the Soviet Republic lie at the basis of this policy." Understandably, Russia, ruined by civil war, is seeking a political and economic *modus vivendi* with the West. But it is the International's task to prepare for the proletarian revolution throughout the whole world. It should therefore be independent of the Soviet government; but instead, the International is its instrument. "Rather than counting on a radical

point for the bourgeoisie." The "theses on the trade union movement" came out in favor of revolutionary trade unions and of wildcat strikes against the workers' bureaucracy, but looked to factory councils rather than a federation of trade unions as the basis of a new socialist society.

25. Two prominent social-patriots, Frossard and Cachin, went to Moscow on a negotiating mission at the time of the Congress. The merger was to be approved shortly afterwards at the Tours Congress in December 1920.

26. For example, the famous 21 "conditions for the admission of parties into the Communist International," adopted at the Second Congress, extols parliamentary and trade union action and is drawn up so as to eliminate certain persons; in fact, it contains no features that were not already contained in the programs of classical Social Democracy, the only difference being in their more "leftist" rhetoric.

communist party working toward a future revolution, Moscow wants to be able to rely on a large organized proletarian force capable of intervening on its behalf now and of bringing pressure on their respective governments.

"Hence it is advocating in Western Europe a policy that does not too blatantly contradict the traditional ideas and methods of the large mass organizations," one that favors the coming to power of leftist governments, with participation of trade unions and of the Communist Party under the aegis of "an organization of councils on the Russian model. . . . The task of communism is to uncover the forces and the tendencies that seek to stop the revolution midway; to show to the masses the way to forge ahead, the way to reach, through impassioned conflict, the ultimate goal of undivided power; to arouse the energies of the proletariat and to deepen the revolutionary course. And it can do all this only if, here and now, it opposes the tendencies to subject itself to the power of the leaders. . . .

"If one accepts the perspective of immediate protection of Soviet Russia, one inevitably accepts this particular idea of the world revolution (seizure of power by the workers' leaders whose sympathies are with the Soviet Union). In effect, if other European countries have political systems similar to Russia's—namely, domination by a workers' bureaucracy based on a system of councils—it will be possible to keep imperialism in check, at least in Europe. Russia, surrounded by friendly workers' republics, would then be able to pursue in peace its economic construction in the direction of communism. Hence, what we regard only as intermediate and inadequate forms to be vigorously opposed is regarded by Moscow as the full realization of the proletarian revolution, the supreme purpose of communist policy.

". . . If those in power in Russia fraternize with the Western European workers' bureaucracy—corrupted by its situation, its opposition to the masses, its compromise with the bourgeois world—and become impregnated with its spirit, the force that is drawing Russia toward communism will evaporate. And similarly, if this group of leaders relies on the peasant proprietors rather than on the workers, there is a danger that bourgeois-agrarian forms will develop, causing the world revolution to stagnate. [27] The source of this stagnation lies in the fact that the political system in Russia, which represents the transitory form of the road toward com-

27. It will be seen here that Pannekoek envisions a "degeneration" of the Soviet leaders through contact with and imitation of the traditional workers' movement and its chiefs. This hypothesis is diametrically opposed to all the judgments reached by observers of all persuasions since then. Without, of course, being able to measure the extent of such a counter-influence, one can trace some real indication of it at the level both of the Communist International and the Communist Party (not to mention the ideological level), particularly in the early 1920s, a period in which the distinctive traits of classical Marxist-Leninism were taking shape.

munism—and which has not yet developed into a full-fledged bureau-cracy—signifies in Western Europe a decidedly reactionary obstacle to revolution. We have already stressed that such a 'workers' government' is incapable of arousing the energy demanded for the construction of communism. But since, after the revolution, the middle and lower middle classes (allied with the peasants) will still hold an inordinate amount of power—a situation very different from that in Russia after the October Revolution—the reaction will have every opportunity to sabotage even the smallest efforts at construction, while the proletarian masses, for their part, will have to redouble their efforts to break away from this system...."

CHAPTER NINE

COMMUNISM AND NATIONAL LIBERATION

Ten years (but what years!) separate the writing of *Tactical Differences* from that of *Communist Tactics*. Ten years before, Pannekoek, like all the international Left, believed it was possible to fight revisionism by radical tactics. Now, however, facts showed that this strategy belonged to a current that was seeking to gain power by imposing on Western Europe the old methods of struggle—i.e., parliamentary and trade union action, both of which were products of the lack of solidarity and the spiritual weakness of the proletariat. On this basis, Pannekoek could predict that the policy of a "workers' government" (or the Popular Front, as it was later called) was doomed to impotence and failure, and, in fact, that it would on occasion help dissipate revolutionary forces.

Another prognosis of the highest importance concerned Russia and, in a more general way, the Asia countries. The revolt against foreign capital, he said, broadening his 1909 views, would henceforth be extended to the bourgeois intellectuals with socialist leanings, but this expansion would depend on the course taken by the proletarian revolution in Western Europe and America. In Russia, the backwardness of the country necessarily entailed the emergence of a bureaucracy in the state and in industry that fused with the old bureaucracy. From this was constituted an independent administrative machinery, a leadership power based on the system of councils. which, in order to survive, had to compromise with the capitalist powers. Hence, while maintaining the unity of the Communist International, the policy pursued in Western Europe had to be free of the least interference from Moscow. Furthermore, the fate of the revolution, the destiny of the contemporary world, depended on the masses' initiative, which it was the Communist Party's mission to express and to stimulate, and not to deflect into actions decided from "above." This "above" represented a body of professionals committed to achieving a compromise between the classes on the basis of immediate forces and by means of specialized procedures—in Parliament, in the arbitration of labor disputes, in municipal councils, in a host of administrative services. Needless to say, its own specific interests carried a certain weight in the measures that it undertook in the name of its "electors."

Such was the twofold criticism that Pannekoek would henceforth make of Social Democracy's basic premise (and therefore equally that of Western European Leninism and, for that matter of every exploitative society): "Someone must lead." And Pannekoek would not base his critique on a popular policy, as a defender of a rival third party, but he would argue in terms of the new organizational forms that had emerged during the great revolutionary crisis of the first half of this century.

There is one further point that should be mentioned here, even though it is only indirectly connected. Pannekoek was aware of the differences among the left-Zimmerwaldians over the national question, yet he did not enter directly into the controversy. At most, he emphasized a little earlier that the independence of the Indies was something that the Communists should demand.

The German left (Luxemburg, Knief, and others), convinced that the era of the bourgeois national liberation wars was over, maintained that in the future the only thing that counted was the class struggle for socialism. What had Pannekoek and his friend Gorter to say about this? Early in 1918, Gorter wrote: "The nations ardently aspire to real self-determination. But however cruel this may seem, the realization of this right, unless it is subordinated to socialism, can be expressed only in imperialism. Capitalism, and in particular imperialism, cannot effectively resolve the problem of nations. Some nations may attain independence, but in that case the small nations become the stake in a conflict between the great nations, or of the small nations among themselves, which seek to subjugate or annex them."

However, Gorter very carefully added the following footnote: "With regard to the right to self-determination, a decided distinction must be made between Western and Eastern Europe, on the one hand, and Asian countries and the colonies, on the other." [1] In the theses which Lenin published in Vorbote, he remarked about a pamphlet on imperialism that Gorter had just published: "Gorter errs when he denies the principle of national self-determination, but he correctly applies this principle when he demands the immediate 'political and national independence' of the Dutch Indies and unmasks the Dutch opportunists who are refusing to formulate this demand and to fight for it." [2]

Lenin, with his eminently practical mind, thus clearly highlighted the basic divergence: what to him was a position of principle was in no way so for the

1. H. Gorter, Die Wereldravolutie (Amsterdam, undated), p. 30.
2. Lenin, "The Socialist Revolution and the Right of Nations to Self-Determination," Works, XXII, p. 164.

Western European Communists. According to them, the slogan of self-determination came from one imperialist group wanting to plunder another,[3] and therefore created confusion; or it came from a rising dominant class, in which case it could be historically progressive (as can be inferred from their analysis of the situation in Asia). But it was not there that the importance lay, at least in regard to the developed industrial world centers of Europe and America.

Lenin once contended that his theses established with particular clarity the connection between the question of self-determination and the general question of the struggle for democratic reforms."[4] Now, at this general level, a decisive question of principle was involved: the Western European communists were rejecting, once and for all, the idea of subordinating the proletarian class struggle to practical reforms to be achieved only by parliamentary action.

Unlike the classical Social Democrats, they made no secret of their sympathy for the national liberation movements in the colonies (movements still almost non-existent in this period); but confined active solidarity with the colonized nations to the framework of the class struggle since this solidarity in itself did not at all constitute a significant force in this struggle.

At the level of theoretical analysis, Gorter clearly distinguishes between the colonies' prospects for national emancipation and those that existed in the major Asian countries. Twenty-five years later, Pannekoek's "Workers' Councils" makes this same distinction but in a changed context: "When socialism grew up, half a century ago, the general expectation was that the liberation of the colonial peoples would take place together with the liberation of the workers. The colonies there and the workers here were exploited by the same capitalism; so they were allies in the fight against the common foe. It is true that their fight for freedom did not mean freedom for the entire people; it meant the rise of a new ruling class. But even then it was commonly accepted, with only occasional doubts, that the working class in Europe and the rising bourgeoisie in the colonies should be allies. For the Communist Party this was still more self-evident; it meant that the new ruling class of Russia looked upon the future ruling classes in the colonies as its natural friends, and tried to help them." At that time, however, Pannekoek says in effect that the forces operating in favor of the liberation of the colonies were very weak.

---

3. Anton Pannekoek, in *Das Wilsonsche Programm* (Vienna, 1919), sees in self-determination "the ideological garb of the world domination of Anglo-American capital," but makes no allusion to the right of self-determination as such.
4. Lenin, *Works*, XXIII, p. 10.

"The essence of colonial policy is exploitation of foreign countries while preserving their primitive forms of production or even lowering their productivity. Here capital is not a revolutionary agent developing production to higher forms; just the reverse. European capital is here a dissolving agent, destroying the old modes of work and life without replacing them by better techniques. European capital, like a vampire, clasps the defenseless tropical peoples and sucks their lifeblood without caring whether the victims succumb. . . .

"The Western bourgeoisie considers its rule over the colonies a natural and lasting state of things, idealizing it into a division of tasks profitable to both parties. The energetic intelligent race from the cool climes, it says, serves as the leaders of production, whereas the lazy, careless colored races execute under their command the unintelligent manual labor. Thus the tropical products, indispensable raw materials and important delicacies, are inserted into the world's commerce. And European capital wins its well deserved profits because by its government it guaranteed to the fatalistic aborigines security, peace and, by its medical service and hygienic measures, health, too. Suppose this idyll of a paternal government, honest illusion or deceptive talk of theorists and officials, was true even though in reality it is impossible under capitalist rule, then still it would be faced with an insoluble dilemma: If by the cessation of wars, epidemics and infant mortality the population increases, there results a shortage of arable land notwithstanding all the irrigation and reclaiming, the conflict is only delayed. Industrialization for export, properly speaking an unnatural way out for the most fertile lands, can give only temporary relief. Every population that is ruled from above must arrive at such a state if left to its own instincts. Every economic system develops its own system of population increase. If an autocratic rule from above suppresses the feelings of responsibility, then any active force of self-restraint and self-rule over the conditions of life is extinguished. The impending clash between the population increase and the restriction of means of subsistence can find its solution only in a strong display of inner energy and will-power among a people, consequence of its self-reliance and freedom, or of an active fight for freedom.

"In the latter part of the 19th century and thereafter it is not the commercial capital in the first place that exploits the colonies. . . . In India, in such towns as Bombay, a class of rich merchants also take part and constitute the burgeonings of a modern Indian bourgeoisie. This Indian industry consists almost exclusively of textile factories; and of all the textile goods consumed in India, nearly 60 percent is imported from England and Japan, 20 percent comes from the cottage industry, and only 20 percent is provided by Indian factories. Yet to exhibit and introduce aspects of modern work and life is sufficient inspiration for a nationalist movement to throw off the yoke of the Western rulers. Its spokesmen are the intellectuals, especially younger ones, who are acquainted with Western science, and who, in order to oppose it, study and emphasize with strong conviction their own national culture.... The movement, of course, is still too weak to throw off the domination of Western capitalism. With the rise of capitalist factories there also arises a class of industrial workers with extremely low wages and an incredibly low standard of living! Strikes have occurred against Indian as well as European employers. But compared with the immense population, all this is an insignificant start, important only as indication of future development.

"With the present world war, colonial exploitation and the problem of liberation acquire a new aspect. A fight for independence in its old meaning has no longer any chance against the enormously increasing power of capitalism. On the other hand, it is likely that, from now on, world capital under American hegemony will act as a revolutionary agent. By a more rational system of exploitation of these hundreds of millions of people, capital will be able to increase its profits considerably—by following another way than the previous primitive impoverishing methods of plunder, by raising labor in the colonies to a higher level of productivity, by better techniques, by improvement of traffic, by investing more capital, by social regulations and progress in education. All of this is not possible without according a large amount of independence or at least self-rule to the colonies.

"Self-rule of the colonies, of India, and of the Malayan islands, has already been announced. It means that European parliaments and viceroys can no longer rule the colonies despotically. It does not mean that politically the working masses will be their own masters, that as free producers they will dispose of their means of production. Self-rule relates only to the upper classes of these colonies; not only will they be inserted into the lower ranks of administration, but they will occupy the leading places, assisted of course by white advisers and experts, to ensure that capital interests are properly served. Already from the upper classes of India a rather large group of intellectuals has emerged, quite capable as ruling officials of modernizing political and social life.

"To characterize modern capitalist production as a system wherein the workers by their own free responsibility and will-power are driven to the utmost exertion, the expression was often used that a free worker is no coolie. The problem of Asia now is to make the coolie a free worker. In China, the process is taking its course; there the workers of olden times possessed a strong individualism. In tropical countries it will be much more difficult to transform the passive downtrodden masses, kept in deep ignorance and superstition by heavy oppression, into active, skilled workers capable of handling the modern productive apparatus and forces. Thus capital is faced with many problems. Modernization of the government apparatus through self-rule is necessary, but more is needed: the possibility of social and spiritual organization and progress, based on political and social rights and liberties, on solid general instruction. Whether world capital will be able and willing to follow this course cannot be foreseen. If it does, then the working classes of these countries will be capable of independent fighting for their class interests and for freedom along with the Western workers.

"To all the peoples and tribes living in primitive forms of production in Africa, in Asia, in Australia, it will, of course, mean an entire change of the world, when the working class will have annihilated capitalism. Instead of as hard exploiting masters and cruel tyrants, the white race will come to them as friends to help them and to teach them how to take part in the progressing development of humanity." [5]

Thus, according to Pannekoek, the colonies as late as 1947 were not capable of liberating themselves by their own means. Of course, a subcontinent such as India had some chance of initiating a really new stage of its development, capable of engendering a complete overthrow of outmoded attitudes; but, in every respect, all this was still remote and depended on the development of Western capitalism. As for the other countries, everything seemed to indicate that these prospects, however tenuous, were closed to them. If salvation was to be, it had to come from the workers of the West. [6] But China — both because of the historical weakness of the traditional "bourgeoisie" and because of the pressure of the peasant masses — in all probability is about to have at its head an exploiting class capable of leading it out of its age-old backwardness: "The Chinese Communist Party, and still more the Red Army, however, consists of rebellious peasants. Not the name stuck on a label outside, but the class character determines the real content of thought and action.... To the red leaders the ideal of the future was a democratic middle-class China, with free peasants as owners, or at least well-to-do farmers of the soil. Under Communist ideas and slogans they were the heralds and champions of the capitalist development of China....

"The ideals and aims for which the working masses of China are fighting will, of course, not be realized. Landowners, exploitation and poverty will not disappear; what disappears are the old stagnant primitive forms of misery,

---

5. Anton Pannekoek, *Workers' Councils, op. cit.*, pp. 195-200.
6. Cf. Franz Fanon, *The Wretched of the Earth* (New York, 1968). Of course, it would be wrong to exaggerate the parallel between the European left-Marxist and the African nationalist.

usury and oppression. The productivity of labor will be enhanced; the new forms of direct exploitation by industrial capital will replace the old ones. The problems facing Chinese capitalism will require central regulations by a powerful government. That means forms of dictatorship in the central government, perhaps complemented by domestic forms of autonomy in the small units of district and village. The introduction of mechanical force into agriculture requires the conjunction of the small lots into large production units; whether by gradual expropriation of the small peasants, or by the foundation of cooperatives or *kolchozes* after the Russian model, will depend on the relative power of the contending classes. This development will not go on without producing deep changes in the economic, and thereby in the social relations, the spiritual life and the old family structure. The dimensions, however, of things there, of the country, of the population, of its misery, of its traditions, of its old cultural life are so colossal, that to change conditions, even if it's done with the utmost energy, will take many dozens of years.

"The intensity of this development of economic conditions will stir the energies and stimulate the activity of the classes. The fight against capitalism will arise simultaneously with capitalism. The fight of the industrial workers will spring up with the growth of factories. And in China, with the strong spirit of organization and great solidarity shown so often by the Chinese proletarians and artisans, a powerful working class movement may be expected to arise more quickly than in Europe. To be sure, the industrial workers will remain a minority compared with the mass of the agrarian population, which is equally subjected to capitalist exploitation, though in different ways. The mechanization of agriculture, however, will weave strong ties between them, manifesting itself in the community of interests and fights. So the character of the fight for freedom and mastery in many regards may take on different aspects in China than in Western Europe and America."[7]

---

7. Anton Pannekoek, *Workers' Councils, op. cit.*, pp. 193-95.

CHAPTER TEN

THE COUNCIL STATE

Pannekoek saw no need to reply specifically to Lenin's pamphlet, *Left-Wing Communism: An Infantile Disorder*, since, as he rightly emphasized, it contained no new line of argument. But Gorter did discuss it, in his *Open Letter to Lenin*. [1] We need not return to it here, except to consider one aspect of the controversy: the accusation of utopianism.

When the accusation came from the Western academic camp, it consisted in ascribing to religious delusions anything in the ideas or activity of a human group that rejected the equation of passive submission to circumstances with active adaptation to the existing order. It involves, therefore, a value judgment whose values themselves need to be judged, were its content not so clear to begin with. Considered from a political viewpoint, however, this assertion sought to defend the old organizational forms by presenting the new forms as an historical accident in normal times, and as a necessary but subordinate element in critical times. Held in common by the spokesmen of both branches of Social Democracy, it was therefore formulated either in classical or radical terminology.

The classical formulation would run along these lines: "Even though Lenin may have been right beyond question at the tactical level, Gorter was right when he maintained that the Russian Revolution was moving to its destruction, toward a new slavery." [2] In other words, the Leninist tactic was excellent so long as it was not applied; if in Russia and in the underdeveloped countries it led to known catastrophes, it would lead to similar fiascos in Western Europe. But, this judgment is itself completely a-historical, since the left-communists had devoted most of their attention to the backward and therefore reactionary character of the old Marxist tactics, both classical and radical. In fact, if these criticisms are of any value today, it is in terms of a battle that was not even theirs: the electoral rivalry between the Socialist

---

1. H. Gorter, *Réponse a Lénine* (Paris, 1930), pp. 26-29, 50-51. Here Gorter takes up the criticisms of trade union and parliamentary action made in *La Tactique Communiste*. Translated and prefaced by André Prudhommeaux, the text first appeared in the *Ouvrier communiste,* organ of a group of Parisian council communists.
2. S. Tas, "Herman Gorter, révolutionnaire et poète," *la Révolution prolétarienne*, 50 (May 1951), p. 172.

Party and the Communist Party, grafted onto the ideological conflict between the two blocs.

From the same basic assumptions, Arthur Rosenberg, a historian and a former Communist deputy, reached a similar judgment. He presented a portrait of the KAP members, which at least sheds light on the feelings of the petty Leninists of his type toward the left communists: "To this movement (utopian extremism) belong the poorest and most hopeless of the workers. They passionately hate not only bourgeois society but all those whose existence is a little less wretched than their own. They reject all diplomacy and all compromise, and accept only extremist action.... It is a purely emotional movement, incapable of elaborating any doctrine or organized action whatsoever. The utopian extremists accept Bolshevist ideas *en masse*." [3]

This in no way prevented Rosenberg from paying homage to Gorter, whom he regarded along with Trotsky and Luxemburg as "representing the future within the proletariat," and as a theoretician who "really raised the essential question" when he challenged the domination of Moscow over the Communist International. [4] Once more, theory, regarded as a good research instrument, was divorced from its practical consequences, was ascribed to particular people, and was approved only to the extent to which it agreed with the views of a Social Democracy, which did not even dare speak its name. [5]

Georg Lukács was, of course, a theorist of a completely different persuasion. He clearly pinpointed the meaning of "the 1912 Pannekoek-Kautsky controversy" when he wrote about Kautsky: "For to adopt the stance of opposition means that the existing order is accepted in all essentials as an immutable foundation and the efforts of the 'opposition' are restricted to making as many gains as possible for the workers within the established system." [6] According to this classical perspective, the state is regarded as the prize in a class war between the bourgeoisie and the proletariat, while for the revolutionary, the state constitutes an element of force against which the proletariat must be mobilized. But what is this revolutionary tactic based on? Lukacs rejected the solution of the German Left since they, along with Rosa Luxemburg, did not acknowledge the council form as "the weapon by which to fight for and gain by force the presuppositions of socialism," [7] and he

---

3. A. Rosenberg, *Histoire du bolchevisme* (Paris, 1936), p. 176.

4. *Ibid.*, pp. 85, and 222-24.

5. Thus one finds Pannekoek's successful "refutation of Lenin" acknowledged "despite his penchant for an orthodox Marxism." M. Rubel, *Karl Marx* (Paris, 1957), p. 324, n. 49.

6. Georg Lukács, *History and Class Consciousness* (Cambridge, Mass., 1976), p. 260.

7. *Ibid.*, p. 280.

stressed that Rosa, "in her criticism of the replacement of the constituent Assembly by the soviets...imagines the proletarian revolution as having the structural forms of the bourgeois revolutions."[8] Curiously, however, he traced this idea to her tendency "to overestimate the importance of spontaneous mass actions,"[9] whereas Luxemburg herself justified participation in the elections in Germany, by the need "to educate the masses," to remedy the "immaturity" of the proletariat.[10]

Lukács invoked this same idea as the theoretical basis of the categories of mediation—party and trade unions. The desire for a synthesis between parliamentary and trade union action and the council form, then animating the German left wing, especially the KPD (against which Pannekoek speaks out in *Communist Tactics*), is therefore shaped on the idea of a specialized kind of Jacobin "political leadership" freed from the influence of backward social categories. In regard to the refusal of the Dutch and the KAP to identify the "dictatorship of the proletariat and dictatorship of the party," Lukács accused them of placing "utopian and exaggerated hopes on the anticipation of subsequent phases of development," and of ignoring "the real structure of forces here and now."[11]

Thus, as Lukács—whose opinion in this matter has varied little—quite recently reaffirmed, utopian sectarianism involves the effort to realize general or final principles independently of a socio-historical development that yields permanent transformations of forms and functions and in which new mediations constantly appear, while the old forms lose their validity or undergo essential modifications.[12] In reality, this is to return "within the established order." The classical tactic, linked with the old form of organization and with the old methods of struggle, could not but become an end in itself, as is shown, for example, in the history of the German Communist Party. Based on the "real structure" (i.e., on the market relationships and the relationships of immediate forces) the parliamentary and trade union tactic takes precedence, in ordinary circumstances, over the new tactic, without the former being able to develop into the latter in time of crisis. Theoretically intended to allow for accomodations, the old tactic in

8. *Ibid.*, p. 284.
9. *Ibid.*, p. 303.
10. Prudhommeaux, *op. cit.*, p. 48.
11. Lukács, *History and Class Consciousness, op. cit.*, p. 296.
12. G. Lukács, "Reflections on the Split," *Studies on the Left*, IV, 1, 1964, p. 25. Lukács here regards the anti-parliamentary position of the 1920 "sectarians" as tantamount to what he calls the "extreme subjectivism" of Stalin and of Mao, which consists of dogmatizing without regard to the "facts." These "facts" are, of course, decided by Lukács in his own way.

practice only strengthens the trade unionist consciousness of the masses, making them forget that they ought to act directly, by themselves.

In contrast, the partisans of the new tactic wanted to develop the initiative of the masses through extra-parliamentary forms of organization. In the 1920s, they were concerned, therefore, with creating or strengthening organs linked with the concrete life of the exploited and with their immediate demands: in the factories, these organs were the factory organizations, the *Revolutionäre Betriebsorganisation* (RBO), which, in theory at least, united workers of all tendencies on the basis of their enterprise; while a little later on, there emerged the action committees (*Aktionsauschüsse*) centered on districts, employment exchanges, etc.[13] Regrouped within the AAU, these organs were animated by militants of the vanguard party, the KAP. The latter did not intend to become a mass party. Its mission was "to point the way through the confusion and the wavering of the proletarian revolution, to keep the course steadily fixed toward Communism." The party, "an organization of the most conscious elements, should attempt to put an end to these waverings, and not allow itself to be drawn into them. Its task is to help the masses to surmount them as quickly and as completely as possible, by the clarity and purity of its conduct, by the consistency between its words and its actions, its presence in the front line of battle, and the correctness of its foresight."[14] Consequently, this party of the elite should show a particularly rigid attitude where principles are concerned. Nothing shows this more clearly than does a letter written by Pannekoek in the fall of 1920, in answer to a proposition made by Eric Mühsam. Mühsam, the anarchist leader, had put forward the idea of a federation of all the groups "who resolutely walk the Bolshevist path to communism, without bowing to the decrees of Moscow."[15]

"If I understand you correctly," Pannekoek wrote, "you blame the [Second] Moscow Congress for having excluded a section of the revolutionaries [notably

---

13. Cf. *Programm und organisations-statut der K.A.P.D.* (Berlin, 1924), pp. 45-47.

14. *Die Hauptfragen der revolutionären Taktik* (Berlin, 1921), pamphlet of the KAPD, pp. 7-8. The party, notes Gorter, is "a nucleus as tough as steel, as pure as crystal." In Gorter, *op. cit.*, p. 98.

15. *Die Aktion*, X:45-46, Nov. 13, 1920. Mühsam was then in prison, after the crushing of the Bavarian Commune. The anarchists, after participating very actively in the operations of the Spartakists in Berlin, the Ruhr, and elsewhere, had for a time separated from both Communist wings. Thus, in March 1919, one of their principal leaders, Rudolf Rocker, declared that the centralism of the Bolsheviks could lead only to a kind of state socialism; in December of the same year he denounced even more vigorously "the Russian 'commissariocracy,' founded on a principle of authority like that of all other class depotisms." Cf. Peter Losche, *Der Bolschevismus im Urteil der deutschen S.D.*, 1903-1920 (West Berlin, 1967), pp. 276ff. For Pannekoek's assessment of anarchism, see the final paragraph of the present chapter.

the KAP] and, by doing so, for having committed the same error and shown the same narrow intolerance as did the Congress of the First International [The Hague, 1872] and of the Second International [London, 1892]. And you propose to all the groups or parties outside the Moscow International that they should form themselves into a free federation, leaving to each of its members complete freedom of agitation and of action. I shall now give the reasons why I am opposed to this idea.

"We regard the Congress as guilty of showing itself to be, not intolerant, but much too tolerant. We do not reproach the leaders of the Third International for excluding us; we censure them for seeking to include as many opportunists as possible. In our criticism, we are not concerned about ourselves, but about the tactics of Communism; we do not criticize the secondary fact that we ourselves were excluded from the community of communists, but rather the primary fact that the Third International is following in Western Europe a tactic both false and disastrous for the proletariat. The exclusion is simply the disagreeable form assumed by the necessary separation from those who want to be able to manifest their opposition freely and are not content to slink furtively away. And yet, struggle of tendencies is necessary, since it enables the proletariat to find its way. The fact that men with ardent revolutionary ideas embrace and congratulate one another on their excellence serves no useful purpose; what is necessary, however, is that the proletariat, the huge masses, clearly see the path and the purpose, cease to hesitate and waver at the mercy of events, and move resolutely into action. This cannot be the fruit of purely sentimental aspirations toward unity. It can only result from a clear and coherent theory of combat—a theory which, in the heat of battle and under the pressure of necessity, ultimately imposes itself, so that the theory and the people become as one.

"The First International in 1872 was therefore right to exclude the anarchists; and, even though opportunism had already risen in its ranks, the Second International was equally justified in repeating this expulsion. The theory of combat which alone can lead the proletariat to victory is none other than Marxism. Precise knowledge about the conditions appropriate to the proletarian revolution can be acquired only by the science of Marxism, a factor in the radical overthrow of ideas. No doubt, in recent years, Marxism has been deformed by those who have misused it in order to exorcise the revolution: first of all, by the conservatives of the Marxist tradition of the USPD type, and then by the *Rote Fahne* following them along the same road. It must therefore be proclaimed with the utmost clarity that the agitation and the tactic of the KAPD, which does not involve Marx at every turn, is linked to a more authentic and more practical Marxism, in which the revolutionary flame of Marx burns more actively and effectually than it does for the spokesmen of the USPD and the KPD, who are constantly paying lip service to Marx.

"Because of this deformation—which is causing many young revolutionaries to turn aside as though Marxism were really a theory of mechanical evolution and fatalistic certitude—the emphasis must constantly be placed on the importance of Marxism for the revolution. This in no way implies that those most learned in the letter of Marxism make the best militants: on the contrary, experience has shown over and over again that theoretical knowledge and enthusiasm for action were linked with dispositions of mind which often made these two qualities incompatible, and that there are many who come to proper revolutionary actions without theory, thanks to intuitive practice. What we mean by the importance of Marxism is that the materialist-revolutionary conception of the world and of society, which was that of Marx, should penetrate the masses in order to make them clearsighted and self-assured.

"You want to create a federation of all the revolutionary groups excluded by Moscow. We disagree, because a federation of this kind would automatically become a declared opponent of Moscow. Although the Congress has excluded our tendency, we feel a solidarity with the Russian Bolsheviks. We reproach them for having insufficient knowledge of the situation in Western Europe, the conditions of class struggle in the key countries, capitalist for centuries, or of not taking sufficient account of them, and with allying themselves with the big opportunist parties in the hope of achieving the world revolution more quickly. And we say to them: the opportunists have no right to be in your ranks; *we* are the ones who should be there. We reproach them for underestimating both the enormous differences between Russia and Western Europe and those between the Bolshevik Party and the Western European parties, and for the error of reinforcing the power of leaders whose exclusion is the first condition for securing revolution in the west. However, it would be an example of the same narrow doctrinaire attitude to commit a similar error by applying to Russian conditions considerations that are valid only for Western Europe, by projecting our analysis of the role of the leaders here on to what it is there, that role being very different because it is exercised under very different conditions. We therefore proclaim our solidarity, not only with the Russian proletariat, but also with their Bolshevik leaders, even while we criticize with the utmost vigor their intervention within international communism. It is from this same position—of complete fraternal solidarity with the Russian communists, linked with an equally categorical rejection of the tactics they are pursuing in Western Europe—that the KAPD has proposed affiliation with the Third International as a 'sympathetic' party."[16]

We shall return to Pannekoek's final analysis of Russian Bolshevism, and also to his definitive ideas about anarchism. But, first, without going into details, we shall attempt to trace the trajectory of the KAP.

From the onset, the party faced a difficult task. This, however, is something it had in common with all the young communist formations of the period, orthodox or not, which were forced out of necessity to compete with the old socialist and trade union organizations. The latter had long years of consummate experience in the manipulation of the masses and in dialogue with the authorities, not to mention the strength they drew from direct participation in state power (ministries, public administrations, police, etc.). They therefore enjoyed a superficial stability which, in turn, won for them the support of the most stable strata of the working class and of a section of the petty bourgeoisie. The KPD, compelled therefore to recruit in the socially less stable strata,[17] was caught between the extreme aspirations of a group often subjected to abrupt and terrible setbacks and those of a group whose sole purpose, in the final analysis, was to enlist as many people as possible by every means possible, from electoral promises to chauvinism. By its nature, the KAP could not increase its audience—the aim of every political organization—by resorting to these means, except for the last one.

In February-March 1921, the Communist International (or some of its leaders) decided to launch an "offensive" in Germany, partly because of an explosive situation in Russia (this was the eve of the Kronstadt rising). Unambiguously invited to prepare an armed insurrection, the *Zentrale* of the

16. *Die Aktion*, XI:11-12, March 19, 1921. We cannot deal in detail here with the various relations of the KAPD with both the Third International and the KPD. The following quotation from Lenin sums up very well the attitude of the Communist International to those whom it had just used—with their consent—as cannon fodder during the "March action" of 1921: "Provided that Communist parties of sufficient strength, experience and influence, have secured firm footholds, at least in the most important countries, then we should tolerate the presence of semi-anarchist (KAP) elements at our international congresses. Their presence may even be useful up to a point, to the extent to which such elements provide a 'discouraging example' to Communists devoid of experience, and also to the extent to which these elements are themselves amenable to instruction.... In Germany, we have tolerated them too long. The Third Congress of the International has delivered an ultimatum with a precise expiration date. If today, they have themselves withdrawn from the Communist International, so much the better.... By arguing with them, we merely provide publicity for their ideas. They are very unintelligent; it is a mistake to take them seriously; it is not worth irritating ourselves over them. They have no influence, nor will they have any if we take a firm line against them." Lenin, "Letter to the German Communists," *Works*, Vol. XXXII.

17. On the considerable fluctuations of KPD membership, see Flechtheim, *op. cit.*, pp. 235-236.

KPD (in the absence of Paul Levi, then touring Italy) complied docilely with the orders. The Moscow emmissaries (Bela Kun, in particular) contacted the KAP's "gang leaders" (to adopt an expression used by one of them),[18] who then gave the green light.

In Saxony, the spirit of revolt remained alive among the workers, and, since the bosses' repressive machinery (spies, private and semi-public militias) proved incapable of coping with it, the Social Democratic authorities, with their usual servility, decided to send in the armed forces. When the police battalions were sent into central Germany to occupy the factories, strikes occurred, with the support of the KPD, and at Mansfeld, at Eisleben, at the Leuna chemical factories (near Merseburg, a bastion of the AAU), the police were met with rifle fire. Amost everywhere in the country, the Kapists sought to unleash strikes, and even resorted to violence in order to induce the recalcitrants to stop work. On the whole, these efforts proved useless and, due to a lack of active solidarity, the insurrection (March 16-31) soon ended in a blood bath.[19]

The leaders of the KAPD saw in the terrorist action (whose results were always ridiculous) a way to give the proletariat confidence in its own strength, "to uproot the belief in the superiority, cohesion and unshakable character of bourgeois power, and to dissipate forever the fear of the omnipotent directors and bosses."[20] And they did not hesitate to present the March action as an indication of the "radicalization" of the KPD militants: "The masses of the Communist Party," they wrote in their central organ,[21] "are adopting our

---

18. Karl Plaetner, *Der mitteldeutsche Bandenführer* (Berlin, 1930). Cf. also Max Hölz, *Vom "Weissen Kreuz" zur Roten Fahne* (Berlin, 1929), pp. 141-71.

19. Here are two viewpoints of the time. First, that of Paul Levi, opposed to Moscow: "Only the will, clearsightedness and resoluteness of the masses themselves can set a mass party in motion, and it is only when this preliminary condition has been met that a good leadership is able to lead. . . . This distrust and this total negation of the Marxist principle regarding relations between the Communists and the masses, has almost automatically engendered. . . the undoubtedly anarchist qualities of the March action. The struggle of the unemployed against the employed, the intervention of the *lumpenproletariat*, the dynamite attempts (an abortive campaign of Max Hölz), followed inevitably. And all this shows the true character of the March movement—the biggest Bakuninest putsch of history." P. Levi, *Unser Weg wider Putschismus* (Berlin, 1921), p. 39. And the viewpoint of the ex-KAPist Reichenbach: "When for months a parliamentary and trade unionist tactic has predominated exclusively and when from one day to the next sees a headlong plunge into revolutionary activity, a central leadership can no doubt adapt to so sudden a change, but not the ensemble of permanent officials, not the mass of the militants. . . . The March action was the last attempt to involve the latent elements of the revolutionary class struggle on a broad basis, with a view to inaugurating the struggle for the conquest of power." Reichenbach, *op. cit.*, pp. 124-25. Recent academic literature on the subject merely reflects the division of the world into two ideological blocs.

20. *Kommunistische Arbeiter Zeitung*, No. 189, Sept 20, 1921.

21. *Ibid.*, No. 181, March 24, 1921.

slogans, and are forcing them on their leaders." (The latter, of course, were keeping well out of the way).

However, the KAP and the AAU constituted only one wing, the bigger and more combative one, of *Rätekommunismus*, or council communism, as it was beginning to be called to distinguish it from *Parlementskommunismus*, or parliamentary communism. The other wing sought to be "a unitary organization" (the AAU-E, which was constituted late in 1920). It rejected the party form (at least in theory), and regarded Bolshevik Russia as a state founded on centralism, "an organizational principle of the bourgeois-capitalist epoch."[22] Otto Rühle, one of its principal theoreticians, harshly criticized the whole March operation, particularly for what he regarded as a bourgeois military type strategy, that of guerrilla warfare by ill-equipped small groups. For this, he would substitute armed self-defense of the factories (in spite of the failure at Leuna).[23]

These differences assumed an immediate practical political character that they certainly never had in Holland. This is why Pannekoek could concentrate on analyzing the real significance of these events. In his view, the special importance of the March operation lay in its being symptomatic of "the internal development of communism," of the limits assigned to its action: "The March movement," he writes,[24] "was a fiasco that resulted from the policy planned by Moscow and from the tactics determined by the Second Congress. That is why an end must be put to the dictatorship of Russia over the Western European revolution." It was a tactical error "such as has often been made in the past, and dearly paid for" by the fighting workers with whom Pannekoek expressed his unqualified solidarity.

To establish a tactical error, the tactic itself and its consequences must be examined, and then it must be traced back to its material and conceptual origins. Pannekoek does this as follows: "In Western Europe, Communism will never successfully progress in the form of a new party—with completely new cadres, slogans and programs—but a party analogous in its internal nature to the old parties, with the same political jobbery, the same blustering leadership tactics, and the same noisy publicity. Certainly, Russia has been a beacon in the darkness and has awakened enduring hope; however, this light could only feebly filter through the thick smokescreen thrown up by lies in the

---

22. O. Rühle, "Bericht über Russland," *Die Aktion*, X:39-40, Oct. 2, 1920.

23. "Das Ende der mitteldeutschen Kampfe," *Die Aktion*, XI:15-16, May 16, 1921; For information on Rühle, see Paul Mattick, "Otto Rühle et le mouvement ouvrier," *Cahiers du communisme de conseil*, No. 3, January 1968.

24. Anton Pannekoek, "Sovjet-Rusland en het West-Europeesche Kommunisme," *De Nieuwe Tijd*, 1921, pp. 436-48.

news; and those who presented themselves here as the emissaries of this light were often too much influenced by the old Second International spirit to be able to contribute effectively toward arousing the necessary enthusiasm. Simply replacing Scheidermann with Levi is not enough to give the workers the courage to face up to death and misery."

Both on the basis of international solidarity and the instinct of self-preservation, he continued, the Russian Communists should have supported the Western European revolution. But they did so only in their own way, that is, by "misinterpreting" the whole situation. And Pannekoek stresses: "What we wrote at the time in *Verbote* about the major catastrophe of the Second International when faced with the war (namely, that this catastrophe signified much more than the fact that the proletariat was still too weak to defeat the bourgeoisie), applies equally to this minor catastrophe of the March action: It signifies that the methods of the Second International period are incapable of raising the material and spiritual force of the proletariat to the strength required to break the power of the dominant class."

Despite its "enormous exemplary value," the Russia of the Soviets, through the Communist International has contributed in no small way to maintain this condition of weakness, Pannekoek says, by imposing a return to parliamentary and trade unionist tactics, at the expense of tactics based on "the factory organizations of Germany and of England, which arose spontaneously and in a more or less deliberate way among the most advanced workers. . . . These tactics consist of building up by means of theoretical propaganda and of practical struggle, organizational forms that exclude any possibility of domination by professional leaders, and that combine, on the basis of the factory, all the wills to combat existing within the proletariat, so as to transform them into forces for action. That these tactics alone can achieve our objective is something which the March experience has just shown."

Its tragic results derived, first of all, from the fact that the German workers were not able to set about finding their way for themselves. Why? Because, Pannekoek writes, "the policy and the tactics of the Third International are closely connected to the state policy of the Soviet Republic. The new orientation of the Russian state policy ought, therefore, to exercise a reciprocal influence on the Third International's practice." Now, this policy is committed to two essential imperatives: at home, to make concessions to capital and to private property; abroad to re-establish trade with the capitalist countries.

At home, "the Russian leaders know that they must foster a spirit of development among the peasantry in order to create a basis for the building of communism. No doubt, this has less to do with a Marxist perspective than with the attitude of the peasants. The sabotage of agricultural production, the peasant uprisings and the Kronstadt insurrection have shown to the Russian government the dangers that it faces. In effect, there is a chance that a peasant counterrevolution may follow the revolution, as has happened in the past (1792, 1848). While the peasants, completely imbued with bourgeois lies, are leaning toward the restoration of a capitalist government, the Russian leaders, of Marxist persuasion, are consciously adapting their policy to economic necessity, while attempting to steer the economy in the direction of communism.

"To summarize this situation, it can be said that the Russian Revolution is a bourgeois revolution, like the French one of 1789: at the economic level, its essential content has been the transformation of the peasantry into freeholders and small producers; at the political level, it represents the coming to power of a new bureaucracy whose primary concern must be to satisfy the interests of these peasants. Of course, there are big differences between these two revolutions in regard to class relationships, degree of development, orientation of the movement and perspectives, which are not taken into account here. Nevertheless, this relationship highlights one important fact, and therefore clarifies the relations between Russia and Western European communism."[25]

Pannekoek then described the NEP, which he refused to regard, as did the Leninist press of the time, as "a major triumph of communism." According to him, the strengthening of private property in the rural areas and in towns, together with the commercial agreements with the capitalist powers, though unavoidable measures, posed serious consequences for the future of comunism in Russia, and were in danger of strengthening the forces of reaction there. "It is to be hoped, however, that the Russian leaders who, of course, are perfectly aware of the danger, will succeed in strangling these forces by means of their political power, by means of 'state capitalism'; but, at the present time, the new capital is about to attempt to bring pressure on the government through doubtful elements of the bureaucracy of the Soviets."

In the final part of this article, Pannekoek once again severely criticizes the German Leninists who were seeking to form joint "workers' governments" with the Social Democrats, who, in other respects, were their professed enemies and, whom, at times during this period, they were actually fighting.

Shortly after the publication of this article, *Nieuwe Tijd* ran out of funds

25. Pannekoek, *op. cit.*, p. 442.

and was forced to cease publication at the very time when the Dutch group, the KAPN, was experiencing repercussions of the crisis that was shaking its (relatively) powerful German equivalent. Begining in 1921, Pannekoek's name appeared only rarely in the journals and magazines of the extreme left. Because of the changed situation, the astronomer took over from the militant thinker. We shall see, however, that there was no question of the theoretician's renouncing the struggle; but simply that the theoretician's intervention, without breaking with the movement (or with what remained of it), took on a less immediate character.

The March 1921 defeat began a period of particularly bestial repression legally sanctioned by a law "for the protection of the Republic." Arrests, tortures, condemnations multiplied; the KAPist newspapers were suspended, their premises seized. The historical drama was redoubled by personal dramas; the enforced disintegration of the practical movement was accompanied by a theoretical stagnation, and "the most active militants, driven underground, resorted to conspiratorial methods that only precipitated the movement's disintegration."[26]

Such were the causes of a sudden and swift decline. But all this does not explain why the council movement was not able to regain its position after the defeat. The KPD also underwent the rigors of repressions, but it then found a permanent *raison d'être* in day-to-day action, first and foremost within the established institutions, and therefore in the ordinary forms of bourgeois politics, where it constituted an effective force. However, the revolutionary elements, disgusted with everything, renounced political activity and abandoned the party *en masse*. [27] The party continued, of course, to recruit but, in fact, it had lost its substance. As a result of this policy, it found itself unable to offer any real resistance to the Nazis—an incapacity whose main cause is most frequently attributed, in a manner as frivolous as it is revealing, to a strategic error, to a refusal to form a common parliamentary front with the Social Democrats for which Stalin alone was to blame.

In any case, the membership of the KAP, once counted in the thousands, in time came to be counted in hundreds. [28] On several occasions, the temptation to resort to a "flexible tactic" was felt in its ranks (especially within the AAU); a temptation to a modified return to trade union practice, to propaganda for immediate demands. The first serious crisis occurred in 1921-22, which ended

26. Paul Mattick, "Otto Rühle...," *op. cit.*, p. 17.
27. In 1927, in the region of Thuringia, nearly 75 percent of the ex-militants of the USPD and of the Spartakusbund had left the party. Cf. the excellent study by Siegfried Bahne, "Die K.P.D." in *Das Ende der Partien* (Dusseldorf, 1960), p. 661.
28: Cf. *Informations Correspondance Ouvrières, op. cit.*, pp. 12-14.

in a new split.[29] In 1927, the problem came up again. In effect, the "ultra-left" wing of the KPD drew close to the KAPD, after its expulsion from the Communist Party.[30] Its militants put the accent on the "anti-parliamentary parliamentarianism," and more especially on the "revolutionary trade unionism" of the early days of the Communist International.

From 1921, Pannekoek remained to a large extent outside the party, and intervened only to emphasize "the need for an intensive propaganda centered on the new situation and the new tasks."[31] He was to return to and develop his arguments in 1927, in an article entitled "Principle and Tactic,"[32] with which we shall now deal.

Pannekoek began by offering this diagnosis: "From 1918 to the present day, every chapter of European history could be headed: *The Defeat of the Revolution.*"

The World War, he continued, had increased to the utmost the distinctive traits of capitalism: exploitation of the masses, militarist oppression, misery and privations. "The collapse occurred first in Russia, the country with the lowest level of capitalist organization. After the revolts in the towns caused by famine, the mutiny of the peasant troops, the overthrow of the Czarist regime, there followed some six months of feverish political development. Petty bourgeois strata and parties succeeded one another in power: the Kadets, the Mensheviks, the socialist-revolutionaries, each showed themselves to be too timorous, too corrupt from the spiritual viewpoint, to take the necessary drastic measures. They lacked the resolution to see things through, to break once and for all out of centuries accumulated misery. The course taken by the revolution did not fit in with these exhausted organizations. Only the Bolsheviks, formed on radical Marxism, carried the revolution on to its uttermost limits, and founded in 1917 the Republic of Soviets; the Communist Party came to power in the form of the dictatorship of the proletariat."

Then, Germany cracked. Soldiers' and workers' councils came into existence, and were immediately coopted by "a whole stratum, almost a class,

29. Cf. H. Gorter, *Die Notwendigkeit der Wiedervereinigung der K.A.P.D.* (Berlin, 1923).

30. Cf. S. Bahne, "Zwischen 'Luxemburgismus' und 'Stalinismus.' Die 'ultra-linke' Opposition in der K.P.D.," *Vierteljahrshefte für Zeitgeschichte*, October, 1961.

31. K. Horner, "Marxismus und Idealismus," *Proletarier* (theoretical organ of the KAPD), 1, 4, February-March 1921.

32. K. Horner, "Prinzip und Taktik," *Proletarier*, No. 7-8, 1927, pp. 141-48 and 178-86. An editorial note states: "Since before the war, the author of this article has defended, within the Social Democratic Party and in concert with Rosa Luxemburg, the Marxist line against reformism. We shall return to various points of this work which demand a reply or additional information."

of permanent officials," the working class having been disciplined by a prolonged Social Democratic and trade union education." Moreover, "there was no party, however small, that was animated by revolutionary class consciousness. The formation of such a party was prevented by circumstances arising as much from questions of personalities as from concrete difficulties. Everywhere, small groups were spontaneously organizing themselves, and through their spokesmen, Liebknecht and Luxemburg, made their appeal to the masses, but there was neither program nor cohesion. The revolutionary workers were defeated after bitter clashes, and their leaders were assassinated. Then began the decline of the revolution. . . .

"Whereas the proletariat was scarcely prepared for its historic mission, the bourgeoisie knew how to exploit proletarian deficiencies to the fullest. . . . Becoming socialist minded, they agreed, without a blow having been struck, to the reforms which they had stubbornly opposed for decades: the Republic, universal suffrage, the eight-hour day, the recognition of the right to trade unions. . . . The republican regime and democracy served solely as means to inaugurate new forms of political domination for the benefit of capital. The worst aspect of this was not that these reforms had been set up by the workers in the course of a revolutionary movement, but the fact that the workers believed that they had gained something by all this. Under modern capitalism, the purpose of democracy, both in terms of its nature and its function, is to nourish this conviction and to weaken the workers' will to action. Thus, democracy, once acquired, was exploited to the full: henceforth, the task of elaborating and implementing reforms and other measures was entrusted exclusively to parliamentarians, to trade union leaders, to ministers. For it is of the essence of democracy to see to it that the working masses are kept away from the political terrain, that they are kept to their routine tasks in the domain of production, and doomed to revolutionary inactivity. And thus, the revolutionary episode was terminated; in effect, revolution is considered to be the intensive, daily and direct political action of the masses themselves. . . .

"The power of the bourgeoisie stems essentially from the immaturity, the fears, the illusions of the proletariat, from lack of proletarian class consciousness, clear vision of purposes, unity and cohesion. Since no one knew to what extent the workers would be capable of powerful and united actions, the bourgeoisie was forced to jettison the ballast." Then, "the revolutionary elite having been decimated," power moved toward the right "as the fear of the proletariat diminished." And the Social Democrats found themselves gradually ousted.

"In Western Europe, the effect of the revolution scarcely went beyond some kind of social reforms (e.g. the eight-hour day); but in Eastern Europe, a very important economic revolution took place, where the big, more or less feudal estates were parceled out, and gave rise in turn to small or medium forms of exploitation. This revolution was made more radical by the fact that modern industry and modern class antagonisms were less developed there. It was in Russia that the revolution went furthest. It is still going on in the neighboring states, which have been re-established or enlarged after the war (Poland, Rumania, Czechoslovakia, etc.). Finally "throughout the whole of Europe, capitalism feels politically strong and self-assured: the specter of socialism, which had terrified it for decades, has been removed...."

Nevertheless, the KAP holds the theory that capitalism has entered a final crisis, "an economic crisis from which capitalism can never emerge and is therefore heading toward its destruction." This thesis, says Pannekoek, has nothing in common with Marxism. "Marx and Engels have constantly and emphatically stressed that only the conscious action of the proletariat, with power acquired through the class struggle and later through the establishment of a new mode of production, could put an end to capitalism.... Socialism is something that concerns people, something that involves the will, the clearsightedness and the energy to seize power and to break all the fetters shackling the new economic development, by overthrowing the political, juridical and ideological system of the bourgeoisie. What happens in the economic domain must first become alive in the minds of men, for only there does the transforming act occur.... Economic causes act as a stimulus to class consciousness, but with an intensity that varies very greatly from case to case. Whereas in phases of proseperity the masses are satisfied with their lot and think only about working, these phases are followed by crises in which discontent grows, revolutionary attitudes gain strength, and the proletariat moves into action.... Favorable and fortuitous circumstances can never compensate the lack of internal vigor, but can merely open up ways."

These are considerations of a general kind. The present great postwar political crisis is over: "minor crises can no doubt still occur in the field of capital, and establish whether it is better to govern through democracy or through reaction. But, as far as the proletariat is concerned, it is for the moment solely a question of economic crisis, for too much credence must not be given to the constant prophesying of world wars. The bourgeoisie is now on its guard. The capitalist world is making every effort to overcome the deep postwar crisis, but the fact is that we are still at the very center of this crisis and that unemployment weighs heavily on the working class.

"What, then, are the prospects for revolutionary development?

It is often alleged that "if we move toward a prolonged and severe economic depression, its effect will be to revolutionize the proletariat and lead to an uninterrupted development of the revolution.

"The idea that the capitalist system is caught up in a permanent and irresolvable crisis has undoubtedly some value—insofar, at least, as it is not just wishful thinking, but is traceable in part to Luxemburg's work on the accumulation of capital, which provides something of a theoretical basis for it. Since her book was published two years before the war, Rosa Luxemburg did not herself formulate this perspective; but, today, this conclusion is drawn from it. It is therefore absolutely necessary to return to this subject.

"In the last section of Book Two of *Capital*, Marx deals with the process of capitalist reproduction. He does so by means of mathematical examples of purely theoretical value, and consequently this section of the book aroused very little attention; but the way that these examples are being invoked at the present time shows the extent to which a clearly abstract question can assume a practical relevance for the tactics of the class struggle. Marx shows in these pages how the capitalist production goes on by its own accord as long as all the products return in the new "circuits" of production, in the form of consumer goods, or of raw materials, or again of the means of production. This holds equally true for the stage when production is constantly expanding; a different distribution suffices for this, according to the branches of production and the types of merchandise—for example, when there is a relatively greater need for means of production. If a correct relationship is established between the different branches, supply and demand will always strike a balance. Of course, this is true only at the level of theoretical abstraction; since capitalist production is decentralized, supply and demand remain unknown quantities and equilibrium is not achieved without certain merchandise remaining unsold. That is why the branch producing such merchandise does not expand, and sometimes goes into a deep depression. And since at the same time, equilibrium is established, capital grows and sets off in quest of new fields of investment; the abstract equilibrium is in perpetual development and is kept in motion through ceaseless creations and trial runs, in quest of a final, self-regulating situation.

"From the theoretical viewpoint, however, it is important that equilibrium be established on an average, for this makes it possible to verify that the capitalist process of production can have, with equal likelihood, a large or a small output, since it is not concerned with consumer needs outside its own cycle. Capitalism does not produce the necessities of life in terms of human needs; what interests it is not the number of men who are starving, but the quantity of workers in its service whose salaries are convertible into necessities of life. In a time of crisis, the whole process contracts; in a time of prosperity, it expands. Of course, the reserves of men and of raw materials available ultimately impose limits on this process, but both also increase in a regular way. For it absorbs the vestiges of the primitive modes of production, small enterprises and sectors where self-consumption still dominates, with which it establishes exchange relationships, and which supply it with merchandise and raw material, while at the same time serving it as resevoirs of work power, and at whose expense it ceaselessly expands.

"In her book on accumulation, Luxemburg believed she had detected an error in Marx's calculations. She therefore concluded that, in the process of capitalist production, supply and demand could not coincide, and that, through the accumulation of capital, there was always an excess of merchandise for which there was no demand—and that all this holds true even at the level of abstract theory. This, therefore, must necessarily produce a marketing crisis that cannot be remedied except by violence and by the opening up of new territories to serve as markets. It is this, then, that is the basic cause of imperialism: because of its internal necessities, the capitalist system is inevitably forced to undertake the conquest of foreign countries.

"It is only a short step from this theory to the idea that the marketing crisis, linked by its very nature to the expansion of production, is bound to assume such breadth and gravity that it becomes impossible to surmount it. Hence, with any amelioration of the situation ruled out, capitalism finds itself in an impasse, and one can most certainly see in this a fatal crisis. We have already pointed out that Luxemburg never concluded that capitalism will one day inevitably find itself face to face with such an insurmountable crisis. She formulated her theory purely as an explanation in economic terms of imperialism and of the reasons why every crisis necessarily leads to an enforced extension of the sphere of imperialism; the fact that today there are no further markets to open up is something that scarcely needs emphasizing.

"In any case, this theory is incorrect. As was pointed out in the *Bremer Bürger-Zeitung*, [33] shortly after the publication of Luxemburg's book, she was

---

33.   Cf. Pannekoek's articles in the Bremen paper—issues for January 29 and 30, 1913 (and also in *Neue Zeit*, XXXI:1, pp. 780-92, and *Nieuwe Tijd*, XXI, 1916, pp. 268-83). Pannekoek returns again to this problem in *Rätekorrespondenz*, No. 1, 1934, pp. 1-20, where he criticizes the important work by Henryk Grossmann: *Das Akkumulations- und Zusammenbruchs-gesetz der kapitalistischen Systems* (Leipzig, 1929). Grossmann also upheld the theses of the inevitable economic collapse, but in a sense different from Luxemburg. In both cases, Pannekoek strongly challenges, on the basis of a simple mathematical treatment of Marxian schemas, the possibility of disproportionalities between the two sectors of production over a long period and with regular growth. According to him, the overthrow of capitalism cannot occur without the massive and conscious intervention of the exploited and of their struggle by and for themselves.

wrong in saying that Marx had made an error in his tables. We cannot dwell here on the details of the theory (already discussed in one of the early numbers of *Proletarier*); suffice it to recall that the accumulation of capital, the perpetual formation of new masses of capital in quest of investments in spheres yielding the highest profits, furnishes a primary and absolutely adequate explanation of the reasons why capitalism is constantly enlarging its domain at the expense of more primitive modes of production, as well as of the means which it uses to achieve this end, with or without recourse to violence according to the existing relationships of forces.

"So, therefore, anyone seeking to base his tactics on the idea that capitalism will embroil itself in a permanent crisis that it will not be able to surmount commits a dangerous error. An illusion of this kind leads one to elaborate, in effect, what is merely a short-term tactic, and the subsequent disillusionment is calculated to breed discouragement. It must also be stressed that this belief has no serious foundation—indeed, no foundation other than wishful thinking and the patent fact that up to now capitalism has not succeeded in surmounting its postwar crisis. But the bases of Marx's theory remain valid: it is entirely possible for capitalism to increase production and thereby surmount a highly unfavorable situation. The difficulty, in fact, is the one that always follows crisis: how to start up production again. For one must first buy in order to be able to sell; each branch of production must therefore wait for the others, since in a period of speculation no one dares to extend credit. However, if there is an upsurge in any one branch that enables it to get under way again, the others begin to get orders, and the expansion begins to spread from branch to branch. Of course, different factors may delay this recovery (for example, the present political restructuring of Europe is, in many ways, shackling economic growth). How and when production will begin a new cycle depends on so many unknown factors that any prediction on the matter would be highly speculative; nevertheless, one thing is certain—that there is no foundation whatever for the idea that there can be no chance of a change in the conjuncture of circumstances now working against capitalism."

Pannekoek cites two factors in favor of an eventual resumption of the production cycle: a large-scale increase in gold production, owing to the discovery of new gold fields, and "the promotion of eastern Asia to the rank of an autonomous sector of capitalist production.... Capitalism is far from being at its last gasp. According to those who think that it is, it is enough simply to wait awhile and then the final victory will come. But this is just sugar coating the pill. The hard fact is that an arduous climb still lies before us; we have only reached the foot of the mountains. It is difficult today to foresee the short-term economic development. If a phase of expansion has just begun, it is equally certain that it will be followed by just as significant a crisis. And with the crisis, the revolution will reappear. The old revolution is finished: we must prepare the new one."

In the second part of this article, Pannekoek attempts to define the nature and the function of the Communist Party, whose task it is to prepare the future. (Clearly, he is concerned with Western European Communism, not with that of the Third International). Later, we shall present a text especially devoted to this subject. However, even at the risk of some repetition, it is interesting to see what he has to say here.

"Since both Social Democracy and communism take as their objective the seizure of social power by the working class, they cannot be distinguished from one another by their aims. Nor can they be distinguished by the methods used to attain this common objective. While it remains true that the communists opt for the method of *revolution* whereas the Social Democrats look to an *evolution* involving the slow maturation of the future state in the womb of the present society, this division is blurred by the fact that they both foresee the possibility of a final class-against-class struggle in order to deliver the final blow after a period of numerous proletarian successes and defeats. Again, a basis for distinguishing between them cannot be that the communists seek to take power by a single blow rather than waiting for power to fall into their hands, like the Social Democrats: this is not the communist idea. We are well aware that the transition to social power constitutes a process full of shifts, of victories and defeats, in many countries and regions of the world — in fact, a whole historical period dominated by a violence whose harbingers have appeared in the course of the events of the last ten years.

"The fundamental difference between these two tendencies lies in the idea they have each formed of the means, of the organs, through which the proletariat will gain power.

"Social Democracy has always viewed the party (linked with the trade unions) as the organ that is to lead the revolution to victory. This does not necessarily imply the exclusive use of electoral methods; in the opinion of the radical wing, the party should combine the pressures of parliamentary and extra-parliamentary means, such as strikes and demonstrations, in order to assert the power of the proletariat. But, when all is said and done, it was the party that directed the battle, called the masses into the streets, or acted as an advance detachment. And if the oppressive mantle of state power were to be whisked off, it is again the party, as representing the proletariat, that must assume power, along with the trade unions who were exercising the basic economic role of executive organs of production.

"That is the reason why, according to this conception, the Social

Democratic Party was quite different from any other party. It was the party of the working class, a party serving as a political organization of the proletariat; in due course, it would prevail over the organizations of the bourgeoisie, and its apparatus in full maturity would then come to power. And it was for this reason that it was necessary to attract more and more workers within the sphere of the party, as militants, as members, and as electors. The party card was to show which side of the barricade one had opted for. Moscow propagated an idea that although basically the same, was carried to grotesque lengths: the idea of the dictatorship of a small party that was the incarnation of the 'dictatorship of the proletariat.' The development of Social Democracy before, during and after the War has shown that it was impossible to fulfill this project. A party that develops in this way, with a corresponding apparatus of permanent officials, takes on a conservative character. Its bureaucracy naturally fears the consequences of a revolution and has an interest in maintaining and improving the established order. Its body of officials hope to succeed the capitalist bureaucracy naturally and peacefully, or to govern in coalition with the latter, at least for some time. Within a democratic party of this kind, exactly as within a democratic state, the mass of militants lack the means to impose their will on a bureaucracy holding all the means of power; and this is all the more true in a dictatorial party of the Moscow type."

Contemporary mass movements "have shown how things happen and must happen, in what way the great conflicts blow up, and have thus confirmed the history of former revolutions. In all of these, it was the gigantic power of immense masses of the people at their highest degree of expansion and unity that overthrew the old order and opened the way to new developments. Such a power does not suddenly appear in a meteoric fashion; it originates from deep and long-felt discontent, from an intense agitation that gives the masses a clear picture of the situation, from a series of experiences that educate the doubters and the hesitant. Frequently, it is preceded by abortive attempts and violent clashes, for only through such things does the power of the masses take shape. In previous revolutions, it was mostly petty bourgeoisie or artisans who intervened on the basis of craft or of district. In the modern proletarian revolutions, the majority belong to the major enterprises; the working masses intervene and make decisions on the basis of their factory. The general assemblies (of a factory, or of the branch of industry as a larger unit) decide on maintaining social peace or on holding a strike or demonstration, deliberate with the other enterprises through delegate assemblies, and pour their members into the street to form a compact nucleus around which the class as a whole crystalizes.

"These experiences have shaped communist thinking about revolution. It is not the party that makes the revolution, but *the class as a whole*. Hence, the party has a completely different function from that ascribed to it in the old Social Democratic conception. It cannot absorb in itself the whole of the class and act for the class; on the contrary, it can only be the avant-garde of the class and remain true to its spiritual orientation. In their places of work, the communists are the ones who see farthest, who have the clearest ideas, and who are the most devoted to cause; that is why they are able to step forward at any time, to propose the best solutions, to size up the situation, to disperse the fears of the hesitant, and to deflect anything liable to set the movement on a wrong course. The party also plays this role in connection with general delegate assemblies charged with taking major decisions, inasmuch as it points out the right road to them and presents a program of action. Again, both during the growth period and the period of rapid development, it is the party that spreads among the masses the slogans needed to show the way, to clarify the situation, and to avoid mistakes.

"All action invariably demands a spiritual battle of the masses aimed at achieving lucidity—a battle in which opposing parties and tendencies meet and clash; and the Communist Party should wage this battle for the workers under the eyes of the workers. In this way, then, the party becomes, at each stage of the class struggle, a primordial organ, as it were, the soul of the revolution. . . .

"Quite simply, the party is the organization of communist militants animated with the same sentiments. Its strength grows through discussions about program and principles, and through the participation of all its members in agitation and in action." There is no question of recruitment at any price. "Quality, correctness of principles, that is what counts most in the eyes of the party. . . ."

Today, certain people call for "flexible tactics calculated to increase the attractiveness of the KAP. Anyone lately involved in the workers' movement and familiar with its literature will read between the lines propositions analogous to those of an earlier period that sought a softening of principles and an adaptation to circumstances. The slogan, 'Let's be done with powerlessness! ,' also constituted, at that time, the point of departure for opportunism. . . . But the party's power to attract does not reside in the party itself, but in its principles. And when the workers do not want to listen—in other words, when conditions are such that no challenge of a revolutionary kind presents itself with any urgency—other principles predominate. In these circumstances, it is useless for the party to try to prevail at any and all costs, for this would signify that it had sacrificed its principles to secure an accomodation with things as they are. Nor does it serve any good to compromise with principles in order to make them appear acceptable to a large number of people; what matters for the future is not the number of adherents who find the principles acceptable, but the communists who understand them and who make them deeply and personally their own."

Hence, according to Pannekoek, "what is of greatest value in the KAP press is not the impassioned appeals, which now interest only a small number of workers, but serious information, critical commentary on the economic situation, and discussion of tactical problems linked with that situation. . . .

"The main objection to carrying out a tactic based on the theoretical principles of Marxism is that the tactic is inapplicable and ineffectual. Those who delve into bookish theory can completely and contentedly accept an attitude strictly in accordance with these principles and with these alone. But the masses, who have not studied the theory, take a very different view: they are concerned only with practical consequences. And if one wishes to win them over, one must bear in mind their objectives and their aspirations: the securing of reforms. It could be said that principle is the salt of practice, but if one over-salts the dishes, the meal becomes inedible.

"However, excessive attachment to one of these mutually opposing positions within the workers' movement involves the danger of overlooking what is *essential*. The difference between a principle-centered tactic and an opportunist tactic is not that the first originates out of fear that the theory may lose its purity through contact with a bad world, whereas the second never leaves the terrain of real life. The alleged dogmatist always guides his tactic toward praxis—revolutionary praxis, that is. The difference between these two tendencies arises from whether the emphasis is placed on short- or long-term tactics. There is no question here of reproaching the opportunists for their fixation on practice in general, but for their limited practice, which takes into account only the present moment and sacrifices what is of permanent value for the future to immediate gains."

In times of prosperity, when the workers are concerned only with securing reforms, opportunism thrives. A mass party will feel the repercussion of this and will inevitably be drawn into opportunism, whatever its past history; German Social Democracy is a case in point, but merely a typical case. "A small party is better able to defend itself against these influences. Faced with a given alternative, it can choose: it can reject the inclinations of the masses, stick firmly to principle, and therefore undergo a shrinkage of size and influence; or it can attempt to increase its membership, win influence, and fall into the morass. We are speaking here only about the spiritual effects of economic circumstances on the workers. Political situations can, of course, also develop and present a party with the same type of choice. A case in point was the Third International when it plunged with both feet into the morass of opportunism, simply to gain a rapid increase of its political influence."

In a revolutionary phase, the picture changes completely. The masses are transformed: "they cease to react in the manner of petty bourgeoisie, who are deeply disturbed by any talk of revolution, and they themselves seek revolution. They demand clear slogans, clear-cut programs, radical objectives and turn increasingly toward the party that can give them these, owing to its principle-centered attitude. It can thus happen that the old parties find themselves abandoned one after the other, and that a small group, hitherto despised as dreamers devoid of common sense and as rigid dogmatists, suddenly comes forward and takes over the direction of the masses in the course of the revolution. This was what occurred in the case of the Bolsheviks during the Russian Revolution; without the rigid, intolerant dogmatism that led Lenin and his comrades to extirpate from their party, during the pre-revolutionary phase, every inclination toward opportunism, the Russian Revolution would not have presented the clear-cut, radical character that carried it to success and made it a model for the proletarian revolution. The subsequent fact that, through the absence of revolution in Europe and through the petty bourgeois structure of Russia itself, a relapse into bourgeois politics inevitably occurred, does not lessen in any way the exemplary value of those first years of the Russian Revolution.

"In thus contrasting the principle-centered tactic with the opportunist type, we have also created a clear distinction between revolutionary periods and reactionary periods." But this is a broad distinction; for, in reality, all kinds of intermediate phases exist. Even in times of crisis, the principle-centered tactic "does not always have the ear of the proletariat, at least as a whole. The unemployed look for temporary assistance, for reforms, so that they may return to being salaried slaves; those who are employed continue to count on the stability and continuance of the capitalist system. Despite their revolt, the masses have not yet the desire to achieve the objective, still lack the feel of their own power and the will to strive toward the ultimate goal—the primary conditions for revolution.... It is therefore impossible to forecast with certainty whether the situation in times of crisis favors or does not favor communist propaganda; there are so many economic, traditional, ideological and other factors at work to make minds receptive or non-receptive, that only by hindsight can one measure what has finally prevailed." But, in any case, to attempt to adapt to a contingent situation is to carry the spirit of an outmoded phase into a new phase of the class struggle.

"However, the principle-centered tactic is not learned from books, or through courses on theory and political formation, but through real life practice of the class struggle. It is true that prior to action, as well as after action, theory can be expressed in concepts that present organized knowledge; but, in order to develop in a real sense, this knowledge itself must be acquired in the hard school of experience, a harsh lived experience that shapes the mind in the full heat of combat. Practical action brings into reality all factors of which the theory speaks, and enables one to see the increasing forces of solidarity, of awareness, but also—through the defeats that the enemy inflicts thanks to its spiritual resources—the weaknesses of one's own class. It is only through the practice of its struggles against capitalism, as Marx in his time already stressed, that the proletariat is transformed into a revolutionary class capable of conquering the capitalist system....

"These reflections are also valid for the struggle against the bosses, and, in this sense, are of particular relevance to the *Allgemeine Arbeiterunion*. Like the KAP, the AAU is essentially an organization for revolution. Under other conditions, during a period of revolutionary ebb, one would not dream of founding such an organization. But it is all that remains from the revolutionary years; the workers who created it and who fought under its banners, do not want the experience of those struggles to be forgotten, and therefore are conserving the AAU as a precious means of future development. That is why a period such as the present one brings even more contradictions for this union than it does for the KAP.

"Were the AAU to decide to act as a trade union organization, we would have simply another *Kraft-Zentrale*. At present, it is AAU policy that, in revolutionary phases, all the members of the various confederations should follow the same path to insure coherent unity of all the factories. And it's clear propaganda for this idea could only founder if the AAU set itself up as a competitor to the other confederations, instead of acting as the proponent of a tactic that completely transcended their aims.

"...It has sometimes been said that the AAU was the proponent of an organizational principle: factory organization as superior to the trade unions." But, in any case, it is not concerned with being an instrument for reanimating a trade union kind of combativeness. "To adopt this objective would be to transform itself into an organization involved out of necessity in compromising with the bosses and in the formation of a bureaucratic stratum, and for these reasons would therefore be drawn onto the path of reformism.... When the struggles for better pay and working conditions led by the trade unions are in accordance with reformist principles, in the manner of carpet sellers or of pleaders before a court, the AAU should subject them to the most severe criticism. If, against the wishes of the trade unions, the workers declare war on the bosses, the AAU should support them with enlightenment and advice and put at their disposal its machinery of agitation; however, in doing so, it must never act as though seeking to fight its competitors, as though attempting to lure members away from the trade unions. It should not, therefore, adopt the attitude of a new organization that places itself at the head of the workers, but, on the contrary, should seek to make the new principles prevail. There is no question, for the AAU, of refusing to assume the leadership of the struggle because its membership is small. On the contrary, indeed, these principles demand that the workers fight, think and decide for themselves, and not that they appeal for direction from organizations other than the trade unions. . . . It will follow the proper course only if all its decisions are in accordance with the principle of not trying to develop as a specific organization, but instead attempting to contribute to the maturation of the workers. This is tantamount to saying that the mission of the AAU is to assist the progress of all social conflicts toward revolution. But it cannot be maintained that the revolution can be achieved through any and every social conflict; and therefore the mission of the AAU must be to transform every conflict into a phase of revolutionary development by raising the level of knowledge and of the will to fight.

"What really matters is that—in the years of decline, of confusion, of deceit—the principles of the class struggle, in the Marxist sense, have been protected by a handful of men welded together; for without this, no revival would be possible. Clear and proven principles and an ardent zeal for struggle are the two pillars on which the revolutionary development must be reconstructed."

To argue that the realities of the situation left room for no other choice is not to lessen the immediate importance of the preceding considerations. The idea of "flexible" (or "dynamic") tactics no doubt embodied a legitimate aspiration to break out of the group-centered life—that framework within which, unable to direct one's aggression effectively against the world, one directed it against the nearest group, and, through lack of numbers, one saw discussions about principles in terms of personal antagonisms. Almost until the last days of *Rätekommunismus*, that was toward the end of 1932—when the Social Democratic repression was directed against the leftist press, while at the same time the different tendencies were uniting against fascism—this question provoked stormy controversies and individual or collective rifts. But the Leninist Communist Party itself, although relatively large, succeeded neither in securing a foothold in the reformist trade unions (a policy urged on it by its impractical masters) nor in creating a really competitive central body.[34]

Pannekoek in no respect sought to develop elaborate formulations. He was interested only in the best hypotheses of development, the only ones really worth envisaging, the others being of no practical value. And he noted, in *Prinzip und Taktik*, that even in the time of crisis, when the inevitable outcome of the situation is "the rapid growth of the party and of its influence, there is a strong probability that one can only prepare the way for the coming revolutionary wave, every phase of this kind constituting merely a stage within a total process."[35]

It is well known that the official workers' movement, with its paramilitary organizations, its rituals and its banners, collapsed before the National Socialists and the petty bourgeoisie, without daring to fling itself into a real battle, and offering as a pretext the argument that the consequences of an extra-parliamentary conflict were hazardous (while the movement itself had done everything to ensure that this was so). And we know what a fearful price the people of Europe have paid for this new bankruptcy—a consequence of an entire tactic, to use Pannekoek's terminology. It will be argued that there were many other causes for the triumph of fascism besides this shameful surrender; but one can argue against this particular cause. And this was what was attempted, though in vain, by the council movement in Germany.

---

34. Under the pressure of the 1929 crisis, the KPD attempted to revive, in its own fashion, the KAPist tactic of the self-activation of the masses by "a twofold organization"—political and trade-unionist. Cf. Flechtheim, *op. cit.*, pp. 161-62. This attempt at adaptation, always linked with the old parliamentary tactic, soon came to nothing.

35. *Ibid.*, 8, p. 183.

CHAPTER ELEVEN

THE RUSSIAN REVOLUTION

Almost all the 'organized' forces of council communism disappeared shortly after the inauguration of the Nazi reign of terror. There remained only isolated elements and small groups scattered throughout the world. Only one group — the *Groep van Internationale Communisten*, or GIC — continued to display at that time any theoretical or practical activity. We shall discuss it later. For the moment, though, let us note that it published several pamphlets by Pannekoek (generally anonymous).[1]

One of these GIC publications was his *Lenin as Philosopher*[2] to which we have already referred. The title is itself revealing, since the pamphlet (subtitled "A Critical Examination of the Philosophical Basis of Leninism") is in effect a critique of Lenin's *Materialism and Empiriocriticism* published in 1908, and issued in German in 1927. Following Marx and Dietzgen, Pannekoek examined the objective character both of matter (in the modern sense, including wave phenomena) and of mental representations (from the simplest to the most complex — a mathematical model, for example), as well as the forms of interaction between the material world and the spiritual world.

Pannekoek follows Marx, we have said, but this needs qualification. In effect, Pannekoek stresses that Marxism is a body of ideas that are by definition revolutionary, and that the politics of Marx, like his theories, developed in close connection with the organic transformation of society. "The method of research that they [Marx and Engels] framed remains up to this day an excellent guide and tool toward the understanding and interpretation of new events;" this method is that of historical materialism, "a

---

1. For instance, in the pamphlet *De Arbeiders, het Parlement en het Kommunisme*, Pannekoek deals in broad outline with the idea of the councils. The table of contents provides a good summary of this pamphlet: crisis and misery; the conflict between work and property; the class struggles; parliamentarianism as an instrument of emancipation; leaders as emancipators; the utility of parliament; the Communist Party; the direct action of the masses; the workers' councils.

2. J. Harper, *Lenin als Philosoph. Kritische Betrachtung der philosophischen Grundlage des Leninismus* (Amsterdam, 1938), mimeographed. The English version appears as Anton Pannekoek, *Lenin as Philosopher* (New York, 1948).

living theory that grows with the proletariat and with the tasks and aims of its struggle."[3]

Pannekoek applies this method to the study of the bourgeois ideas of the world, whose development rests primarily on the idea of the natural sciences, "the spiritual basis of capitalism." These ideas, he says, took on a materialist character as long as the bourgeoisie fought for political power against feudal absolutism and religion, the latter still being at that time the spiritual basis of the former. But when the bourgeoisie had come into power and the class struggle had emerged, the new dominant class stressed the weaknesses of materialism and the limits of science.

And it is in this context, with Marx having "stated that realities determine thought, that Dietzgen established the relationship between reality and thought." He was to show, in effect, that spiritual and material phenomena "constitute the entire real world, a coherent entity in which matter determines mind" (that is, thoughts are "material for our brain activity of forming concepts") and mind, through human activity, determines matter. We are therefore dealing with what "may rightly be called monism"—a monism that Pannekoek was to take up on his own account, adapting it to the evolution of the exact sciences.[4]

Pannekoek therefore examines, from this monist and materialist perspective, the epistemological theories of Mach and of Avenarius. We can deal here with only one aspect of this masterly account, which certainly deserves to be published in full. Mach, whose philosophical work made a considerable contribution to the development of quantitative physics, reduced the world to a system of objects, the knowledge of which was a matter of sensations of a predominantly intersubjective character—not the interaction of, but the near-identity of matter and mind. To this, Pannekoek answers, in line with Marxism, that knowledge does not originate in personal meditation (as Avenarius holds) or only in the activity of the professional philosopher alone (as Mach holds), but in social labor, in the interaction of man and nature in general.

Continuing with a close analysis of this anti-Machist work by Lenin, Pannekoek shows that the latter, who was in no way equipped to understand modern physics—and therefore the ideas of the Austrian physicist—thoroughly misinterprets and misunderstands it, and, by way of refutation, can only indulge in invective. According to Lenin, "the philosophical

---

3. *Ibid.*, p. 13.
4. *Ibid.*, pp. 24-25. Pierre Naville finds in the Pannekoek pamphlet, which has "some good chapters," a "vague realism," then a "dualism," and finally an "existentialism"! Cf. P. Naville, *Psychologie, Marxisme, materialisme* (Paris, 1947), pp. 141-45.

expression of objective reality" covers only physical matter, whereas *matter* "in Historical Materialism [is] the designation of all that is really existing in the world."[5] But, says Pannekoek, what must be specially noted is the identity relationship that Lenin establishes between Marx and Engels, on the one hand, and the bourgeois materialists, on the other (with the exception of three points—namely, the "mechanistic materialism" of the bourgeois thinkers; "the anti-dialectical character of their philosophy;" and the "non-intelligibility of historical materialism").[6] In this connection, Pannekoek points out: "Of course, theoretical ideas must be criticized by theoretical arguments. But the social consequences are emphasized with such vehemence, the social origins of the contested ideas should not be left out of consideration. This most essential character of Marxism does not seem to exist for Lenin."[7]

Lenin, in speaking of a book by Haeckel, the materialist popularizer, says: "This little book has become a weapon in the class struggle."[8] But what class struggle does he mean, at what period and under what conditions? Pannekoek comments as follows: "Socialist workers embraced the social doctrines of Marx and the materialism of natural science with equal interest. Their labor under capitalism, their daily experience and their awakening understanding of social forces contributed greatly toward undermining traditional religion. Then to solve their doubts, the need for scientific knowledge grew, and the workers became the most zealous readers of the works of Buechner and Haeckel. . . . This, by the way, concurs with the fact that the working-class movement had not yet reached beyond capitalism, that in practice the class struggle only tended to secure its place within capitalist society, and that the democratic solutions of the early bourgeois movements were also accepted as valid for the working class. The full comprehension of revolutionary Marxist theory is possible only in connection with revolutionary practice."[9]

"Wherein, then, do bourgeois materialism and Historical Materialism stand opposed to one another?

"Both agree insofar as they are materialist philosophies, that is both recognize the primacy of the experienced material world: both recognize that spiritual phenomena, sensation, consciousness, ideas, are derived from the former. They are opposite in that bourgeois materialism bases itself upon natural science, whereas Historical Materialism is primarily the science of

---

5. Pannekoek, *ibid.*, p. 61.
6. Lenin, *Materialisme et empiriocriticisme* (Paris, 1956), pp. 205-206.
7. Pannekoek, *Lenin as Philosopher*, *op. cit.*, p. 64.
8. Lenin, *Materialisme et empiriocriticisme, op. cit.*, p. 306.
9. Pannekoek, *Lenin as Philosopher, op. cit.*, pp. 17-18.

society. Bourgeois scientists observe man only as an object of nature, the highest of the animals, determined by natural laws. For an explanation of man's life and action, they have only general biological laws and, in a wider sense, the laws of chemistry, physics and mechanics. With these means little can be accomplished in the way of understanding social phenomena and ideas. Historical Materialism, on the other hand, lays bare the specific evolutionary laws of human society and shows the interconnection between ideas and society.

"The axiom of materialism that the spiritual is determined by the material world, has therefore entirely different meanings for the two doctrines. For bourgeois materialism it means that ideas are products of the brain, are to be explained out of the structure and the changes of the brain substance, finally out of the dynamics of the atoms of the brain. For Historical Materialism, it means that the ideas of man are determined by his social conditions; society is his environment which acts upon him through his sense organs. This postulates an entirely different kind of problem, a different approach, a different line of thought, hence, also a different theory of knowledge.

"For bourgeois materialism the problem of the meaning of knowledge is a question of the relationship of a spiritual phenomenon to the physico-chemical-biological phenomena of the brain matter. For Historical Materialism it is a question of the relationship of our thoughts to the phenomena that we experience as the external world. Now man's position in society is not simply that of an observing being; he is a dynamic force who reacts upon his environment and changes it."[10]

It is precisely this attitude of bourgeois materialism that Pannekoek traces in Lenin and in his teacher, Plekhanov, after having shown its connection with conditions that made possible the emergence of classical Social Democracy. When Plekhanov identified the ideas of Marx as an extension of those of Feuerbach,[11] he was, in a certain sense, uttering a simple truism; but he also highlights the basic and distinctive trait of the Marxist theory of knowledge, which "proceeds from the action of society, this self-made material world of man, upon the mind, and so belongs to the proletarian class struggle."[12] It was on this basis that Pannekoek wrote the chapter "The Russian Revolution," which follows.

"The basic philosophical agreement of Lenin and Plekhanov and their common divergence from Marxism points to their common origin in Russian

---

10. *Ibid.*, pp. 18-19.
11. In this connection, Pannekoek uses many citations from Plekhanov's *Questions fondamentales du marxisme* (Paris, undated), 2nd ed. pp. 15-21.
12. Pannekoek, *Lenin as Philosopher, op. cit.*, pp. 66-67.

social conditions. The name and garb of doctrine or theory depend on its spiritual descent; they indicate the earlier thinker to whom we feel most indebted and whom we think we follow. The real content, however, depends on its material origin and is determined by the social conditions under which it developed and has to work. Marxism itself says that the main social ideas and spiritual trends express the aims of the classes, i.e., the needs of social development, and change with the class struggles themselves. So they cannot be understood isolated from society and class struggle. This holds for Marxism itself.

"In their early days Marx and Engels stood in the first ranks of the opposition to German absolutism — an opposition that was still unified, containing both the bourgeoisie and the working class. Their development toward Historical Materialism, then, was the theoretical reflection of the development of the working class toward independent action against the bourgeoisie. The practical class-antagonism found its expression in the theoretical antagonism. The fight of the bourgeoisie against feudalism was expressed by middle-class materialism, the cognate of Feuerbach's doctrine, which used natural science to fight religion as the consecration of the old powers. The working class in its own fight has little use for natural science, the instrument of its foe; its theoretical weapon is social science, the science of social development. To fight religion by means of natural science has no significance for the workers; they know, moreover, that its roots will be cut off anyhow first by capitalist development, then by their own class struggle. Nor have they any use for the obvious fact that thoughts are produced by the brain. They have to understand how ideas are produced by society. This is the content of Marxism as it grows among the workers as a living and stirring power, as the theory expressing their growing power of organization and knowledge. When in the second half of the 19th century capitalism gained complete mastery in Western and Central Europe as well as in America, bourgeois materialism disappeared. Marxism was the only materialist class-view remaining.

"In Russia, however, matters were different. Here the fight against czarism was analogous to the former fight against absolutism in Europe. In Russia, too, church and religion were the strongest supports of the system of government; they held the rural masses, engaged in primitive agrarian production, in complete ignorance and superstition. The struggle against religion was here a prime social necessity. Since in Russia there was no significant bourgeoisie that could take up the fight as a future ruling class, the task fell to the intelligentsia; during scores of years it waged a strenuous fight for enlightenment of the masses against czarism. Among the Western bourgeoisie, now reactionary and anti-materialist, it could find no support whatever in this struggle. It had to appeal to the socialist workers, who alone sympathized with it, and it took over their acknowledged theory, Marxism. Thus it came about that even intellectuals who were spokesmen of the first rudiments of a Russian bourgeoisie, such as Peter Struve and Tugan Baranovski, presented themselves as Marxists. They had nothing in common with the proletarian Marxism of the West; what they learned from Marx was the doctrine of social development with capitalism as the next phase. A revolutionary force emerged in Russia for the first time when the workers took up the fight, first by strikes alone, then in combination with political demands. Now the intellectuals found a revolutionary class to join up with, in order to become its spokesmen in a socialist party.

"Thus the proletarian class struggle in Russia was at the same time a struggle against czarist absolutism, under the banner of socialism. So Marxism in Russia, developing as the theory of those engaged in the social conflict, necessarily assumed a different character than it had in Western Europe. It was still the theory of a fighting working class; but this class had to fight first and foremost for what in Western Europe had been the function and work of the bourgeoisie, with the help of the intellectuals. So the Russian intellectuals, in adapting the theory to this local task, had to find a form of Marxism in which criticism of religion stood in the forefront. They found it in an approach to earlier forms of materialism, and in the first writings of Marx from the time when in Germany the fight of the bourgeoisie and the workers against absolutism was still undivided."[13]

Plekhanov, Pannekoek recalls, was the first to adopt this approach, and to establish a close relationship between the materialism of Marx and the theories both of the major French materialists and of Feuerbach. In the ranks of German socialism, "Plekhanov was known as the herald of the Russian working-class struggle, which he predicted theoretically at a time when practically there was hardly any trace." Nearer as he was to the Western socialists, Plekhanov "was determined by Russian conditions less than was Lenin."

---

13. *Ibid.*, pp. 67-68. An expert Sovietologist, the Dominican priest Bochenski, citing this passage, approves of its content in so far as it pertains to the importance attached to the struggle against religion by the Russian revolutionaries. But he reproaches Pannekoek, on the one hand, for not seeing in Lenin a "classic" materialist, rarely "original" but "rather less crude then Engels;" and on the other, for confining to "religious values" only the hate that Lenin had for all "values." Finally, he says Pannekoek focuses too much on the conditions that determined the personality of Lenin, and not sufficiently on this personality itself. Cf. Bochenski, *Der Sowjetrussische dialektische Materialisme* (Bern, 1950), pp. 41-44. Thus, Pannekoek, too "existentialist" for Naville, is not sufficiently so for this priest.

Above all else, Pannekoek writes, Lenin and the Bolshevik Party saw as the first task "the annihilation of czarism and of the backward, barbarous social system of Russia. Church and religion were the theoretical foundations of that system"—hence the need for "a relentless fight against them." "The struggle against religion stood in the center of Lenin's theoretical thought; any concession, however small, to 'fideism' was an attack on the life-nerve of the movement." This fight "was very similar to the former fight of the bourgeoisie and intellectuals in Western Europe. . . . In Russia, however, it was the working class that had to wage the fight; so the fighting organization had to be a socialist party, proclaiming Marxism as its creed, and taking from Marxism what was necessary for the Russian Revolution: the doctrine of social development from capitalism to socialism, and the doctrine of class war as its moving force. Hence Lenin gave to his materialism the name and garb of Marxism, and assumed it to be the real Marxism.

"This identification was supported by still another circumstance. In Russia capitalism had not grown up gradually from small-scale production in the hands of a middle class, as it had in Western Europe. Big industry was imported from outside as a foreign element by Western capitalism, exploiting the Russian workers. Moreover, Western financial capital, by its loans to the czar, exploited the entire agrarian Russian people, who were heavily taxed to pay the interest. Western capital here assumed the character of colonial capital, with the czar and his officials as its agents. In countries exploited as colonies all the classes have a common interest in throwing off the yoke of the usurious foreign capital, to establish their own free economic development, leading as a rule to home capitalism. This fight is waged against world-capital, hence often under the name of socialism; and the workers of the Western countries, who stand against the same foe, are the natural allies. Thus in China, Sun-Yat-sen was a socialist; since, however, the Chinese bourgeoisie, for whom he was a spokesman, was a large and powerful class, his socialism was 'national' and he opposed the 'errors' of Marxism.

"Lenin, on the contrary, had to rely on the working class, and because his fight had to be implacable and radical, he espoused the radical ideology of the Western proletariat fighting world-capitalism—Marxism, in other words. Since, however, the Russian Revolution showed a mixture of two characters (bourgeois revolution in its immediate aims, proletarian revolution in its active forces), the appropriate bolshevist theory likewise had to present two characters, bourgeois materialism in its basic philosophy, proletarian evolutionism in its doctrine of class struggle. This mixture was termed Marxism. But it is clear that Lenin's Marxism, as determined by the special Russian attitude toward capitalism, had to be fundamentally different from the real Marxism growing as the basic view of the worker in the countries of big capital. Marxism in Western Europe is the worldview of a working class confronting the task of converting a most highly developed capitalism, its own world of life and action, into communism. The Russian workers and intellectuals could not make this their object: they had first to open the way for a free development of a modern industrial society. To the Russian Marxists the nucleus of Marxism is not contained in Marx's thesis that social reality determines consciousness, but in the sentence of young Marx, inscribed in big letters in the Moscow People's House, that religion is the opium of the people.

"It may happen that in a theoretical work there appear, not the immediate surroundings and tasks of the author, but more general and remote influences and wider tasks. In Lenin's book, however, nothing of the sort is perceptible. It is a manifest and exclusive reflection of the Russian Revolution at which he was aiming. Its character so entirely corresponds to bourgeois materialism that, had it been known at the time in Western Europe (only confused rumors on the internal strifes of Russian socialism penetrated here) and had it been properly interpreted, one could have predicted that the Russian Revolution must somehow result in a kind of capitalism based on a workers' struggle.

"There is a widespread opinion that the Bolshevist Party was Marxist, and that it was only for practical reasons that Lenin, the great scholar and leader of Marxism, gave to the revolution a direction other than what Western workers called communism—thereby showing his realistic Marxian insight. The critical opposition to the Russian and Communist Party politics tries indeed to oppose the despotic practice of the present Russian government—termed Stalinism—to the 'true' Marxist principles of Lenin and old Bolshevism. Wrongly so. Not only because in practice these politics were inaugurated already by Lenin. But also because the alleged Marxism of Lenin and the Bolshevist Party is nothing but a legend. Lenin never knew real Marxism. Whence should he have taken it? Capitalism he knew only as colonial capitalism; social revolution he knew only as the annihilation of big land ownership and czarist despotism. Russian Bolshevism cannot be reproached for having abandoned the way of Marxism, for it was never on that way. Every page of Lenin's philosophical work is there to prove it; and Marxism itself, by its thesis that theoretical opinions are determined by social relations and necessities, makes it clear that it could not be otherwise. Marxism, however, at the same time shows the necessity of the legend; every bourgeois revolution, requiring working class and peasant support, needs the illusion that it is something different, larger, more universal. Here it was the illusion that the Russian Revolution was the first step of world revolution liberating the entire proletarian class from capitalism; its theoretical expression was the legend of Marxism.

"Of course Lenin was a pupil of Marx; from Marx he learned what was most essential for the Russian Revolution, the uncompromising proletarian class struggle. Just as for similar reasons, the social democrats were pupils of Marx. And surely the fight of the Russian workers, in their mass actions and their soviets, was the most important practical example of modern proletarian warfare. That, however, Lenin did not understand Marxism as the theory of proletarian revolution, that he did not understand capitalism, bourgeoisie, proletariat in their highest modern development, was shown strikingly when from Russia, by means of the Third International, the world revolution was to be begun, and the advice and warnings of Western Marxists were entirely disregarded. An unbroken series of blunders, failures and defeats that resulted in the present weakness of the workers' movement showed the unavoidable shortcoming of the Russian leadership."[14]

Thus, Pannekoek links Russian conditions to Lenin's fragmentary development of Marxism. But, according to Pannekoek, Lenin regarded ideas as truths having an existence independent of society, without seeing in them "generalizations of former experiences and necessities;" he thus assigns to them "an unlimited validity" and, under the guise of restoring Marxism in view of idealist tendencies, he hardens them into the dogmas of bourgeois materialism—divinized abstractions: matter, energy and causality in nature; freedom and progress in social life—replaced in our day by the cult "of the state and of the nation."

The sphere of influence of Leninism is not limited to Russia, Pannekoek wrote in 1938: "The aim of the Communist Party[15]—which is called world revolution—is to bring to power, by means of the fighting force of the workers, a stratum of leaders who institute planned production by means of state power; in its essence it coincides with the aims of social democracy. The social ideals of well-ordered organization of production for use under the direction of technical and scientific experts inspire "daring radicalism of materialist thought. Thus the Communist Party sees in this class a natural ally, and seeks to draw it into its camp. By means of a suitable propaganda, it tries therefore to withdraw the intelligentsia from the spiritual influences of the bourgeoisie and of private capitalism in decline, and to win them over to a revolution destined to give them their true place as a new dominant class. At the philosophical level, this means winning them over to materialism. A

---

14. Pannekoek, *op. cit.,* pp. 65-72.
15. The reference is, of course, to the Communist Party in the generic sense.

revolution is incompatible with the soft-centered and conciliatory ideology of an idealist system; it needs the exciting and audacious radicalism of materialism.

"There is, of course, the difficulty that the intellectual class is too limited in number, too heterogeneous in social position, and hence too feeble to be able single-handedly to seriously threaten capitalist domination. Neither are the leaders of the Second and the Third Internationals a match for the power of the bourgeoisie, even if they could impose themselves by strong and clear politics instead of being rotten through opportunism. When, however, capitalism is tumbling into a heavy economic or political crisis that rouses the masses, when the working class has taken up the fight and succeeds in shattering capitalism in an initial victory—then their time will come. Then they will intervene and slide themselves in as leaders of the revolution, nominally to give their aid by taking part in the fight, in reality to deflect the action in the direction of their party aims. Whether or not the defeated bourgeoisie will then rally with them to save what can be saved of capitalism, their intervention in any case comes down to cheating the workers, leading them off the road to freedom." [16]

In his major work, *Workers' Councils*, Pannekoek deals with the Russian Revolution as follows:

"The Russian Revolution was an important episode in the development of the working class movement—first, as already mentioned, by the display of new forms of political strike, instruments of revolution. Moreover, in a higher degree, by the first appearance of new forms of self-organization of the fighting workers, known as soviets, i.e., councils. In 1905 they were hardly noticed as a special phenomenon and they disappeared with the revolutionary activity itself. In 1917 they reappeared with greater power; now their importance was grasped by the workers of Western Europe, and they played a role here in the class struggles after World War I.

"The soviets, essentially, were simply the strike committees, such as always arise in wide strikes. Since the strikes in Russia broke out in large factories and

---

16. Pannekoek, *op. cit.*, pp. 78-79. Karl Korsch, in a laudatory account of Pannekoek's work, clarifies the "sliding" of historical materialism into dialectical materialism, under the aegis of Lenin, who fitted the Hegelian dialectic to the old bourgeois materialism and pointed out the close link existing between the latter and the Jacobin political form (state, party dictatorship) of Russian and international Bolshevism. Cf. Korsch, "Lenin's Philosophy," *Living Marxism,* IV:5 (November 1938), pp. 138-44. Cf. also Mousso and Philippe, "Politique et philosophie de Lénine a Harper," *Internationalisme*, 30 (January 1948), pp. 28-36; Philippe, *ibid.*, pp. 31-33. Both reproach Pannekoek for seeing the October Revolution as a purely bourgeois movement, and for reducing the whole works of Lenin to a philosophic exposé "of more than doubtful quality," and consequently neglecting the "political positions" of the Bolsheviks, the most advanced positions of that time, we are told.

rapidly expanded over towns and districts, the workers had to keep in continual touch. In the shops the workers assembled and talked regularly after the close of work, or in times of tension even continually, the entire day. They sent their delegates to other factories and to the central committees, where information was interchanged, difficulties discussed, decisions taken, and new tasks considered.

"But here the tasks proved more encompassing than in ordinary strikes. The workers had to throw off the heavy oppression of czarism; they felt that their action was changing Russian society at its foundations. They had to consider not only wages and labor conditions in their shops, but all questions related to society at large. They had to find their own way in these realms and to take decisions on political matters. When the strike flared up, extended over the entire country, stopped all industry and traffic and paralyzed governmental functions, the soviets were confronted with new problems. They had to regulate public life, they had to take care of public security and order, they had to provide the indispensable public utilities and services. They had to perform governmental functions; what they decided was executed by the workers, whereas the government and police stood aloof, conscious of their impotence against the rebellious masses. Then the delegates of other groups, of intellectuals, of peasants, of soldiers, who came to join the central soviets, took part in the discussions and decisions. But all this power was like a flash of lightning, like a passing meteor. When at last the czarist government mustered its military forces and beat down the movement, the soviets disappeared.

"Thus it was in 1905. In 1917 the war had weakened government through the defeats at the front and the hunger in the towns, and now the soldiers, mostly peasants, took part in the action. Besides the workers' councils in the towns, soldiers' councils were formed in the army; the officers were shot when they did not acquiesce to the soviets taking all power into their hands to prevent entire anarchy. After half a year of vain attempts on the part of politicians and military commanders to impose new governments, the soviets, supported by the socialist parties, were master of society.

"Now the soviets stood before a new task. From organs of revolution they had to become organs of reconstruction. The masses were their own master and of course began to build up production according to their needs and life interest. What they wanted and did was not determined, as always in such cases, by inculcated doctrines, but by their own class character, by their conditions of life. What were these conditions? Russia was a primitive agrarian country with only the beginnings of industrial development. The masses of the people were uncivilized and ignorant peasants, spiritually dominated by a gold, glittering church, and even the industrial workers were strongly connected with their old villages. The village soviets arising everywhere were self-governing peasant committees. They seized the large estates of the former large landowners and divided them up. The development went in the direction of small holders with private property, and displayed already the distinctions between larger and smaller properties, between influential wealthy and more humble poor farmers.

"In the towns, on the other hand, there could be no development to private capitalist industry because there was no bourgeoisie of any significance. The workers wanted some form of socialist production, the only one possible under these conditions. But their minds and character, only superficially touched by the beginnings of capitalism, were hardly adequate to the task of themselves regulating production. So their foremost and leading elements, the socialists of the Bolshevist Party—organized and hardened by years of devoted fight, their leaders in the revolution—became the leaders in the reconstruction. Moreover, were these working class tendencies not to be drowned by the flood of aspirations for private property coming from the land, a strong central government had to be formed, able to restrain the peasants' tendencies. In this heavy task of organizing industry, of organizing the defensive war against counterrevolutionary attacks, of subduing the resistance of capitalist tendencies among the peasants, and of educating them to modern scientific ideas instead of their old beliefs, all the capable elements among the workers and intellectuals, supplemented by such of the former officials and officers as were willing to cooperate, had to combine in the Bolshevist Party as the leading body. It formed the new government. The soviets gradually were eliminated as organs of self-rule, and reduced to subordinate organs of the government apparatus. The name of Soviet Republic, however, was preserved as a camouflage, and the ruling party retained the name of Communist Party."[17]

Pannekoek then goes on to describe the manner in which a system of state capitalist production developed in Russia, but we cannot do more than mention it here. His account concludes with the following, which is highly characteristic of his method: "For the working class, the significance of the Russian Revolution must be looked for in quite different directions. Russia showed to the European and American workers, confined within reformist ideas and practice, first how an industrial working class by a gigantic mass action of wild strikes is able to undermine and destroy an obsolete state power; and second, how in such actions the strike committees develop into

---

17. Pannekoek, *Workers' Councils, op. cit.,* pp. 83-85.

workers' councils, organs of fight and of self-management, acquiring political tasks and functions."[18]

It is on the same basis that, in *Lenin as Philosopher,* Pannekoek defines what he means by revolutionary Marxism. Here again, he is not at all concerned with restoring a body of ideas, still less with polemics, but he reasons in accordance with the real conditions and the final purpose of an all-out working class struggle in the developed capitalist countries: "In reality, for the working class in the countries of developed capitalism, in Western Europe and America, matters are entirely different. Its task is not the overthrow of a backward absolutist monarchy. Its task is to vanquish a ruling class commanding the mightiest material and spiritual forces the world ever knew. Its object cannot be to replace the domination of stockbrokers and monopolists over a disorderly production by the domination of state officials over a production regulated from above. Its object is to be itself master of production and itself to regulate labor, the basis of life. Only then is capitalism really destroyed. Such an aim cannot be attained by an ignorant mass, the confident disciples of a party that presents itself as expert leadership. It can be attained only if the workers themselves, the entire class, understand the conditions, ways and means of their fight; when every man knows from his own judgment what to do. They must, every one of them, act themselves, decide themselves, hence think out and know for themselves. Only in this way will a real class organization be built up from below, having the form of something like workers' councils. It is of no avail that they have been convinced that their leaders know what is afoot and have gained the point in theoretical discussion—an easy thing when each is acquainted with the writings of his own party only. Out of the contest of arguments they have to form a clear opinion themselves. There is not truth lying ready at hand that has only to be imbibed; in every new case truth must be contribed by exertion of one's own brain.

"This does not mean, of course, that every worker should judge on scientific arguments in fields that can be mastered only by professional study. It means first, that all workers should give attention not only to their direct working and living conditions but also to the great social issues connected with their class struggle and the organization of labor and whould know how to take decisions here. But it implies, secondly, a certain standard of argument in propaganda and political strife. When the views of the opponent are distorted because the willingness or the capacity to understand them is lacking, then in the eyes of the believing adherents you may score a success; but the only result—which in party strife is even intended—is to bind them with stronger

18. *Ibid.,* p. 86.

fanaticism to the party. For the workers, however, what is of importance is not the increase of party power but the increase of their own capacity to seize power and to establish their mastery over society. Only when, in arguing and discussing, the opponent is given his full pound, when in weighing arguments against one another each solid opinion is understood out of social class relations, will the participant hearers gain such well-founded insight as is necessary for a working class to assure its freedom.

"The working class needs Marxism for its liberation. Just as the results of natural science are necessary for the technical construction of capitalism, so the results of social science are necessary for the organizational construction of communism. What was needed first was political economy, that part of Marxism that expounds the structure of capitalism, the nature of exploitation, the class-antagonism, the tendencies of economic development. It gave, directly, a solid basis to the spontaneously arising fight of the workers against the capitalist masters. Then, in the further struggle, by its theory of the development of society from primitive economy through capitalism to communism, it gave confidence an enthusiasm through the prospect of victory and freedom. When the not yet numerous workers took up their first difficult fight, and the hopeless indifferent masses had to be roused, this insight was the first thing needed.

"When the working class has grown more numerous, more powerful, and society is full of the proletarian class struggle, another part of Marxism has to come to the forefront. That they should know that they are exploited and have to fight is not the main point any more; they must know how to fight, how to overcome their weakness, how to build up their unity and strength. Their economic position is so easy to understand, their exploitation so manifest that their unity in struggle, their common will to seize power over production should presumably result at once. What hampers them is chiefly the power of the inherited and infused ideas, the formidable spiritual power of the middle-class world, enveloping their minds into a thick cloud of beliefs and ideologies, dividing them, and making them uncertain and confused. The process of enlightenment, of clearing up and vanquishing this world of old ideas and ideologies is the essential process of building the working class power, is the progress of revolution. Here that part of Marxism is needed that we call its *philosophy*, the relation of ideas to reality."[19]

Pannekoek applied to anarchism this evolutionary conception of Marxism linked with the new character of the class struggle. In the earlier sections of the present collection,[20] we have seen that he reproached anarchism for

---

19.   *Lenin as Philosopher, op. cit.,* pp. 75-76.
20.   Although the answer to Mühsam says nothing specific, its author is clearly against the

slowing down events. After World War II, he returned to this, but this time he ascribed a different motivation to it. This is shown by a letter to the Australian publisher of "Workers' Councils:"[21]

"In the present times of increasing submission by the workers to powerful state tyranny, it is natural that more sympathy is directed toward anarchism, with its propaganda of freedom. Just as social democracy, its opponents, it had its roots in 19th-century capitalism. One took its necessity from exploitation and capitalist competition, the other from the entire enslaving and suppression of personality; one found its force in the need for and propaganda of organization, the other in the need for and propaganda of freedom. Since the former was felt most immediately and overwhelmingly by the workers, social democracy won the masses an anarchism could not compete with it. Now under rising state capitalism it seems to have a better chance. But we have to bear in mind that both in the same way carry the mark of their origin out of the primitive conditions of the 19th century. The principle of freedom, originating from bourgeois conditions of early capitalism, freedom of trade and enterprise, is not adequate to the working class. The problems or goals for the workers are to combine freedom and organization. Anarchism, by setting up freedom as its goal, forgets that the free society of workers can only exist by a strong feeling of community as the prominent character of the collaborating producers. This new character, coming forth as strong solidarity in the workers' fights already, is the basis of organization—without compulsion from above. The self-made organization by free collaborating workers is the basis at the same time of their personal freedom, i.e., of their feeling as free masters of their own work. Freedom as the chief content of anarchist teaching may awake strong sympathies now, but it is only a part, not even the basic part, of the goal of the working class, which is expressed by self-rule, self-determination, by means of council organization. It seems, then, that in the present times there is in anarchism a certain approach toward the idea of workers' councils, especially where it involves groups of workers. But the old pure anarchist doctrine is too narrow to be of value for the workers' class struggle now."

---

idea of common action with the anarchists. A year later, when a section of the KAPD proposed to create a new anti-Moscow International, it was Gorter who drew up its manifesto, *Die kommunistische Arbeiter Internationale* (Berlin, 1921). The attempt had little impact, except in Holland, of course, and in Bulgaria, where a KAP of a thousand members was set up after the sabotage by the Leninist Communist Party of a rail workers' strike in 1919-1920. Cf. Joseph Rothschild, *The Communist Party of Bulgaria* (New York, 1959), pp. 99, 155, 296.

21. "Anarchism Not Suitable," *Southern Advocate for Workers' Councils*, 42 (February 1948). The title is J. A. Dawson's, editor of the paper, who also published studies by other council communists (Mattick, Korsch) and by non-conformist anarchists (Lain Diez, translator of *Lenin as Philosopher* into Spanish, and Kennafick).

CHAPTER TWELVE

PARTY AND WORKING CLASS

Needless to say, the GIC [1] hammered out its ideas by criticizing other political organizations, including the KAP. In its view, the basic condition for a new world was "control over the natural course of production and distribution" by the workers' councils. This demanded a definitive break with the classical party form, since the latter was regarded as a de facto leadership organ representing the councils—a role that the KAPD (and its various factions) effectively sought to corner for itself. However, the GIC in no way questioned the need for an autonomous communist body of ideas; in fact, it envisioned political organization in the form of a federation of "work groups." [2] These groups, functioning as "organs of collective thought," lived and multiplied by their own activity: theoretical elaboration. But this activity was possible only when linked with mass actions, with actions arising spontaneously from the contradictions of modern society and not at anyone's beck and call [3]—as, for instance, in the Amsterdam disturbances of 1934.

Of course, this viewpoint was criticized. One criticism was concerned particularly with the need for a more intensive, more concrete participation in the conflicts, and therefore with the need for a political group endowed with a coherence greater than that of a simple federation. [4] Pannekoek intervened in the discussion a little later, with an article entitled "Partei und Arbeiterklasse" ("The Party and the Working Class"), [5] which follows.

"We are only at the very earliest stages of a new workers' movement. The old movement was embodied in parties, and today belief in the party constitutes the most powerful check on the working class' capacity for action. That is why we are not trying to create a new party. This is so, not because our numbers are small—a party of any kind begins with a few people—but

1. On the history of this group, cf. "Aperçu sur l'histoire des communistes de conseils en Hollande," *Informations et liaisons ouvrières*, 30, May 6, 1959.
2. "Ueber die Notwendigkeit einer Partei," *Der Kampfruf* (organ of the AAU—Berlin), 3-4, January 1930.
3. "Das Werden einer neuen Arbeiterbewegung," *Raetekorrespondenz*, 8-9, April-May 1935, pp. 1-28.
4. *Ibid.*, 10-11, July-August 1935, pp. 22-26.
5. Anton Pannekoek, "Partei und Arbeiterklasse," *ibid.*, 15, March 1936, pp. 1-6. All articles in *Raetekorrespondenz* were published anonymously.

because, in our day, a party cannot be other than an organization aimed at directing and dominating the proletariat. To this type of organization we oppose the principle that the working class can effectively come into its own and prevail only by taking its destiny into its own hands. The workers are not to adopt the slogans of any group whatsoever, not even our own groups; they are to think, decide and act for themselves. Therefore, in this transitional period, the natural organs of education and enlightenment are, in our view, work groups, study and discussion circles, which have formed of their own accord and are seeking their own way.

"This view directly contradicts the traditional ideas about the role of the party as an essential educational organ of the proletariat. Hence it is resisted in many quarters where, however, there is no further desire to have dealings either with the Socialist Party or the Communist Party. This, no doubt, is to be partly explained by the strength of tradition: when one has always regarded the class war as a party war and a war between parties, it is very difficult to adopt the exclusive viewpoint of class and of the class war. But partly, too, one is faced with the clear idea that, after all, it is incumbent on the party to play a role of the first importance in the proletarian struggle for freedom. It is this idea we shall now examine more closely.

"The whole question pivots, in short, on the following distinction: a party is a group based on certain ideas held in common, whereas a class is a group united on the basis of common interests. Membership in a class is determined by function in the production process, a function that creates definite interests. Membership in a party means being one of a group having identical views about the major social questions.

"In recent times, it was supposed for theoretical and practical reasons that this fundamental difference would disappear within a class party, the 'workers' party.' During the period when Social Democracy was in full growth, the current impression was that this party would gradually unite all the workers, some as militants, others as sympathizers. And since the theory was that identical interests would necessarily engender identical ideas and aims, the distinction between class and party was bound, it was believed, to disappear. Social Democracy remained a minority group, and moreover became the target of attack by new workers' groups. Splits occurred within it, while its own character underwent radical change and certain articles of its program were either revised or interpreted in a totally different sense. Society does not develop in a continuous way, free from setbacks, but through conflicts and antagonisms. While the working class battle is widening in scope, the enemy's strength is increasing. Uncertainty about the way to be followed constantly and repeatedly troubles the minds of the combatants;

and doubt is a factor in division, of internal quarrels and conflicts within the workers' movement.

"It is useless to deplore these conflicts as creating a pernicious situation that should not exist and which is making the workers powerless. As has often been pointed out, the working class is not weak because it is divided; on the contrary, it is divided because it is weak. And the reason why the proletariat ought to seek new ways is that the enemy has strength of such a kind that the old methods are ineffectual. The working class will not secure these ways by magic, but through a great effort, deep reflection, through the clash of divergent opinions and the conflict of impassioned ideas. It is incumbent upon it to find its own way, and precisely therein is the *raison d'être* of the internal differences and conflicts. It is forced to renounce outmoded ideas and old chimeras, and it is indeed the difficulty of this task that engenders such big divisions.

"Nor should the illusion be nursed that such impassioned party conflicts and opinion clashes belong only to a transitional period such as the present one, and that they will in due course disappear, leaving a unity stronger than ever. Certainly, in the evolution of the class struggle, it sometimes happens that all the various elements of strength are merged in order to snatch some great victory, and that revolution is the fruit of this unity. But in this case, as after every victory, divergences appear immediately when it comes to deciding on new objectives. The proletariat then finds itself faced with the most arduous tasks: to crush the enemy, and more, to organize production, to create a new order. It is out of the question that all the workers, all categories and all groups, whose interests are still far from being homogeneous, should think and feel in the same way, and should reach spontaneous and immediate agreement about what should be done next. It is precisely because they are committed to finding for themselves their own way ahead that the liveliest differences occur, that there are clashes among them, and that finally, through such conflict, they succeed in clarifying their ideas.

"No doubt, if certain people holding the same ideas get together to discuss the prospects for action, to hammer out ideas by discussion, to indulge in propaganda for these attitudes, then it is possible to describe such groups as parties. The name matters little, provided that these parties adopt a role distinct from that which existing parties seek to fulfill. Practical action, that is, concrete class struggle, is a matter for the masses themselves, acting as a whole, within their natural groups, notably the work gangs, which constitute the units of effective combat. It would be wrong to find the militants of one tendency going on strike, while those of another tendency continued to work. In that case, the militants of each tendency should present their viewpoints to the factory floor, so that the workers as a whole are able to reach a decision based on knowledge and facts. Since the war is immense and the enemy's strength enormous, victory must be attained by merging all the forces at the masses' disposal — not only material and moral force with a view to action, unity and enthusiasm, but also the spiritual force born of mental clarity. The importance of these parties or groups resides in the fact that they help to secure this mental clarity through their mutual conflicts, their discussions, their propaganda. It is by means of these organs of self-clarification that the working class can succeed in tracing for itself the road to freedom.

"That is why parties *in this sense* (and also their ideas) do not need firm and fixed structures. Faced with any change of situation, with new tasks, people become divided in their views, but only to reunite in new agreement; while others come up with other programs. Given their fluctuating quality, they are always ready to adapt themselves to the new.

"The present workers' parties are of an absolutely different character. Besides, they have a different objective: to seize power and to exercise it for their sole benefit. Far from attempting to contribute to the emancipation of the working class, they mean to govern for themselves, and they cover this intention under the pretence of freeing the proletariat. Social Democracy, whose ascendent period goes back to the great parliamentary epoch, sees this power as government based on a parliamentary majority. For its part, the Communist Party carries its power politics to its extreme consequences: party dictatorship.

"Unlike the parties described above, these parties are bound to have formations with rigid structures, whose cohesion is assured by means of statutes, disciplinary measures, admission and dismissal procedures. Designed to dominate, they fight for power by orienting the militants toward the instruments of power that they possess and by striving constantly to increase their sphere of influence. They do not see their task as that of educating the workers to think for themselves; on the contrary, they aim at drilling them, at turning them into faithful and devoted adherents of their doctrines. While the working class needs unlimited freedom of spiritual development to increase its strength and to conquer, the basis of party power is the repression of all opinions that do not conform to the party line. In 'democratic' parties, this result is secured by methods that pay lip service to freedom; in the dictatorial parties, by brutal and avowed repression.

"A number of workers are already aware that domination by the Socialist Party or the Communist Party would simply be a camouflaged supremacy of the bourgeois class, and would thus perpetuate exploitation and servitude. But, according to these workers, what should take its place is a 'revolutionary party' that would really aim at creating proletarian power and communist society. There is no question here of a party in the sense we defined above, i.e., of a group whose sole objective is to educate and enlighten, but of a party in the current sense, i.e., a party fighting to secure power and to exercise it with a view to the liberation of the working class, and all this as a vanguard, as an organization of the enlightened revolutionary minority.

"The very expression 'revolutionary party' is a contradiction in terms, for a party of this kind could not be revolutionary. If it were, it could only be so in the sense in which we describe revolutionary as a change of government resulting from somewhat violent pressures, e.g., the birth of the Third Reich. When we use the word 'revolution,' we clearly mean the proletarian revolution, the conquest of power by the working class.

"The basic theoretical idea of the 'revolutionary party' is that the working class could not do without a group of leaders capable of defeating the bourgeoisie for them and of forming a new government, in other words, the conviction that the working class is itself incapable of creating the revolution. According to this theory, the leaders will create the communist society by means of decrees; in other words, the working class is still incapable of administering and organizing for itself its work and production.

"Is there not a certain justification for this thesis, at least provisionally? Given that at the present time the working class as a mass is showing itself to be unable to create a revolution, is it not necessary that the revolutionary vanguard, the party, should make the revolution on the working class' behalf? And is not this valid so long as the masses passively submit to capitalism?

"This attitude immediately raises two questions. What type of power will such a party establish through the revolution? What will occur to conquer the capitalist class? The answer is self-evident: an uprising of the masses. In effect, only mass attacks and mass strikes lead to the overthrow of the old domination. Therefore, the 'revolutionary party' will get nowhere without the intervention of the masses. Hence, one of two things must occur.

"The first is that the masses persist in action. Far from abandoning the fight in order to allow the new party to govern, they organize their power in the factories and workshops and prepare for new battles, this time with a view to the final defeat of capitalism. By means of workers' councils, they form a community that is increasingly close-knit, and therefore capable of taking on the administration of society as a whole. In a word, the masses prove that they are not as incapable of creating the revolution as was supposed. From this moment, conflict inevitably arises between the masses and the new party, the latter seeking to be the only body to exercise power and convinced that the party should lead the working class, that self-activity among the masses is only a factor of disorder and anarchy. At this point, either the class movement has become strong enough to ignore the party or the party, allied with bourgeois elements, crushes the workers. In either case, the party is shown to be an obstacle to the revolution, because the party seeks to be something other than an organ of propaganda and of enlightenment, and because it adopts as its specific mission the leadership and government of the masses.

"The second possibility is that the working masses conform to the doctrine of the party and turn over to it control of affairs. They follow directives from above and, persuaded (as in Germany in 1918) that the new government will establish socialism or communism, they get on with their day-to-day work. Immediately, the bourgeoisie mobilizes all its forces: its financial power, its enormous spiritual power, its economic supremacy in the factories and the large enterprises. The reigning party, too weak to withstand such an offensive, can maintain itself in power only by multiplying concessions and withdrawals as proof of its moderation. Then the idea becomes current that for the moment this is all that can be done, and that it would be foolish for the workers to attempt a violent imposition of utopian demands. In this way, the party, deprived of the mass power of a revolutionary class, is transformed into an instrument for the conservation of bourgeois power.

"We have just said that, in relation to the proletarian revolution, a 'revolutionary party' is a contradiction in terms. This could also be expressed by saying that the term 'revolutionary' in the expression 'revolutionary party' necessarily designates a bourgeois revolution. On every occasion, indeed, that the masses have intervened to overthrow a government and have then handed power to a new party, it was a bourgeois revolution that took place—a substitution of a new dominant category for an old one. So it was in Paris when, in 1830, the commercial bourgeoisie took over from the big landed proprietors; and again, in 1848, when the industrial bourgeoisie succeeded the financial bourgeoisie; and again in 1871 when the whole body of the bourgeoisie came to power. So it was during the Russian Revolution, when the party bureaucracy monopolized power in its capacity as a governmental category. But in our day, both in Western Europe and in America, the bourgeoisie is too deeply and too solidly rooted in the factories and the banks to be removed by a party bureaucracy. Now as always, the only means of conquering the bourgeoisie is to appeal to the masses, the latter taking over the factories and forming their own complex of councils. In this case, however, it seems that the real strength is in the masses who destroy the domination of capital in proportion as their own action widens and deepens.

"Therefore, those who contemplate a 'revolutionary party' are learning only a part of the lessons of the past. Not unaware that the workers' parties—the Socialist Party and Communist Party—have become organs of domination serving to perpetuate exploitation, they merely conclude from this that it is only necessary to improve the situation. This is to ignore the fact that the failure of the different parties is traceable to a much more general cause—namely, the basic contradiction between the emancipation of the class, as a body and by their own efforts, and the reduction of the activity of the masses to powerlessness by a new pro-workers' power. Faced with the passivity and indifference of the masses, they come to regard themselves as a revolutionary vanguard. But, if the masses remain inactive, it is because, while instinctively sensing both the colossal power of the enemy and the sheer magnitude of the task to be undertaken, they have not yet discerned the mode of combat, the way of class unity. However, when circumstances have pushed them into action, they must undertake this task by organizing themselves autonomously, by taking into their own hands the means of production, and by initiating the attack against the economic power of capital. And once again, every self-styled vanguard seeking to direct and to dominate the masses by means of a 'revolutionary party' will stand revealed as a reactionary factor by reason of this very conception."

In *Workers' Councils*, Pannekoek does not discuss the need for a party with an extremely flexible structure. Perhaps this was because he saw this book as itself a party work, an instrument "of propaganda and of enlightenment." However, while he was not concerned with coining a new word to express the idea of party as a loose body of 'work groups,' the idea itself is present in all his political writings.

In 1947, for example, in "Five Theses on the Fight of the Working Class against Capitalism," a work that is remarkably concise, he writes that the function of parties is "to spread insight and knowledge, to study, discuss and formulate social ideas, and by their propaganda to enlighten the minds of the masses. The workers' councils are the organs for practical action and fight of the working class; to the parties falls the task of the building up of its spiritual power. Their work forms an indispensable part in the self-liberation of the working class."[6]

A few years later, Pannekoek wrote a letter to a Paris group which, pursuing its own path of development, had come upon the idea of workers' councils. In this letter, he emphasized yet again that the theoretical activity "of a party or group" by means "of study and discussion" is linked with one "primordial task: to go out and speak to the workers."[7]

---

6. Anton Pannekoek, "Five Theses on the Fight of the Working Class against Capitalism," *Southern Advocate for Workers' Councils*, May 1947; recently published as an appendix to: *The Mass Strike in France May-June 1968*, Root and Branch Pamphlet 3 (1970), pp. 55-58.

7. *Socialisme ou Barbarie*, IV:14, April-June 1954, pp. 39-43.

CHAPTER THIRTEEN

PRINCIPLES OF ORGANIZATION

Besides the Dutch "work groups," there were similar groups in the United States, especially in areas of German emigration. In the review *Living Marxism* [1] Pannekoek published various articles, many of which were excerpts from *Workers' Councils*, [2] the only one of his books that he considered to be definitively political. Unfortunately, the limits of the present book do not allow us to reproduce long extracts, much less whole chapters. However, their substance is contained in the following articles: [3]

"Organization is the chief principle in the working class fight for emancipation. Hence the forms of this organization constitute the most important problem in the practice of the working class movement. It is clear that these forms depend on the conditions of society and the aims of the fight. They cannot be the invention of theory, but have to be built up spontaneously by the working class itself, guided by its immediate necessities.

"With expanding capitalism the workers first built their trade unions. The isolated worker was powerless against the capitalist; so he had to unite with his fellows in bargaining and fighting over the price of his labor-power and the hours of labor. Capitalists and workers have opposite interests in capitalistic production; their class struggle is over the division of the total product between them. In normal capitalism, the workers' share is the value of their labor power, i.e., what is necessary to sustain and restore continually their capacities to work. The remaining part of the product is the surplus value, the share of the capitalist class. The capitalists, in order to increase their profit, try to lower wages and increase the hours of labor. Where the workers were powerless, wages were depressed below the existence minimum; the hours of labor were lengthened until the bodily and mental health of the working class deteriorated so as to endanger the future of society. The formation of unions and of laws regulating working conditions—features rising out of the bitter fight of workers for their very lives—were necessary to

---

1. Review "for theory and discussion," first published under the title *International Council Correspondence*, and later became *New Essays*. At the center of this review was the ex-KAPist, Paul Mattick.

2. Anton Pannekoek, *Workers' Councils* (Melbourne, 1950).

3. J. Harper, "General Remarks on the Question of Organization," *Living Marxism*, IV:5, November 1938, pp. 144-53.

restore normal conditions of work in capitalism. The capitalist class itself recognized that trade unions are necessary to direct the revolt of the workers into regular channels to prevent them from breaking out in sudden explosions.

"Similarly, political organizations have grown up, though not everywhere in exactly the same way, because the political conditions are different in different countries. In America, where a population of farmers, artisans and merchants free from feudal bonds could expand over a continent with endless possibilities, conquering the natural resources, the workers did not feel themselves a separate class. They were imbued, as were the whole of the people, with the bourgeois spirit of individual and collective fight for personal welfare, and the conditions made it possible to succeed to a certain extent. Except at rare moments or among recent immigrant groups, no need was seen for a separate working class party. In the European countries, on the other hand, the workers were dragged into the political struggle by the fight of the rising bourgeoisie against feudalism. They soon had to form working class parties and, together with part of the bourgeoisie, had to fight for political rights: for the right to form unions, for free press and speech, for universal suffrage, for democratic institutions. A political party needs general principles for its propaganda; for its fight with other parties it wants a theory having definite views about the future of society. The European working class, in which communistic ideas had already developed, found its theory in the scientific work of Marx and Engels, explaining the development of society through capitalism toward communism by means of the class struggle. This theory was accepted in the programs of the Social Democratic Parties of most European countries; in England, the Labor Party formed by the trade unions, professed analogous but vaguer ideas about a kind of socialist commonwealth as the aim of the workers.

"In their program and propaganda, the proletarian revolution was the final result of the class struggle; the victory of the working class over its oppressors was to be the beginning of a communistic or socialist system of production. But so long as capitalism lasted, the practical fight had to center on immediate needs and the preservation of standards in capitalism. Under parliamentary government parliament is the battlefield where the interests of the different classes of society meet; big and small capitalists, land owners, farmers, artisans, merchants, industrialists, workers, all have their special interests that are defended by their spokesmen in parliament, all participate in the struggle for power and for their part in the total product. The workers have to take part in this struggle. Socialist or labor parties have the special task of fighting by political means for the immediate needs and interests of the workers within capitalism. In this way they get the votes of the workers and grow in political influence.

"With the modern development of capitalism, conditions have changed. The small workshops have been superseded by large factories and plants with thousands and tens of thousands of workers. With this growth of capitalism and of the working class, its organizations also had to expand. From local groups the trade unions grew to national federations with hundreds of thousands of members. They had to collect large funds for support in big strikes, and still larger ones for social insurance. A large staff of managers, administrators, presidents, secretaries, editors of their papers, an entire bureaucracy of organization leaders developed. They had to haggle and bargain with the bosses; they became the specialists acquainted with methods and circumstances. Eventually they became the real leaders, the masters of the organizations, masters of the money as well as of the press, while the members themselves lost much of their power. This development of the organizations of the workers into instruments of power over them has many examples in history; when organizations grow too large, the masses lose control of them.

"The same change takes place in the political organizations, when from small propaganda groups they grow into big political parties. The parliamentary representatives are the leading politicians of the party. They have to do the real fighting in the representative bodies; they are the specialists in that field; they make up the editorial, propaganda, and executive personnel; their influence determines the politics and tactical line of the party. The members may send delegates to debate at party congresses, but their power is nominal and illusory. The character of the organization resembles that of the other political parties — organizations of politicians who try to win votes for their slogans and power for themselves. Once a socialist party has a large number of delegates in parliament it allies with others against reactionary parties to form a working majority. Soon socialists become ministers, state officials, mayors and aldermen. Of course, in this position they cannot act as delegates of the working class, governing for the workers against the capitalist class. The real political power and even the parliamentary majority remain in the hands of the capitalist class. Socialist ministers have to represent the interests of the present capitalist society, i.e., of the capitalist class. They can attempt to initiate measures for the immediate interests of the workers and try to induce the capitalist parties to acquiesce. They become middlemen, mediators pleading with the capitalist class to consent to small reforms in the interests of the workers, and then try to convince the workers that these are important reforms that they should accept. And then the Socialist Party, as an instrument in the hands of these leaders, has to support them and also, instead of calling upon the workers to fight for their interests, seeks to pacify them, deflect them from the class struggle.

"Indeed, fighting conditions have grown worse for the workers. The power of the capitalist class has increased enormously with its capital. The concentration of capital in the hands of a few captains of finance and industry, the coalition of the bosses themselves, confronts the trade unions with a much stronger and often nearly unassailable power. The fierce competition of the capitalists of all countries over markets, raw materials and world power, the necessity of using increasing parts of the surplus value for this competition, for armaments and welfare, the falling rate of profit, compel the capitalists to increase the rate of exploitation, i.e., to lower the working conditions for the workers. Thus the trade unions meet increasing resistance, the old methods of struggle grow useless. In their bargaining with the bosses the leaders of the organization have less success; because they know the power of the capitalists, and because they themselves do not want to fight—since in such fights the funds and the whole existence of the organization might be lost—they must accept what the bosses offer. So their chief task is to assuage the workers' discontent and to defend the proposals of the bosses as important gains. Here also the leaders of the workers' organizations become mediators between the opposing classes. And when the workers do not accept the conditions and strike, the leaders either must oppose them or allow a sham fight, to be broken off as soon as possible.

"The fight itself, however, cannot be stopped or minimized; the class antagonism and the depressing forces of capitalism are increasing, so that the class struggle must go on, the workers must fight. Time and again they break loose spontaneously without asking the union and often against their decisions. Sometimes the union leaders succeed in regaining control of these actions. This means that the fight will be gradually smothered in some new arangement between the capitalists and labor leaders. This does not mean that without this interference such wildcat strikes would be won. They are too restricted. Only indirectly does the fear of such explosions tend to foster caution by the capitalists. But these strikes prove that the class fight between capital and labor cannot cease, and that when the old forms are not practicable any more, the workers spontaneously try out and develop new forms of action. In these actions revolt against capital is also revolt agains the old organizational forms.

"The aim and task of the working class is the abolition of capitalism. Capitalism in its highest development, with its ever deeper economic crises, its imperialism, its armaments, its world wars, threatens the workers with misery and destruction. The proletarian class fight, the resistance and revolt against these conditions, must go on until capitalist domination is overthrown and capitalism is destroyed.

"Capitalism means that the productive apparatus is in the hands of the capitalists. Because they are the masters of the means of production, and hence of the products, they can seize the surplus value and exploit the working class. Only when the working class itself is master of the means of production does exploitation cease. Then the workers control entirely their conditions of life. The production of everything necessary for life is the common task of the community of workers, which is then the community of mankind. This production is a collective process. First each factory, each large plant, is a collective of workers, combining their efforts in an organized way. Moreover, the totality of world production is a collective process; all the separate factories have to be combined into a totality of production. Hence, when the working class takes possession of the means of production, it has at the same time to create an organization of production.

"There are many who think of the proletarian revolution in terms of the former revolutions of the middle class, as a series of consecutive phases: first, conquest of government and installment of a new government, then expropriation of the capitalist class by law, and then a new organization of the process of production. But such events could lead only to some kind of state capitalism. As the proletariat rises to dominance it develops simultaneously its own organization and the forms of the new economic order. These two developments are inseparable and form the process of social revolution. Working class organization into a strong body capable of united mass actions already means revolution, because capitalism can rule only unorganized individuals. When these organized masses stand up in mass fights and revolutionary actions, and the existing powers are paralyzed and disintegrated, then simultaneously the leading and regulating functions of former governments fall to the workers' organizations. And the immediate task is to carry on production, to continue the basic process of social life. Since the revolutionary class fight against the bourgeoisie and its organs is inseparable from the seizure of the productive apparatus by the workers and its application to production, the same organization that unites the class for its fight also acts as the organization of the new productive process.

"It is clear that the organizational forms of trade union and political party, inherited from the period of expanding capitalism, are useless here. They developed into instruments in the hands of leaders unable and unwilling to engage in revolutionary fight. Leaders cannot make revolutions: labor leaders abhor a proletarian revolution. For the revolutionary fights the workers need new forms of organization in which they keep the powers of action in their own hands. It is pointless to try to construct or to imagine these new forms; they can originate only in the practical fight of the workers themselves. They have already originated there; we have only to look into practice to find its beginnings everywhere that the workers are rebelling against the old powers.

"In a wildcat strike, the workers decide all matters themselves through regular meetings. They choose strike committees as central bodies, but the members of these committees can be recalled and replaced at any moment. If the strike extends over a large number of shops, they achieve unity of action by larger committees consisting of delegates of all the separate shops. Such committees are not bodies to make decisions according to their own opinion, and over the workers; they are simply messengers, communicating the opinions and wishes of the groups they represent, and conversely, bringing to the shop meetings, for discussion and decision, the opinion and arguments of the other groups. They cannot play the roles of leaders, because they can be momentarily replaced by others. The workers themselves must choose their way, decide their actions; they keep the entire action, with all its difficulties, its risks, its responsibilities, in their own hands. And when the strike is over, the committees disappear.

"The only examples of a modern industrial working class as the moving force of a political revolution were the Russian Revolutions of 1905 and 1917. Here the workers of each factory chose delegates, and the delegates of all the factories together formed the 'soviet,' the council where the political situation and necessary actions were discussed. Here the opinions of the factories were collected, their desires harmonized, their decisions formulated. But the councils, though a strong directing influence for revolutionary education through action, were not commanding bodies. Sometimes a whole council was arrested and reorganized with new delegates; at times, when the authorities were paralyzed by a general strike, the soviets acted as a local government, and delegates of free professions joined them to represent their field of work. Here we have the organization of the workers in revolutionary action, though of course only imperfectly, groping and trying for new methods. This is possible only when all the workers with all their forces participate in the action, when their very existence is at stake, when they actually take part in the decisions and are entirely devoted to the revolutionary fight.

"After the revolution this council organization disappeared. The proletarian centers of big industry were small islands in an ocean of primitive agricultural society where capitalist development had not yet begun. The task of initiating capitalism fell to the Communist Party. Simultaneously, political power centered in its hands and the soviets were reduced to subordinate organs with only nominal powers.

"The old forms of organization, the trade union and political party and the new form of councils (soviets), belong to different phases in the development of society and have different functions. The first has to secure the position of the working class among the other classes within capitalism and belongs to the period of expanding capitalism. The latter has to secure complete dominance for the workers, to destroy capitalism and its class divisions, and belongs to the period of declining capitalism. In a rising and prosperous capitalism, council organization is impossible because the workers are entirely occupied in ameliorating their conditions, which is possible at that time through trade unions and political action. In a decaying crisis-ridden capitalism, these efforts are useless and faith in them can only hamper the increase of self-action by the masses. In such times of heavy tension and growing revolt against misery, when strike movements spread over whole countries and hit at the roots of capitalist power, or when, following wars or political catastrophes, the government authority crumbles and the masses act, the old organizational forms fail against the new forms of self-activity of the masses.

"Spokesmen for socialist or communist parties often admit that, in revolution, organs of self-action by the masses are useful in destroying the old domination; but then they say these have to yield to parliamentary democracy to organize the new society. Let us compare the basic principles of both forms of political organization of society.

"Original democracy in small towns and districts was exercised by the assembly of all the citizens. With the big population of modern towns and countries this is impossible. The people can express their will only by choosing delegates to some central body that represents them all. The delegates for parliamentary bodies are free to act, to decide, to vote, to govern after their own opinion by 'honor and conscience,' as it is often called in solemn terms.

"The council delegates, however, are bound by mandate; they are sent simply to express the opinions of the workers' groups who sent them. They may be called back and replaced at any moment. Thus the workers who gave them the mandate keep the power in their own hands.

"On the other hand, members of parliament are chosen for a fixed number of years; only at the polls are the citizens masters—on this one day when they choose their delegates. Once this day has passed, their power has gone and the delegates are independent, free to act for a term of years according to their own 'conscience,' restricted only by the knowledge that after this period they have to face the voters anew; but then they count on catching their votes in a noisy election campaign, bombing the confused voters with slogans and demagogic phrases. Thus not the voters but the parliamentarians are the real masters who decide politics. And the voters do not even send persons of their own choice as delegates; they are presented to them by the political parties. And then, if we suppose that people could select and send persons of their own choice, these persons would not form the government; in parliamentary democracy the legislative and the executive powers are separated. The real government dominating the people is formed by a bureaucracy of officials so far removed from the people's vote as to be practically independent. That is how it is possible that capitalistic dominance is maintained through general suffrage and parliamentary democracy. This is why in capitalistic countries, where the majority of the people belongs to the working class, this democracy cannot lead to a conquest of political power. For the working class, parliamentary democracy is a sham democracy, whereas council representation is real democracy: the direct rule of the workers over their own affairs.

"Parliamentary democracy is the political form in which the different important interests in a capitalist society exert their influence upon government. The delegates represent certain classes: farmers, merchants, industrialists, workers; but they do not represent the common will of their voters. Indeed, the voters of a district have no common will; they are an assembly of individuals, capitalists, workers, shopkeepers, by chance living at the same place, having partly opposing interests.

"Council delegates, on the other hand, are sent out by a homogeneous group to express its common will. Councils are not only made up of workers, having common class interests; they are a natural group, working together as the personnel of one factory or section of a large plant, and are in close daily contact with each other, having the same adversary, having to decide their common actions as fellow workers in which they have to act in united fashion; not only on the questions of strike and fight, but also in the new organization of production. Council representation is not founded upon the meaningless grouping of adjacent villages or districts, but upon the natural groupings of workers in the process of production, the real basis of society.

"However, councils must not be confused with the so-called corporative representation propagated in fascist countries. This is a representation of the different professions or trades (masters and workers combined), considered as fixed constituents of society. This form belongs to a medieval society with fixed classes and guilds, and in its tendency to petrify interest groups it is even worse than parliamentarism, where new groups and new interests rising up in the development of capitalism soon find their expression in parliament and government.

"Council representation is entirely different because it is the representation of a class engaged in revolutionary struggle. It represents working class interests only, and prevents capitalist delegates and capitalist interests from participation. It denies the right of existence to the capitalist class in society and tries to eliminate capitalists by taking the means of production away from them. When in the progress of revolution the workers must take up the functions of organizing society, the same council organization is their instrument. This means that the workers' councils then are the organs of the dictatorship of the proletariat. This dictatorship of the proletariat is not a shrewdly devised voting system artificially excluding capitalists and the bourgeoisie from the polls. It is the exercise of power in society by the natural organs of the workers, building up the productive apparatus as the basis of society. In these organs of the workers, consisting of delegates of their various branches in the process of production, there is no place for robbers or exploiters standing outside productive work. Thus the dictatorship of the working class is at the same time the most perfect democracy, the real workers' democracy, excluding the vanishing class of exploiters.

"The adherents of the old forms of organization exalt democracy as the only right and just political form, as against dictatorship, an unjust form. Marxism knows nothing of abstract right or justice; it explains the political forms in which mankind expresses its feelings of political right, as consequences of the economic structure of society. In Marxian theory we can find also the basis of the difference between parliamentary democracy and council organization. As bourgeois democracy and proletarian democracy respectively they reflect the different character of these two classes and their economic systems.

"Bourgeois democracy is founded upon a society consisting of a large number of independent small producers. They want a government to take care of their common interests: public security and order, protection of commerce, uniform systems of weight and money, administering of law and justice. All these things are necessary in order that everybody can do his business in his own way. Private business takes the whole attention, forms the life interests of everybody, and those political factors are, though necessary, only secondary and demand only a small part of their attention. The chief content of social life, the basis of existence of society, the production of all the goods necessary for life, is divided up into private business of the separate citizens, hence it is natural that it takes nearly all their time, and that politics, their collective affair, is a subordinate matter, providing only for auxiliary conditions. Only in bourgeois revolutionary movements do people take to the streets. But in ordinary times politics are left to a small group of specialists, politicians, whose work consists just of taking care of these general, political conditions of bourgeois business.

"The same holds true for the workers, as long as they think only of their direct interests. In capitalism they work long hours, all their energy is exhausted in the process of exploitation, and little mental power and fresh thought is left them. Earning their wage is the most immediate necessity of life; their political interests, their common interest in safeguarding their interests as wage earners may be important, but are still secondary. So they leave this part of their interests also to specialists, to their party politicians and their trade union leaders. By voting as citizens or members the workers may give some general directions, just as middle-class voters may influence their politicians, but only partially, because their chief attention must remain concentrated upon their work.

"Proletarian democracy under communism depends upon just the opposite economic conditions. It is founded not on private but on collective production. Production of the necessities of life is no longer a personal business, but a collective affair. The collective affairs, formerly called political affairs, are no longer secondary, but the chief object of thought and action for everybody. What was called politics in the former society—a domain for specialists—has become the vital interest of every worker. It is not the securing of some necessary conditions of production, it is the process and the regulation of production itself. The separation of private and collective affairs and interests has ceased. A separate group or class of specialists taking care of the collective affairs is no longer necessary. Through their council delegates, which link them together, the producers themselves are managing their own productive work.

"The two forms of organization are not distinguished in that the one is founded upon a traditional and ideological basis, and the other on the material productive basis of society. Both are founded upon the material basis of the system of production, one on the declining system of the past, the other on the growing system of the future. Right now we are in the period of transition, the time of big capitalism and the beginnings of the proletarian revolution. In big capitalism the old system of production has already been destroyed in its foundations; the large class of independent producers has disappeared. The main part of production is collective work of large groups of workers; but the control and ownership have remained in a few private hands. This contradictory state is maintained by the strong power factors of the capitalists, especially the state power exerted by the governments. The task of the proletarian revolution is to destroy this state power; its real content is the seizure of the means of production by the workers. The process of revolution is an alternation of actions and defeats that builds up the organization of the proletarian dictatorship, which at the same time is the dissolution, step by step, of the capitalist state power. Hence it is the process of the replacement of the organization system of the past by the organization system of the future.

"We are only in the beginnings of this revolution. The century of class struggle behind us cannot be considered a beginning as such, but only a preamble. It developed invaluable theoretical knowledge, it found gallant revolutionary words in defiance of the capitalist claim of being a final social system; it awakened the workers from the hopelessness of misery. But its actual fight remained bound within the confines of capitalism, it was action through the medium of leaders and sought only to set easy masters in the place of hard ones. Only a sudden flickering of revolt, such as political or mass strikes breaking out against the will of the politicians, now and then announced the future of self-determined mass action. Every wildcat strike, not taking its leaders and catchwords from the offices of parties and unions, is an indication of this development, and at the same time a small step in its direction. All the existing powers in the proletarian movement, the socialist and communist parties, the trade unions, all the leaders whose activity is bound to the bourgeois democracy of the past, denounce these mass actions as anarchistic disturbances. Because their field of vision is limited to their old forms of organization, they cannot see that the spontaneous actions of the workers bear in them the germs of higher forms of organization. In fascist countries, where bourgeois democracy has been destroyed, such spontaneous mass actions will be the only form of future proletarian revolt. Their tendency will not be a restoration of the former middle class democracy but an advance in the direction of the proletarian democracy, i.e., the dictatorship of the working class."

Pannekoek repeats here the essential arguments of his "Social Democracy and Communism," sometimes almost verbatim. The difference, it should also be noted, consists in the inevitable alteration of perspective. The first article was linked with immediate problems; the second takes a long-term view of them. The *Living Marxism* article appeared at a time when one could no longer doubt that World War II was imminent. When, after the war, Pannekoek returned, in *Workers' Councils*, to the whole body of questions dealt with in the above article, his attitude had scarcely changed. This is understandable, in a sense, since, while the war had transformed capitalism, these transformations were only germinally perceptible at the end of the preceding period (the consequences, however, being then more or less discernible). And this was also true of the class struggle.

Nevertheless, it might be useful to supplement this article with extracts concerning democratic ideology and its historic role, first during the Spanish Civil War—of which Pannekoek does not seem to have seen all the aspects—and then during the period that followed and in which we are still living, at least at the ideological level.

"Something analogous, on a minor scale, was what happened in the civil war in Spain, 1935-1936. In the industrial town of Barcelona the workers, having at the revolt of the generals stormed the barracks and drawn the soldiers to their side, were master of the town. Their armed groups dominated the street, maintained order, took care of the food provision, and, while the chief factories were kept at work under the direction of their syndicalist unions, waged war upon the fascist troops in adjoining provinces. Then their leaders entered into the democratic government of the Catalan republic, consisting of middle-class republicans allied with socialist and communist politicians. This meant that instead of fighting for their class, the workers had to join in and adapt to the common cause. Weakened by democratic illusions and inner dissension, their resistance was crushed by armed troops of the Catalan government. And soon, as a symbol of restored bourgeois order, you could see as in olden times workers' women, waiting before the bakers' shops, brutalized by mounted police. The working class once more was down, the first step in the downfall of the republic that finally led to the dictatorship of the military leaders.

"In social crisis and political revolution, when a government breaks down, power falls into the hands of the working masses; and for the propertied class, for capitalism arises the problem of how to wrest it out of their hands. So it was in the past, so it may happen in the future. Democracy is the means, the appropriate instrument of persuasion. The arguments of formal and legal quality have to induce the workers to give up their power and to let their organization be inserted as a subordinate part into the state structure.

"Against this the workers have to carry in them a strong conviction that council organization is a higher and more perfect form of equality.... The equal right in deciding needs not to be secured by any formal regulating paragraph; it is realized in that the work, in every part, is regulated by those who do the work....

"It is often said that in the modern world the point of dispute is between democracy and dictatorship; and that the working class has to throw in its full weight for democracy. The real meaning of this statement of contrast is that capitalist opinion is divided as to whether capitalism should maintain its sway with soft, deceitful democracy or with hard dictatorial constraint. It is the old problem of whether rebellious slaves are kept down better by kindness or by terror. If asked, the slaves of course prefer kind treatment to terror; but if they let themselves be fooled so as to mistake soft slavery for freedom, it is pernicious to the cause of their freedom. For the working class in the present time the real issue is between council organization, the true democracy of labor, and the apparent, deceitful bourgeois democracy of formal rights. In proclaiming council democracy, the workers transfer the fight from political form to economic contents. Or rather—since politics is only form and means for economy—for the sounding political slogan they substitute the revolutionizing political deed, the seizure of the means of production. The slogan of political democracy serves to detract the attention of the workers from their true goal. It must be the concern of the workers, by putting up the principle of council organization, of actual democracy of labor, to give true expression to the great issue now moving society." [4]

---

4. Anton Pannekoek, *Workers' Councils, op. cit.,* pp. 152-53.

CHAPTER FOURTEEN

DIRECT ACTION IN CONTEMPORARY SOCIETIES

For a long time, capitalism has dominated at every level. After the war, it was already climbing toward its triumphant restoration. Under these conditions, communism could be represented only by a handful of theoreticians. Here and there, however, intellectuals with advanced ideas were posing questions, and it was only to be expected that they should come up with the idea of the workers councils—and equally inevitable that they should finally judge it to be impractical. In effect, this was an idea directed toward the future, toward another phase of the struggle; in a phase of decline—that is, a phase of relative harmony among the classes—this idea could more or less explain the past, and be used especially to indicate some advance signs of a very slow reversal of the situation. But, in such a period, this body of theory can scarcely open up perspectives of immediate action to writers, sociologists and philosophers eager to fight for the still-threatened cause of democracy and freedom. Far from doing so, it concerned itself only with details, with wildcat strikes, for example, with actions that generally have no future. After having aroused a vague interest, followed by disillusionment, it was quickly passed over. Such was the case with the editors of *Politics*, a New York review that provided a platform for post-Marxists, post-Freudians, post-anarchists, and many others, and in whose columns the names Karl Korsch and Paul Mattick were to appear several times. Pannekoek published an article in this review, "The Failure of the Working class." [1] Here is the full text:

"In former issues of *Politics* the problem has been posed: why did the working class fail its historical task? Why did it not offer resistance to National Socialism in Germany? Why is there no trace of any revolutionary movement among the workers of America? What has happened to the social vitality of the world working class? Why do the masses all over the globe no longer seem capable of initiating anything new aimed at their own self-liberation? Some light may be thrown upon this problem by the following considerations.

"It is easy to ask: why did the workers not rise against threatening fascism?

---

1. "The Failure of the Working Class," *Politics*, III, 8, Sept. 1946, pp. 270-72.

To fight you must have a positive aim. Opposed to fascism there were two alternatives: either to maintain or to return to the old capitalism, with its unemployment, its crises, its corruption, its misery—whereas National Socialism presented itself as an anti-capitalist reign of labor, without unemployment, a reign of national greatness, of community politics that could lead to a socialist revolution. Thus, indeed, the deeper question is: why did the German workers not make their revolution?

"Well, they had experienced a revolution: 1918. But it had taught them the lesson that neither the Social Democratic Party, nor the trade unions was the instrument of their liberation; both turned out to be instruments of restoring capitalism. So what were they to do? The Communist Party did not show a way either; it propagated the Russian system of state-capitalism, with its still worse lack of freedom.

"Could it have been otherwise? The avowed aim of the Socialist Party in Germany—and then in all countries—was state socialism. According to program the working class had to conquer political dominance, and then by its power over the state, had to organize production into a state-directed planned economic system. Its instrument was to be the Socialist Party, developed already into a huge body of 300,000 members, with a million trade-union members and three million voters behind them, led by a big apparatus of politicians, agitators, editors, eager to take the place of the former rulers.[2] According to program, then, they should expropriate by law the capitalist class and organize production in a centrally directed planned system.

"It is clear that in such a system the workers, though their daily bread may seem to be secured, are only imperfectly liberated. The upper echelons of society have been changed, but the foundations bearing the entire building remain the old ones: factories with wage-earning workers under the command of directors and managers. So we find it described in the English socialist G. D. H. Cole, who after World War I strongly influenced the trade unions by his studies of guild socialism and other reforms of the industrial system. He says: 'The whole people would be no more able than the whole body of shareholders in a great enterprise to manage an industry.... It would be necessary, under socialism as much as under large scale capitalism, to entrust the actual management of industrial enterprise to salaried experts, chosen for their specialized knowledge and ability in particular branches of work.... There is no reason to suppose that the methods of appointing the actual managers in socialized industries would differ widely from those already in force in large scale capitalist enterprise.... There is no reason to

---

2. By and large, the period in question is around 1903.

suppose that the socialization of any industry would mean a great change in its managerial personnel.'

"Thus the workers will have new masters instead of the old ones. Good, humane masters instead of the bad, rapacious masters of today. Appointed by a socialist government or at best chosen by themselves. But, once chosen, they must be obeyed. The workers are not master over their shops, they are not master of the means of production. Above them stands the commanding power of a state bureaucracy of leaders and managers. Such a state of affairs can attract the workers as long as they feel powerless over against the power of the capitalists; so in their first rise during the 19th century this was put up as the goal. They wer not strong enough to drive the capitalists out of the command over the production installations; so their way out was state socialism, a government of socialists expropriating the capitalists.

"Now that the workers begin to realize that state socialism means new fetters, they face the difficult task of finding and opening new roads. This is not possible without a deep revolution of ideas, accompanied by much internal strife. No wonder that the vigor of the fight slackens, that they hesitate, divided and uncertain, and seem to have lost their energy.

"Capitalism, indeed, cannot be annihilated by a change in the commanding persons; but only by the abolition of commanding. The real freedom of the workers consists in their direct mastery over the means of production. The essence of the future free world community is not that the working masses get enough food, but that they direct their work themselves, collectively. For the real content of their life is their productive work; the fundamental change is not a change in the passive realm of consumption, but in the active realm of production. Before them now the problem arises of how to unite freedom and organization; how to combine mastery of the workers over the work with the binding up of all this work into a well-planned social entirety. How to organize production, in every shop as well as over the whole of world economy, in such a way that they themselves as parts of a collaborating community regulate their work. Mastery over production means that the personnel, the bodies of workers, technicians and experts that by their collective effort run the shop and put into action the technical apparatus are at the same time the managers themselves. The organization into a social entity is then performed by delegates of the separate plants, by so-called workers councils, discussing and deciding on the common affairs. The development of such a council organization will afford the solution of the problem; but this development is a historical process, taking time and demanding a deep transformation of outlook and character.

"This new vision of a free communism is only beginning to take hold of the minds of the workers. And so now we begin to understand why former promising workers' movements could not succeed. When the aims are too narrow there can be no real liberation. When the aim is a semi- or mock-liberation, the inner forces aroused are insufficient to bring about the fundamental results. So the German socialist movement, unable to provide the workers with arms powerful enough to fight successfully monopolistic capital, had to succumb. The working class had to search for new roads. But the difficulty of disentangling itself from the net of socialist teachings imposed by old parties and old slogans made it powerless against aggressive capitalism, and brought about a period of continuous decline, indicating the need for a new orientation.

"Thus what is called the failure of the working class is the failure of its narrow socialist aims. The real fight for liberation has yet to begin; what is known as the workers' movement in the century behind us, seen in this way, was only a series of skirmishes of advance guards. Intellectuals, who are wont to reduce the social struggle to the most abstract and simple formulas, are inclined to underrate the tremendous scope of the social transformation before us. They think how easy it would be to put the right name into the ballot box. They forget what deep inner revolution must take place in the working masses; what amount of clear insight, of solidarity, of perseverance and courage, of proud fighting spirit is needed to vanquish the immense physical and spiritual power of capitalism.

"The workers of the world nowadays have two mighty foes, two hostile and suppressing capitalist powers against them: the monopolistic capitalism of America and England, and Russian state capitalism. The former is drifting toward social dictatorship camouflaged in democratic forms; the latter proclaims dictatorship openly, formerly with the addition 'of the proletariat,' although nobody believes that any more. They both try to keep the workers in a state of obedient well-drilled followers, acting only at the command of the party leaders, the former by the aid of the socialist program of socialist parties, the latter by the slogans and wily tricks of the Communist party. The tradition of glorious struggle helps them keep spiritually dependent on obsolete ideas. In the competition for world domination, each tries to keep the workers in its fold, by shouting against capitalism here, against dictatorship there.

"In the awakening resistance to both, the workers are beginning to perceive that they can fight successfully only by adhering to and proclaiming exactly the opposite principle—the principle of devoted collaboration of free and equal personalities. Theirs is the task of finding out the way in which the principle can be carried out in their practical action."

"The paramount question here is whether there are indications of an existing or awakening fighting spirit in the working class. So we must leave the field of political party strife, now chiefly intended to fool the masses, and turn to the field of economic interests, where the workers intuitively fight their bitter struggle for living conditions. Here we see that with the development of small business into big business, the trade unions cease to be instruments of the workers' struggle. In modern times these organizations ever more turn into the organs by which monopoly capital dictates its terms to the working class.

"When the workers begin to realize that the trade unions cannot direct their fight against capital they face the task of finding and practicing new forms of struggle. These new forms are the wildcat strikes. Here they shake off direction by the old leaders and the old organizations; here they take the initiative in their own hands; here they have to think out time and ways, to take the decisions, to do all the work of propaganda, of extension, of directing their action themselves. Wildcat strikes are spontaneous outbursts, the genuine practical expression of class struggle against capitalism, though without wider aims as yet; but they embody a new character already in the rebellious masses: self-determination instead of determination by leaders, self-reliance instead of obedience, fighting spirit instead of accepting the dictates from above, unbreakable solidarity and unity with the comrades instead of duty imposed by membership. The unit in action and strike is, of course, the same as the unit of daily productive work, the personnel of the shop, the plant, the docks; it is the common work, the common interest against the common capitalist master that compels them to act as one. In these discussions and decisions all the individual capabilities, all the forces of character and mind of all the workers, exalted and strained to the utmost, are cooperating toward the common goal.

"In the wildcat strikes we can see the beginnings of a new practical orientation of the working class, a new tactic, the method of direct action. They represent the only actual rebellion of man against the deadening weight of world-dominating capital. Surely, on a small scale such strikes mostly have to be broken off without success—warning signs only. Their efficiency depends on their extension over larger masses; only fear for such indefinite extension can compel capital to make concessions. If the pressure by capitalist exploitation grows heavier—and we can be sure it will—resistance will be aroused ever anew and will involve ever larger masses. When the strikes take on such dimensions as to disturb seriously the social order, when they assail capitalism in its inner essence, the mastery of the shops, then the workers will have to confront state power with all its resources. Then their strikes must assume a political character; they have to broaden their social outlook; their strike committees, embodying their class community, assume wider social functions, taking the character of workers' councils. Then the social revolution, the breakdown of capitalism, comes into view.

"Is there any reason to expect such a revolutionary development in coming times, through conditions that were lacking until now? It seems that we can, with some probability, indicate such conditions. In Marx's writings we find the sentence: a production system does not perish before all its innate possibilities have developed. In the persistence of capitalism, we now begin to detect some deeper truth in this sentence than was suspected before. As long as the capitalist system can keep the masses alive, they feel no stringent necessity to do away with it. And it is able to do so as long as it can grow and expand its realm over wider parts of the world. Hence, so long as half the world's population stands outside capitalism, its task is not finished. The many hundreds of millions thronged in the fertile plains of Eastern and Southern Asia are still living in pre-capitalistic conditions. As long as they can afford a market to be provided with rails and locomotives, with trucks, machines and factories, capitalist enteprise, especially in America, may prosper and expand. And henceforth it is on the working class of America that world revolution depends.

"This means that the necessity of revolutionary struggle will impose itself once capitalism engulfs the bulk of mankind, once a further significant expansion is hampered. The threat of wholesale destruction in this last phase of capitalism makes this fight a necessity for all the producing classes of society, the farmers and intellectuals as well as the workers. What is condensed here in these short sentences is an extremely complicated historical process covering a period of revolution, prepared and accompanied by spiritual fights and fundamental changes in basic ideas. These developments should be carefully studied by all those to whom communism without dictatorship, social organization on the basis of community-minded freedom, represents the future of mankind."

With the exception of one important aspect, to which we shall return shortly, the major outlines of the council idea are now clear. Of course, certain essential aspects of this idea have been, are being and will be highlighted both by historical evolution and by other militant theoreticians. But, as far as Pannekoek is concerned, his writings, from *Workers' Councils* to his death, deal consistently with the same major themes. However, to stress yet again the absence of all conceptual metaphysics in his thought, here is an extract from one of his letters to the editor of a small leftist socialist review.[3]

3. "Ueber Arbeiterāte," *Funken*, III:1, June 1952, pp. 14-15.

"Workers' councils does not designate a form of organization whose lines are fixed once and for all, and which requires only the subsequent elaboration of the details. It is concerned with a principle — the principle of the workers' self-management of enterprises and of production. This principle can in no way be implemented by a theoretical discussion about the best practical forms it should take. It concerns a practical struggle against the apparatus of capitalist domination. In our day, 'workers' councils,' certainly does not mean a brotherhood that is its own end and purpose; 'workers' councils' is synonymous with the class struggle (where brotherhood plays its part), with revolutionary action against state power. Revolutions cannot, of course, be summoned at will; they arise spontaneously in moments of crisis, when the situation becomes intolerable. They occur only on two conditions: first, if a feeling of intolerability exercises greater and greater pressures on the masses; second, if simultaneously a certain generally accepted awareness of what ought to be done grows up among them. It is at this level that propaganda and public discussion play their part. And these actions cannot secure a lasting success unless large sections of the working class have a clear understanding of the nature and purposes of their warfare; hence the necessity for making the workers councils a theme for discussion.

"So, therefore, the idea of workers councils does not involve a program of practical objectives to be realized tomorrow or next year. It serves solely as a guide for the long and severe fight for freedom, which still lies ahead for the working class. Marx, it will be remembered, said that the hour of capitalism has sounded; but he was careful to add that, in his view, this hour would cover a whole historical period."

CHAPTER FIFTEEN

PRODUCTION AND DISTRIBUTION IN THE NEW WORLD

One criticism that the Dutch "work groups" leveled at the different tendencies in the German council movement stands out as essential. While not denying the importance of the fight against the "former workers' movement" (the Second and Third Internationals, trade unions), the GIC accentuated the council form, and saw the study of "the economic form of communism" as a primary theoretical task. In 1929, the communist council press published a circular with the following conclusions: "The program and the principles of the various closed groups that profess allegiance to the idea of the councils base themselves on analyses, satisfactory or otherwise, of the present course of capitalist society. It is obvious, however, that, if a new world is to be constructed, its foundations must first be clearly determined. Suppression of the capitalist merchant economy does not automatically reveal the laws of movement of the communist society—the society destined to succeed it. What will be the bases of this new society? The council movement must be able to answer this question if it intends to contribute to a conscious transformation of the economic process."[1]

The result of these reflections was published shortly afterward.[2] It contained primarily a critique of the anarchist viewpoint (Sébastien Faure), that of the Social Democratic (Kautsky, Otto Leichter) and that of the radical (Lenin, Eugène Varga), as well as a critique of Bolshevik practice during the first years of the Soviet regime. The point at issue was that all these handed the management of the new society over to a central body, with no thought for any active intervention by the workers. A second volume of this work proposed a unit of calculation serving to organize the circulation of use values produced within the new world. This unit of calculation is none other than time, the average social working hour, as Marx and Engels several times pointed out.[3]

To carry out this principle, based on the reduction of the various categories of work to one category of *labor* pure and simple, means to abolish the salary

---

1. Cf. *Proletarischer Zeitgeist* (published by the AAUE of Zwickqu), VII:2, January 1929.
2. Kollektivarbeit der GIK (Holland), *Grundprinzipien kommujnistischer Produktion und Verteilung* (Berlin, 1930).
3. Cf. especially Karl Marx, *Critique of the Gotha Program* and Engels, *Anti-Dühring*.

form, which embodies the separation of the producer from the means of production. This abolition is conceivable only if the various enterprises are linked by a system of living relationships—the workers councils—so that, by means of this working time common to all, "the social relationships of men in their various works and their relationship with the end products of their labor remain simple and transparent both in production and in distribution."[4] Clearly, the functioning of this principle demands that the workers be directly responsible for social activities. It is on this latter point that the contribution of the GIC was to prove particularly original and fruitful, and was to go beyond the framework of a mere restoration of principles.

We cannot examine here the objections that this idea may raise from the viewpoint of radical Marxism-Leninism,[5] nor, still less, can we deal with the development both of attitudes and techniques and of the theory itself, in the second half of the twentieth century. Before discussing the terms of a problem these terms themselves should be clearly set out. This is precisely what Pannekoek has attempted in *Workers' Councils*,[6] and what he has to say will serve as a conclusion to the present book.

Within the organization of councils, he writes, all the workers, whatever their rank in production, have their say both in the management of the enterprise and in the control of the jobs. "All working personnel, men and women, young and old, take their part as equal companions in this shop organization, in the actual work as well as in the general regulation. Of course, there will be many differences in the personal tasks, easier or more difficult according to strengths and talents, different in character according to inclination and ability. And, of course, the differences in general insight will give a preponderance to the advice of the most intelligent. Initially, as an inheritance of capitalism, there are large differences in education and training, and the lack of good technical and general knowledge in the masses will be felt as a heavy deficiency. Then the small number of highly trained professional technicians and scientists must act as technical leaders, without thereby acquiring a commanding or socially leading position, without gaining privileges other than the esteem of their companions and the moral authority that always accompanies skill and knowledge.

"The organization of a shop is the conscious arrangement and connection of all the separate procedures into one whole. All these interconnections of mutually adapted operations may be represented in a well-ordered scheme, a mental image of the actual process. . . . In numerical form this is done by

4. Karl Marx, *Kapital*, Vol. 1.
5. Mitchel, "Problèmes de la période de transition," *Bilan*, especially nos. 34-36, 1936.
6. Anton Pannekoek, *Workers' Councils, op. cit.*, p. 29.

bookkeeping. Bookkeeping registers and fixes all that happens in the process of production.... In comprehensive accounts, it allows continually to compare the results with the previous estimates in planning, so that production in the shop is made into a mentally controlled process.

"Capitalist management of enterprises also controls production mentally. Here, too, the process involves calculation and bookkeeping. But there is the fundamental diference that capitalist calculation is adapted entirely to the viewpoint of the production of profit. Prices and costs are its fundamental data; work and wages are only factors in calculating the resulting profit on the yearly balance on account. In the new system of production, on the other hand, the work hour is the fundamental datum, whether it is still expressed, in the beginning, in money units, or in its own true form. In capitalist production calculation and bookkeeping is a management secret. It is no concern of the workers; they are objects of exploitation, they are only factors in the calculation of cost and production, accessories to the machines. In the production under common ownership the bookkeeping is a public matter; it lies open to all. The workers always have a complete view of the course of the whole process. Only in this way are they able to discuss matters in the sectional assemblies and in the shop committees, and to decide on what has to be done. The numerical results are made visible, moreover, by statistical tables, by graphs and pictures that display the situation at a glance. This information is not restricted to the shop personnel; it is a public matter, open to all outsiders. Every shop is only a member in the social production, and the connection of its doings with the work outside is expressed in the bookkeeping. Thus insight in the production going on in every enterprise is common knowledge for all the producers.

"Labor is a social process. Each enterprise is part of the productive body of society. The total social production is formed by their connection and collaboration. Like the cells that constitute a living organism, they cannot exist isolated and cut off from the body. So the organization of the work inside the shop is only half of the task of the workers. Over it, a still more important task, stands the joining of the separate enterprises, their combination into a social organization.

"Whereas organization within the shop already existed under capitalism and had only to be replaced by another form of organization based on a new foundation, social organizations of all the shops into one whole is, or was until recent years, something entirely new, without precedent. So utterly new, that during the entire 19th century the establishment of this organization, under the name of 'socialism' was considered the main task of the working class. Capitalism consisted of an unorganized mass of independent enterprises—'a jostling crowd of separate private employers,' as the program of the Labor Party expresses it—connected only by the chance relations of market and competion, resulting in bankruptcies, overproduction and crisis, unemployment and an enormous waste of materials and labor power. To abolish it, the working class should conquer the political power and use it to organize industry and production. This state-socialism was considered, then, as the first step into a new development.

"In the last years the situation has changed insofar that capitalism itself had made a beginning with state-run organizations. . . . The political power of the state officials is greatly strengthened by their economic power, by their command over the means of production, the foundation of society.

"The principle of the working class is in every respect the exact opposite. The organization of production by the workers is founded on free collaboration: no masters, no servants. The combination of all the enterprises into one social organization takes place according to the same principle. The mechanism for this purpose must be built up by the workers.

"Given the impossibility of calling all the workers into one meeting, they can only express their will by means of delegates. Lately, such bodies of delegates have been called workers councils. Every collaborating group designates the members who have to express its opinion and its wishes in the council assemblies. These took an active part themselves in the deliberations of this group, they came to the front as able defenders of the views that carried the majority. Now they are sent as the spokesmen of the group to confront these views with those of other groups in order to come to a collective decision. Though their personal abilities play a role in persuading their colleagues and in clearing problems, their weight does not lie in their individual strength, but in the strength of the community that delegated them. What carries weight are not simple opinions, but still more the will and the readiness of the group to act accordingly. Different persons will act as delegates according to the different questions raised and the forthcoming problems.

"The chief problem, the basis of all the rest, is production itself. Its organization has two sides, the establishment of general rules and norms and the practical work itself. Norms and rules must be established for the mutual relations in the work, for the rights and duties. Under capitalism the norm consisted in the command of the master, the director. Under state capitalism it consisted in the mightier command of the leader, the central government. Now, however, all producers are free and equal. Now in the economic field of labor the same change takes place as occurred in former centuries in the political field, with the rise of the bourgeoisie. When the rule of the citizens came in place of the rule of the absolute monarch, this could not mean that for his arbitrary will the arbitrary will of everybody was substituted. It meant that, henceforth, laws established by the common will should regulate the public rights and duties. So now, in the realm of labor, the command of the master gives way to rules fixed in common, to regulate the social rights and duties, in production and consumption. To formulate them will be the first task of the workers councils. This is not a difficult task, not a matter of profound study or serious discord. For every worker these rules will immediately spring up in his consciousness as the natural basis of the new society: everyone's duty to take part in the production in accordance with his forces and capacities, everyone's right to enjoy his adequate part of the collective product.

"How will the quantities of labor spent and the quantities of product to which he is entitled be measured? In a society where the goods are produced directly for consumption there is no market to exchange them; and no value as expression of the labor contained in them establishes itself automatically out of the processes of buying and selling. Here the labor spent must be expressed in a direct way by the number of hours. The administration keeps records of the hours of labor contained in every piece or unit quantity of product, as well as of the hours spent by each of the workers. In the averages of all workers of a factory and finally, of all the factories of the same category, the personal differences are smoothed out and results are compared.

"In the first times of transition when there is much devastation to be repaired, the first problem is to build up the production apparatus and to keep people alive. It is quite possible that the habit, imposed by war and famine, of having the indispensable foodstuffs distributed without distinction is simply continued. It is most probable that, in those times of reconstruction, when all the forces must be exerted to the utmost, when, moreover, the new moral principles of common labor are only gradually forming, the right of consumption will be tied to the performance of work. The old popular saying that whoever does not work shall not eat expresses an instinctive feeling of justice. Here is not only the recognition that labor is the basis of all human life, but also the proclamation that now there is an end to capitalist exploitation and to appropriating the fruits of foreign labor by property titles of an idle class.

"This does not mean, of course, that now the total product is distributed among the producers, according to the time given by each. Or, expressed in another way, that every worker receives products equivalent to the quantity of hours of labor spent in working. A considerable part of the work must be spent on the common property, on the perfection and enlargement of the productive apparatus. Under capitalism part of the surplus value served this purpose; the capitalist had to use part of his profit, accumulated into new capital, to innovate, expand and modernize his technical equipment, in his case driven by the need to keep up with his competitors. So the progress in techniques took place in forms of exploitation. Now, in the new form of production, this progress is the common concern of the workers. Keeping themselves alive is the most immediate, but building the basis of future production is the most glorious part of their task. They will have to settle what part of their total labor shall be spent on the making of better machines and more efficient tools, on research and experiment, for facilitating the work and improving the production.

"Moreover, part of the total time and labor of society must be spent on activities that are productive but are still necessary—i.e., general administration, education, medical services. Children and old people will receive their share of the product without corresponding achievements. People incapable of work must be sustained; and especially in the initial phase there will be a large number of human wrecks left by the former capitalist world. Probably the rule will prevail that the productive work is the task of the younger adults; or, in other words, is the task of everybody during that period of his life when both the tendency and the capacity for vigorous activity are greatest. By the rapid increase of the productivity of labor this part, the time needed to produce all the necessities of life will continually decrease, and an increasing part of life will be available for other purposes and activities.

"The basis of the social organization of production consists in careful administration, in the form of statistics and bookkeeping.

"...The function and the place numerical administration occupies in society depends on the character of this society. Financial administration of states was always necessary as part of the central government, and the computing officials were subordinate servants of the kings or other rulers. Where in modern capitalism production is subjected to an encompassing central organization, those who have the central administration in their hands will be the leading directors of economy and develop into a ruling bureaucracy. When in Russia the revolution of 1917 led to a rapid expansion of industry, and hosts of workers still permeated by the barbarous ignorance of the villages crowded into the new factories, they lacked the power to check the rising dominance of the bureaucracy then organizing into a new ruling class. When in 1933 in Germany, a sternly organized party conquered the state power, it took control of the organization of all the forces of capitalism as its means of central administration.

"Conditions are entirely different when the workers are masters of their labor and organize production as free producers. Administration by means of bookkeeping and computing is a special task of certain persons, just as hammering steel or baking bread is a special task of other persons, all equally useful and necessary. The workers in the computing offices are neither servants nor rulers. They are not officials in the service of the workers councils, obediently having to perform their orders. They are groups of workers, like other groups collectively regulating their work themselves, disposing of their implements, performing their duties, as does every group, in continual connection with the needs of the whole. They are the experts who have to provide the basic data of the discussions and decisions in the assemblies of workers and of councils. They have to collect the data, to present it in an easily intelligible form of tables, of graphs, of pictures, so that every worker at every moment has a clear image of the state of things. Their knowledge is not a private property giving them power; they are not a body with exclusive administrative knowledge that thereby somehow could exert a deciding influence. The product of their labor, the numerical insight needed for the work's progress, is available to all. This general knowledge is the foundation of all the discussions and decisions of the workers and their councils by which the organization of labor is performed.

"For the first time in history the economic life, in general and in detail, lies as an open book before the eyes of mankind. The foundations of society, under capitalism a huge mass hidden in the dark depths, dimly lighted here and there by statistics on commerce and production, now has entered into the full daylight and shows its detailed structure. Here we dispose of a science of society consisting of a well-ordered knowledge of facts, out of which leading causal relations are readily grasped. It forms the basis of the social organization of labor just as the knowledge of the facts of nature, also condensed into causal relations, forms the basis of the technical organization of labor. As a knowledge of the common simple facts of daily life it is available to everyone and enables him to survey and grasp the necessities of the whole as well as his own part in it. It forms the spiritual equipment through which the producers are able to direct the production and to control their world. . . ."

But this form of organization is not destined to continue in force throughout the ages. It contains within itself, the elements of its own dissolution. Without, of course, dwelling on the question, Pannekoek nevertheless has this to say:

"The workers' councils are the form of self-government which in the times to come will replace the forms of government of the old world. Of course not for all time; no such form is for eternity. When life and work in community are natural habit, when mankind entirely controls its own life, necessity gives way to freedom and the strict rules of justice established before dissolve into spontaneous behavior. Workers' councils are the form of organization during the transition period in which the working class is fighting for dominance, is destroying capitalism and is organizing social production." [7]

An anthology must of necessity contain more or less arbitrary cuts and omissions. But perhaps this defect is less important in an anthology such as this one than is the inevitable distortion of historical realities — a distortion occasioned by the ascription to a particular theoretician of a body of ideas that is primarily a product of the class struggle and therefore only secondarily ascribable to any individual.

Council communism belongs to the past. To raise the banner of a disinherited name is, quite frankly, a futile occupation; to attempt to revive certain outmoded ideas, to passively seek a signpost to present conduct in a history forever past and gone, can only feed dogma (or harmless dreams). But this having been said, it is proper to point to one idea — "the failure of the working class" — which, for specific reasons, has disappeared from contemporary societies, and which reappears, in diverse aspects, as soon as new conditions establish themselves. The idea of councils is the fruit of an immense, but already remote, effort at emancipation. As such, it is something with both a positive and a negative legacy, and the critical discussion of this can in itself have value for action. Pannekoek himself has expressed this idea very clearly: "The importance of the past lies in the fact that it enables lessons to be drawn of a kind that can throw light on the future." [8]

The anthology form offers precisely the advantage of showing by a cross-section of history what is no longer valid in yesterday's ideas, even though they might have been the most advanced of their own day. The anthology form also highlights the fact that we cannot easily shake off the old forms of thought and organization — certainly not by seeking to reinstate them exactly as they were. Still more, this form stresses the fundamental fact that only the development of new organizational forms makes it possible to pass beyond the old forms, provided there was a decisive break with the existing institutional world, with all its organs of dialogue (political parties, trade unions).

Consider the situation in which the producers are led to fight against

---

7. *Ibid.*, p. 47.
8. Anton Pannekoek, "Prinzip und Taktik," *op. cit.*, p. 178.

capital, but to do so outside their traditional organizations and ultimately against them; a lull occurs, but then this fight is resumed more intensively and finally becomes one of unparalleled bitterness. The outcome of such a great historical battle depends in large measure on how deeply the producers are aware of the meaning and the purposes of their action. From this perspective, the transmission of teachings from the past—essentially as positive ideas, as general principles—can furnish, in conjunction with other elements of knowledge, a means of discerning more clearly and more quickly, in the autonomous battles of the present, the traits of mass actions and of a new world still in gestation; in other words, it can be an element of orientation. In this sense, pages from a long history of conflicts can serve, first, as matter for reflection and discussion, and then as weapons of propaganda.

If one can speak of the personal genius of Anton Pannekoek, this is not because of any accurate predictions he made (for, in that case, one would have to overlook certain serious errors or gaps in his thinking about the evolution of capitalism). Rather, his genius consists in having set out clearly and boldly toward the end of a particular phase of the struggle for freedom what had been attained by that particular pahse. Pannekoek summarized this theme in the final paragraphs of his *Workers' Councils*;

"Socialism, as inherited from the 19th century, was the creed of a social mission for the leaders and politicians: to transform capitalism into a system of a state-directed economy without exploitation, producing abundance for all. It was the creed of class struggle for the workers, the belief that by transferring government into the hands of these socialists they would assure their freedom. Why did it not happen? Because the casting of a secret vote was too insignificant an effort to count as real class struggle. Because the socialist politicians, alone in the entire capitalist fabric of society, stood against the immense power of the capitalist mastery of the production apparatus, with the workers' masses only looking on, expecting them, little squad, to upset the world. What could they do other than run the affair in the usual way, and, by reforming the worst abuses, save their conscience? Now it is seen that socialism in the sense of state-directed planned economy means state capitalism, and that socialism in the sense of workers' emancipation is only possible as a new orientation. The new orientation of socialism is self-direction of production, self-direction of the class-struggle, by means of workers' councils.

"What is called the failure of the working class and what alarms many socialists—i.e., the contradiction between the economic breakdown of capitalism and the inability of the workers to seize power and establish the new order—is no real contradiction. Economic changes only gradually produce changes in the mind. The workers educated in the belief in socialism stand bewildered now that they see that its very opposite, heavier slavery, is the outcome. To grasp that socialism and communism now both mean doctrines of enslavement is a hard job. New orientation needs time; maybe only a new generation will comprehend its full scope.

"At the end of World War I revolution seemed near; the working class arose full of hope and expectation that now its old dreams would come true. But they were dreams of imperfect freedom, they could not be realized. Now at the end of World War II only slavery and destruction seem near; hope is far distant; but there still looms a task, the greater aim of real freedom. More powerful than before, the working class has to rise in its fight for mastery over the world. Capitalism has found more powerful forms of suppression. . . .

"A century ago, when the workers were a small class of downtrodden, helpless individuals, the call was heard: workers of the world unite! You have nothing to lose but your chains; you have a world to win. Since then they have become the largest class; and they have united; but only imperfectly. Only in groups, smaller or larger, not yet as one class unity. Only superficially, in outer forms, not yet in deep essence. And still they have nothing to lose but their chains; what else they have they cannot lose by fighting, only by timidly submitting. And the world to be won begins to be perceived dimly. At that time no clear goal could be depicted around which to unite; so their organizations in the end became tools of capitalism. Now the goal becomes distinct; against the stronger domination of the state-directed planned economy of the new capitalism stands what Marx called the association of free and equal producers. So the call for unity must be supplemented by an indication of the goal: take the factories and machines; assert your mastery over the productive apparatus; organize production by means of workers' councils."[9]

---

9. Anton Pannekoek, *Workers' Councils, op. cit.*, pp. 230-31.